CONFUSION AT CALVARY

MISUNDERSTANDING JEHOVAH

JERALD L. MANLEY

Confusion at Calvary was written after over five decades of study and interaction as a Baptist pastor with the practical impact of doctrinal beliefs on churches and in the lives of believers and non-believers. The innumerable articles and books that have been read over those decades undoubtedly have influenced my choices for wording, as have the uncountable conversations and discussions on this topic that have occurred over these years. A diligent effort was made to provide the proper and deserved credit for thoughts and quotes that are known to have originated with someone else. It is not my intention to claim originality for that labor which others have given.

The Authorized Version, commonly called the King James Version, is the source for all of my Biblical quotations.

Biblical references in citations from other authors are their choices and must be their responsibility.

Alas! and did my Savior bleed,
And did my Sovereign die?
Would He devote that sacred head
For such a worm as I?

Was it for crimes that I had done
He groaned upon the tree?
Amazing pity, grace unknown,
And love beyond degree!

Well might the sun in darkness hide
And shut his glories in
When God, the mighty Maker, died
For man the creature's sin.

Thus might I hide my blushing face
While His dear cross appears,
Dissolve my heart in thankfulness,
And melt mine eyes to tears.

But drops of grief can ne'er repay
The debt of love I owe;
Here, Lord, I give myself away,
'Tis all that I can do.

Isaac Watts, 1674–1748

DEDICATION

For almost as long as I have known him, he has taken the role as chief among my supporters and encouragers. Whatever I have attempted, he was convinced from the beginning of the endeavor that it would succeed and contributed his assisting efforts energetically. His involvement and strength has made me feel a better man and likely to have enabled me to accomplish more than I would have otherwise. I value his friendship and his counsel beyond measure.

Confusion at Calvary is dedicated to our younger son, John.

Jerald L. Manley

CONTENTS

INTRODUCTION

The topic presented in *Confusion at Calvary* has been somewhat of a Gordian knot for me. During the darkened hours when Jesus of Nazareth was suspended on that Roman cross just outside the gates of Jerusalem, did GOD the Father forsake GOD the Son? Good godly preachers and Bible students, individuals that I respect with esteem, have written and preached that He did.

It is preached and taught that believers are to take comfort in GOD the Father forsaking His Son, so that He would never forsake His children. Certainly, it appears that Jesus of Nazareth was forsaken; however, was He?

I offer one passage of Scripture for my reader to mediate upon as he reads *Confusion at Calvary.*

> John 8:28 Then said Jesus unto them, **When** ye have lifted up the Son of man, **then** shall ye know that I am *he*, and *that* I do nothing of myself; but as my Father hath taught me, I speak these things. 29 And he that sent me is with me: **the Father hath not left me alone**; for I do always those things that please him.

In the context of the *lifting up* of the Son of man, the LORD Jesus speaks of the Father never leaving Him alone. That statement is impossible to reconcile with the Father turning His back on Jesus of Nazareth at Calvary. In fact, the attempt to reconcile these irreconcilable statements produces a Gordian knot that requires solution by a Sword.

Allegedly, Gordius, king of Phrygia and the father of Midas of the golden touch, tied a knot that defied every attempt to untie. It was asserted, according to the legend that the man who could untie that knot would become the future king. The *Merriam-Webster 11th Collegiate Dictionary* notes that the knot tied by Gordius has become a term for "an intricate problem; especially a problem insoluble in its own terms."

Three centuries before the birth of Jesus of Nazareth, Alexander the Great invaded Asia Minor to fulfill his ambition to conquer the world. In the central mountains of modern Turkey, he overwhelmed the kingdom of Phrygia. In the town of Gordium, he found the famous ox cart of Gordius at the Temple of Zeus. Shown the knot that had defied all efforts for a full century, Alexander, at the age of twenty-three, solved the Gordian knot. He unsheathed his sword and sliced straight through the Gordian knot.

The two-edged Sword of the word of GOD applied to the problem of whether or not GOD the Father deserted and disowned GOD the Son at Calvary severed the Gordian knot for me. *Confusion at Calvary* presents my understanding that GOD the Son was not confused at Calvary and that GOD the Father did not abandon the Son of GOD in the darkness of the cross.

CHAPTER 1

I SAW ONE HANGING ON A TREE

> Christ hath redeemed us from the curse of the
> law, being made a curse for us: for it is writ-
> ten, Cursed *is* every one that hangeth on a
> tree:[1]
>
> Galatians 3:13

Isaiah 53

Who hath believed our report?
and to whom is the arm of the LORD revealed?

For he shall grow up before him
as a tender plant,
and as a root out of a dry ground:
he hath no form nor comeliness;
and when we shall see him,
there is no beauty that we should desire him.

He is despised and rejected of men;
a man of sorrows,
and acquainted with grief:
and we hid as it were *our* faces from him;
he was despised,
and we esteemed him not.

Surely he hath borne our griefs,

1

and carried our sorrows:
yet we did esteem him stricken,
smitten of God, and afflicted.

But he *was* wounded for our transgressions,
he was bruised for our iniquities:
the chastisement of our peace *was* upon him;
and with his stripes we are healed.

All we like sheep have gone astray;
we have turned every one to his own way;
and the LORD hath laid on him
the iniquity of us all.

He was oppressed, and he was afflicted,
yet he opened not his mouth:
he is brought as a lamb to the slaughter,
and as a sheep before her shearers is dumb,
so he openeth not his mouth.

He was taken from prison and from judgment:
and who shall declare his generation?

for he was cut off out of the land of the living:
for the transgression of my people
was he stricken.

And he made his grave with the wicked,
and with the rich in his death;
because he had done no violence,
neither *was any* deceit in his mouth.

Yet it pleased the LORD to bruise him;
he hath put *him* to grief:
when thou shalt make his soul
an offering for sin,
he shall see *his* seed,
he shall prolong *his* days,
and the pleasure of the LORD
shall prosper in his hand.

He shall see of the travail of his soul,
and shall be satisfied:
by his knowledge shall
my righteous servant justify many;

for he shall bear their iniquities.
Therefore will I divide him
a portion with the great,
and he shall divide the spoil with the strong;
because he hath poured out his soul
unto death:
and he was numbered with the transgressors;
and he bare the sin of many,
and made intercession for the transgressors.

There He hangs.

The Word, full of grace and truth, Who was made flesh to dwell among men, so that those who saw Him might behold the glory of GOD and that we reading the Gospels might also behold that glory. The glory of the only begotten of the Father is hanging on that tree.

There He hangs.

He Who spake as never man spake and quieted the wind and stilled the sea, He Whose touch gave sight to the blind, hearing to the deaf, and speech to the dumb is hanging on that tree.

There He hangs.

He Who cured infirmities and plagues, restored withered limbs, healed the sick of all manner of diseases, cast out devils, and even called the dead from the grave is hanging on that tree.

There He hangs.

He Who went about doing good, feeding the hungry caring for the poor and needy and comforting the brokenhearted is hanging on that tree.

There He hangs.

The Mediator between GOD and men, the man Christ Jesus, Who cried, "Come unto me, all ye that labour and are heavy laden, and I will give you rest" is hanging on that tree.

There He hangs.

The One Who said, "For God so loved the world, that He gave His only begotten Son, that whosoever believeth in Him should not perish, but have everlasting life. For God sent not His Son into the world to condemn the world; but that the world through Him might be saved. He that believeth on Him is not condemned: but he that believeth not is condemned already, because he hath not believed in the name of the only begotten Son of God" is hanging on that tree.

There He hangs.

Esteemed not, forsaken by His disciples, despised and rejected by His nation, accused by the priests, and condemned by the government, He is hanging on that tree.

There He hangs.

Suspended between heaven and earth, with body beaten and bruised and bloodied, with face swollen and slashed and stained, with hands and feet held in place by bronze nails, the sacrifice bound to the altar with the cords of love is hanging on that tree.

There He hangs.

The dust from the streets, the spittle of the crowd, and the sweat of His brow and His body mingle with His blood and steadily drips in swelling drops onto the ground as He is hanging on that tree.

His suffering is beyond the capacity of words to convey; and yet, dumb before His tormentors, He is hanging on that tree.

The night before, in the Garden, He had resisted against sin to the point of sweating great drops of blood as He prayed to the Father for deliverance from the cup of Satan. He prayed to live that He might accomplish the will of the Father and continue His journey to this very cross. The Scripture records that the Father heard His prayer and that the Son of GOD was indeed strengthened for this very hour;[2] but He is hanging on that tree.

There He hangs.

One might begin with those drops of blood that fell where He prayed in the Garden and from those blots begin to follow a trail of bloody stains back across the brook Cedron, and on up from the valley inside the house of Annas. From there that trail of blood would lead around to the house of Caiaphas. The splotches then move across the city to Pilate's Hall. From there, the trail moves back to Herod's Palace and then returns to Pilate; and finally winds along through the narrow streets of Jerusalem to this hill called Calvary. The crimson trail of His blood finds an end on this rugged hill at the foot of this rugged Roman cross where a jeering crowd has gathered to watch Him hanging on that tree.

There He hangs.

Exposed and humiliated, fixed in position, nailed into place, His skin is torn; the flesh exposed. His back is lacerated until it resembles a butchered side of beef. The meat of His chest and rib cage is exposed to show splotches of the white of bone. The stomach is distended. He is hanging on that tree.

Under the climbing blazing Judean sun, with the hordes of flies and gnats swarming undeterred about His bruised and battered and swollen face, He is hanging on that tree.

The very hair has been plucked from that face. His eyes are puffed and matted. The fists and the reeds have lashed and sliced and mutilated His features. His arms are stretched until his legs must support His weight from an unnatural position. Every muscle, every joint, every tendon, every nerve is strained and aching. The very bones hurt. His mouth and throat are dry—the tongue is thick and beginning to swell. The lungs are on fire. Every breath requires willpower as He is hanging on that tree.

There He hangs.

Inhumane the behavior, inexcusable the treatment, indescribable the horror, inexpressible the suffering, unspeakable the agony, that is the Son of GOD hanging on that tree.

All things were made by Him; and without Him was not any thing made that was made. He was in the world, and the world was made by Him, and the world knew Him not. He came unto His own, and His own received Him not. The Creator is hanging on that tree.

He, by Whom all things consist and for Whom all things were made, entered this world as a tiny, tender, helpless baby. He removed, as it were, the robes of deity to put on the clothes of humanity. The Son of GOD exchanged the streets of gold to walk the sandy trails of Galilee. He left the companionship of holy angels to eat with publicans and sinners. The Son of man is hanging on that tree.

Poverty—He felt it.

Privation—He knew it.

Hunger—He endured it.

Thirst—He felt it.

6

Weariness—He lived it.

Pain—He bore it.

Loneliness—He accepted it.

Abuse—that too was His lot.

From the stable to the cross, He was laughed at, ridiculed, and mocked. He Who wore the diadem of glory had quietly accepted the Crown of thorns. He Who had enjoyed the splendor of heaven now wordlessly allowed the spittle of the priests and from the soldiers. He Who had received the praise of angels silently now tolerates the mockery of the crowds as He is hanging on that tree.

There He hangs.

Calvary was torment, torture, anguish, and agony—but it was even more. It was indeed the culmination of the Life that was a light for men as He hangs upon that tree.

Hours before in the Upper Room, He had described how *and* why *and* when *and* where He now is—accursed, nailed through feet and hands, and hanging on that tree. Even after His explanation, as those men that He had called friends were seated at the Passover table with Jesus of Nazareth, they began quibbling among themselves as to which one among them should be the greatest.[3] They even dare to dispute with Him when He says one will betray Him and, in unison, they swore their loyalty to Him, even unto death.

The night before when Jesus of Nazareth and these men enter the Garden where they had often come to pray,[4] He tells them that His soul is sorrowful even unto death. Those men, His friends, after a long day and a heavy meal fall quickly into a deep slumber. While His disciples slept, He sweats great drops of blood resisting against the attack of Satan.[5]

Following that bloody time of prayer, when His friend Judas,[6] coming to betray Him, arrives with the armed and boisterous mob, these self-proclaimed martyrs forsake Him and scattered each to his own fearful for self-preservation.[7]

The Son of GOD, arrested and bound as if He were a common criminal, is led roughly[8] through the streets as a Lamb to the slaughter and is brought first to the house of Annas and then to the house of Caiaphas.

In the presence of the high priest, He was slapped and buffeted—that word buffet is used to describe the badgering and beating that a ship takes from the waves slamming into it in a storm[9]—and this irreligious and repulsive act was in the presence of the high priest.

After the unlawful—and I mean by that contrary to the Mosaic Law, which the high priest and the Sanhedrin knew to the very letter—after this improper, illegal mistreatment, Caiaphas and the Council have Him taken to the Roman governor's house. After he subjects Jesus of Nazareth to public humiliation, Pilate sends Him to King Herod, who finding Him unresponsive to questions or prodding, mocks Him and joined with his soldiers to strip Him of His clothing. Herod then provides the means to decorate Jesus of Nazareth in a gorgeous royal robe. He then returned Him to Pilate.[10]

When Pilate received Him back, in an apparent effort to placate the mob, he had Jesus of Nazareth scourged, an act which was one of expediency and not justice. Pilate violated Roman jurisprudence in attempting to placate the Jews and perhaps in hoping to please his wife when He had Jesus of Nazareth scourged *before* he declared Him to be guilty. However, that scourging was prophesied by the psalmist: "The plowers plowed upon my back: they made long their furrows."[11]

Scourging made use of a whip with several long lashes of leather affixed to a wooden handle. Each strip of leather was pierced with pieces of glass and metal and thorns and stones and tied with knots.

Some have identified this whip as *the cat of nine tails.* These devilish weapons are swung with such violence that they wrap around the body of the victim, who is tied so that his arms are extended upward, stretching taunt the skin and flesh and muscles.

Those lashes would reach from the loins to the face and they could rip and tear the body, even to exposing the bones. Not a few men died under the beating. A Roman scourging disemboweled many a man.

Someone among those soldiers, we know not who, made a crown woven from spiked thorns and crushed it into his brow piercing the scalp, causing more blood to flow. Who among men could have had such hatred for the Son of GOD?

Pilate presents the abused Son of man *in gorgeous royal purple bloodstained robe with a crown of thorns* to the assembled rabble—"Behold the man." Tthe instant response, agitated by the by the chief priests, is the chilling cry for Him to be crucified. The religious leaders had accused Jesus of Nazareth of making Himself a King;[12] and now they charge that "he made himself the Son of God."[13]

After interviewing Jesus of Nazareth again and though having thrice declared Him innocent, Pilate washes his hands before all and sends Jesus of Nazareth to be crucified. Pilate gives Him to his soldiers to prepare for the crucifixion.

They bow, bending their knees and crying "Hail King of the Jews." They slap Him. They beat Him with reeds that split and splinter on impact with the resulting slicing of the body as it with a series of those lacerations that we know as *paper cuts*.

Finally, not because of mercy, but due to the pressure of time, the preparation for crucifixion is ended. After nearly 6 hours of this unspeakable repulsive maltreatment, the Son of GOD is led away to be crucified. He leaves the Judgment Hall of Pilate with the bitterly caustic words of the priests still ringing and laying so heavily on His heart.

These men trained to represent the holy, the just, and the merciful GOD of Heaven, and educated to offer sacrifices to obtain forgiveness, positioned to lead praise to the loving-kindness and tender mercies of GOD, required to know the word of GOD, and expected to be watching for the Messiah, were shouting the most hateful words possible: "Away with Him! His blood be upon us and upon our children. We will not have *this man* to reign over us. Crucify Him!"

With the sentence pronounced, the Son of man was led from Pilate's Hall through the narrow streets of the city of David and then through the gates, beyond the City called Peace, to that *Place of a Skull* to be crucified.

Scripture is nearly silent regarding this arduous, exhausting, grievous walk through the narrow streets of Jerusalem, which at times would have become a jeering, abusing gauntlet. Responding to a groping of women along the way, He gave a neglected, overlooked prophecy of judgment to come. [14]

Somewhere along the way, the cross was taken from Jesus of Nazareth and forced upon Simon of Cyrene, who was compelled to bear that cross to the *Place of a Skull*. Whatever the reason for the transposition of the cross from Jesus of Nazareth to Simon of Cyrene, it was not because the lord Jesus was overcome by weakness or exhaustion, making Him unable to fulfill His journey to Golgotha. **There statement, not even a hint, in the Biblical record that Jesus of Nazareth stumbled and *fell beneath His load* on the way to Calvary.**[15] The suggestion that the Son of GOD needed the assistance of Simon in order to get to Golgotha is simply a fabrication.[16]

As the soldiers and those to be crucified began to move[17] through Jerusalem, someone, *we know not who or why*, decided that since this Man was the King of the Jews, He deserved a servant to carry the cross. Perhaps, as the little company pushed its way through the narrow crowded streets, someone saw a man among the shuffling throngs pulling back to let the soldiers through and, as he saw him, his racist mind thought this black man looked exactly like the suitable servant for the King of the Jews. However it was that it happened, let me remind you that Jesus of Nazareth needed no human assistance to climb Calvary's Mount.

It is written that "when the time was come that he should be received up, he stedfastly set his face to go to Jerusalem." He had said, "for this cause came I unto this hour."[18] The Son of GOD manifest in the flesh was not in the need of support to arrive at Calvary.

When He came to the brow of Golgotha, the Son of man lay down His life. It was not taken from Him.[19] Jesus of Nazareth was nailed to the middle of three crosses, but it was not the strength of the bronze nails that held the Son of GOD on that cross.

11

The cross was lifted into the air and dropped some two or three feet into the hole prepared to hold that instrument of death.

The jolt would rip and tear the flesh, wrenching the tendons and muscles, and dislocating joints.[20] Everything connected with a crucifixion was designed intentionally to cause suffering and death.[21] The cross was an instrument of torture as much as it was one of death.

There hangs Jesus of Nazareth.

Isaiah looking through the long prophetic lens declares that as the Righteous Servant was hanging on that cross, His appearance was so marred that He was unrecognizable as a human being.[22]

What the Son of GOD endured is beyond the capacity of words to describe. How the Son of man must have looked as He was hanging on that tree is an impossible picture for any artist to paint. No writer, no sculptor, no artist has ever been able to depict or to portray exactly and accurately the crucifixion of the Son of GOD. Isaiah records "when we shall see him, *there is* no beauty that we should desire him" and that "He is despised and rejected of men; a man of sorrows, and acquainted with grief: and we hid as it were *our* faces from him; he was despised, and we esteemed him not."[23]

Isaiah is speaking of this time of beatings, a scourging, and the crucifixion. Jesus of Nazareth on that cross makes the one hide the face. The Holy Spirit testified of these sufferings through the prophets.[24]

Uninformed, unthinking, ignorant men sometimes declare that they have seen or experienced hell in some event in life or some place on earth; however, there is only one time in all of history when hell has ever been on the surface of the earth.

In some very real sense, when the LORD Jesus was hanging on that tree, when the Son of GOD was suspended between heaven and earth on that old rugged hill called Calvary, He Who knew no sin took our sin upon Himself; and there at Calvary, He endured our hell.

The LORD Jesus endured the full penalty of my sin and of your sin. By Himself, He purged our sins, yours and mine.

Do you understand this?

Every slap of the hand was for you.

Every strike of the fist was for you.

Every stripe of the whip was for you.

Every slash of the reed was for you.

A lifetime filled with lies was tolerated for you. Years of gossip were endured for you. Tongues with vicious slander were suffered for you.

He endured those six judicial examinations[25] that night; all of which were tainted with illegalities and perjuries, for you.

Those were the least of what He endured for you.

The piercing of the flesh, the plucking of the hair, the plunging of the spear, all of the bruising, all of the buffeting, all of the battering, all of the beating was for you.

The pain, the agony, the suffering, the shame was all borne for you.

Every blow of the hammer on each nail through His flesh and into that cross was for you, each thorn of the Crown was for you; each tear of a muscle was for you; each drop of blood was for you.

If you feel that I am being personal, I am. I mean for you to consider this issue very personal.

With legions of angels watching in silence, the heavy woven curtains of utter darkness fall suddenly and humanity is prevented from seeing—and for three hours silence reigns on that old rugged hill as the wrath that all sinners ought to receive was poured out on that One hanging there—the horrors of hell descended upon that One hanging on that tree.

In the silent solitude of that utter blackness, the Son of GOD received what I should endure and what you ought to bear—*He tasted death for every man—He tasted death for me—He tasted death for you.*[26]

There He hangs—suspended between heaven and earth.

His body is beaten and bruised and bloodied. His face is swollen and slashed and stained. His hands and feet are held in place by bronze nails; but the sacrifice is bound to the altar with the cords of love.[27]

There He hangs.

What is our response? Here I stand and there you sit! How are we unmoved? Should it not stir us that you and I could raise more emotion over a fabricated story about an abused puppy or a mutilated kitten that over the death of Jesus of Nazareth?

Tree huggers will cry over an oak being felled, while you and I shed no tears for the Son of GOD Who endured all of this for us.

Where are our tears for the Son of man?

Why are we so unresponsive?

How dare we remain so complacent?

Are we that ungrateful?

How have we grown so calloused?

It is time for the text.

The solemn question that I submit and that you must answer was asked by the Psalmist in Psalm 116:12: What shall I render unto the LORD for all his benefits toward me?

You must answer it in light of the declaration of the Apostle Paul in 2 Corinthians 5:15: And that he died for all, that they which live should not henceforth live unto themselves, but unto him which died for them, and rose again.

The LORD Jesus did all of that for you. The one question that you must answer is "What have you done for Him?"

In evil long I took delight,
Unawed by shame or fear,
Till a new object struck my sight,
And stopped my wild career.

I saw One hanging on a tree,
In agony and blood,
Who fixed His languid eyes on me,
As near His cross I stood.

Sure, never to my latest breath,
Can I forget that look;
It seemed to charge me with His death,
Though not a word He spoke.

My conscience felt and owned the guilt,
And plunged me in despair,
I saw my sins His blood had spilt,
And helped to nail Him there.

A second look He gave, which said,
"I freely all forgive;
This blood is for thy ransom paid;
I die that thou mayst live."

Thus, while His death my sin displays
In all its blackest hue,
Such is the mystery of grace,
It seals my pardon too.[28]

Dear Reader, I do not know you; but this I do know if you have never accepted the atonement that the Lamb of GOD provided for you on that Tree of Calvary then you are the very person that this chapter was intended to reach.

Will you right now receive the gift of eternal life? There will never be a better time or a better place. That tugging desire in your heart for a right relationship with the GOD of Heaven comes from the working of the Holy Spirit of GOD. The GOD of Heaven loves you and wants to be your Heavenly Father.

I would not put words in your mouth, but perhaps I might guide you with some encouragement. I assure you that the GOD of Heaven knows your thoughts and hears your words.

If you realize that you have sinned against the GOD of Heaven, then confess that to Him.

It you understand that you cannot work your way to Heaven, then acknowledge that to GOD.

If you believe that Jesus died on that cross and rose from the grave so that you might be saved, then tell that to the GOD of Heaven.

If you desire to receive the gift of eternal life that was purchased by the atoning blood of the LORD Jesus, then do so right now.

Romans 10:9 That if thou shalt confess with thy mouth the Lord Jesus, and shalt believe in thine heart that GOD hath raised him from the dead, thou shalt be saved.

¹ Deuteronomy 21:22 And if a man have committed a sin worthy of death, and he be to be put to death, and thou hang him on a tree: 23 His body shall not remain all night upon the tree, but thou shalt in any wise bury him that day; (for he that is hanged is accursed of God;) that thy land be not defiled, which the LORD thy God giveth thee for an inheritance.

Acts 5:31 Him hath God exalted with his right hand to be a Prince and a Saviour, for to give repentance to Israel, and forgiveness of sins. 32 And we are his witnesses of these things; and so is also the Holy Ghost, whom God hath given to them that obey him.

Acts 10:39 And we are witnesses of all things which he did both in the land of the Jews, and in Jerusalem; whom they slew and hanged on a tree: 40 Him God raised up the third day, and shewed him openly;

Acts 13:29 And when they had fulfilled all that was written of him, they took him down from the tree, and laid him in a sepulchre. 30 But God raised him from the dead:

1 Peter 2:24 Who his own self bare our sins in his own body on the tree, that we, being dead to sins, should live unto righteousness: by whose stripes ye were healed.

² Hebrews 5:7 Who in the days of his flesh, when he had offered up prayers and supplications with strong crying and tears unto him that was able to save him from death, and was heard in that he feared;

John 12:27 Now is my soul troubled; and what shall I say? Father, save me from this hour: but for this cause came I unto this hour.

³ Luke 22:14 And when the hour was come, **he sat down, and the twelve apostles with him**. 15 And he said unto them, With desire I have desired to eat this passover with you before I suffer: 16 For I say unto you, I will not any more eat thereof, until it be fulfilled in the kingdom of God. 17 And he took the cup, and gave thanks, and said, Take this, and divide *it* among yourselves: 18 For I say unto you, I will not drink of the fruit of the vine, until the kingdom of God shall come. 19 And he took bread, and gave thanks, and brake *it*, and gave unto them, saying, This is my body which is given for you: this do in remembrance of me. 20 Likewise also the cup after supper, saying, This cup *is* the new testament in my blood, which is shed for you. 21 But, behold, the hand of him that betrayeth me *is* with me on the table. 22 And truly the Son of man goeth, as it was determined: but woe unto that man by whom he is betrayed! 23 And they began to inquire among themselves, which of them it was that should do this thing. **24 And there was also a strife among them, which of them should be accounted**

the greatest. 25 And he said unto them, The kings of the Gentiles exercise lordship over them; and they that exercise authority upon them are called benefactors. 26 But ye *shall* not *be* so: but he that is greatest among you, let him be as the younger; and he that is chief, as he that doth serve. 27 For whether *is* greater, he that sitteth at meat, or he that serveth? *is* not he that sitteth at meat? but I am among you as he that serveth. 28 Ye are they which have continued with me in my temptations. 29 And I appoint unto you a kingdom, as my Father hath appointed unto me; 30 That ye may eat and drink at my table in my kingdom, and sit on thrones judging the twelve tribes of Israel. 31 And the Lord said, Simon, Simon, behold, Satan hath desired *to have* you, that he may sift *you* as wheat: 32 But I have prayed for thee, that thy faith fail not: and when thou art converted, strengthen thy brethren. 33 And he said unto him, **Lord, I am ready to go with thee, both into prison, and to death.** 34 And he said, I tell thee, Peter, the cock shall not crow this day, before that thou shalt thrice deny that thou knowest me. 35 And he said unto them, When I sent you without purse, and scrip, and shoes, lacked ye any thing? And they said, Nothing. 36 Then said he unto them, But now, he that hath a purse, let him take *it*, and likewise *his* scrip: and he that hath no sword, let him sell his garment, and buy one. 37 For I say unto you, that this that is written must yet be accomplished in me, And he was reckoned among the transgressors: for the things concerning me have an end. 38 And they said, Lord, behold, here *are* two swords. And he said unto them, It is enough.

Matthew 26:33 Peter answered and said unto him, Though all *men* shall be offended because of thee, *yet* will I never be offended. 34 Jesus said unto him, Verily I say unto thee, That this night, before the cock crow, thou shalt deny me thrice. 35 Peter said unto him, Though I should die with thee, yet will I not deny thee. Likewise also said all the disciples. 36 Then cometh Jesus with them unto a place called Gethsemane, and saith unto the disciples, Sit ye here, while I go and pray yonder. 37 And he took with him Peter and the two sons of Zebedee, and began to be sorrowful and very heavy.

4 John 18:1 When Jesus had spoken these words, he went forth with his disciples over the brook Cedron, where was a garden, into the which he entered, and his disciples. 2 And Judas also, which betrayed him, knew the place: for Jesus ofttimes resorted thither with his disciples.

5 Hebrews 12:3 For consider him that endured such contradiction of sinners against himself, lest ye be wearied and faint in your minds. 4 Ye have not yet resisted unto blood, striving against sin.

Luke 22:44 And being in an agony he prayed more earnestly: and his sweat was as it were great drops of blood falling down to the ground.

Hebrews 5:7 Who in the days of his flesh, when he had offered up prayers and supplications with strong crying and tears unto him that was able to save him from death, and was heard in that he feared;

6 Matthew 26:50 And Jesus said unto him, Friend, wherefore art thou come? Then came they, and laid hands on Jesus, and took him.

7 Matthew 26:56 But all this was done, that the scriptures of the prophets might be fulfilled. Then all the disciples forsook him, and fled.

Mark 14:50 And they all forsook him, and fled.

John 16:32 Behold, the hour cometh, yea, is now come, that ye shall be scattered, every man to his own, and shall leave me alone: and yet I am not alone, because the Father is with me.

8 In 2004, Mel Gibson, known for his drunken anti-Semitic rants, produced *The Passion of the Christ*, constructed largely upon the *The Dolorous Passion of Our Lord Jesus Christ* by Anne Catherine Emmerich. I have not viewed the film. Based upon the reviews and a synopsis, the character of Jesus in the film is mauled and tortured between the Garden and the house of the high priest. He was not handled with gentleness, but the film exceeds the Scriptures and I wish to be clear that my use of the word *roughly* is not meant to convey what now is the common conception in the minds of those who have been influenced by the film.

9 This transitive verb is defined by the Merriam-Webster 11th Collegiate Dictionary as "to strike sharply especially with the hand ... to strike repeatedly: BATTER 'the waves buffeted the shore'... to drive, force, move, or attack by or as if by repeated blows."

10 Luke 23:11 And Herod with his men of war set him at nought, and mocked *him*, and arrayed him in a gorgeous robe, and sent him again to Pilate.

11 Psalm 129:3 The plowers plowed upon my back: they made long their furrows.

John 19:1 Then Pilate therefore took Jesus, and scourged *him*. 2 And the soldiers platted a crown of thorns, and put *it* on his head, and they put on him a purple robe, 3 And said, Hail, King of the Jews! and they smote him with their hands. 4 Pilate therefore went forth again, and saith unto them, Behold, I bring him forth to you, that ye may know that I find no fault in him. 5 Then came Jesus forth, wearing the crown of thorns, and the purple robe. And *Pilate* saith unto them, Behold the man!

Matthew 27:26 Then released he Barabbas unto them: and when he had scourged Jesus, he delivered *him* to be crucified. 27 Then the soldiers of the governor took Jesus into the common hall, and gathered unto him the whole band *of soldiers.* 28 And they stripped him, and put on him a scarlet robe. 29 And when they had platted a crown of thorns, they put *it* upon his head, and a reed in his right hand: and they bowed the knee before him, and mocked him, saying, Hail, King of the Jews! 30 And they spit upon him, and took the reed, and smote him on the head. 31 And after that they had mocked him, they took the robe off from him, and put his own raiment on him, and led him away to crucify *him.*

Mark 15:15 And *so* Pilate, willing to content the people, released Barabbas unto them, and delivered Jesus, when he had scourged *him,* to be crucified. 16 And the soldiers led him away into the hall, called Praetorium; and they call together the whole band. 17 And they clothed him with purple, and platted a crown of thorns, and put it about his *head,* 18 And began to salute him, Hail, King of the Jews! 19 And they smote him on the head with a reed, and did spit upon him, and bowing *their* knees worshipped him. 20 And when they had mocked him, they took off the purple from him, and put his own clothes on him, and led him out to crucify him.

¹² Luke 23:2 And they began to accuse him, saying, We found this *fellow* perverting the nation, and forbidding to give tribute to Caesar, saying that he himself is Christ a King.

¹³ John 19:7 The Jews answered him, We have a law, and by our law he ought to die, because he made himself the Son of God.

¹⁴ Luke 23:27 And there followed him a great company of people, and of women, which also bewailed and lamented him. 28 But Jesus turning unto them said, Daughters of Jerusalem, weep not for me, but weep for yourselves, and for your children. 29 For, behold, the days are coming, in the which they shall say, Blessed *are* the barren, and the wombs that never bare, and the paps which never gave suck. 30 Then shall they begin to say to the mountains, Fall on us; and to the hills, Cover us. 31 For if they do these things in a green tree, what shall be done in the dry?

¹⁵ Ira F. Stamphill wrote the song *Follow Me,* which contains the lines: "My feet were also weary, upon the Calvary road; The cross became so heavy, I fell beneath the load." The song is often used because of its missionary lines: Oh Jesus if I die upon a foreign field someday, 'Twould be no more than love demands, no less could I repay." It is a pleasant song, but the LORD Jesus did not fall beneath the load. I wish Stamphill had written "bowed beneath the load." That would have been poetic license, but it would not have violated the Scriptures by

following Roman Catholic tradition. Strangely, Simon of Cyrene is not accorded official recognition as a saint by the Roman Catholic Church. The song is under copyright restrictions for use.

16 The idea is the product of a works based soteriology. It is the suggestion that Christ alone is not sufficient for salvation, but that another intercessor is needed or that baptism must remove sin or that works are required.

17 Matthew 27:32 And as they came out, they found a man of Cyrene, Simon by name: him they compelled to bear his cross.

Mark 15:21 And they compel one Simon a Cyrenian, who passed by, coming out of the country, the father of Alexander and Rufus, to bear his cross.

Luke 23:26 And as they led him away, they laid hold upon one Simon, a Cyrenian, coming out of the country, and on him they laid the cross, that he might bear it after Jesus.

18 Luke 9:51

John 12:27 Now is my soul troubled; and what shall I say? Father, save me from this hour: but for this cause came I unto this hour.

19 John 10:17 Therefore doth my Father love me, because I lay down my life, that I might take it again. 18 No man taketh it from me, but I lay it down of myself. I have power to lay it down, and I have power to take it again. This commandment have I received of my Father.

Were these verses to be read and believed, then the issue of the Jews being responsible for the death of Jesus of Nazareth would never be present. *No man taketh it from me*—while that statement certainly declares that He was a willing sacrifice and that the soldiers did not have to force Him to the cross, it goes beyond that to declare that His life was not taken by the action of any collection of humanity. However, those gathered on that day would have killed Him had they been able to do so and they are rightly held to be guilty for the intent of the deed.

Acts 2:23 Him, being delivered by the determinate counsel and foreknowledge of God, ye have taken, and by wicked hands have crucified and slain:

Acts 3:13 The God of Abraham, and of Isaac, and of Jacob, the God of our fathers, hath glorified his Son Jesus; whom ye delivered up, and denied him in the presence of Pilate, when he was determined to let *him* go. 14 But ye denied the Holy One and the Just, and desired a murderer to be granted unto you; 15 And killed the Prince of life, whom God hath raised from the dead; whereof we are witnesses.

Acts 4:10 Be it known unto you all, and to all the people of Israel, that by the name of Jesus Christ of Nazareth, whom ye crucified, whom God raised from the dead, *even* by him doth this man stand here before you whole. 11 This is the stone which was set at nought of you builders, which is become the head of the corner.

Acts 5:30 The God of our fathers raised up Jesus, whom ye slew and hanged on a tree.

Acts 7:52 Which of the prophets have not your fathers persecuted? and they have slain them which shewed before of the coming of the Just One; of whom ye have been now the betrayers and murderers:

In the offering of the burnt offering and the sin offering, a required and important step was for the offerer to lay his hand upon the head of the animal signifying his identification with the sacrifice and the identification of the sacrifice with him; however, it also signified the responsibility of the offerer for the death of the sacrifice. (Leviticus 1:4 And he shall put his hand upon the head of the burnt offering; and it shall be accepted for him to make atonement for him.) The sins were laid upon the head of animal so that the atonement achieved by the shed blood of the animal might be laid on the offerer. This was the type, the example, of how our sins are laid upon Christ so that the atonement obtained by His shed blood might be imputed to us. All of the Levitical offerings, as well as those offerings presented before the Law was given are types of the one offering of the LORD Jesus. Paul wrote that Christ is our Passover and He is sacrificed for us (1 Corinthians 5:7). It is also true that Christ is our burnt offering, our meat offering, our peace offering, our sin offering, our trespass offering, our morning and evening sacrifice offering, and our Day of Atonement offering.

In accepting the atonement that is in Christ as *my presented Sacrifice,* I then also accept the responsibility for the death of the Sacrifice. Who is responsible for the death of Jesus of Nazareth, I am and so are all that receive Him as their salvation. Those who reject Him surely are like those that Paul describes in Hebrews 10:29 as treading on the Person of the Son of GOD and counts the blood of the covenant an unholy thing worthy of contempt and disdain.

[20] Psalm 22:14 I am poured out like water, and all my bones are out of joint: my heart is like wax; it is melted in the midst of my bowels. 15 My strength is dried up like a potsherd; and my tongue cleaveth to my jaws; and thou hast brought me into the dust of death. 16 For dogs have compassed me: the assembly of the wicked have inclosed me: they pierced my hands and my feet. 17 I may tell all my bones: they look *and* stare upon me.

21 "Death by Roman crucifixion was a result of the whole body weight being supported by the stretched arms. When nailed to the cross there was a massive strain put on the wrists, arms and shoulders often resulting in a dislocation of the shoulder and elbow joints. The rib cage was constrained in a fixed position, which made it extremely difficult to exhale, and impossible to take a full breath. The victim would continually try to draw himself up by his feet to allow for inflation of the lungs enduring terrible pain in his feet and legs. The pain in the feet and legs became unbearable and the victim was forced to trade breathing for pain. The length of time required to die from crucifixion could range from hours to a number of days."

"The main cause of death by Roman crucifixion was due to asphyxiation. Asphyxiation results from lack of exchange of oxygen and carbon dioxide due to respiratory failure or disturbance, resulting in insufficient brain oxygen, which leads to unconsciousness and death. The execution method of Roman Crucifixion could produce death from a number of other causes, including physical shock caused by the scourging that preceded the crucifixion shock from the process of being nailed to the cross, dehydration or exhaustion."

Alchin, L.K., Tribunes and Triumphs. Roman Punishment. Retrieved January 29, 2014 from www.tribunesandtriumphs.org

22 Isaiah 52:14 As many were astonied at thee; his visage was so marred more than any man, and his form more than the sons of men.

23 Isaiah 52:2, 3

24 1 Peter 1:11 Searching what, or what manner of time the Spirit of Christ which was in them did signify, when it testified beforehand the sufferings of Christ, and the glory that should follow.

As an example of these prophesies, consider these verses from Psalm 69.

1 Save me, O God; for the waters are come in unto *my* soul. 2 I sink in deep mire, where *there is* no standing: I am come into deep waters, where the floods overflow me. 3 I am weary of my crying: my throat is dried: mine eyes fail while I wait for my God. 4 They that hate me without a cause are more than the hairs of mine head: they that would destroy me, *being* mine enemies wrongfully, are mighty: then I restored *that* which I took not away. ... 7 Because for thy sake I have borne reproach; shame hath covered my face. 8 I am become a stranger unto my brethren, and an alien unto my mother's children. 9 For the zeal of thine house hath eaten me up; and the reproaches of them that reproached thee are fallen upon me. ... 20 Reproach hath broken my heart; and I am full of heaviness: and I looked *for some* to take pity, but *there was* none; and for comforters, but I

found none. 21 They gave me also gall for my meat; and in my thirst they gave me vinegar to drink.

25 Jesus of Nazareth faces six judicial sessions of examination during the time between the arrest in Gethsemane and the washing of his hands by Pilate and his condemning Jesus of Nazareth to death. Those sessions are the examination before Annas, the examination before Caiaphas, the examination before the Sanhedrin, the first examination before Pilate, the examination before Herod, and the second examination before Pilate.

26 The LORD Jesus taught "If a man keep my saying, he shall never see death." The scribes and Pharisees (John 8:3, 13) responded to that statement by quoting Him as having said "If a man keep my saying, he shall never taste of death."

> John 8:51 Verily, verily, I say unto you, If a man keep my saying, he shall never see death. 52 Then said the Jews unto him, Now we know that thou hast a devil. Abraham is dead, and the prophets; and thou sayest, If a man keep my saying, he shall never taste of death.

The phrase "see death" would have been familiar to these religiously trained scribes and Pharisees, who were steeped in "the law of Moses, and *in* the prophets, and *in* the Psalms" (Luke 24:44). Paul would later use the same phrase in writing primarily to a Jewish audience.

> Psalm 89:48 What man *is he that* liveth, and shall not see death? shall he deliver his soul from the hand of the grave? Selah.

> Hebrews 11:5 By faith Enoch was translated that he should not see death; and was not found, because God had translated him: for before his translation he had this testimony, that he pleased God.

However, these men did not hear the phrase that way. They heard *taste* instead of *see*. Either these men were using a common Jewish phrase that appears in the Talmud (*SwordSearcher;* A. T. Robertson's *Word Pictures in the New Testament;* John 8:52), but not in the Old Testament or they were quoting what the LORD Jesus had told His disciples in a session immediately before the time of the Transfiguration.

> Matthew 16:28 Verily I say unto you, There be some standing here, which shall not taste of death, till they see the Son of man coming in his kingdom.

> Mark 9:1 And he said unto them, Verily I say unto you, That there be some of them that stand here, which shall not taste of death, till they have seen the kingdom of God come with power.

> Luke 9:27 But I tell you of a truth, there be some standing here, which shall not taste of death, till they see the kingdom of God.

While the commentaries follow the first potential, I lean to the latter understanding. The scribes and Pharisees, along with the Sadducees, took careful notice of every word that the Son of man said; they had their spies in every gathering of disciples to catch Him in His words. I believe they had knowledge of what He had taught the disciples only a few weeks before.

The LORD Jesus is referencing the second death, eternal death, not physical death. The second death is connected with the Lake of Fire.

> Revelation 2:11 He that hath an ear, let him hear what the Spirit saith unto the churches; He that overcometh shall not be hurt of the second death. ... 20:6 Blessed and holy *is* he that hath part in the first resurrection: on such the second death hath no power, but they shall be priests of God and of Christ, and shall reign with him a thousand years. ... 14 And death and hell were cast into the lake of fire. This is the second death. ... 21:8 But the fearful, and unbelieving, and the abominable, and murderers, and whoremongers, and sorcerers, and idolaters, and all liars, shall have their part in the lake which burneth with fire and brimstone: which is the second death.

The LORD Jesus tasted death so that those who believe on Him would never taste of death.

> Hebrews 2:9 But we see Jesus, who was made a little lower than the angels for the suffering of death, crowned with glory and honour; that he by the grace of God should taste death for every man.

This concept is fully in keeping with the statements of Christ in John 11.

> 1 Now a certain *man* was sick, *named* Lazarus, of Bethany, the town of Mary and her sister Martha. 2 (It was *that* Mary which anointed the Lord with ointment, and wiped his feet with her hair, whose brother Lazarus was sick.) 3 Therefore his sisters sent unto him, saying, Lord, behold, he whom thou lovest is sick. 4 When Jesus heard *that*, he said, This sickness is not unto death, but for the glory of God, that the Son of God might be glorified thereby. 5 Now Jesus loved Martha, and her sister, and Lazarus. 6 When he had heard therefore that he was sick, he abode two days still in the same place where he was. 7 Then after that saith he to *his* disciples, Let us go into Judaea again. 8 *His* disciples say unto him, Master, the Jews of late sought to stone thee; and goest thou

thither again? 9 Jesus answered, Are there not twelve hours in the day? If any man walk in the day, he stumbleth not, because he seeth the light of this world. 10 But if a man walk in the night, he stumbleth, because there is no light in him. 11 These things said he: and after that he saith unto them, Our friend Lazarus sleepeth; but I go, that I may awake him out of sleep. 12 Then said his disciples, Lord, if he sleep, he shall do well. 13 Howbeit Jesus spake of his death: but they thought that he had spoken of taking of rest in sleep. 14 Then said Jesus unto them plainly, Lazarus is dead. 15 And I am glad for your sakes that I was not there, to the intent ye may believe; nevertheless let us go unto him. 16 Then said Thomas, which is called Didymus, unto his fellowdisciples, Let us also go, that we may die with him. 17 Then when Jesus came, he found that he had *lain* in the grave four days already. 18 Now Bethany was nigh unto Jerusalem, about fifteen furlongs off: 19 And many of the Jews came to Martha and Mary, to comfort them concerning their brother. 20 Then Martha, as soon as she heard that Jesus was coming, went and met him: but Mary sat *still* in the house. 21 Then said Martha unto Jesus, Lord, if thou hadst been here, my brother had not died. 22 But I know, that even now, whatsoever thou wilt ask of God, God will give *it* thee. 23 Jesus saith unto her, Thy brother shall rise again. 24 Martha saith unto him, I know that he shall rise again in the resurrection at the last day. 25 Jesus said unto her, **I am the resurrection, and the life: he that believeth in me, though he were dead, yet shall he live: 26 And whosoever liveth and believeth in me shall never die. Believest thou this?** 27 She saith unto him, Yea, Lord: I believe that thou art the Christ, the Son of God, which should come into the world.

[27] Psalm 118:27 God is the LORD, which hath shewed us light: bind the sacrifice with cords, even unto the horns of the altar.

[28] John Newton. In Public Domain.

CHAPTER 2

CONFUSION AT CALVARY

I have long been intrigued with the pattern of noticeable paradoxes found in Scripture. It is not that I have found inconsistency or illogicality; my mindset is that I do not consider contradictions as having a possibility of existence within Scripture, while conceding that I do not comprehend the entirety of Scripture.

Even so, this traceable pattern of paradox does exist where the expected is replaced by the neglected, where the obvious is supplanted by the unseen, or where the primary gives place to the secondary.[1] Nothing that the Eternal TRINITY does may be said to have fallen accidentally into place; happenstance is not a Biblical word or concept, even though the natural eye may see it so.[2]

Two relatively minor episodes in my early ministry helped me settle the issue of the possibility of confusion[3] within Scripture.

The first incident was when, as a young preacher, I read that GOD spoke with a tongue that never stammered and wrote with a pen that

29

never skipped. I found the word of GOD to be a safe harbor more than fifty years ago, so I dropped anchor; and it has never slipped and I have never felt the need to weigh anchor. In the years since, there have been winds and waves aplenty; but that solid anchorage has held safely and securely.

Examples of paradoxes are easily found in Scripture; perhaps among the more familiar would be: "[the] first shall be last; and the last first"[4]; and that losing life for Christ's sake means that it will be found.[5] However, the student of Scripture must also be intrigued with the passages that relate the following unusual stories.

1. The judge who was told he had too many men to go into battle against a vastly superior force.[6]
2. The widow who had a great debt and the prophet told her to borrow more.[7]
3. The man whose ears could not hear and into whose ears the LORD Jesus stuck His fingers.[8]
4. The man whose eyes were blind and on whose unseeing eyes the LORD Jesus placed clay.[9]
5. The man dead four days, already decomposing, bound hand and foot, being called upon to come out of the grave.[10]

I may be confounded in trying to explain the *how* or the *why* of what the Bible says; but I am confident that there is no confusion in what the Bible says: ***"Whatever the Bible says is so."***[11]

The second experience that helped me anchor my confidence in the Bible came when I heard Dr. John R. Rice call attention to the fact that GOD handles problems differently than do we. I listened, considered, and began that day to apply the principle that GOD gave Isaiah[12] in a far wider scope as well as a more mundane way than ever before. I previously rather used that doctrine for salvation and the great things of Scripture. From that sermon, I began to see that it is generally descriptive of the methodology of GOD's providence, which I understand to be His watchcare for His creation and especially for His children.

From that message forward, I have noticed that it applies even to the least aspect of my living. His ways are infinitely higher than my ways; and, though I often do not comprehend the *why* of His ways, I have learned that He does indeed also think of me in higher ways than I do myself.

Simply put, human reasoning or even earthly experience cannot satisfactorily explain the events of life. Observation does not always reveal the truth of what is actually transpiring. Without the revelation that GOD has given us in His word, we would never be able to evaluate the enigma of living; but with that revelation in that very Book, we may have confidence that the GOD of Heaven knows what He is doing.

This Book that we call the Bible and that identifies itself as the word of GOD has no error of inclusion and no blunder of exclusion. There is no dross in the word of GOD for it is as silver *purified seven times*. It is as *fine gold*: pure gold without the admixture of any alloy within. [13]

The psalmist described the word of GOD as perfect, sure, right, pure, clean, and true and righteous altogether. That last word "altogether" has the English synonyms of "completely, wholly, totally, thoroughly," and, the one I especially like, "when all is said and done." The same continuity is found in the Hebrew. The "altogether" goes back to the "perfect," includes "sure, right, pure, clean, true, and righteous," but it continues forward to the day when all of the word of GOD is *that was said is fully and finally done.*[14]

We need have no fear that the word of GOD is contaminated and corrupted. Men have attempted to pollute the words of the word of GOD for centuries; however, GOD has preserved His word through all of those centuries, because it is His words.[15]

Since this Book did not arise "by the will of man," **but** "proceedeth out of the mouth of God," was spoken by "holy men of God ... as they were moved by the Holy Ghost," was "written for the generation to come" "for our learning, that we through patience and comfort of the scriptures might have hope," **because** "all these things happened unto them for ensamples: and they are written for our admonition, upon whom the ends of the world are come."[16] It is, therefore, ours to search the Scriptures with a readiness of mind to receive what is written therein.[17]

Therefore, as we study what is perhaps the greatest perplexity—the paradox of paradoxes—let us do so with the confidence that our GOD "is the Rock, his work is perfect: for all his ways are judgment: a GOD of truth and without iniquity, just and right is he."[18] There is no iniquity—no counterfeit—involved with GOD.

Just as importantly, there is no inconsistency with GOD.[19] As He was to Adam, He was to Moses and that is what He is *to all generations.* James was moved to tell us that there is no shadow of turning with GOD.[20] He is described as the Rock, which speaks of stability and unchangeableness. It was that constancy and permanence that was the comfort for the psalmist.[21]

It is that immutability that is at question in the discussion of what occurred on the hill called

Golgotha. Did GOD the Father abandon GOD the Son at Calvary?

All of my church attending life, I have heard a variety of preachers and teachers declare that GOD the Father turned His back on Jesus of Nazareth when He hung upon that cross on the hill called Calvary.[22] It is often stated that GOD cannot look upon sin, therefore, when the LORD Jesus "was made to be sin,"[23] the Father *had* to turn His back and look away.

That concept has never sat well with me. It simply has not gone down, as my father would have said. The thought simply did not make sense; it did not seem to be logical. If GOD cannot look upon sin, how then is it possible that "The eyes of the LORD *are* in every place, **beholding the evil and the good**"?[24]

Why would it be recorded eighteen times that a kings did *evil **in the sight** of the LORD*?

Why would the prophet write, "Behold, **the eyes of the Lord GOD *are* upon** the sinful kingdom, and I will destroy it from off the face of the earth; saving that I will not utterly destroy the house of Jacob, saith the LORD"?[25]

More essentially, how would it be possible for the Incarnation to have taken place? Was not Jesus of Nazareth GOD manifest in the flesh?[26]

Jesus of Nazareth is declared to have the "fullness of the GODHEAD dwelling in Him.[27] Yet, GOD is said not to be able to look on sin. Did He not **see** both those hidden sins of the hearts[28] as well as the overt sins of the people?[29] How is it then possible to teach that Jesus of Nazareth is the Word, Who is GOD, made flesh, but then to advocate that GOD cannot look upon sin?[30]

Scripture is absolute in its consistency; it must be inviolable in all efforts of Biblical interpretation. The LORD Jesus affirmed "the scripture cannot be broken."[31] Even a maverick prophet such as Balaam understood that the words of GOD were incapable of being changed or of being in conflict with the other words of GOD.

> Numbers 22:18 And Balaam answered and said unto the servants of Balak, If Balak would give me his house full of silver and gold, I cannot go beyond the word of the LORD my God, to do less or more. ... 23:19 God *is* not a man, that he should lie; neither the son of man, that he should repent: hath he said, and shall he not do *it?* or hath he spoken, and shall he not make it good? 20 Behold, I have received *commandment* to bless: and he hath blessed; and I cannot reverse it.

Any confliction that *appears* to exist between two or more passages of Scripture is due to misconception of one or more of those passages on our part. Any presentation of a passage from the word of GOD that purports to be Biblical but that contradicts another passage of Scripture is erroneous in its facts as well as in its origin. The words of the word of GOD "proceedeth out of the mouth of the LORD";[32] therefore, it is impossible for there to be a contradiction among the words of Scripture. The error is that of the human interpreter, regardless of assumed stature.

> Psalm 89:34 My covenant will I not break, nor alter the thing that is gone out of my lips.

The *good and perfect gift* identified by James as *from above,* coming *down from the Father of lights, with Whom is no variableness, neither shadow of turning*[33] is described with the eloquence of Hebrew poetry, in Psalm 19.

> 7 The law of the LORD *is* **perfect**, converting the soul: the testimony of the LORD *is* sure, making wise the simple. 8 The statutes of the LORD *are* **right**, rejoicing the heart: the commandment of the LORD *is* **pure**, enlightening

the eyes. 9 The fear of the LORD *is* **clean**, enduring for ever: the judgments of the LORD *are* **true** *and* **righteous altogether**. 10 More to be desired *are they* than gold, yea, than much fine gold: sweeter also than honey and the honeycomb.

The GOD of the Bible is not the author of confusion;[34] therefore, whenever there is confusion in presentation or in understanding, that confusion did not originate with GOD and it was not produced by the Spirit of GOD.

It seems to me that to introduce a separation between JEHOVAH on earth and JEHOVAH in heaven[35] by suggesting that something transpired that *changed* the Son of GOD so that GOD the Father had to cast Him out of His sight is to introduce the confusion of contradiction regarding the relationship of JEHOVAH in heaven and JEHOVAH on the cross. JEHOVAH the Holy Spirit is never introduced into the formula. The unity of the TRINITY is ruptured. When this is allowed, the TRINITY is misunderstood and therefore misrepresented in occurred that day at Golgotha.

Confusion at Calvary is written to set aside the authority of the views of men—*even very good men*—and to let the Scriptures stand as they proceeded from the mouth of GOD, speaking for themselves. It is prayerfully sent with the desire that it might remove the confusion that exists as to what GOD the Father did when Jesus of Nazareth died outside the gate of Jerusalem at the place of a skull.[36]

Abraham asked, "Shall not the Judge of all the earth do right?"[37] That is the question that rests before us.

Was their Confusion at Calvary?

---

[1] I am using the word *paradox* in the sense of "a statement that is seemingly contradictory or opposed to common sense" "contrary to expectation" (Merriam-Webster) and in accordance with the medical definition from the American Heritage Medical Dictionary "That which is apparently, though not actually, inconsistent with or opposed to the known facts in any case."

One passage that quickly illustrates this pattern of paradox by using one in each verse—is 2 Corinthians 4:16 For which cause we faint not; but though our outward man perish, yet the inward man is renewed day by day. 17 For our light affliction, which is but for a moment, worketh for us a far more exceeding and eternal weight of glory; 18 While we look not at the things which are seen, but at the things which are not seen: for the things which are seen are temporal; but the things which are not seen are eternal.

[2] 1 Corinthians 2:14 But the natural man receiveth not the things of the Spirit of God: for they are foolishness unto him: neither can he know *them*, because they are spiritually discerned.

John 8:43 Why do ye not understand my speech? *even* because ye cannot hear my word.

Proverbs 14:6 A scorner seeketh wisdom, and *findeth it* not: but knowledge *is* easy unto him that understandeth.

[3] Under the general title of confusion, I include, whether intentional or accidental, mistakes, errors, inaccuracies, missteps, lapses, gaffes, blunders, slips, faults, oversteps, miscalculations, blemishes, omissions, flaws, defects, imperfections, deficiencies, misstatements, weaknesses, shortcomings, exaggerations, embellishments, overstatements, understatements, deceptions, deceits, duplicities, trickery, or falsenesses of any class, kind, category, type, manner, sort, form, or nature whatsoever.

[4] Mark 10:31 But many *that are* first shall be last; and the last first.

Matthew 19:30 But many *that are* first shall be last; and the last *shall be* first.

Matthew 20:16 So the last shall be first, and the first last: for many be called, but few chosen.

Luke 13:30 And, behold, there are last which shall be first, and there are first which shall be last.

[5] Matthew 10:39 He that findeth his life shall lose it: and he that loseth his life for my sake shall find it.

Matthew 16:25 For whosoever will save his life shall lose it: and whosoever will lose his life for my sake shall find it.

6 Judges 7:2 And the LORD said unto Gideon, The people that *are* with thee *are* too many for me to give the Midianites into their hands, lest Israel vaunt themselves against me, saying, Mine own hand hath saved me. 3 Now therefore go to, proclaim in the ears of the people, saying, Whosoever *is* fearful and afraid, let him return and depart early from mount Gilead. And there returned of the people twenty and two thousand; and there remained ten thousand. 4 And the LORD said unto Gideon, The people *are* yet *too* many; bring them down unto the water, and I will try them for thee there: and it shall be, *that* of whom I say unto thee, This shall go with thee, the same shall go with thee; and of whomsoever I say unto thee, This shall not go with thee, the same shall not go. 5 So he brought down the people unto the water: and the LORD said unto Gideon, Every one that lappeth of the water with his tongue, as a dog lappeth, him shalt thou set by himself; likewise every one that boweth down upon his knees to drink. 6 And the number of them that lapped, *putting* their hand to their mouth, were three hundred men: but all the rest of the people bowed down upon their knees to drink water. 7 And the LORD said unto Gideon, By the three hundred men that lapped will I save you, and deliver the Midianites into thine hand: and let all the *other* people go every man unto his place.

7 2 Kings 4:1 Now there cried a certain woman of the wives of the sons of the prophets unto Elisha, saying, Thy servant my husband is dead; and thou knowest that thy servant did fear the LORD: and the creditor is come to take unto him my two sons to be bondmen. 2 And Elisha said unto her, What shall I do for thee? tell me, what hast thou in the house? And she said, Thine handmaid hath not any thing in the house, save a pot of oil. 3 Then he said, Go, borrow thee vessels abroad of all thy neighbours, *even* empty vessels; borrow not a few. 4 And when thou art come in, thou shalt shut the door upon thee and upon thy sons, and shalt pour out into all those vessels, and thou shalt set aside that which is full. 5 So she went from him, and shut the door upon her and upon her sons, who brought *the vessels* to her; and she poured out. 6 And it came to pass, when the vessels were full, that she said unto her son, Bring me yet a vessel. And he said unto her, *There is* not a vessel more. And the oil stayed. 7 Then she came and told the man of God. And he said, Go, sell the oil, and pay thy debt, and live thou and thy children of the rest.

8 Mark 7:33 And he took him aside from the multitude, and put his fingers into his ears, and he spit, and touched his tongue;

9 John 9:6 When he had thus spoken, he spat on the ground, and made clay of the spittle, and he anointed the eyes of the blind man with the clay,

10 John 11:43 And when he thus had spoken, he cried with a loud voice, Lazarus, come forth.

11 A favorite saying of Dr. Bob Jones Sr. particularly as he addressed his "preacher boys."

12 Isaiah 55:8 For my thoughts *are* not your thoughts, neither *are* your ways my ways, saith the LORD. 9 For *as* the heavens are higher than the earth, so are my ways higher than your ways, and my thoughts than your thoughts.

13 Psalms 19:10 More to be desired *are they* than gold, yea, than much fine gold: sweeter also than honey and the honeycomb.

Psalms 119:127 Therefore I love thy commandments above gold; yea, above fine gold.

14 Psalm 12:6 The words of the LORD *are* pure words: *as* silver tried in a furnace of earth, purified seven times.

Psalm 19:7 The law of the LORD *is* perfect, converting the soul: the testimony of the LORD *is* sure, making wise the simple. 8 The statutes of the LORD *are* right, rejoicing the heart: the commandment of the LORD *is* pure, enlightening the eyes. 9 The fear of the LORD *is* clean, enduring for ever: the judgments of the LORD *are* true *and* righteous altogether. 10 More to be desired *are they* than gold, yea, than much fine gold: sweeter also than honey and the honeycomb. 11 Moreover by them is thy servant warned: *and* in keeping of them *there is* great reward.

Isaiah 55:11 So shall my word be that goeth forth out of my mouth: it shall not return unto me void, but it shall accomplish that which I please, and it shall prosper *in the thing* whereto I sent it.

15 Isaiah 59:21 As for me, this *is* my covenant with them, saith the LORD; My spirit that *is* upon thee, and my words which I have put in thy mouth, shall not depart out of thy mouth, nor out of the mouth of thy seed, nor out of the mouth of thy seed's seed, saith the LORD, from henceforth and for ever.

16 Deuteronomy 8:3 And he humbled thee, and suffered thee to hunger, and fed thee with manna, which thou knewest not, neither did thy fathers know; that he might make thee know that man doth not live by bread only, but by every *word* that proceedeth out of the mouth of the LORD doth man live.

Matthew 4:4 But he answered and said, It is written, Man shall not live by bread alone, but by every word that proceedeth out of the mouth of God.

2 Peter 1:21 For the prophecy came not in old time by the will of man: but holy men of God spake *as they were* moved by the Holy Ghost.

Psalm 102:18 This shall be written for the generation to come: and the people which shall be created shall praise the LORD.

Romans 15:4 For whatsoever things were written aforetime were written for our learning, that we through patience and comfort of the scriptures might have hope.

1 Corinthians 10:11 Now all these things happened unto them for ensamples: and they are written for our admonition, upon whom the ends of the world are come.

[17] John 5:39 Search the scriptures; for in them ye think ye have eternal life: and they are they which testify of me.

Acts 17:10 And the brethren immediately sent away Paul and Silas by night unto Berea: who coming *thither* went into the synagogue of the Jews.

[18] Deuteronomy 32:4 *He is* the Rock, his work *is* perfect: for all his ways *are* judgment: a God of truth and without iniquity, just and right *is* he.

[19] Malachi 3:6 For I *am* the LORD, I change not; therefore ye sons of Jacob are not consumed.

James 1:17 Every good gift and every perfect gift is from above, and cometh down from the Father of lights, with whom is no variableness, neither shadow of turning.

1 Samuel 15:29 And also the Strength of Israel will not lie nor repent: for he is not a man, that he should repent.

Isaiah 46:10 Declaring the end from the beginning, and from ancient times the things that are not yet done, saying, My counsel shall stand, and I will do all my pleasure: 11 Calling a ravenous bird from the east, the man that executeth my counsel from a far country: yea, I have spoken it, I will also bring it to pass; I have purposed it, I will also do it.

Hebrews 1:11 They shall perish; but thou remainest; and they all shall wax old as doth a garment; 12 And as a vesture shalt thou fold them up, and they shall be changed: but thou art the same, and thy years shall not fail.

Psalm 33:11 The counsel of the LORD standeth for ever, the thoughts of his heart to all generations.

[20] James 1:17 Every good gift and every perfect gift is from above, and cometh down from the Father of lights, with whom is no variableness, neither shadow of turning.

[21] Deuteronomy 32:4 *He is* the **Rock**, his work *is* perfect: for all his ways *are* judgment: a God of truth and without iniquity, just and right *is* he. ... 15 But Jeshurun waxed fat, and kicked: thou art waxen fat, thou art grown thick, thou art covered *with fatness*; then he forsook God *which* made him, and lightly esteemed the **Rock** of his salvation. 16 They provoked him to jealousy with strange *gods*, with abominations provoked they him to anger. 17 They sacrificed unto devils, not to God; to

gods whom they knew not, to new *gods that* came newly up, whom your fathers feared not. 18 Of the **Rock** *that* begat thee thou art unmindful, and hast forgotten God that formed thee. ... 31 For their rock *is* not as our **Rock**, even our enemies themselves *being* judges. 32 For their vine *is* of the vine of Sodom, and of the fields of Gomorrah: their grapes *are* grapes of gall, their clusters *are* bitter:

2 Samuel 22:2 And he said, The LORD *is* my **rock**, and my fortress, and my deliverer; 3 The God of my **rock**; in him will I trust: *he is* my shield, and the horn of my salvation, my high tower, and my refuge, my saviour; thou savest me from violence. ... 31 *As for* God, his way *is* perfect; the word of the LORD *is* tried: he *is* a buckler to all them that trust in him. 32 For who *is* God, save the LORD? and who *is* a **rock**, save our God? ... 47 The LORD liveth; and blessed *be* my **rock**; and exalted be the God of the **rock** of my salvation.

Psalm 18:2 The LORD *is* my **rock**, and my fortress, and my deliverer; my God, my strength, in whom I will trust; my buckler, and the horn of my salvation, *and* my high tower. ... 31 For who *is* God save the LORD? or who *is* a **rock** save our God? ... 46 The LORD liveth; and blessed *be* my **rock**; and let the God of my salvation be exalted.

28:1 Unto thee will I cry, O LORD my **rock**; be not silent to me: lest, *if* thou be silent to me, I become like them that go down into the pit.

31:2 Bow down thine ear to me; deliver me speedily: be thou my strong **rock**, for an house of defence to save me. ... 3 For thou *art* my **rock** and my fortress; therefore for thy name's sake lead me, and guide me.

42:9 I will say unto God my **rock**, Why hast thou forgotten me? why go I mourning because of the oppression of the enemy?

61:2 From the end of the earth will I cry unto thee, when my heart is overwhelmed: lead me to the **rock** *that* is higher than I.

62:2 He only *is* my **rock** and my salvation; *he is* my defence; I shall not be greatly moved. ... 6 He only *is* my **rock** and my salvation: *he is* my defence; I shall not be moved. ... 7 In God *is* my salvation and my glory: the **rock** of my strength, *and* my refuge, *is* in God.

71:3 Be thou my strong habitation, whereunto I may continually resort: thou hast given commandment to save me; for thou *art* my **rock** and my fortress.

78:35 And they remembered that God *was* their **rock**, and the high God their redeemer.

89:26 He shall cry unto me, Thou *art* my father, my God, and the **rock** of my salvation.

92:15 To shew that the LORD *is* upright: *he is* my **rock**, and *there is* no unrighteousness in him.

94:22 But the LORD is my defence; and my God *is* the **rock** of my refuge.

95:1 O come, let us sing unto the LORD: let us make a joyful noise to the **rock** of our salvation.

[22] "He didn't just feel forsaken; he was forsaken. For Jesus to become the curse, he had to be completely forsaken by the Father. It was as if there was a cry from heaven, as if Jesus heard the words "God damn you," because that's what it meant to be cursed and under the anathema of the Father. I don't understand that, but I know that it's true." R. C. Sproul, http://www.ligonier.org/blog/forsaken-jesus-became-curse/

Some of us think at times that we could cry, "My God, My God, why hast Thou forsaken me?" There are season when the brightness of our Father's smile is eclipsed by clouds and darkness; but let us remember that God never does really forsake us. It is only a seeming forsaking with us, but in Christ's case it was a real forsaking. We grieve at a little withdrawal of our Father's love; but the real turning away of God's face from His Son, who shall calculate how deep the agony which it caused Him? In our case, our cry is often dictated by unbelief: in His case, it was the utterance of a dreadful fact, for God had really turned away from Him for a season. O thou poor, distressed soul, who once lived in the sunshine of God's face, but now art in darkness, remember that He has not really forsaken thee. God in the clouds is as much our God as when He shines forth in all the lustre *[sic]* of His grace; but since even the thought that He has forsaken us gives us agony, what must the woe of the Saviour have been when He exclaimed, "My God, My God, why hast Thou forsaken me? Charles Haddon Spurgeon. *SwordSearcher; Spurgeon's Morning and Evening Devotional* Psalms 22:1; for April 15.

[23] 2 Corinthians 5:21 For he hath made him *to be* sin for us, who knew no sin; that we might be made the righteousness of God in him.

[24] Proverbs 15:3

[25] Amos 9:8

[26] 1 Timothy 3:16 And without controversy great is the mystery of godliness: God was manifest in the flesh, justified in the Spirit, seen of angels, preached unto the Gentiles, believed on in the world, received up into glory.

[27] Colossians 1:19 For it pleased *the Father* that in him should all fulness dwell ... 2:9 For in him dwelleth all the fulness of the Godhead bodily.

[28] John 2:24 But Jesus did not commit himself unto them, because he knew all *men*, 25 And needed not that any should testify of man: for he knew what was in man.

[29] Luke 22:60 And Peter said, Man, I know not what thou sayest. And immediately, while he yet spake, the cock crew. 61 And the Lord turned, and looked upon Peter. And Peter remembered the word of the Lord, how he had said unto him, Before the cock crow, thou shalt deny me thrice.

John 19:10 Then saith Pilate unto him, Speakest thou not unto me? knowest thou not that I have power to crucify thee, and have power to release thee? 11 Jesus answered, Thou couldest have no power *at all* against me, except it were given thee from above: therefore he that delivered me unto thee hath the greater sin.

[30] John 1:1 In the beginning was the Word, and the Word was with God, and the Word was God. ... 14 And the Word was made flesh, and dwelt among us, (and we beheld his glory, the glory as of the only begotten of the Father,) full of grace and truth.

[31] John 10:35 If he called them gods, unto whom the word of God came, and the scripture cannot be broken;

[32] Deuteronomy 8:3 And he humbled thee, and suffered thee to hunger, and fed thee with manna, which thou knewest not, neither did thy fathers know; that he might make thee know that man doth not live by bread only, but by every *word* that proceedeth out of the mouth of the LORD doth man live.

Matthew 4:4 But he answered and said, It is written, Man shall not live by bread alone, but by every word that proceedeth out of the mouth of God.

[33] While James is not directly addressing Scripture in 1:17, the Scriptures are indeed *from above* and they are *good* and *perfect,* coming *from the unchangeable Father of lights.*

James 1:17 Every good gift and every perfect gift is from above, and cometh down from the Father of lights, with whom is no variableness, neither shadow of turning.

[34] The archaic meaning of the word confuse is *"to bring to ruin.* Merriam-Webster 11th Collegiate Dictionary. While modern readers do not understand the word in that light, that usage is the end result of confusing the word of GOD.

1 Corinthians 14:33 For God is not *the author* of confusion, but of peace, as in all churches of the saints.

[35] Genesis 19:24 Then the LORD rained upon Sodom and upon Gomorrah brimstone and fire from the LORD out of heaven;

The Son of GOD, LORD, in a pre-incarnate form is on the earth and He brings the judgment of brimstone and fire upon Sodom and Gomorrah that comes from the LORD in heaven.

Matthew 3:13 Then cometh Jesus from Galilee to Jordan unto John, to be baptized of him. 14 But John forbad him, saying, I have need to be baptized of thee, and comest thou to me? 15

And Jesus answering said unto him, Suffer *it to be so* now: for thus it becometh us to fulfil all righteousness. Then he suffered him. 16 And Jesus, when he was baptized, went up straightway out of the water: and, lo, the heavens were opened unto him, and he saw the Spirit of God descending like a dove, and lighting upon him: 17 And lo a voice from heaven, saying, This is my beloved Son, in whom I am well pleased.

GOD the Father in Heaven speaks His approval of GOD the Son on earth and did so on three separate occasions: at the baptism, at the Mount of Transfiguration, and when the Saviour was teaching.

Matthew 3:17 And lo a voice from heaven, saying, This is my beloved Son, in whom I am well pleased. ... 17:5 While he yet spake, behold, a bright cloud overshadowed them: and behold a voice out of the cloud, which said, This is my beloved Son, in whom I am well pleased; hear ye him.

Mark 9:7 And there was a cloud that overshadowed them: and a voice came out of the cloud, saying, This is my beloved Son: hear him.

Luke 9:35 And there came a voice out of the cloud, saying, This is my beloved Son: hear him.

John 12:27 Now is my soul troubled; and what shall I say? Father, save me from this hour: but for this cause came I unto this hour. 28 Father, glorify thy name. Then came there a voice from heaven, *saying*, I have both glorified *it*, and will glorify *it* again.

2 Peter 1:17 For he received from God the Father honour and glory, when there came such a voice to him from the excellent glory, This is my beloved Son, in whom I am well pleased.

36 Hebrews 13:12 Wherefore Jesus also, that he might sanctify the people with his own blood, suffered without the gate.

Matthew 27:33 And when they were come unto a place called Golgotha, that is to say, a place of a skull,

37 Genesis 18:25 That be far from thee to do after this manner, to slay the righteous with the wicked: and that the righteous should be as the wicked, that be far from thee: Shall not the Judge of all the earth do right?

CHAPTER 3

WAS NABOTH FORSAKEN?

Naboth was a godly Bible-quoting man who owned property that Ahab the king coveted. Queen Jezebel had Naboth taken before a crooked court with a religious formality[1] and took his property from him through perjured testimony. Naboth and his sons were then stoned; their blood soaked corpses are left outside the city, while his wife and their mother is left destitute and homeless.[2]

> 1 Kings 21:1 And it came to pass after these things, *that* Naboth the Jezreelite had a vineyard, which *was* in Jezreel, hard by the palace of Ahab king of Samaria. 2 And Ahab spake unto Naboth, saying, Give me thy vineyard, that I may have it for a garden of herbs, because it *is* near unto my house: and I will give thee for it a better vineyard than it; *or*, if it seem good to thee, I will give thee the worth of it in money. 3 And Naboth said to Ahab, The LORD forbid it me, that I should give the inheritance of my fathers unto thee.

Naboth had a prime piece of real estate that bordered the land of King Ahab. When Ahab presented his offer to buy the property, Naboth respectfully declined and based his refusal not upon the terms of sale, which were fair and even generous, but upon the commands of GOD that (1) the land was not his to sell and (2) the property could not be transferred from one tribe to another.

> Leviticus 25:23 The land shall not be sold for ever: for the land is mine; for ye are strangers and sojourners with me.

> Numbers 36:7 So shall not the inheritance of the children of Israel remove from tribe to tribe: for every one of the children of Israel shall keep himself to the inheritance of the tribe of his fathers.

Naboth was a man that knew what GOD had established regarding the sale and transfer of the lot-apportioned land[3] and that determined to live his life based upon the word of GOD. Had he chosen, with this transaction, Naboth could have gained the royal favor and at the same time, he could have made a sizeable financial profit or he could have gained a better and larger piece of property. All that he had to do was to be willing to evade or to compromise the command of GOD.

This Naboth would not do for he could not disobey the commands of his GOD. Instead, he honored the word of GOD above his personal advantage and even the potential betterment of his family. He was committed to do the will of GOD even to the point of resisting the will of the king. He did this knowing the temperament of King Ahab and his Queen, Jezebel.

He was a GOD-fearing man living in an ungodly nation during the reign of an ungodly king. He had to know there would be repercussions for honoring GOD above the king.

Naboth was right in his decision. He correctly understood the words of GOD. The land was not his to sell.

The GOD of Israel had clearly promised to honor those that obey His commands. This was recorded in the Law just as the instruction not to sell the land was written in the Law.

> Deuteronomy 11:27 A blessing, if ye obey the commandments of the LORD your God, which I command you this day: 28 And a curse, if ye will not obey the commandments of the LORD your God, but turn aside out of the way which I command you this day, to go after other gods, which ye have not known.

However, because he chose to obey the LORD, Naboth is slandered; his reputation is destroyed and he is murdered following a mock trial. Not only did he die, but also Naboth saw his sons sentenced to death.[4] Ahab could not take possession as long as they lived.

Naboth also would have understood that his wife would now be a destitute dispossessed widow left to the mercy of others. As he died under the stoning, he would do so knowing that all of this happened to him, to his children, and to his wife solely because he chose to follow the command of his GOD obediently and faithfully.

One wonders if Naboth knew Elijah and knew something as to how the LORD had protected and provisioned the prophet. Did that knowledge give him encouragement to defy the king and to stand on Scripture?

No miracle of protection came. Naboth dies apparently forsaken by GOD and without a friend.

When Elijah was sent by the LORD to confront Ahab, the mercy of GOD gives Ahab a reprieve.[5] This surely must have caused those neighbors and friends who knew the story to be confused. They may well have asked the question that I now pose, "Was Naboth deceived?" Did His GOD forsake him?

¹ Jezebel gave instructions for a *fast* (not a feast) to be held. The implication is that some terrible sin had been committed and was bringing a blight on Jezreel. The citizens were called upon to fast. The implication was that some horrible calamity had befallen the city. The fast was to seek divine guidance as to how to expiate the evil and to restore the blessings. Naboth is set on high; that is, he is brought before the tribunal as one accused. The Biblical text to support this is in the next footnote.

² 1 Kings 21:1 And it came to pass after these things, *that* Naboth the Jezreelite had a vineyard, which *was* in Jezreel, hard by the palace of Ahab king of Samaria. 2 And Ahab spake unto Naboth, saying, Give me thy vineyard, that I may have it for a garden of herbs, because it *is* near unto my house: and I will give thee for it a better vineyard than it; *or*, if it seem good to thee, I will give thee the worth of it in money. 3 And Naboth said to Ahab, The LORD forbid it me, that I should give the inheritance of my fathers unto thee. 4 And Ahab came into his house heavy and displeased because of the word which Naboth the Jezreelite had spoken to him: for he had said, I will not give thee the inheritance of my fathers. And he laid him down upon his bed, and turned away his face, and would eat no bread. 5 But Jezebel his wife came to him, and said unto him, Why is thy spirit so sad, that thou eatest no bread? 6 And he said unto her, Because I spake unto Naboth the Jezreelite, and said unto him, Give me thy vineyard for money; or else, if it please thee, I will give thee *another* vineyard for it: and he answered, I will not give thee my vineyard. 7 And Jezebel his wife said unto him, Dost thou now govern the kingdom of Israel? arise, *and* eat bread, and let thine heart be merry: I will give thee the vineyard of Naboth the Jezreelite. 8 So she wrote letters in Ahab's name, and sealed *them* with his seal, and sent the letters unto the elders and to the nobles that *were* in his city, dwelling with Naboth. 9 And she wrote in the letters, saying, Proclaim a fast, and set Naboth on high among the people: 10 And set two men, sons of Belial, before him, to bear witness against him, saying, Thou didst blaspheme God and the king. And *then* carry him out, and stone him, that he may die. 11 And the men of his city, *even* the elders and the nobles who were the inhabitants in his city, did as Jezebel had sent unto them, *and* as it *was* written in the letters which she had sent unto them. 12 They proclaimed a fast, and set Naboth on high among the people. 13 And there came in two men, children of Belial, and sat before him: and the men of Belial witnessed against him, *even* against Naboth, in the presence of the people, saying, Naboth did blaspheme God and the king. Then they carried him forth out of the city, and stoned him with stones, that he died. 14 Then they sent to

Jezebel, saying, Naboth is stoned, and is dead. 15 And it came to pass, when Jezebel heard that Naboth was stoned, and was dead, that Jezebel said to Ahab, Arise, take possession of the vineyard of Naboth the Jezreelite, which he refused to give thee for money: for Naboth is not alive, but dead. 16 And it came to pass, when Ahab heard that Naboth was dead, that Ahab rose up to go down to the vineyard of Naboth the Jezreelite, to take possession of it.

3 Numbers 26:52 And the LORD spake unto Moses, saying, 53 Unto these the land shall be divided for an inheritance according to the number of names. 54 To many thou shalt give the more inheritance, and to few thou shalt give the less inheritance: to every one shall his inheritance be given according to those that were numbered of him. 55 Notwithstanding the land shall be divided by lot: according to the names of the tribes of their fathers they shall inherit. 56 According to the lot shall the possession thereof be divided between many and few.

Numbers 33:54 And ye shall divide the land by lot for an inheritance among your families: *and* to the more ye shall give the more inheritance, and to the fewer ye shall give the less inheritance: every man's *inheritance* shall be in the place where his lot falleth; according to the tribes of your fathers ye shall inherit.

Numbers 36:7 So shall not the inheritance of the children of Israel remove from tribe to tribe: for every one of the children of Israel shall keep himself to the inheritance of the tribe of his fathers.

Joshua 19:17 *And* the fourth lot came out to Issachar, for the children of Issachar according to their families. 18 And their border was toward Jezreel, and Chesulloth, and Shunem, 19 And Hapharaim, and Shion, and Anaharath, 20 And Rabbith, and Kishion, and Abez, 21 And Remeth, and Engannim, and Enhaddah, and Bethpazzez; 22 And the coast reacheth to Tabor, and Shahazimah, and Bethshemesh; and the outgoings of their border were at Jordan: sixteen cities with their villages. 23 This *is* the inheritance of the tribe of the children of Issachar according to their families, the cities and their villages.

4 2 Kings 9:25 Then said *Jehu* to Bidkar his captain, Take up, *and* cast him in the portion of the field of Naboth the Jezreelite: for remember how that, when I and thou rode together after Ahab his father, the LORD laid this burden upon him; 26 Surely I have seen yesterday the blood of Naboth, and the blood of his sons, saith the LORD; and I will requite thee in this plat, saith the LORD. Now therefore take *and* cast him into the plat *of ground*, according to the word of the LORD.

5 Elijah certainly knew about Naboth and even knew where his vineyard was located.

1 Kings 21:17 And the word of the LORD came to Elijah the Tishbite, saying, 18 Arise, go down to meet Ahab king of Israel, which *is* in Samaria: behold, *he is* in the vineyard of Naboth, whither he is gone down to possess it. 19 And thou shalt speak unto him, saying, Thus saith the LORD, Hast thou killed, and also taken possession? And thou shalt speak unto him, saying, Thus saith the LORD, In the place where dogs licked the blood of Naboth shall dogs lick thy blood, even thine. 20 And Ahab said to Elijah, Hast thou found me, O mine enemy? And he answered, I have found *thee*: because thou hast sold thyself to work evil in the sight of the LORD. 21 Behold, I will bring evil upon thee, and will take away thy posterity, and will cut off from Ahab him that pisseth against the wall, and him that is shut up and left in Israel, 22 And will make thine house like the house of Jeroboam the son of Nebat, and like the house of Baasha the son of Ahijah, for the provocation wherewith thou hast provoked *me* to anger, and made Israel to sin. 23 And of Jezebel also spake the LORD, saying, The dogs shall eat Jezebel by the wall of Jezreel. 24 Him that dieth of Ahab in the city the dogs shall eat; and him that dieth in the field shall the fowls of the air eat. 25 But there was none like unto Ahab, which did sell himself to work wickedness in the sight of the LORD, whom Jezebel his wife stirred up. 26 And he did very abominably in following idols, according to all *things* as did the Amorites, whom the LORD cast out before the children of Israel. 27 And it came to pass, when Ahab heard those words, that he rent his clothes, and put sackcloth upon his flesh, and fasted, and lay in sackcloth, and went softly. 28 And the word of the LORD came to Elijah the Tishbite, saying, 29 Seest thou how Ahab humbleth himself before me? because he humbleth himself before me, I will not bring the evil in his days: *but* in his son's days will I bring the evil upon his house.

CHAPTER 4

WAS JOB FORSAKEN?

Job was a man that feared GOD and eschewed evil.[1] That word eschew is not one that is used every day, but it is a very good word. If we use only the context of the word and guess at the meaning, we would likely assume that it means something akin to hate. That works for the sentence, but a dictionary would tell us that we missed the importance of the word.

This word eschew has the synonyms of avoid, shun, steer clear of it, have nothing to do with, abstain from, give a wide berth, and turn the back upon. It is defined as "abstain from: to avoid doing or using something on principle or as a matter of course." It would be to our advantage if we eschewed evil.[2]

Job was a righteous man of prayer; the Book bearing his name clearly reveals his character and provides examples of his prayers. James tells us that the prayers of a righteous man availeth much;[3] but the prayers of Job did nothing for Job; those prayers were not answered.

51

Job suffered the loss of his children. His wealth was taken away. His health was destroyed. Our picture of Job is of a man sitting in the ashes at the city dump scraping his sores with a piece of broken pottery. The Biblical description of his disease could well be that of leprosy.[4] What a paradox that is: a godly man inflicted with the disease that is the picture of sin.

The Book of Job covers far more than a day or so in the life of Job. The events in chapter one that would require only that day or so; but there is a matter of considerable time between the two appearances of Satan before GOD. The Jewish rabbis of old held that there was a full year between the chapters. While that might appear to be an exceptionally long time, some time definitely passed. It is only after the attack on Job's health that his three friends make plans to visit him. Coordination of those plans took additional time. When they arrived, a full seven days passed before they said a word.

Over these days that turned into weeks and months, perhaps even into years, Job was a man begging for deliverance from his burdens or, at least, for an explanation of why he was suffering, but neither explanation or deliverance came.

You and I know that Job received eventual deliverance, but Job never receives an explanation. You and I know the story, but we still have no explanation as to why the GOD of Heaven gave Satan His permission to do those things to the children of Job and to Job himself. Remember that while GOD did not give permission to Satan to take the life of Job, GOD made no such restriction concerning the lives of Job's sons, his daughters, or of his servants.

While no explanation was given to Job and none is offered to us, you and I view his journey through his troubles in the light of the recovery and we labor with the discussions between Job and his friends as they wrestle with the problems of Job's life.

However, suppose you were Job and

1. after all of the grieving over the deaths of your four sons and three daughters,

2. after the loss of all your wealth and the means of gaining an income,

3. after all of your kin and friends (except for the four that came to comfort you) have ignored you, and

4. after the uncountable days of personal physical suffering with an incurable horrific disease,

that you discovered that the deaths of your children, the loss of your wealth and friends, and even the painful disfiguring disease that you are enduring are all because GOD has given permission to Satan to do those things.

What would you think to learn that Satan has the consent from GOD to do anything to you that he desires, except to take your life. In fact, if you were Job, you would discover that it certainly seems that GOD called Satan's attention to you.

Considering that context can you conceive how you would feel? Would you be able to reconcile your experiences with what you believe the Bible teaches about the character of GOD?

During those interminable days upon days of grieving, hurting, crying, and praying, Job was considered by all that saw him or that heard of him to be forsaken by GOD. He testified that he felt that way himself.

Was Job forsaken by the GOD of Heaven?

---

[1] Job 1:1 There was a man in the land of Uz, whose name *was* Job; and that man was perfect and upright, and one that feared God, and eschewed evil.

[2] Merriam-Webster 11th Collegiate Dictionary

[3] James 5:16 Confess *your* faults one to another, and pray one for another, that ye may be healed. The effectual fervent prayer of a righteous man availeth much.

[4] The Scriptural description fits with a diagnosis of leprosy. Job 7:4 When I lie down, I say, When shall I arise, and the night be gone? and I am full of tossings to and fro unto the dawning of the day. 5 My flesh is clothed with worms and clods of dust; my skin is broken, and become loathsome. ... 20 I have sinned; what shall I do unto thee, O thou preserver of men? why hast thou set me as a mark against thee, so that I am a burden to myself? 21 And why dost thou not pardon my transgression, and take away mine iniquity? for now shall I sleep in the dust; and thou shalt seek me in the morning, but I *shall* not *be.*

Job 13:14 Wherefore do I take my flesh in my teeth, and put my life in mine hand? ... 28 And he, [describing himself] as a rotten thing, consumeth, as a garment that is moth eaten.

16:8 And thou hast filled me with wrinkles, *which* is a witness *against me*: and my leanness rising up in me beareth witness to my face. ... 16 My face is foul with weeping, and on my eyelids *is* the shadow of death;

17:1 My breath is corrupt, my days are extinct, the graves *are ready* for me.

19:17 My breath is strange to my wife, though I intreated for the children's *sake* of mine own body. ... 20 My bone cleaveth to my skin and to my flesh, and I am escaped with the skin of my teeth.

30:10 They abhor me, they flee far from me, and spare not to spit in my face. ... 17 My bones are pierced in me in the night season: and my sinews take no rest. 18 By the great force *of my disease* is my garment changed: it bindeth me about as the collar of my coat. ... 30 My skin is black upon me, and my bones are burned with heat.

Albert Barnes wrote an extensive discussion of the disease that Satan inflicted upon Job describing it as leprosy. Other commentaries make the same connection, but not with the detail as does the New School Presbyterian Barnes.

"In regard to the disease of Job, we may learn some of its characteristics, not only from the usual meaning of the word, but from the circumstances mentioned in the book itself. It was such that he took a potsherd to scrape himself with, such as to make his nights restless, and full of tossings to and fro and to clothe his flesh with clods of dust, and with worms, and to break his flesh, or to constitute a running sore or ulcer; such as to make him bite his flesh for pain, , and to make him like a rotten thing, or a garment that is moth eaten; such that his face was foul with weeping, and such as to fill him with wrinkles, and to make his flesh lean; such as to make his breath corrupt, and his bones cleave to his skin; such as to pierce his bones with pain in the night, and to make his skin black, and to burn up his bones with heat.

"It has been commonly supposed that the disease of Job was a species of black leprosy commonly called "elephantiasis," which prevails much in Egypt. This disease received its name from ελεφας *elefas*, "an elephant," from the swelling produced by it, causing a resemblance to that animal in the limbs; or because it rendered the skin like that of the elephant, scabtons and dark colored. It is called by the Arabs *judham* (Dr. Good), and is said to produce in the countenance a grim, distorted, and "lion-like" set of features, and hence has been called by some "Leontiasis." It is known as the black leprosy, to distinguish it from a more common disorder called "white leprosy" - an affection which the Greeks call "Leuce," or "whiteness." The disease of Job seems to have been a universal ulcer; producing an eruption over his entire person, and attended with violent pain, and constant restlessness. A universal bile or groups of biles ever the body would accord with the account of the disease in the various parts of the book. In the elephantiasis the skin is covered with incrustations like those of an elephant. It is a chronic and contagious disease, marked by a thickening of the legs, with a loss of hair and feeling, a swelling of the face, and a hoarse nasal voice. It affects the whole body; the bones as well as the skin are covered with spots and tumors, at first red, but afterward black. "Coxe, Ency. Webster." It should be added that the leprosy in all its forms was regarded as contagious, and of course involved the necessity of a separation from society; and all the circumstances attending this calamity were such as deeply to humble a man of the former rank and dignity of Job. *SwordSearcher: Albert Barnes' Notes on the Bible* Job 2:7."

http://www.ccel.org/ccel/barnes)

CHAPTER 5

WAS JEREMIAH FORSAKEN?

J eremiah is one of the Old Testament types of the LORD Jesus and his most recognized description from the Bible commentators is *the man of sorrows* or *the weeping prophet*. Jeremiah was a priest and a prophet, but his long ministry of perhaps seventy-seven years[1] was not a success in terms of numbers of converts or in evidence of miracles and signs.

It is not recorded that He ever witnessed a miracle. Instead, he witnessed the utter destruction of the nation of Judah, the complete devastation of the city of Jerusalem, and the demolition of the Temple.

There would seem to be only three named individuals that were willing to identify with Jeremiah publically before the nation fell:

(1) Baruch,[2] the man who recorded the words of Jeremiah,

(2) Ebedmelech,[3] the man who cared enough for Jeremiah to let down some old cast clouts (cast away material used to patch clothing) and old rags to protect his body

and armpits when he was pulled from the mire into which he had sunk at the bottom of that miry pit, and

(3) Ahikam,[4] who was willing to stand against Jehoiakim the king and the other officials to protect the life of Jeremiah.

When Nebuchadnezzar conquered Judah, he made Gedaliah, the son of Ahikam, the governor and Nebuchadnezzar placed Jeremiah in the care of Gedaliah. Gedaliah may be considered to have been a friend of his father's friend, Jeremiah.

Jeremiah's family and his home city, a community of priests, wanted him imprisoned or dead. His words describing the treachery of his kin and his fellow priests are filled with the pain and grief of betrayal and isolation.

Jeremiah 11:19 But I *was* like a lamb *or* an ox *that* is brought to the slaughter; and I knew not that they had devised devices against me, *saying*, Let us destroy the tree with the fruit thereof, and let us cut him off from the land of the living, that his name may be no more remembered. ... 21 Therefore thus saith the LORD of the men of Anathoth, that seek thy life, saying, Prophesy not in the name of the LORD, that thou die not by our hand:

Jeremiah 12: 6 For even thy brethren, and the house of thy father, even they have dealt treacherously with thee; yea, they have called a multitude after thee: believe them not, though they speak fair words unto thee.

Jeremiah 18:18 Then said they, Come, and let us devise devices against Jeremiah; for the law shall not perish from the priest, nor counsel from the wise, nor the word from the prophet. Come, and let us smite him with the tongue, and let us not give heed to any of his words.

Jeremiah 20:10 For I heard the defaming of many, fear on every side. Report, *say they*, and we will report it. All my familiars watched for my halting, *saying,* Peradventure he will be enticed, and we shall prevail against him, and we shall take our revenge on him.

It is understandable why Jeremiah is known as *the weeping prophet;* this was not because of public weeping, because his tears were shed privately. Jeremiah was indeed the *man of sorrows,* who was *acquainted with grief.*

In the fifty-two chapters of Jeremiah, which is the longest Book of the Bible from a single author[5] and the five chapters of Lamentations covering more over six decades of ministry, there is no record of a victory gained through prayer. Jeremiah does not testify of miracle or answered prayers. Read his testimony:

Jeremiah 14:11 Then said the LORD unto me, Pray not for this people for their good.[6]

Lamentations 3:8 Also when I cry and shout, he shutteth out my prayer. ... 44 Thou hast covered thyself with a cloud, that our prayer should not pass through.

If you wish to read a story of absolute desolation and utter forsakenness and unanswered prayer, read the Book of Lamentations. Consider just the closing of the Book:

Lamentations 5:20 Wherefore dost thou forget us for ever, and forsake us so long time? 21 Turn thou us unto thee, O LORD, and we shall be turned; renew our days as of old. 22 But thou hast utterly rejected us; thou art very wroth against us.

Jeremiah loved GOD and he had a heart to serve the LORD in spite of opposition and obstacles. There is no rebuke administered to Jeremiah for disobedience to the commands of his GOD.

Jeremiah was faithful under extremely *unfavorable-to-faithfulness* conditions. Born during the final years of Judah's worst king Manasseh,

Jeremiah lived as a child through Amon's two wicked years and continued serving God during the reigns of Josiah, Jehoahaz, Jehoiakim, Jehoiakin, and Zedekiah, and at least thirty-seven years into the Captivity. He should be noted for his persevering faithfulness.

Even during the reign of Josiah, the ministry of Jeremiah was not appreciated. He began his ministry in the thirteenth year of Josiah[7] and twenty-three years later in the fourth year of the reign of Jehoiakim, Jeremiah would lament that his message was ignored.

> Jeremiah 25:3 From the thirteenth year of Josiah the son of Amon king of Judah, even unto this day, that *is* the three and twentieth year, the word of the LORD hath come unto me, and I have spoken unto you, rising early and speaking; but ye have not hearkened.

When the young Jeremiah was called to his ministry, he received a personal promise of protection and deliverance.

> Jeremiah 1:7 But the LORD said unto me, Say not, I am a child: for thou shalt go to all that I shall send thee, and whatsoever I command thee thou shalt speak. 8 Be not afraid of their faces: **for I am with thee to deliver thee**, saith the LORD. ... 18 For, behold, I have made thee this day a defenced city, and an iron pillar, and brasen walls against the whole land, against the kings of Judah, against the princes thereof, against the priests thereof, and against the people of the land. 19 And they shall fight against thee; **but they shall not prevail against thee; for I *am* with thee, saith the LORD, to deliver thee**.

However, more than thirty years later as he is no longer a young man, Jeremiah is pulled out of the sucking mire of a dungeon pit by the hands of an Ethiopian using "old cast clouts and old rotten rags to soften the ropes under his armpits" and not by the hand of GOD. I remember that at the time the city was under a mind-numbing siege so I comprehend that the best that Ebedmelech could do was to find some discarded clothing and rotted rags, but the deliverance of Jeremiah from his pit does not match that of Daniel from his lion's den.[8]

He is hated by his family and his fellow priests. He is mistreated or ignored by the kings, the priests, and the people. His life is such a jumble of persecution and prison that one wonders if he ever had a comfortable bed in which to sleep. His record is one of faithfulness in spite of a lack of blessings and not because of blessings.

His final years were not filled with peace and comforts as he is forced to join renegades in their flight into Egypt. There he continues to deliver the message from GOD, rebuking the Jews and prophesying that Babylon would conquer Egypt.[9]

The man was faithful under the worst imaginable conditions. His only comfort or satisfaction lay in the knowledge that he had been faithful.

His death is unrecorded. Two legends have survived. One is that his people grew tired of his incessant negative preaching and stoned him to death in Egypt. The other is that Nebuchadnezzar found him in Egypt and returned him to Babylon as he had supposedly offered to Jeremiah when he captured Jerusalem.

Early in his ministry, Jeremiah had been instructed that he was not to marry.

> Jeremiah 16:2 Thou shalt not take thee a wife, neither shalt thou have sons or daughters in this place.

This would have been a heavy blow to Jeremiah when it came. Perhaps, in later years under the privations and in the face of the hatred, he

61

assented to the wisdom. Nevertheless, this man was denied even the solace of a family.

As to his professional life, it would appear that Jeremiah, though trained for the priesthood, never served as a priest. He was hated by his priestly relatives, who desired to kill him; he would never be welcomed to participate in any priestly function and there is no evidence that he did.

His city would have made him of priestly line of Abiathar, whom Solomon removed as high priest. Thus, it may have been that any deviation from the normal expectations, any overt action that called attention to the family, and especially any appearance of disloyalty to the royal family would have been scrupulously avoided by the family. Jeremiah's failure in all of these areas would have been sufficient reasons for suspicion and hatred from his family.

As a patriot, Jeremiah loved his nation. Yet, he was considered a traitor from the days of Josiah to the end of his life.

All of these conditions were the result of the obedient faithfulness of Jeremiah to GOD. The GOD that called him and promised him that in spite of all opposition he would prevail **and** that he would be delivered. Jeremiah never saw evidence of either occurring in his entire lengthy life of ministry.

Jeremiah was a steady plodder. He was faithful. He was obedient. Even so, he seems to have died forsaken by GOD.

Was Jeremiah deceived by his GOD?

Was Jeremiah forsaken by his GOD?

[1] The ministry of Jeremiah extended through the forty years of the reigns of the last five kings of Judah under Josiah—**18 years**, Jehoahaz—**3 months**, Jehoiakim—**11 years**, Jehoiakin—**3 months**, and Zedekiah—**11 years= a total of 40 years under the kings**) and beyond because Jeremiah ministered after the fall of Jerusalem. Perhaps for as much as **thirty-seven years** in Egypt giving him a lengthy ministry of **77 years**.

He began his ministry in the 13th year of Josiah's reign: To whom the word of the LORD came in the days of Josiah the son of Amon king of Judah, in the thirteenth year of his reign. Jeremiah 1:2

His ministry extended through the 37th year of the captivity—*if Jeremiah wrote the closing verses of the Book bearing his name*: And it came to pass in the seven and thirtieth year of the captivity of Jehoiachin king of Judah, in the twelfth month, in the five and twentieth day of the month, that Evilmerodach king of Babylon in the first year of his reign lifted up the head of Jehoiachin king of Judah, and brought him forth out of prison, Jeremiah 52:31

18 years of Josiah + 11 years of Jehoiakim + 6 months (Jehoahaz and Jehoiakin) + 11 years of Zedekiah + 37 years of captivity = 77 years

Jeremiah would have entered the priesthood at the age of twenty. If the assumption is made that the events of his calling as a prophet, recorded in Jeremiah chapter 1, are in his first year of priesthood, then he would have been 97 at the writing of Jeremiah 52. That is not inconceivable. I see no reason to assume that an editor (even Ezra) added to the words of Jeremiah.

[2] Jeremiah 36:4 Then Jeremiah called Baruch the son of Neriah: and Baruch wrote from the mouth of Jeremiah all the words of the LORD, which he had spoken unto him, upon a roll of a book.

[3] Jeremiah 38:11 So Ebedmelech took the men with him, and went into the house of the king under the treasury, and took thence old cast clouts and old rotten rags, and let them down by cords into the dungeon to Jeremiah. 12 And Ebedmelech the Ethiopian said unto Jeremiah, Put now *these* old cast clouts and rotten rags under thine armholes under the cords. And Jeremiah did so.

[4] Jeremiah 26:24 Nevertheless the hand of Ahikam the son of Shaphan was with Jeremiah, that they should not give him into the hand of the people to put him to death.

[5] This is the longest book in the Bible coming from a single writer; only the Psalms has greater length and the Holy Spirit used several individuals to record the different Psalms. Only

Moses, Paul, and Luke were used to record more of the words of
Scripture than Jeremiah.

6 It is recorded two additional times, that the LORD instructed Jeremiah not to pray for Judah.

Jeremiah 7:16 Therefore pray not thou for this people, neither
lift up cry nor prayer for them, neither make intercession to me:
for I will not hear thee.

Jeremiah 11:14 Therefore pray not thou for this people, neither
lift up a cry or prayer for them: for I will not hear *them* in the
time that they cry unto me for their trouble.

7 Jeremiah 1:1 The words of Jeremiah the son of Hilkiah, of
the priests that *were* in Anathoth in the land of Benjamin: 2 To
whom the word of the LORD came in the days of Josiah the son
of Amon king of Judah, in the thirteenth year of his reign.

8 Take note that Daniel was also taken up out of the den.
Daniel 6:23 Then was the king exceeding glad for him, and
commanded that they should take Daniel up out of the den. So
Daniel was taken up out of the den, and no manner of hurt was
found upon him, because he believed in his God.

9 Jeremiah' final messages are significant in that he did not
hesitate to deliver them *even as what amounted to being a
captive in the land of Egypt.*

Jeremiah 43:1 And it came to pass, *that* when Jeremiah had
made an end of speaking unto all the people all the words of the
LORD their God, for which the LORD their God had sent him to
them, *even* all these words, 2 Then spake Azariah the son of
Hoshaiah, and Johanan the son of Kareah, and all the proud
men, saying unto Jeremiah, Thou speakest falsely: the LORD
our God hath not sent thee to say, Go not into Egypt to sojourn
there: 3 But Baruch the son of Neriah setteth thee on against
us, for to deliver us into the hand of the Chaldeans, that they
might put us to death, and carry us away captives into Babylon.
4 So Johanan the son of Kareah, and all the captains of the
forces, and all the people, obeyed not the voice of the LORD, to
dwell in the land of Judah. 5 But Johanan the son of Kareah,
and all the captains of the forces, took all the remnant of
Judah, that were returned from all nations, whither they had
been driven, to dwell in the land of Judah; 6 *Even* men, and
women, and children, and the king's daughters, and every
person that Nebuzaradan the captain of the guard had left with
Gedaliah the son of Ahikam the son of Shaphan, and Jeremiah
the prophet, and Baruch the son of Neriah. 7 So they came into
the land of Egypt: for they obeyed not the voice of the LORD:
thus came they *even* to Tahpanhes. 8 Then came the word of
the LORD unto Jeremiah in Tahpanhes, saying, 9 Take great
stones in thine hand, and hide them in the clay in the brickkiln,
which *is* at the entry of Pharaoh's house in Tahpanhes, in the
sight of the men of Judah; 10 And say unto them, Thus saith

the LORD of hosts, the God of Israel; Behold, I will send and take Nebuchadrezzar the king of Babylon, my servant, and will set his throne upon these stones that I have hid; and he shall spread his royal pavilion over them. 11 And when he cometh, he shall smite the land of Egypt, *and deliver* such *as are* for death to death; and such *as are* for captivity to captivity; and such *as are* for the sword to the sword. 12 And I will kindle a fire in the houses of the gods of Egypt; and he shall burn them, and carry them away captives: and he shall array himself with the land of Egypt, as a shepherd putteth on his garment; and he shall go forth from thence in peace. 13 He shall break also the images of Bethshemesh, that *is* in the land of Egypt; and the houses of the gods of the Egyptians shall he burn with fire.

Jeremiah 44:1 The word that came to Jeremiah concerning all the Jews which dwell in the land of Egypt, which dwell at Migdol, and at Tahpanhes, and at Noph, and in the country of Pathros, saying, 2 Thus saith the LORD of hosts, the God of Israel; Ye have seen all the evil that I have brought upon Jerusalem, and upon all the cities of Judah; and, behold, this day they *are* a desolation, and no man dwelleth therein, 3 Because of their wickedness which they have committed to provoke me to anger, in that they went to burn incense, *and* to serve other gods, whom they knew not, *neither* they, ye, nor your fathers. 4 Howbeit I sent unto you all my servants the prophets, rising early and sending *them*, saying, Oh, do not this abominable thing that I hate. 5 But they hearkened not, nor inclined their ear to turn from their wickedness, to burn no incense unto other gods. 6 Wherefore my fury and mine anger was poured forth, and was kindled in the cities of Judah and in the streets of Jerusalem; and they are wasted *and* desolate, as at this day. 7 Therefore now thus saith the LORD, the God of hosts, the God of Israel; Wherefore commit ye *this* great evil against your souls, to cut off from you man and woman, child and suckling, out of Judah, to leave you none to remain; 8 In that ye provoke me unto wrath with the works of your hands, burning incense unto other gods in the land of Egypt, whither ye be gone to dwell, that ye might cut yourselves off, and that ye might be a curse and a reproach among all the nations of the earth? 9 Have ye forgotten the wickedness of your fathers, and the wickedness of the kings of Judah, and the wickedness of their wives, and your own wickedness, and the wickedness of your wives, which they have committed in the land of Judah, and in the streets of Jerusalem? 10 They are not humbled *even* unto this day, neither have they feared, nor walked in my law, nor in my statutes, that I set before you and before your fathers. 11 Therefore thus saith the LORD of hosts, the God of Israel; Behold, I will set my face against you for evil, and to cut off all Judah. 12 And I will take the remnant of Judah, that have set their faces to go into the land of Egypt to sojourn there, and they shall all be consumed, *and* fall in the land of Egypt; they shall *even* be consumed by the sword *and* by the famine: they shall die, from the least even unto the greatest, by the sword and by the famine: and they shall be an execration, *and* an astonishment, and a curse, and a reproach. 13 For I will punish them that dwell in the land of Egypt, as I have punished Jerusalem, by the sword, by the famine, and by the pestilence: 14 So that none of the remnant of Judah, which are gone into the land of Egypt to sojourn there, shall escape or remain, that they should return into the land of Judah, to the which they have a desire to return to dwell there: for none shall return but such as shall escape. 15 Then all the men which knew that their wives had burned incense unto other gods, and all the women that stood by, a great multitude, even all the people that dwelt in the land of Egypt, in Pathros, answered Jeremiah, saying, 16 As for the word that thou hast spoken unto us in the name of the LORD, we will not hearken unto thee. 17 But we will certainly do whatsoever thing goeth forth out of our own mouth, to burn incense unto the queen of heaven, and to pour out drink offerings unto her, as we have done, we, and our fathers, our kings, and our princes, in the cities of Judah, and in the streets of Jerusalem: for *then* had we plenty of victuals, and were well, and saw no evil. 18 But since we left off to burn incense to the queen of heaven, and to pour out drink offerings unto her, we have wanted all *things*, and have been consumed by the sword and by the famine. 19 And when we burned incense to the queen of heaven, and poured out drink offerings unto her, did we make her cakes to worship her, and pour out drink offerings unto her, without our men? 20 Then Jeremiah said unto all the people, to the men, and to the women, and to all the people which had given him *that* answer, saying, 21 The incense that ye burned in the cities of Judah, and in the streets of Jerusalem, ye, and your fathers, your kings, and your princes, and the people of the land, did not the LORD remember them, and came it *not* into his mind? 22 So that the LORD could no longer bear, because of the evil of your doings, *and* because of the abominations which ye have committed; therefore is your land a desolation, and an astonishment, and a curse, without an inhabitant, as at this day. 23 Because ye have burned incense, and because ye have sinned against the LORD, and have not obeyed the voice of the LORD, nor walked in his law, nor in his statutes, nor in his testimonies; therefore this evil is happened unto you, as at this day. 24 Moreover Jeremiah said unto all the people, and to all the women, Hear the word of the LORD, all Judah that *are* in the land of Egypt: 25 Thus saith the LORD of hosts, the God of Israel, saying; Ye and your wives have both spoken with your mouths, and fulfilled with your hand, saying, We will surely perform our vows that we have vowed, to burn incense to the queen of heaven, and to pour out drink offerings unto her: ye will surely accomplish your vows, and surely perform your vows. 26 Therefore hear ye the word of the LORD, all Judah that dwell in the land of Egypt; Behold, I have sworn by my great name, saith the LORD, that my name shall no more be named in the mouth of any man of Judah in all the land of Egypt, saying, The Lord GOD liveth. 27 Behold, I will watch over them for evil, and not for good: and all the men of Judah that *are* in the land of Egypt shall be consumed by the sword and by the famine, until there be an end of them. 28 Yet a small number that escape the sword shall return out of the land of Egypt into the land of Judah, and all the remnant of Judah, that are gone into the land of Egypt to sojourn there, shall know whose words shall stand, mine, or theirs. 29 And this *shall be* a sign unto you, saith the LORD, that I will punish you in this place, that ye may know that my words shall surely stand against you for evil: 30 Thus saith the LORD; Behold, I will give Pharaohhophra king of Egypt into the hand of his enemies, and into the hand of them that seek his life; as I gave Zedekiah king of Judah into the hand of Nebuchadrezzar king of Babylon, his enemy, and that sought his life.

CHAPTER 6

WAS JOHN THE BAPTIST FORSAKEN?

John the Baptist is the forerunner of the LORD Jesus. He announces and introduces the Lamb of GOD to Israel. John the Baptist is the pivot man of all history.[1] He was sent by the direct commission of GOD and he did not hesitate to say so in the firmest of terms.

> John 1:29 The next day John seeth Jesus coming unto him, and saith, Behold the Lamb of God, which taketh away the sin of the world. 30 This is he of whom I said, After me cometh a man which is preferred before me: for he was before me. 31 And I knew him not: but that he should be made manifest to Israel, therefore am I come baptizing with water. 32 And John bare record, saying, I saw the Spirit descending from heaven like a dove, and it abode upon him. 33 And I knew him not: but he that sent me to baptize with water, the same said unto me, Upon whom thou shalt see the Spirit descending, and remaining on him, the same is he which baptizeth with the Holy Ghost. 34 And I saw, and bare record that this is the Son of GOD. 35 Again the next

69

day after John stood, and two of his disciples;
36 And looking upon Jesus as he walked, he
saith, Behold the Lamb of God!

Of John, the LORD Jesus testified that no
prophet was greater than was he—not Moses, not
Isaiah, not Daniel, not David.

> Matthew 11:10 For this is *he*, of whom it is
> written, Behold, I send my messenger before
> thy face, which shall prepare thy way before
> thee. 11 Verily I say unto you, Among them
> that are born of women **there hath not risen
> a greater**[2] than John the Baptist: notwith-
> standing he that is least in the kingdom of
> heaven is greater than he. 12 And from the
> days of John the Baptist until now the king-
> dom of heaven suffereth violence, and the vio-
> lent take it by force. 13 For all the prophets
> and the law prophesied until John.

His birth was announced by an angel and his
commission was an exalted one.[3] His father is told
that he would be "great in the sight of the Lord,"
"filled with the Holy Ghost," "many of the children
of Israel shall he turn to the Lord their God," and
"make ready a people prepared for the Lord." He
will accomplish this by turning "the hearts of the
fathers to the children, and the disobedient to the
wisdom of the just." His father was filled with the
Holy Spirit and prophesied that "thou, child, shalt
be called the prophet of the Highest: for thou
shalt go before the face of the Lord to prepare his
ways; To give knowledge of salvation unto his
people by the remission of their sins."

However, the statements of his father are not
the commission that John himself received. We do
not have the record of the actual event or the full
account of when "the word of God came unto
John the son of Zacharias in the wilderness."
However, John testifies that "he that sent me to
baptize with water" also instructed him to watch

70

for the Holy Spirit to descend and remain upon the Son of GOD.[4]

> John 1:32 And John bare record, saying, I saw the Spirit descending from heaven like a dove, and it abode upon him. 33 And I knew him not: but he that sent me to baptize with water, the same said unto me, Upon whom thou shalt see the Spirit descending, and remaining on him, the same is he which baptizeth with the Holy Ghost. 34 And I saw, and bare record that this is the Son of God.

Perhaps the same angelic messenger that gave the announcement to his father Zacharias came to John and conveyed the commission to John. From that time forward, John was "the burning and shining light" to the nation of Israel.[5]

John never sought fame or popularity. John *resided* in the wilderness and he preached and conducted the *baptismal services* in the Jordan near Bethabara and AEnon near to Salim.[6] We have no record of his having ever preached in any city. Those who heard John did not go to the village square; they *resorted*[7] to him in the wilderness; they had to travel. In the contemporary world, in which we live, John the Baptist would not have been considered *seeker friendly* and he could never be identified as an *emergent Christian*. The message of John the Baptist was restrictive and rigid.[8]

> O generation of vipers, who hath warned you to flee from the wrath to come? Bring forth therefore fruits worthy of repentance, ... now also the axe is laid unto the root of the trees: every tree therefore which bringeth not forth good fruit is hewn down, and cast into the fire. ... one mightier than I cometh ... Whose fan *is* in his hand, and he will throughly purge his floor, and will gather the wheat into his garner; but the chaff he will burn with fire unquenchable.

Behold the Lamb of God, which taketh away the sin of the world. ... ... this is the Son of GOD. ... Behold the Lamb of God! ... He must increase, but I *must* decrease. ... For he whom God hath sent speaketh the words of God: ... The Father loveth the Son, and hath given all things into his hand. He that believeth on the Son hath everlasting life: and he that believeth not the Son shall not see life; but the wrath of God abideth on him.

John the Baptist would have been described in a previous generation as a *hell-fire and damnation preacher.*

It is true that John impacted the nation. It is true that he prepared the men that the LORD Jesus called as His apostles. However, it also true that John is arrested, imprisoned, and beheaded; because he dared to preach and to apply the Law of GOD to the life of the king. He rebuked Herod the king to his face with "It is not lawful for thee to have her." The law involved was not a Roman law, nor a Jewish civil law; it was the Law of GOD.

From the time of his arrest to his death is most likely no less than six months and would not be more than some sixteen to eighteen months, based upon the chronology chosen.[9] However long it was that John was imprisoned, it must have been a very difficult time. What mental and emotional strain confinement in a dungeon with a limited view, if any at all, of the world would be to a man of the wilderness, you and I can only imagine.

Jesus of Nazareth, the One that he introduced and Whom he encouraged his own disciples to follow as the Messiah and Who was his cousin, *never* visited him, *never* inquired about him, *never* sent a messenger to him. From all appearances, it would seem that Jesus of Nazareth ignored or abandoned him, in effect forsaking him to his fate.

The LORD Jesus identified John as the one fulfilling the promise of Elijah being sent before the Messiah.[10] Elijah was given water to drink when the nation was in a drought, was fed by ravens, was sustained by a widow through a continuing miracle, raised the dead, saw the fire fall from heaven, and was taken to heaven by a whirlwind and the chariot of the LORD.

John the Baptist, the man who, from a human viewpoint, was *the* key to the ministry of Jesus of Nazareth, died as *a party favor.*[11] To any onlooker, he was apparently forsaken by both the Father and the Son.

Was John the Baptist deceived?

Was John the Baptist forsaken?

---

[1] Matthew 11:11 Verily I say unto you, Among them that are born of women there hath not risen a greater than John the Baptist: notwithstanding he that is least in the kingdom of heaven is greater than he. 12 And from the days of John the Baptist until now the kingdom of heaven suffereth violence, and the violent take it by force. 13 For all the prophets and the law prophesied until John.

Luke 16:16 The law and the prophets *were* until John: since that time the kingdom of God is preached, and every man presseth into it.

[2] Luke 7:28 For I say unto you, Among those that are born of women there is not a greater prophet than John the Baptist: but he that is least in the kingdom of God is greater than he.

[3] Luke 1:13 But the angel said unto him, Fear not, Zacharias: for thy prayer is heard; and thy wife Elisabeth shall bear thee a son, and thou shalt call his name John. 14 And thou shalt have joy and gladness; and many shall rejoice at his birth. 15 For he shall be great in the sight of the Lord, and shall drink neither wine nor strong drink; and he shall be filled with the Holy Ghost, even from his mother's womb. 16 And many of the children of Israel shall he turn to the Lord their God. 17 And he shall go before him in the spirit and power of Elias, to turn the hearts of the fathers to the children, and the disobedient to the wisdom of the just; to make ready a people prepared for the Lord. ... 67 And his father Zacharias was filled with the Holy Ghost, and prophesied, saying, 68 Blessed *be* the Lord God of Israel; for he hath visited and redeemed his people, 69 And hath raised up an horn of salvation for us in the house of his servant David; 70 As he spake by the mouth of his holy prophets, which have been since the world began: 71 That we should be saved from our enemies, and from the hand of all that hate us; 72 To perform the mercy *promised* to our fathers, and to remember his holy covenant; 73 The oath which he sware to our father Abraham, 74 That he would grant unto us, that we being delivered out of the hand of our enemies might serve him without fear, 75 In holiness and righteousness before him, all the days of our life. 76 And thou, child, shalt be called the prophet of the Highest: for thou shalt go before the face of the Lord to prepare his ways; 77 To give knowledge of salvation unto his people by the remission of their sins, 78 Through the tender mercy of our God; whereby the dayspring from on high hath visited us, 79 To give light to them that sit in darkness and *in* the shadow of death, to guide our feet into the way of peace.

[4] Luke 3:1 Now in the fifteenth year of the reign of Tiberius Caesar, Pontius Pilate being governor of Judaea, and Herod being tetrarch of Galilee, and his brother Philip tetrarch of

Ituraea and of the region of Trachonitis, and Lysanias the tetrarch of Abilene, 2 Annas and Caiaphas being the high priests, **the word of God came unto John the son of Zacharias in the wilderness.** 3 And he came into all the country about Jordan, preaching the baptism of repentance for the remission of sins; 4 As it is written in the book of the words of Esaias the prophet, saying, The voice of one crying in the wilderness, Prepare ye the way of the Lord, make his paths straight.

John 1:15 John bare witness of him, and cried, saying, This was he of whom I spake, He that cometh after me is preferred before me: for he was before me. 16 And of his fulness have all we received, and grace for grace. 17 For the law was given by Moses, *but* grace and truth came by Jesus Christ. 18 No man hath seen God at any time; the only begotten Son, which is in the bosom of the Father, he hath declared *him.* 19 And this is the record of John, when the Jews sent priests and Levites from Jerusalem to ask him, Who art thou? 20 And he confessed, and denied not; but confessed, I am not the Christ. 21 And they asked him, What then? Art thou Elias? And he saith, I am not. Art thou that prophet? And he answered, No. 22 Then said they unto him, Who art thou? that we may give an answer to them that sent us. What sayest thou of thyself? 23 He said, I *am* the voice of one crying in the wilderness, Make straight the way of the Lord, as said the prophet Esaias. 24 And they which were sent were of the Pharisees. 25 And they asked him, and said unto him, Why baptizest thou then, if thou be not that Christ, nor Elias, neither that prophet? 26 John answered them, saying, I baptize with water: but there standeth one among you, whom ye know not; 27 He it is, who coming after me is preferred before me, whose shoe's latchet I am not worthy to unloose. 28 These things were done in Bethabara beyond Jordan, where John was baptizing. 29 The next day John seeth Jesus coming unto him, and saith, Behold the Lamb of God, which taketh away the sin of the world. 30 This is he of whom I said, After me cometh a man which is preferred before me: for he was before me. 31 And I knew him not: but that he should be made manifest to Israel, therefore am I come baptizing with water. 32 And John bare record, saying, I saw the Spirit descending from heaven like a dove, and it abode upon him. 33 And I knew him not: but **he that sent me to baptize with water, the same said unto me**, Upon whom thou shalt see the Spirit descending, and remaining on him, the same is he which baptizeth with the Holy Ghost. 34 And I saw, and bare record that this is the Son of God. 35 Again the next day after John stood, and two of his disciples; 36 And looking upon Jesus as he walked, he saith, Behold the Lamb of God!

3:23 And John also was baptizing in AEnon near to Salim, because there was much water there: and they came, and were baptized. 24 For John was not yet cast into prison. 25 Then there arose a question between *some* of John's disciples and the Jews about purifying. 26 And they came unto John, and said unto him, Rabbi, he that was with thee beyond Jordan, to whom thou barest witness, behold, the same baptizeth, and all *men* come to him. 27 John answered and said, A man can receive nothing, except it be given him from heaven. 28 Ye yourselves bear me witness, that I said, I am not the Christ, but that I am sent before him. 29 He that hath the bride is the bridegroom: but the friend of the bridegroom, which standeth and heareth him, rejoiceth greatly because of the bridegroom's voice: this my joy therefore is fulfilled. 30 He must increase, but I *must* decrease. 31 He that cometh from above is above all: he that is of the earth is earthly, and speaketh of the earth: he that cometh from heaven is above all. 32 And what he hath seen and heard, that he testifieth; and no man receiveth his testimony. 33 He that hath received his testimony hath set to his seal that God is true. 34 For he whom God hath sent speaketh the words of God: for God giveth not the Spirit by measure *unto him.* 35 The Father loveth the Son, and hath given all things into his hand. 36 He that believeth on the Son hath everlasting life: and he that believeth not the Son shall not see life; but the wrath of God abideth on him.

5 John 5:33 Ye sent unto John, and he bare witness unto the truth. 34 But I receive not testimony from man: but these things I say, that ye might be saved. 35 He was a burning and a shining light: and ye were willing for a season to rejoice in his light.

6 Matthew 3:1 In those days came John the Baptist, preaching in the wilderness of Judaea, ... 13 Then cometh Jesus from Galilee to Jordan unto John, to be baptized of him. ... 11:7 And as they departed, Jesus began to say unto the multitudes concerning John, What went ye out into the wilderness to see? A reed shaken with the wind?

Mark 1:4 John did baptize in the wilderness, and preach the baptism of repentance for the remission of sins...9 And it came to pass in those days, that Jesus came from Nazareth of Galilee, and was baptized of John in Jordan

Luke 3:2 Annas and Caiaphas being the high priests, the word of God came unto John the son of Zacharias in the wilderness. ... 7:24 And when the messengers of John were departed, he began to speak unto the people concerning John, What went ye out into the wilderness for to see? A reed shaken with the wind?

John 1:28 These things were done in Bethabara beyond Jordan, where John was baptizing. ... 3:23 And John also was baptizing in AEnon near to Salim, because there was much water there: and they came, and were baptized.

7 John 10:41 And many resorted unto him, and said, John did no miracle: but all things that John spake of this man were true.

8 The content of all of John the Baptist's recorded sermons is smaller than one might think.

Matthew 3:1 In those days came John the Baptist, preaching in the wilderness of Judaea, 2 And saying, Repent ye: for the kingdom of heaven is at hand.

Mark 6:17 For Herod himself had sent forth and laid hold upon John, and bound him in prison for Herodias' sake, his brother Philip's wife: for he had married her. 18 For John had said unto Herod, It is not lawful for thee to have thy brother's wife. 19 Therefore Herodias had a quarrel against him, and would have killed him; but she could not:

Luke 3:7 Then said he to the multitude that came forth to be baptized of him, O generation of vipers, who hath warned you to flee from the wrath to come? 8 Bring forth therefore fruits worthy of repentance, and begin not to say within yourselves, We have Abraham to *our* father: for I say unto you, That God is able of these stones to raise up children unto Abraham. 9 And now also the axe is laid unto the root of the trees: every tree therefore which bringeth not forth good fruit is hewn down, and cast into the fire. 10 And the people asked him, saying, What shall we do then? 11 He answereth and saith unto them, He that hath two coats, let him impart to him that hath none; and he that hath meat, let him do likewise. 12 Then came also publicans to be baptized, and said unto him, Master, what shall we do? 13 And he said unto them, Exact no more than that which is appointed you. 14 And the soldiers likewise demanded of him, saying, And what shall we do? And he said unto them, Do violence to no man, neither accuse *any* falsely; and be content with your wages. 15 And as the people were in expectation, and all men mused in their hearts of John, whether he were the Christ, or not; 16 John answered, saying unto *them* all, I indeed baptize you with water; but one mightier than I cometh, the latchet of whose shoes I am not worthy to unloose: he shall baptize you with the Holy Ghost and with fire: 17 Whose fan *is* in his hand, and he will throughly purge his floor, and will gather the wheat into his garner; but the chaff he will burn with fire unquenchable. 18 And many other things in his exhortation preached he unto the people. 19 But Herod the tetrarch, being reproved by him for Herodias his brother Philip's wife, and for all the evils which Herod had done, 20 Added yet this above all, that he shut up John in prison.

John 1:19 And this is the record of John, when the Jews sent priests and Levites from Jerusalem to ask him, Who art thou? 20 And he confessed, and denied not; but confessed, I am not the Christ. 21 And they asked him, What then? Art thou Elias?

And he saith, I am not. Art thou that prophet? And he answered, No. 22 Then said they unto him, Who art thou? that we may give an answer to them that sent us. What sayest thou of thyself? 23 He said, I *am* the voice of one crying in the wilderness, Make straight the way of the Lord, as said the prophet Esaias. 24 And they which were sent were of the Pharisees. 25 And they asked him, and said unto him, Why baptizest thou then, if thou be not that Christ, nor Elias, neither that prophet? 26 John answered them, saying, I baptize with water: but there standeth one among you, whom ye know not; 27 He it is, who coming after me is preferred before me, whose shoe's latchet I am not worthy to unloose. 28 These things were done in Bethabara beyond Jordan, where John was baptizing. 29 The next day John seeth Jesus coming unto him, and saith, Behold the Lamb of God, which taketh away the sin of the world. 30 This is he of whom I said, After me cometh a man which is preferred before me: for he was before me. 31 And I knew him not: but that he should be made manifest to Israel, therefore am I come baptizing with water. 32 And John bare record, saying, I saw the Spirit descending from heaven like a dove, and it abode upon him. 33 And I knew him not: but he that sent me to baptize with water, the same said unto me, Upon whom thou shalt see the Spirit descending, and remaining on him, the same is he which baptizeth with the Holy Ghost. 34 And I saw, and bare record that this is the Son of God. 35 Again the next day after John stood, and two of his disciples; 36 And looking upon Jesus as he walked, he saith, Behold the Lamb of God! 37 And the two disciples heard him speak, and they followed Jesus.

John 3:23 And John also was baptizing in AEnon near to Salim, because there was much water there: and they came, and were baptized. 24 For John was not yet cast into prison. 25 Then there arose a question between *some* of John's disciples and the Jews about purifying. 26 And they came unto John, and said unto him, Rabbi, he that was with thee beyond Jordan, to whom thou barest witness, behold, the same baptizeth, and all *men* come to him. 27 John answered and said, A man can receive nothing, except it be given him from heaven. 28 Ye yourselves bear me witness, that I said, I am not the Christ, but that I am sent before him. 29 He that hath the bride is the bridegroom: but the friend of the bridegroom, which standeth and heareth him, rejoiceth greatly because of the bridegroom's voice: this my joy therefore is fulfilled. 30 He must increase, but I *must* decrease. 31 He that cometh from above is above all: he that is of the earth is earthly, and speaketh of the earth: he that cometh from heaven is above all. 32 And what he hath seen and heard, that he testifieth; and no man receiveth his testimony. 33 He that hath received his testimony hath set to his seal that God is true. 34 For he whom God hath sent speaketh the words of God: for God giveth not the Spirit by measure *unto him*. 35 The Father loveth the Son, and hath given all things into his hand. 36 He that believeth on the Son hath everlasting life: and he that believeth not the Son shall not see life; but the wrath of God abideth on him.

⁹ My preference for a chronology of the Gospels is *The Harmony of the Four Gospels* by Edward Robinson as edited by Benjamin Davies. No attempt to chronologize the Gospels is infallible. In this arrangement, John the Baptist is imprisoned no more than a year after the baptism of the LORD Jesus. His death. John is held in prison for some sixteen to eighteen months before he is beheaded. Other chronologies will set the imprisonment from a few weeks to several months.

¹⁰ Malachi 3:1 Behold, **I will send my messenger, and he shall prepare the way before me: and the Lord**, whom ye seek, shall suddenly come to his temple, even the messenger of the covenant, whom ye delight in: behold, he shall come, saith the LORD of hosts. ... 4:5 Behold, **I will send you Elijah the prophet** before the coming of the great and dreadful day of the LORD: 6 And he shall turn the heart of the fathers to the children, and the heart of the children to their fathers, lest I come and smite the earth with a curse.

Isaiah 40:3 The voice of him that crieth in the wilderness, Prepare ye the way of the LORD, make straight in the desert a highway for our God.

Matthew 11:11 Verily I say unto you, Among them that are born of women there hath not risen a greater than John the Baptist: notwithstanding he that is least in the kingdom of heaven is greater than he. 12 And from the days of John the Baptist until now the kingdom of heaven suffereth violence, and the violent take it by force. 13 For all the prophets and the law prophesied until John. 14 And if ye will receive *it*, **this is Elias, which was for to come**.

Matthew 17:11 And Jesus answered and said unto them, Elias truly shall first come, and restore all things. 12 **But I say unto you, That Elias is come already, and they knew him not, but have done unto him whatsoever they listed**. Likewise shall also the Son of man suffer of them.

Mark 9:12 And he answered and told them, Elias verily cometh first, and restoreth all things; and how it is written of the Son of man, that he must suffer many things, and be set at nought. 13 **But I say unto you, That Elias is indeed come, and they have done unto him whatsoever they listed, as it is written of him**.

Luke 1:17 And he shall go before him **in the spirit and power of Elias**, to turn the hearts of the fathers to the children, and the disobedient to the wisdom of the just; to make ready a people prepared for the Lord.

11 Matthew 14:3 For Herod had laid hold on John, and bound him, and put *him* in prison for Herodias' sake, his brother Philip's wife. 4 For John said unto him, It is not lawful for thee to have her. 5 And when he would have put him to death, he feared the multitude, because they counted him as a prophet. 6 But when Herod's birthday was kept, the daughter of Herodias danced before them, and pleased Herod. 7 Whereupon he promised with an oath to give her whatsoever she would ask. 8 And she, being before instructed of her mother, said, Give me here John Baptist's head in a charger. 9 And the king was sorry: nevertheless for the oath's sake, and them which sat with him at meat, he commanded *it* to be given *her*. 10 And he sent, and beheaded John in the prison. 11 And his head was brought in a charger, and given to the damsel: and she brought *it* to her mother. 12 And his disciples came, and took up the body, and buried it, and went and told Jesus.

Mark 6:17 For Herod himself had sent forth and laid hold upon John, and bound him in prison for Herodias' sake, his brother Philip's wife: for he had married her. 18 For John had said unto Herod, It is not lawful for thee to have thy brother's wife. 19 Therefore Herodias had a quarrel against him, and would have killed him; but she could not: 20 For Herod feared John, knowing that he was a just man and an holy, and observed him; and when he heard him, he did many things, and heard him gladly. 21 And when a convenient day was come, that Herod on his birthday made a supper to his lords, high captains, and chief *estates* of Galilee; 22 And when the daughter of the said Herodias came in, and danced, and pleased Herod and them that sat with him, the king said unto the damsel, Ask of me whatsoever thou wilt, and I will give *it* thee. 23 And he sware unto her, Whatsoever thou shalt ask of me, I will give *it* thee, unto the half of my kingdom. 24 And she went forth, and said unto her mother, What shall I ask? And she said, The head of John the Baptist. 25 And she came in straightway with haste unto the king, and asked, saying, I will that thou give me by and by in a charger the head of John the Baptist. 26 And the king was exceeding sorry; *yet* for his oath's sake, and for their sakes which sat with him, he would not reject her. 27 And immediately the king sent an executioner, and commanded his head to be brought: and he went and beheaded him in the prison, 28 And brought his head in a charger, and gave it to the damsel: and the damsel gave it to her mother. 29 And when his disciples heard *of it*, they came and took up his corpse, and laid it in a tomb.

CHAPTER 7

WAS LAZARUS FORSAKEN?

The passage is familiar. Within Scripture, there are certain passages that are recognizable to any group of believers. Alongside Psalm 23 and Isaiah 53, among others, stands John 11 with the story of the raising of Lazarus from the dead. However, as so often happens with Scripture, Christians concentrate on the exciting parts and skip through the details. When the believer slowly and carefully studies John 11, the story introduces some disquieting thoughts that produce disturbing questions.

Since you and I already know the end of the story, we do not devote our attention to the mundane details. Yet in those neglected details lies doctrinal truth that would help us face life with a different perspective if we only knew them.

Jesus of Nazareth receives a call for help from a family that was very involved in His ministry. Their home was the one place in Judea in which He was always welcomed. The chapter twice reminds us, verse 3 and verse 5, that Jesus of Nazareth loved Lazarus and his sisters. Mary and Martha send a messenger to tell the LORD that

81

Lazarus was sick. Consider the words carefully. Look for the small details.

> 1 Now a certain *man* was sick, *named* Laza-
> rus, of Bethany, the town of Mary and her sis-
> ter Martha. 2 (It was *that* Mary which anoint-
> ed the Lord with ointment, and wiped his feet
> with her hair, whose brother Lazarus was
> sick.) 3 Therefore his sisters sent unto him,
> saying, Lord, behold, he whom thou lovest is
> sick. 4 When Jesus heard *that*, he said, This
> sickness is not unto death, but for the glory of
> God, that the Son of GOD might be glorified
> thereby. 5 Now Jesus loved Martha, and her
> sister, and Lazarus. 6 When he had heard
> therefore that he was sick, he abode two days
> still in the same place where he was.

When the message comes, notice how Jesus of Nazareth responds. He does not send an answer; He stayed "in the same place where He was" for two entire additional days. During that time, the LORD Jesus apparently did not delay because of any pressing activity. There is no record of any teaching or miracles.

From the viewpoint of Mary and Martha, He ignored their request. From the viewpoint of Lazarus, He did not seem to care enough to come; He appears to have abandoned him. It would appear that Jesus of Nazareth forsook Lazarus and his sisters. When others had rejected Him, they believed Him. When others hesitated or openly doubted Him, these three had wholeheart-edly followed Him. With faith and *in expectation*, they sent Him word of their urgent need. His immediate actions and comments seem to ignore their need and their request.

When that request arrived, Jesus of Nazareth told His disciples, "This sickness is not unto death." He continued to explain that the sickness was "for the glory of God, that the Son of GOD might be glorified thereby." In our language, He said for them not to be concerned because the sickness was "not unto death."

They would have understood this to mean that Lazarus was not going to die. As they watched Him conduct a normal schedule for the next two days,[1] they would have thought that the matter was settled; Lazarus was not going to die. They would have understood that a*ll would be well for Lazarus.*

If they even thought about Lazarus, they would have remembered that the Master had assured them that the sickness was for the glory of GOD. Even more, that sickness was expressly designed so that the Son of GOD would be glorified.

I speak with reverence, but I want us to have the mindset of the disciples as well as that of Mary, Martha, and Lazarus. The message was brought by a messenger; it was not telephoned or mailed. That messenger surely would have heard the comments of Jesus of Nazareth and certainly would have returned with the good news: *all will be well for Lazarus.*

Even if the messenger carried the exact words of LORD Jesus, Mary, Martha, *and Lazarus* would have heard that the sickness was not unto death, but for the glory of GOD. Moreover, they would have rejoiced in that the Son of GOD would be glorified. Imagine the reception of this news; it would have brought comfort and hope. *All will be well for Lazarus.*

The disciples would have accepted His words to mean that Lazarus was going to get well; and yet, taken and viewed in the time position that it was spoken, that answer also must have sounded more than a little cold and uncaring, perhaps even a little self-serving. *Lazarus is suffering; his sisters are burdened, but I will be glorified.* Taken as an isolated comment, a perception of a sentiment almost arrogant could be taken.

Because we have read the end of the story, we know what the LORD was going to do and we understand what He was saying; but the disciples knew only what they heard and what they saw. We view with hindsight and benefit from having the end of the story in our knowledge. None of the participants in this story is able to view those words and His actions beyond the single snapshot of that moment, that place, and that event.

Taking only a single frame snapshot from a lengthy video will always give a terribly distorted understanding or misleading interpretation of the entire story. A given photograph does not represent an entire vacation. A single picture cannot present an entire day, much less a whole life.

The comment of the Master on this day in that setting would have been understood to convey hope of recovery from the sickness in a glorious way. The return of the messenger with the words of the LORD Jesus would have given encouragement to Lazarus and to his sisters. The disciples would have felt the relief of having the hope of Lazarus's complete recovery. That is the snapshot of that time and that event—it is quite accurate at the time, but it does not tell the whole of the story.

Two days after the message arrived, the LORD said that Lazarus was sleeping and that He will take the disciples to visit Lazarus to wake him from that sleep. Remember the mindset of the disciples. They would accept this statement as the announcement that Lazarus was now through the crisis of the sickness and on the road to full recovery. They had His words and His actions to give them this confidence.

"Lord, if he sleep, he shall do well." They are convinced that sleeping is the good sign that Lazarus is going to recover: "he shall do well." He believed that Lazarus was getting better; however, their rejoicing and their relief is destroyed quickly when Jesus of Nazareth bluntly says. "Lazarus is dead."

How startled and shaken they must have been when the LORD said, "Lazarus is dead." He had told them only two days previously that Lazarus was not going to die and now He says that Lazarus is dead.

We know the end of the story and we know that Jesus meant that the purpose or the outcome of the sickness was not the death of Lazarus; *but they did not know the end of the story.* Since they were only human, they would have thought, as you and I would have thought, that the LORD made a mistake—or even worse, that He had made a promise that He could not keep. They would have questioned the knowledge and the power of Jesus of Nazareth.

Those disciples would have had difficulty in reconciling the two declarations of the LORD: "this sickness is not unto death" and "Lazarus is dead." Those statements appear to be in conflict, even direct opposition. Taken as they stand, those are simply *irreconcilable* pronouncements. These incompatible words produce thoughts that are terrible to think and so reprehensible that we would struggle, as they must have struggled, not to allow the uncomfortable thought to be completed.

How could it be that Jesus could be so mistaken?

Why would He give them a false hope?

Have I been deceived into leaving my home and my occupation for this?

Could I have misunderstood?

Could all of us have misunderstood?

How? Why?

The snapshot is this: Lazarus seems forsaken in his grave; Mary and Martha appear to be let down or ignored in their grief, and the disciples are unsettled and confused.

That perplexity must have only increased when the LORD took *an additional* two full days to travel to Bethany.[2] This implies a leisurely journey: Lazarus is dead and the LORD is not in any hurry to give any comfort to the grieving family.

He even stops in Jerusalem, only fifteen furlongs from Bethany, just an eighth of a mile less than two miles, long enough for word of His coming to reach Bethany. After receiving the news of the sickness, He had not broken His schedule for two entire days and now He takes two days in traveling. The words and the conduct of Jesus of Nazareth must have troubled the disciples, as it surely would have bothered Lazarus and his sisters.

I believe we have evidence of the struggle in the hearts of Mary and Martha and their friends.

> John 11:21 Then said Martha unto Jesus, Lord, if thou hadst been here, my brother had not died. 22 But I know, that even now, whatsoever thou wilt ask of God, God will give it thee. ... 32 Then when Mary was come where Jesus was, and saw him, she fell down at his feet, saying unto him, Lord, if thou hadst been here, my brother had not died. ... 37 And some of them said, Could not this man, which opened the eyes of the blind, have caused that even this man should not have died?

Martha affirms her faith in Jesus as the Christ and I do not wish to imply otherwise; even so, I cannot avoid what *else* her words say. She seems to be saying something like this: "My brother is dead, but he did not have to die. You could have prevented his death if you had come when we sent for you. Even now, if you would only ask, then GOD would fix all of this." That is a version of the oft-repeated "GOD, why did you let this happen to me?"

Even the family friends reveal their confusion: "Could not this man ... have caused that ... this man should not have died?" If He could have, why did He not do so? In other words, why did Jesus let this man die? That was not the last time that this question has been asked.

Lazarus is sick. Mary and Martha send a message to Jesus seeking His help. What happened to Lazarus?

He suffered and then he died.

Mary and Martha are left grieving.

The friends are questioning?

The disciples anticipated that Lazarus would be healed; they are disappointed.

With only the knowledge given us when Jesus of Nazareth arrived in Bethany, it appears that Lazarus, his sisters, and the disciples were told that Lazarus would recover; however, Lazarus died. The promise of restored health certainly seems to have been broken.

To all appearances, Lazarus was forsaken by Jesus; Mary and Martha were abandoned by Jesus and the disciples were misled. Were all of these followers of Jesus deceived? In particular, was Lazarus forsaken?

---

[1] John 11:6 When he had heard therefore that he was sick, he abode two days still in the same place where he was.

[2] John 11:17 Then when Jesus came, he found that he had *lain* in the grave four days already.

CHAPTER 8

WERE THE DISCIPLES FORSAKEN?

C onsider the first generation of the followers of Jesus of Nazareth. According to the extant historical records many of them died a martyr's death. No chronicler of the first or second century Christians wrote of an apostle that died a natural death with one possible exception. Every account presents the apostles as having been slain for their testimony. There are variations, but the central truth that their common lot was martyrdom is ever present. Largely these accounts are evaluated by modern historians as traditions.

While it is a legitimate assessment that not all traditions are true,[1] it is also necessary to remember that some traditions are true.[2] Where traditions do not conflict with Scripture or with authenticated truth, the tradition should be respected, at least. The LORD Jesus would seem to have indicated that the apostles would face martyrdom when He spoke with His disciples the night before He was crucified as we find in the Gospel of John, chapter 16.

1 These things have I spoken unto you, that ye should not be offended. 2 They shall put you out of the synagogues: yea, **the time cometh, that whosoever killeth you will think that he doeth God service**. 3 And these things will they do unto you, because they have not known the Father, nor me. 4 But these things have I told you, that when the time shall come, ye may remember that I told you of them. And these things I said not unto you at the beginning, because I was with you.

The tradition that the apostles were martyred, therefore, does not conflict with the word of GOD. The Scriptures only record the death of one of the apostles; history's traditions provide accounts of the others. In the approximate chronological order of their deaths and with the accounts abbreviated and summarized, these are the commonly advanced methods of death for the apostles:

Some ten years or so after the stoning of Stephen and the deaths of some 2000 others[3], James is arrested by Herod and beheaded. He is the first of the apostles to be martyred. Peter is arrested a short while later, but he escapes death as he is delivered from prison in a miraculous way.

Acts 12:1 Now about that time Herod the king stretched forth *his* hands to vex certain of the church. 2 And he killed James the brother of John with the sword. 3 And because he saw it pleased the Jews, he proceeded further to take Peter also. (Then were the days of unleavened bread.) 4 And when he had apprehended him, he put *him* in prison, and delivered *him* to four quaternions of soldiers to keep him; intending after Easter to bring him forth to the people. 5 Peter therefore was kept in prison: but prayer was made without ceasing of the church unto God for him. 6 And when Herod would have brought him forth, the same night Peter was sleeping between two soldiers, bound with two chains: and the keepers before the door kept the prison. 7 And, behold, the angel of the Lord came upon *him*, and a light shined in the prison: and he smote Peter on the side, and raised him up, saying, Arise up quickly. And his chains fell off from *his* hands. 8 And the angel said unto him, Gird thyself, and bind on thy sandals. And so he did. And he saith unto him, Cast thy garment about thee, and follow me. 9 And he went out, and followed him; and wist not that it was true which was done by the angel; but thought he saw a vision. 10 When they were past the first and the second ward, they came unto the iron gate that leadeth unto the city; which opened to them of his own accord: and they went out, and passed on through one street; and forthwith the angel departed from him. 11 And when Peter was come to himself, he said, Now I know of a surety, that the Lord hath sent his angel, and hath delivered me out of the hand of Herod, and *from* all the expectation of the people of the Jews. 12 And when he had considered *the thing*, he came to the house of Mary the mother of John, whose surname was Mark; where many were gathered together praying. 13 And as Peter knocked at the door of the gate, a damsel came to hearken, named Rhoda. 14 And when she knew Peter's voice, she opened not the gate for gladness, but ran in, and told how Peter stood before the gate. 15 And they said unto her, Thou art mad. But she constantly affirmed that it was even so. Then said they, It is his angel. 16 But Peter continued knocking: and when they had opened *the door*, and saw him, they were astonished. 17 But he, beckoning unto them with the hand to hold their peace, declared unto them how the Lord had brought him out of the prison. And he said, Go shew these things unto James, and to the brethren. And he departed, and went into another place. 18 Now as soon as it was day, there was no small stir among the soldiers, what was become of Peter. 19 And when Herod had sought for him, and found him not, he examined the keepers, and commanded that *they* should be put to death. And he went down from Judaea to Caesarea, and *there* abode.

The death of James is the only martyrdom of an apostle recorded in Scripture. We find both Paul[4] and Peter[5] writing about their approaching martyrdom, but the deaths are not mentioned. For those accounts, we must turn to history and its traditions.

Philip was scourged, thrown into prison, and afterwards crucified in A.D. 54. Matthew was slain with a halberd, a battle-ax.

James the Less, at the age of ninety-four, was beaten and stoned in Jerusalem; and finally had his brains dashed out with a fuller's club. Matthias was stoned at Jerusalem and then beheaded.

Andrew was crucified on a cross, the two ends of which were fixed transversely in the ground. Hence, the derivation of the term, St. Andrew's Cross. Peter, as one of the last living apostles, was crucified upside down.

Jude was also crucified. Bartholomew was either cruelly beaten, and then crucified or he was flayed, which is a polite word for having the skin removed. Thomas was thrust through with a spear. Simon Zelotes was crucified and that date is given as 74.

John the beloved, the only disciple not murdered or executed, is thrown into boiling oil; when he survived, he was exiled to the isolated penal colony of Patmos. After living with unbelievable disfiguration and indescribable pain—imagine the full body scarring, consider trying to use the feet or the fingers after immersion in boiling oil—John is said to have died in Ephesus about the year 95.

Perhaps one might stretch the definition and call his death as one caused by natural causes.

Among other early leaders, Paul was beheaded; Mark was dragged to pieces by the people of Alexandria; and Luke was hanged on an olive tree.

I remind us that these methods of the deaths of the followers of the Saviour are, except for Stephen and James, brought down through the ages through tradition. Being of human origin and depending upon human transmission, most traditions and legends will have elements of fiction comingled with actual occurrences. As example, since the Scriptures place the apostle Peter in Babylon[6] very late in life, I am not convinced that he was crucified in Rome. He most certainly had not been in Rome through the time that the apostle Paul wrote the Epistle to the Romans. I have no vested interest, as do some, in placing Peter in Rome when Peter places himself in Babylon.

However, the LORD Jesus plainly prophesied that Peter would not die a peaceful death, but that he would die as a prisoner being led to the execution.[7] The word picture best fits a governmental execution. Saul of Tarsus led believers bound to their death under the commission of the high priest.[8]

All of these men had left everything that they possessed in order to follow Jesus of Nazareth. Except for Paul, all of those that I listed had heard the LORD Jesus make very specific and somewhat detailed promises that they had counted upon as they followed His command to preach the Gospel into all the world. Among those commitments that Jesus of Nazareth made to His disciples were these: (Parallel passages are included.)

Matthew 11:27 All things are delivered unto me of my Father: and no man knoweth the

Son, but the Father; neither knoweth any man the Father, save the Son, and *he* to whomsoever the Son will reveal *him.*

Luke 10:22 All things are delivered to me of my Father: and no man knoweth who the Son is, but the Father; and who the Father is, but the Son, and *he* to whom the Son will reveal *him.*

Matthew 21:22 And all things, whatsoever ye shall ask in prayer, believing, ye shall receive.

Matthew 28:18 And Jesus came and spake unto them, saying, All power is given unto me in heaven and in earth. 19 Go ye therefore, and teach all nations, baptizing them in the name of the Father, and of the Son, and of the Holy Ghost: 20 Teaching them to observe all things whatsoever I have commanded you: and, lo, I am with you alway, even unto the end of the world. Amen.

Mark 16:18 They shall take up serpents; and if they drink any deadly thing, it shall not hurt them; they shall lay hands on the sick, and they shall recover.

Luke 10:19 Behold, I give unto you power to tread on serpents and scorpions, and over all the power of the enemy: and nothing shall by any means hurt you.

Luke 21:17 And ye shall be hated of all men for my name's sake. 18 But there shall not an hair of your head perish.

John 3:35 The Father loveth the Son, and hath given all things into his hand.

John 14:13 And whatsoever ye shall ask in my name, that will I do, that the Father may be glorified in the Son.

John 16:23 And in that day ye shall ask me nothing. Verily, verily, I say unto you, Whatsoever ye shall ask the Father in my name, he will give it you.

Those are not nebulous generalities nor are they gratuitous platitudes. Those are precise statements of commitment. He Who said that *all things were delivered* to Him by the Father and Who claimed that the Father had *given Him all power* affirmed to these men that neither *poison* nor *serpents and scorpions* could hurt them and that they had *power over that enemy* and that "nothing shall by any means hurt you."

Trusting in those promises these men placed themselves "in jeopardy every hour"[9] and "hazarded their lives for" just preaching "the name of" the LORD Jesus,[10] but they died for doing so.

Moreover, their lives were not *flowery beds of ease* their deaths were not pleasant, quiet, calm scenes but horrific, terrifying, raucous events. They did not die in their beds whit family and friends in attendance. Those men *sailed through bloody seas* and died in pain and died alone.[11] To all who observed them, they appeared to be forsaken by GOD.

Were those eye and ear witnesses that had touched and been touched by Jesus of Nazareth deceived?[12] Did they die forsaken?

---

[1] Matthew 15:2 Why do thy disciples transgress the tradition of the elders? for they wash not their hands when they eat bread. 3 But he answered and said unto them, Why do ye also transgress the commandment of God by your tradition?

Mark 7:8 For laying aside the commandment of God, ye hold the tradition of men, *as* the washing of pots and cups: and many other such like things ye do. 9 And he said unto them, Full well ye reject the commandment of God, that ye may keep your own tradition.

1 Peter 1:18 Forasmuch as ye know that ye were not redeemed with corruptible things, *as* silver and gold, from your vain conversation *received* by tradition from your fathers;

Colossians 2:8 Beware lest any man spoil you through philosophy and vain deceit, after the tradition of men, after the rudiments of the world, and not after Christ.

[2] 2 Thessalonians 2:15 Therefore, brethren, stand fast, and hold the traditions which ye have been taught, whether by word, or our epistle.

2 Thessalonians 3:6 Now we command you, brethren, in the name of our Lord Jesus Christ, that ye withdraw yourselves from every brother that walketh disorderly, and not after the tradition which he received of us.

[3] This figure comes from *SwordSearcher:Fox's Book of Martyrs*, Edited by William Byron Forbush, as do the accounts of the traditional methods of the deaths of the apostles.

Since not all have access to *Fox's Book of Martyrs*, chapter one is provided. The book is in the public domain.

Chapter I History of Christian Martyrs to the First General Persecutions Under Nero

Christ our Savior, in the Gospel of St. Matthew, hearing the confession of Simon Peter, who, first of all other, openly acknowledged Him to be the Son of God, and perceiving the secret hand of His Father therein, called him (alluding to his name) a rock, upon which rock He would build His Church so strong that the gates of hell should not prevail against it. In which words three things are to be noted: First, that Christ will have a Church in this world. Secondly, that the same Church should mightily be impugned, not only by the world, but also by the uttermost strength and powers of all hell. And, thirdly, that the same Church, notwithstanding the uttermost of the devil and all his malice, should continue.

Which prophecy of Christ we see wonderfully to be verified, insomuch that the whole course of the Church to this day may seem nothing else but a verifying of the said prophecy. First, that Christ hath set up a Church, needeth no declaration.

Secondly, what force of princes, kings, monarchs, governors, and rulers of this world, with their subjects, publicly and privately, with all their strength and cunning, have bent themselves against this Church! And, thirdly, how the said Church, all this notwithstanding, hath yet endured and holden its own! What storms and tempests it hath overpast, wondrous it is to behold: for the more evident declaration whereof, I have addressed this present history, to the end, first, that the wonderful works of God in His Church might appear to His glory; also that, the continuance and proceedings of the Church, from time to time, being set forth, more knowledge and experience may redound thereby, to the profit of the reader and edification of Christian faith.

As it is not our business to enlarge upon our Savior's history, either before or after His crucifixion, we shall only find it necessary to remind our readers of the discomfiture of the Jews by His subsequent resurrection. Although one apostle had betrayed Him; although another had denied Him, under the solemn sanction of an oath; and although the rest had forsaken Him, unless we may except "the disciple who was known unto the high-priest"; the history of His resurrection gave a new direction to all their hearts, and, after the mission of the Holy Spirit, imparted new confidence to their minds. The powers with which they were endued emboldened them to proclaim His name, to the confusion of the Jewish rulers, and the astonishment of Gentile proselytes.

St. Stephen [sic]

St. Stephen suffered the next in order. His death was occasioned by the faithful manner in which he preached the Gospel to the betrayers and murderers of Christ. To such a degree of madness were they excited, that they cast him out of the city and stoned him to death. The time when he suffered is generally supposed to have been at the passover which succeeded to that of our Lord's crucifixion, and to the era of his ascension, in the following spring.

Upon this a great persecution was raised against all who professed their belief in Christ as the Messiah, or as a prophet. We are immediately told by St. Luke, that "there was a great persecution against the church which was at Jerusalem;" and that "they were all scattered abroad throughout the regions of Judaea and Samaria, except the apostles."

About two thousand Christians, with Nicanor, one of the seven deacons, suffered martyrdom during the "persecution that arose about Stephen."

James the Great

The next martyr we meet with, according to St. Luke, in the History of the Apsotles' Acts, was James the son of Zebedee, the elder brother of John, and a relative of our Lord; for his mother

Salome was cousin-german to the Virgin Mary. It was not until ten years after the death of Stephen that the second martyrdom took place; for no sooner had Herod Agrippa been appointed governor of Judea, than, with a view to ingratiate himself with them, he raised a sharp persecution against the Christians, and determined to make an effectual blow, by striking at their leaders. The account given us by an eminent primitive writer, Clemens Alexandrinus, ought not to be overlooked; that, as James was led to the place of martyrdom, his accuser was brought to repent of his conduct by the apostle's extraordinary courage and undauntedness, and fell down at his feet to request his pardon, professing himself a Christian, and resolving that James should not receive the crown of martyrdom alone. Hence they were both beheaded at the same time. Thus did the first apostolic martyr cheerfully and resolutely receive that cup, which he had told our Savior he was ready to drink. Timon and Parmenas suffered martyrdom about the same time; the one at Philippi, and the other in Macedonia. These events took place A.D. 44.

Philip

Was born at Bethsaida, in Galilee and was first called by the name of "disciple." He labored diligently in Upper Asia, and suffered martyrdom at Heliopolis, in Phrygia. He was scourged, thrown into prison, and afterwards crucified, A.D. 54.

Matthew

Whose occupation was that of a toll-gatherer, was born at Nazareth. He wrote his gospel in Hebrew, which was afterwards translated into Greek by James the Less. The scene of his labors was Parthia, and Ethiopia, in which latter country he suffered martyrdom, being slain with a halberd in the city of Nadabah, A.D. 60.

James the Less

Is supposed by some to have been the brother of our Lord, by a former wife of Joseph. This is very doubtful, and accords too much with the Catholic superstition, that Mary never had any other children except our Savior. He was elected to the oversight of the churches of Jerusalem; and was the author of the Epistle ascribed to James in the sacred canon. At the age of ninety-four he was beat and stoned by the Jews; and finally had his brains dashed out with a fuller's club.

Matthias

Of whom less is known than of most of the other disciples, was elected to fill the vacant place of Judas. He was stoned at Jerusalem and then beheaded.

Andrew

Was the brother of Peter. He preached the gospel to many Asiatic nations; but on his arrival at Edessa he was taken and crucified on a cross, the two ends of which were fixed transversely in the ground. Hence the derivation of the term, St. Andrew's Cross.

St. Mark *[sic]*

Was born of Jewish parents of the tribe of Levi. He is supposed to have been converted to Christianity by Peter, whom he served as an amanuensis, and under whose inspection he wrote his Gospel in the Greek language. Mark was dragged to pieces by the people of Alexandria, at the great solemnity of Serapis their idol, ending his life under their merciless hands.

Peter

Among many other saints, the blessed apostle Peter was condemned to death, and crucified, as some do write, at Rome; albeit some others, and not without cause, do doubt thereof. Hegesippus saith that Nero sought matter against Peter to put him to death; which, when the people perceived, they entreated Peter with much ado that he would fly the city. Peter, through their importunity at length persuaded, prepared himself to avoid. But, coming to the gate, he saw the Lord Christ come to meet him, to whom he, worshipping, said, "Lord, whither dost Thou go?" To whom He answered and said, "I am come again to be crucified." By this, Peter, perceiving his suffering to be understood, returned into the city. Jerome saith that he was crucified, his head being down and his feet upward, himself so requiring, because he was (he said) unworthy to be crucified after the same form and manner as the Lord was.

Paul

Paul, the apostle, who before was called Saul, after his great travail and unspeakable labors in promoting the Gospel of Christ, suffered also in this first persecution under Nero. Abdias, declareth that under his execution Nero sent two of his esquires, Ferega and Parthemius, to bring him word of his death. They, coming to Paul instructing the people, desired him to pray for them, that they might believe; who told them that shortly after they should believe and be baptised at His sepulcher. This done, the soldiers came and led him out of the city to the place of execution, where he, after his prayers made, gave his neck to the sword.

Jude

The brother of James, was commonly called Thaddeus. He was crucified at Edessa, A.D. 72.

Bartholomew

Preached in several countries, and having translated the Gospel of Matthew into the language of India, he propagated it in that country. He was at length cruelly beaten and then crucified by the impatient idolaters.

Thomas

Called Didymus, preached the Gospel in Parthia and India, where exciting the rage of the pagan priests, he was martyred by being thrust through with a spear.

Luke

The evangelist, was the author of the Gospel which goes under his name. He travelled with Paul through various countries, and is supposed to have been hanged on an olive tree, by the idolatrous priests of Greece.

Simon

Surnamed Zelotes, preached the Gospel in Mauritania, Africa, and even in Britain, in which latter country he was crucified, A.D. 74.

John

The "beloved disciple," was brother to James the Great. The churches of Smyrna, Pergamos, Sardis, Philadelphia, Laodicea, and Thyatira, were founded by him. From Ephesus he was ordered to be sent to Rome, where it is affirmed he was cast into a cauldron of boiling oil. He escaped by miracle, without injury. Domitian afterwards banished him to the Isle of Patmos, where he wrote the Book of Revelation. Nerva, the successor of Domitian, recalled him. He was the only apostle who escaped a violent death.

Barnabas

Was of Cyprus, but of Jewish descent, his death is supposed to have taken place about A.D. 73.

And yet, notwithstanding all these continual persecutions and horrible punishments, the Church daily increased, deeply rooted in the doctrine of the apostles and of men apostolical, and watered plenteously with the blood of saints.

4 2 Timothy 4:6 For I am now ready to be offered, and the time of my departure is at hand. 7 I have fought a good fight, I have finished *my* course, I have kept the faith: 8 Henceforth there is laid up for me a crown of righteousness, which the Lord, the righteous judge, shall give me at that day: and not to me only, but unto all them also that love his appearing.

5 2 Peter 1:13 Yea, I think it meet, as long as I am in this tabernacle, to stir you up by putting *you* in remembrance; 14 Knowing that shortly I must put off *this* my tabernacle, even as our Lord Jesus Christ hath shewed me. 15 Moreover I will endeavour that ye may be able after my decease to have these things always in remembrance.

6 1 Peter 5:13 The *church that is* at Babylon, elected together with *you*, saluteth you; and *so doth* Marcus my son.

7 John 21:18 Verily, verily, I say unto thee, When thou wast young, thou girdedst thyself, and walkedst whither thou

wouldest: but when thou shalt be old, thou shalt stretch forth thy hands, and another shall gird thee, and carry *thee* whither thou wouldest not. 19 This spake he, signifying by what death he should glorify God. And when he had spoken this, he saith unto him, Follow me.

8 Acts 8:3 As for Saul, he made havock of the church, entering into every house, and haling men and women committed *them* to prison.

Acts 9:1 And Saul, yet breathing out threatenings and slaughter against the disciples of the Lord, went unto the high priest, 2 And desired of him letters to Damascus to the synagogues, that if he found any of this way, whether they were men or women, he might bring them bound unto Jerusalem.

Acts 9:13 Then Ananias answered, Lord, I have heard by many of this man, how much evil he hath done to thy saints at Jerusalem: 14 And here he hath authority from the chief priests to bind all that call on thy name.

Acts 9:21 But all that heard *him* were amazed, and said; Is not this he that destroyed them which called on this name in Jerusalem, and came hither for that intent, that he might bring them bound unto the chief priests?

2 Peter 1:13 Yea, I think it meet, as long as I am in this tabernacle, to stir you up by putting *you* in remembrance; 14 Knowing that shortly I must put off *this* my tabernacle, even as our Lord Jesus Christ hath shewed me. 15 Moreover I will endeavour that ye may be able after my decease to have these things always in remembrance.

9 1 Corinthians 15:30 And why stand we in jeopardy every hour?

10 Acts 15:26 Men that have hazarded their lives for the name of our Lord Jesus Christ.

11 Isaac Watts: Am I a Soldier of the Cross

Am I a soldier of the cross,
A follower of the Lamb,
And shall I fear to own His cause,
Or blush to speak His Name?
Must I be carried to the skies
On flowery beds of ease,
While others fought to win the prize,
And sailed through bloody seas?
Are there no foes for me to face?
Must I not stem the flood?
Is this vile world a friend to grace,
To help me on to God?
Sure I must fight if I would reign;
Increase my courage, Lord.
I'll bear the toil, endure the pain,

101

Supported by Thy Word.
Thy saints in all this glorious war
Shall conquer, though they die;
They see the triumph from afar,
By faith's discerning eye.
When that illustrious day shall rise,
And all Thy armies shine
In robes of victory through the skies,
The glory shall be Thine.

12 Luke 1:2 Even as they delivered them unto us, which from the beginning were eyewitnesses, and ministers of the word;

2 Peter 1:16 For we have not followed cunningly devised fables, when we made known unto you the power and coming of our Lord Jesus Christ, but were eyewitnesses of his majesty. 17 For he received from God the Father honour and glory, when there came such a voice to him from the excellent glory, This is my beloved Son, in whom I am well pleased. 18 And this voice which came from heaven we heard, when we were with him in the holy mount.

1 John 1:1 That which was from the beginning, which we have heard, which we have seen with our eyes, which we have looked upon, and our hands have handled, of the Word of life;

CHAPTER 9

WHERE THE *OTHERS* FORSAKEN?

Among the more difficult passages of Scripture to understand enough to explain is the one found in the closing verses of that chapter so often entitled *The Heroes of the Faith,* Hebrews 11. The first thirty-one verses are a captivating compilation of the majestic triumphs of the men and women of the Old Testament as in ways supernatural, they were given assistance through insurmountable obstacles, deliverances from incomprehensible perplexities, guidance through impenetrable wildernesses, comfort with immeasurable burdens, and victories in impossible battles.

However, as the time allotted for the assembling together begins to fail and the apostle Paul draws toward the close of his message, he begins to compress and to summarize what he does not have sufficient time to explore in this sermon.

32 And what shall I more say? for the time would fail me to tell of Gedeon, and *of* Barak, and *of* Samson, and *of* Jephthae; *of* David also, and Samuel, and *of* the prophets: 33 Who through faith subdued kingdoms, wrought righteousness, obtained promises, stopped the

mouths of lions, 34 Quenched the violence of fire, escaped the edge of the sword, out of weakness were made strong, waxed valiant in fight, turned to flight the armies of the aliens. 35 Women received their dead raised to life again:

Across these three and a half verses, one can repeatedly write in bold letters, as over the previous verses of the chapter, the single descriptive word *victorious*. Every name and every event continues the listing of a plurality of miracles, wonders, and signs. There is not a single dark cloud, not even one the size of a man's hand through the middle of the thirty-fifth verse of this chapter. That thirty-fifth verse, however, is broken right at its midpoint and a colon is placed there. The smooth flow of the chapter is interrupted with a punctuation mark that calls for a pause and an expectation that what comes next is important.

That well-placed colon identifies a complete change in the story. From that punctuation mark to the end of the passage, there are no victories, no deliverances, no successes, no miracles, and not even one instance of even a minor or temporary relief is recorded. We are introduced in these few verses to the untold stories of *The Others*, all of whom are unnamed by the apostle.

and **others** were tortured, not accepting deliverance; that they might obtain a better resurrection: 36 And **others** had trial of cruel mockings and scourgings, yea, moreover of bonds and imprisonment: 37 They were stoned, they were sawn asunder, were tempted, were slain with the sword: they wandered about in sheepskins and goatskins; being destitute, afflicted, tormented; 38 (Of whom the world was not worthy:) they wandered in deserts, and in mountains, and in dens and caves of the earth. 39 And these all, having obtained a good report through faith, received not the promise:

These anonymous *others* will be identified with certainty in eternity. On earth, we may surmise of only a few. We know that Zechariah, the son of Jehoiada the priest, was stoned by order of the king in the very court of the house of GOD.[1]

The old *Jewish Encyclopedia*[2] contains the traditions from the ancient rabbis that the prophet Isaiah was sawn asunder by King Manasseh after having been *inserted* into in a hollowed cedar tree. According to the rabbis, the execution by being sawn asunder was begun at the head apparently as an act of compassion to cause death more quickly.

Among those included within the title of *The Others* must surely be the believers that suffered so horrendously during the intertestmental period just before the time of the Maccabeans. The sufferings from that time of persecution under the ungodly Antiochus were unspeakable in their horrors and very likely not matched until the days of the Third Reich and the equally ungodly Adolph Hitler.

Dr. Harry Ironside in his *Lectures on The Intertestamental Period* gives a sufficient description of those darkened days.

> Antiochus and his minions knew no mercy. They spared neither age, sex, nor condition. Young and old, men and women, priests and people, rich and poor, suffered alike in those fearful days of vengeance. Women who attempted to keep the law and circumcise their sons, were led publicly through the city with their babes at their breasts and flung bodily from the city walls, thus being literally broken to pieces. Any who were discovered observing

the Sabbath day were apprehended and burnt alive.

Josephus' account of those dire and sorrowful times remarkably coincides with the epistle to the Hebrews' account of former saints' sufferings. Says the Jewish historian: "They were whipped with rods, and their bodies were torn to pieces, and were crucified while they were still alive and breathed." The apostle wrote of the same heroes of faith: "They were tortured, not accepting deliverance, that they might obtain a better resurrection; and others had trial of cruel mockings and scourgings, yea, moreover of bonds and imprisonment. They were stoned, they were sawn asunder, were tempted, were slain with the sword: they wandered about in sheepskins and goatskins; being destitute, afflicted, tormented (of whom the world was not worthy); they wandered in deserts and mountains, and dens and caves of the earth,"

While I am not certain, I believe that the changes in this verse are simply the result of Dr. Ironside writing from memory. I have not located any translation that has the reading.

One incident will show how truly these words applied to the faithful among the Jews in this time of trouble. One woman and her seven sons were apprehended together and dragged before the vile and infamous king, who commanded them to cast off their faith and to become worshipers of his gods. As they boldly refused, the first son was seized in the presence of his heroic mother and his six brethren, his tongue torn out, his members cut off, and he burned alive over a slow fire. Again, the alternative was presented to worship the demon-gods and live, or be faithful to Jehovah and die. Unyielding, the second son was taken and flayed alive before the eyes of the rest. And so the horrid trial went on till but one son was left, and he the youngest. The king

106

personally pleaded with him to renounce his faith and bow to the gods, promising riches, ease and honor for himself and his mother if he obeyed. Fearing he might weaken, the devoted woman encouraged his heart in the Lord, saying, "O my son, have pity upon me that bare thee ... I beseech thee, my son, look upon heaven and earth, and all that is therein, and consider that God made them of things that were not; and so was mankind made likewise. Fear not this tormentor, but be worthy of thy brethren; take thy death, that I may receive thee again in mercy with thy brethren." How strong was this testimony to the Jewish faith in the resurrection when uncorrupted by Sadducean influence!

The youth, thus encouraged, defied the king, rebuked him for his iniquity, and predicted his final judgment, till the wretched monarch was so enraged that, we are told, he "handled him worse than all the rest," and "this man died undefiled, and put his whole trust in the Lord." The mother was then despatched, and the eight faithful spirits rested together in Abraham's bosom.

It would only be soul harrowing to dwell longer on details such as these. The night was indeed dark; the storm raged relentlessly; hope almost died within the breasts of the faithful; when, like the shining forth of the star of morning, arose Mattathias who dwelt in Modin.

This man was the father of five sons, and he and his sons are the Maccabees of everlasting renown. The name means, "The hammer of God," and was originally the appellation given to the third son Judas, but is generally now applied to them all.

Those *others* did not receive deliverance. No pillar guided them by day or night. No seas parted for their escape. No sons were raised to life. No ravens brought food. No mouths of lions were stopped. No victories came; yet they were victorious.

All of these individuals received "a good report,"[3] but they did not receive relief from sufferings or rescue from death. They refused the deliverance of fiving up their faith and they received no deliverance from heaven. They did not see the supernatural, except in the sense of the terrible power of Satan that fell unleashed upon them. Those who observed them in their wretchedness and their sufferings would surely have concluded that they were forsaken by GOD.

Were these *others* deceived?

Were they forsaken?

---

[1] 2 Chronicles 24:20 And the Spirit of God came upon Zechariah the son of Jehoiada the priest, which stood above the people, and said unto them, Thus saith God, Why transgress ye the commandments of the LORD, that ye cannot prosper? because ye have forsaken the LORD, he hath also forsaken you. 21 And they conspired against him, and stoned him with stones at the commandment of the king in the court of the house of the LORD.

[2] Now available for research online at http://www.jewishencyclopedia.com/

[3] Matthew 25:21 His lord said unto him, Well done, *thou* good and faithful servant: thou hast been faithful over a few things, I will make thee ruler over many things: enter thou into the joy of thy lord. ... 23 His lord said unto him, Well done, good and faithful servant; thou hast been faithful over a few things, I will make thee ruler over many things: enter thou into the joy of thy lord.

CHAPTER 10

ARE WE FORSAKEN?

Is it possible that you and I have misunderstood the word of GOD or could it be that the GOD of Heaven might have deceived us? Is it possible that He might forsake us?

It would be possible, if all of these individuals that we have considered were deceived. If they all misunderstand what they heard GOD say to them or what they read in His word, then it is assuredly possible that you and I might also misunderstand what GOD has said to us in His word, because they were the ones that He used to transmit that word to us.

The importance of these questions is beyond measurement. There are both temporal and eternal reasons to ask whether these multiple individuals—literally the thousands identified in the texts and the millions more implied—were deliberately deceived by the GOD of Heaven or whether they *all* innocently misunderstood (1) what the Holy Spirit had moved them or others to record or (2) what they had heard with their own ears from the mouth of Jesus of Nazareth.

Were they actually forsaken by the LORD?

111

Did the GOD of Heaven actually turn His back upon those that faithfully followed His commands?

Would He do that to us?

Could He do that to us?

When the following unchallengeable facts are considered, these questions become imperative, because the issue is personal.

1. The command by GOD to obey the commands of GOD is not found in an obscure passage of Scripture or limited to a single occurrence.[1]

2. The sacred record of a person being *murdered* for obeying even one command of JEHOVAH began in the Book of Genesis with Abel[2] and continues without interruption into the Book of the Revelation.[3] Subsequent records of history reveal that the pattern has continued to the present hour.

3. A sizeable number of the most identifiable and honored followers of GOD are included in the sacred listing of those who severely suffered for obeying GOD as shown by our previous comments. Since the closing of the record of Scripture, innumerable honorable godly women and men have undergone severe trials for the testimony of their faith. The blood of multitudes has stained the earth as they have sealed their testimonies with their lives.

4. It is impossible to accept the premise that all of these men and women were anomalies, merely statistical errors.

5. It is equally impossible that all of these man and women misunderstood what

they heard from the mouth of the LORD Jesus, one of the prophets of GOD, or read in the word of GOD.

Additionally, since you and I have accepted the premise that the words of Scripture are properly understood in the literal sense of the meaning, we have a strong vested interest in asking these questions; because we may be called upon to endure persecutions and sufferings and even to pay for our own decision to obey the commands of the LORD with our life. [4] If anything ought to be clear to presently living believers, it is that this world system hates the GOD of Heaven. That visceral hatred extends to all that would place Him first in the life.

Christians live in and on a battlefield. The warfare is spiritual and the weapons of the believer are not carnal. [5] However, the weaponry of the adversary is both spiritual and carnal. [6] We have a tendency to read the caution of Peter and to mentally assign it as meant for the apostles or some exceptionally sanctified believer high above our station and never consider that it is addressed to us.

> 1 Peter 5:8 Be sober, be vigilant; because your adversary the devil, as a roaring lion, walketh about, seeking whom he may devour: 9 Whom resist stedfast in the faith, knowing that the same afflictions are accomplished in your brethren that are in the world.

The battlefield is real. It is in our minds, in our bodies, and in our homes. The enemy launches attacks in our occupations, in our encounters, and through our companions. The battle is being fought on our video screens, in our web access, and on the billboards along our routes. Through music and speech, the enemy comes at us. Those are only the spiritual and mental level attacks.

The physical attacks may sometimes today come in the form of sicknesses, but, for the most part, American Christians have avoided the physical persecutions that believers in other nations are enduring. How long it might be before Biblical standards will bring Bible-following Christians into such conflict with the prevailing winds of *societal evolution* that the persecution will escalate beyond rhetoric and the occasional financial blow is not determinable. However, what can be determined is that the acceleration has increased. The land of the pilgrim's pride is rapidly becoming ashamed of the pilgrims that founded her.

When the pressures build and the persecutions come, will it be possible that our Heavenly Father might forsake us? Should we be concerned that He might? That question is not a hypothetical nebulous collection of words. The reality of future persecution looms on the horizon of American Christians.

In words that are couched in common colloquial terms, when we face the darkness of the coming hours, we need to know if we can rely on JEHOVAH to keep the covenants recorded in Scripture.

Have we been deceived?

Will GOD forsake us?

---

[1] While this list is not comprehensive, it is sufficient to validate the statement.

Exodus 15:26 And said, If thou wilt diligently hearken to the voice of the LORD thy God, and wilt do that which is right in his sight, and wilt give ear to his commandments, and keep all his statutes, I will put none of these diseases upon thee, which I have brought upon the Egyptians: for I *am* the LORD that healeth thee. ... 20:3 Thou shalt have no other gods before me. 4 Thou shalt not make unto thee any graven image, or any likeness *of any thing* that *is* in heaven above, or that *is* in the earth beneath, or that *is* in the water under the earth: 5 Thou shalt not bow down thyself to them, nor serve them: for I the LORD thy God *am* a jealous God, visiting the iniquity of the fathers upon the children unto the third and fourth *generation* of them that hate me; 6 And shewing mercy unto thousands of them that love me, and keep my commandments.

Leviticus 22:31 Therefore shall ye keep my commandments, and do them: I *am* the LORD. ... 26:3 If ye walk in my statutes, and keep my commandments, and do them;

Deuteronomy 4:2 Ye shall not add unto the word which I command you, neither shall ye diminish *ought* from it, that ye may keep the commandments of the LORD your God which I command you. ... 40 Thou shalt keep therefore his statutes, and his commandments, which I command thee this day, that it may go well with thee, and with thy children after thee, and that thou mayest prolong *thy* days upon the earth, which the LORD thy God giveth thee, for ever. ... 5:29 O that there were such an heart in them, that they would fear me, and keep all my commandments always, that it might be well with them, and with their children for ever! ... 6:2 That thou mightest fear the LORD thy God, to keep all his statutes and his commandments, which I command thee, thou, and thy son, and thy son's son, all the days of thy life; and that thy days may be prolonged. ... 17 Ye shall diligently keep the commandments of the LORD your God, and his testimonies, and his statutes, which he hath commanded thee. ... 7:9 Know therefore that the LORD thy God, he *is* God, the faithful God, which keepeth covenant and mercy with them that love him and keep his commandments to a thousand generations; ... 11 Thou shalt therefore keep the commandments, and the statutes, and the judgments, which I command thee this day, to do them. ... 8:2 And thou shalt remember all the way which the LORD thy God led thee these forty years in the wilderness, to humble thee, *and* to prove thee, to know what *was* in thine heart, whether thou wouldest keep his commandments, or no. ... 6 Therefore thou shalt keep the commandments of the LORD thy God, to walk in his ways, and to fear him. ... 10:12 And now, Israel, what doth the LORD thy

God require of thee, but to fear the LORD thy God, to walk in all his ways, and to love him, and to serve the LORD thy God with all thy heart and with all thy soul, To keep the commandments of the LORD, and his statutes, which I command thee this day for thy good? ... 11:1 Therefore thou shalt love the LORD thy God, and keep his charge, and his statutes, and his judgments, and his commandments, alway. ... 8 Therefore shall ye keep all the commandments which I command you this day, that ye may be strong, and go in and possess the land, whither ye go to possess it; ... 18 Therefore shall ye lay up these my words in your heart and in your soul, and bind them for a sign upon your hand, that they may be as frontlets between your eyes. 19 And ye shall teach them your children, speaking of them when thou sittest in thine house, and when thou walkest by the way, when thou liest down, and when thou risest up. 20 And thou shalt write them upon the door posts of thine house, and upon thy gates: 21 That your days may be multiplied, and the days of your children, in the land which the LORD sware unto your fathers to give them, as the days of heaven upon the earth. 22 For if ye shall diligently keep all these commandments which I command you, to do them, to love the LORD your God, to walk in all his ways, and to cleave unto him; ... 27 A blessing, if ye obey the commandments of the LORD your God, which I command you this day: 28 And a curse, if ye will not obey the commandments of the LORD your God, but turn aside out of the way which I command you this day, to go after other gods, which ye have not known. ... 13:4 Ye shall walk after the LORD your God, and fear him, and keep his commandments, and obey his voice, and ye shall serve him, and cleave unto him. ... 18 When thou shalt hearken to the voice of the LORD thy God, to keep all his commandments which I command thee this day, to do *that which is* right in the eyes of the LORD thy God. ... 26:16 This day the LORD thy God hath commanded thee to do these statutes and judgments: thou shalt therefore keep and do them with all thine heart, and with all thy soul. ... 28:9 The LORD shall establish thee an holy people unto himself, as he hath sworn unto thee, if thou shalt keep the commandments of the LORD thy God, and walk in his ways. ... 45 Moreover all these curses shall come upon thee, and shall pursue thee, and overtake thee, till thou be destroyed; because thou hearkenedst not unto the voice of the LORD thy God, to keep his commandments and his statutes which he commanded thee: ... 30:2 And shalt return unto the LORD thy God, and shalt obey his voice according to all that I command thee this day, thou and thy children, with all thine heart, and with all thy soul; ... 8 And thou shalt return and obey the voice of the LORD, and do all his commandments which I command thee this day. ... 10 If thou shalt hearken unto the voice of the LORD thy God, to keep his commandments and his statutes which are written in this book of the law, *and* if thou turn unto the LORD thy God with all thine heart, and with all thy soul. 11 For this commandment which I command thee this day, it *is* not hidden from thee, neither *is* it far off. 12 It *is* not in heaven, that thou shouldest say, Who shall go up for us to heaven, and bring it unto us, that we may hear it, and do it? 13 Neither *is* it beyond the sea, that thou shouldest say, Who shall go over the sea for us, and bring it unto us, that we may hear it, and do it? 14 But the word *is* very nigh unto thee, in thy mouth, and in thy heart, that thou mayest do it. 15 See, I have set before thee this day life and good, and death and evil; ... 30:16 In that I command thee this day to love the LORD thy God, to walk in his ways, and to keep his commandments and his statutes and his judgments, that thou mayest live and multiply: and the LORD thy God shall bless thee in the land whither thou goest to possess it.

Joshua 22:5 But take diligent heed to do the commandment and the law, which Moses the servant of the LORD charged you, to love the LORD your God, and to walk in all his ways, and to keep his commandments, and to cleave unto him, and to serve him with all your heart and with all your soul.

1 Samuel 12:14 If ye will fear the LORD, and serve him, and obey his voice, and not rebel against the commandment of the LORD, then shall both ye and also the king that reigneth over you continue following the LORD your God: 15 But if ye will not obey the voice of the LORD, but rebel against the commandment of the LORD, then shall the hand of the LORD be against you, as *it was* against your fathers.

1 Kings 2:3 And keep the charge of the LORD thy God, to walk in his ways, to keep his statutes, and his commandments, and his judgments, and his testimonies, as it is written in the law of Moses, that thou mayest prosper in all that thou doest, and whithersoever thou turnest thyself: ... 3:14 And if thou wilt walk in my ways, to keep my statutes and my commandments, as thy father David did walk, then I will lengthen thy days. ... 6:12 *Concerning* this house which thou art in building, if thou wilt walk in my statutes, and execute my judgments, and keep all my commandments to walk in them; then will I perform my word with thee, which I spake unto David thy father: ... 8:58 That he may incline our hearts unto him, to walk in all his ways, and to keep his commandments, and his statutes, and his judgments, which he commanded our fathers. ... 61 Let your heart therefore be perfect with the LORD our God, to walk in his statutes, and to keep his commandments, as at this day. ... 9:4 And if thou wilt walk before me, as David thy father walked, in integrity of heart, and in uprightness, to do according to all that I have commanded thee, *and* wilt keep my statutes and my judgments: ... 17:13 Yet the LORD testified against Israel, and against Judah, by all the prophets, *and by* all the

seers, saying, Turn ye from your evil ways, and keep my commandments *and* my statutes, according to all the law which I commanded your fathers, and which I sent to you by my servants the prophets.

Jeremiah 7:23 But this thing commanded I them, saying, Obey my voice, and I will be your God, and ye shall be my people: and walk ye in all the ways that I have commanded you, that it may be well unto you. ... 11:4 Which I commanded your fathers in the day *that* I brought them forth out of the land of Egypt, from the iron furnace, saying, Obey my voice, and do them, according to all which I command you: so shall ye be my people, and I will be your God:

Nehemiah 1:9 But *if* ye turn unto me, and keep my commandments, and do them; though there were of you cast out unto the uttermost part of the heaven, *yet* will I gather them from thence, and will bring them unto the place that I have chosen to set my name there.

Psalm 78:7 That they might set their hope in God, and not forget the works of God, but keep his commandments: ... 103:18 To such as keep his covenant, and to those that remember his commandments to do them. ... 119:4 Thou hast commanded *us* to keep thy precepts diligently. ... 60 I made haste, and delayed not to keep thy commandments. ... 115 Depart from me, ye evildoers: for I will keep the commandments of my God.

Daniel 9:4 And I prayed unto the LORD my God, and made my confession, and said, O Lord, the great and dreadful God, keeping the covenant and mercy to them that love him, and to them that keep his commandments;

John 14:15 If ye love me, keep my commandments. ... 15:10 If ye keep my commandments, ye shall abide in my love; even as I have kept my Father's commandments, and abide in his love.

1 John 2:3 And hereby we do know that we know him, if we keep his commandments. ... 3:22 And whatsoever we ask, we receive of him, because we keep his commandments, and do those things that are pleasing in his sight. ... 5:2 By this we know that we love the children of God, when we love God, and keep his commandments. ... 3 For this is the love of God, that we keep his commandments: and his commandments are not grievous.

Revelation 14:12 Here is the patience of the saints: here *are* they that keep the commandments of God, and the faith of Jesus.

[2] Genesis 4:3 And in process of time it came to pass, that Cain brought of the fruit of the ground an offering unto the LORD. 4 And Abel, he also brought of the firstlings of his flock and of the fat thereof. And the LORD had respect unto Abel and

to his offering: 5 But unto Cain and to his offering he had not respect. And Cain was very wroth, and his countenance fell. 6 And the LORD said unto Cain, Why art thou wroth? and why is thy countenance fallen? 7 If thou doest well, shalt thou not be accepted? and if thou doest not well, sin lieth at the door. And unto thee *shall be* his desire, and thou shalt rule over him. 8 And Cain talked with Abel his brother: and it came to pass, when they were in the field, that Cain rose up against Abel his brother, and slew him.

3 Revelation 6:9 And when he had opened the fifth seal, I saw under the altar the souls of them that were slain for the word of God, and for the testimony which they held: ... 11:7 And when they shall have finished their testimony, the beast that ascendeth out of the bottomless pit shall make war against them, and shall overcome them, and kill them. 8 And their dead bodies shall lie in the street of the great city, which spiritually is called Sodom and Egypt, where also our Lord was crucified. 9 And they of the people and kindreds and tongues and nations shall see their dead bodies three days and an half, and shall not suffer their dead bodies to be put in graves. ... 13:15 And he had power to give life unto the image of the beast, that the image of the beast should both speak, and cause that as many as would not worship the image of the beast should be killed. ... 14:13 And I heard a voice from heaven saying unto me, Write, Blessed are the dead which die in the Lord from henceforth: Yea, saith the Spirit, that they may rest from their labours; and their works do follow them. ... 18:24 And in her was found the blood of prophets, and of saints, and of all that were slain upon the earth.

4 John 15:18 If the world hate you, ye know that it hated me before *it hated* you. 19 If ye were of the world, the world would love his own: but because ye are not of the world, but I have chosen you out of the world, therefore the world hateth you. 20 Remember the word that I said unto you, The servant is not greater than his lord. If they have persecuted me, they will also persecute you; if they have kept my saying, they will keep yours also. 21 But all these things will they do unto you for my name's sake, because they know not him that sent me. 22 If I had not come and spoken unto them, they had not had sin: but now they have no cloke for their sin. 23 He that hateth me hateth my Father also. ... 16:1 These things have I spoken unto you, that ye should not be offended. 2 They shall put you out of the synagogues: yea, the time cometh, that whosoever killeth you will think that he doeth God service. 3 And these things will they do unto you, because they have not known the Father, nor me.

Luke 21:12 But before all these, they shall lay their hands on you, and persecute *you*, delivering *you* up to the synagogues, and into prisons, being brought before kings and rulers for my name's sake. 13 And it shall turn to you for a testimony. 14 Settle *it* therefore in your hearts, not to meditate before what ye shall answer: 15 For I will give you a mouth and wisdom, which all your adversaries shall not be able to gainsay nor resist. 16 And ye shall be betrayed both by parents, and brethren, and kinsfolks, and friends; and *some* of you shall they cause to be put to death. 17 And ye shall be hated of all *men* for my name's sake. 18 But there shall not an hair of your head perish.

5 2 Corinthians 10:3 For though we walk in the flesh, we do not war after the flesh: 4 (For the weapons of our warfare *are* not carnal, but mighty through God to the pulling down of strong holds;)

6 Matthew 23:34 Wherefore, behold, I send unto you prophets, and wise men, and scribes: and *some* of them ye shall kill and crucify; and *some* of them shall ye scourge in your synagogues, and persecute *them* from city to city:

Ephesians 2:2 Wherein in time past ye walked according to the course of this world, according to the prince of the power of the air, the spirit that now worketh in the children of disobedience: 3 Among whom also we all had our conversation in times past in the lusts of our flesh, fulfilling the desires of the flesh and of the mind; and were by nature the children of wrath, even as others.

CHAPTER 11

SEARCHING FOR AN ANSWER

If we are candid in our admission, you and I will confess that we have wondered why we have often experienced difficulties in our efforts in witnessing, oppositions in our expression of a testimony, and pressures to compromise our beliefs. I have found myself in the same spiritual struggle that engulfed Asaph.

Psalm 73:1 Truly God *is* good to Israel, *even* to such as are of a clean heart. 2 But as for me, my feet were almost gone; my steps had well nigh slipped. 3 For I was envious at the foolish, *when* I saw the prosperity of the wicked. 4 For *there are* no bands in their death: but their strength *is* firm. 5 They *are* not in trouble *as other* men; neither are they plagued like *other* men. 6 Therefore pride compasseth them about as a chain; violence covereth them *as* a garment. 7 Their eyes stand out with fatness: they have more than heart could wish. 8 They are corrupt, and speak wickedly *concerning* oppression: they speak loftily. 9 They set their mouth against the heavens, and their tongue walketh through the earth. 10 Therefore his people return hither: and waters of a

121

full *cup* are wrung out to them. 11 And they say, How doth God know? and is there knowledge in the most High? 12 Behold, these *are* the ungodly, who prosper in the world; they increase *in* riches. 13 Verily I have cleansed my heart *in* vain, and washed my hands in innocency. 14 For all the day long have I been plagued, and chastened every morning. 15 If I say, I will speak thus; behold, I should offend *against* the generation of thy children. 16 When I thought to know this, it *was* too painful for me;[1]

Asaph was trying very diligently to serve his GOD and nothing was going right. He had so many difficulties in just living that he was convinced that he was *plagued.* Nothing that he desired to do seemed doable. He was incompetent in his attempts and a failure in his efforts, but he knew that he had been able to do those very things before and had accomplished them. Now, he was plagued; everything he had or was had been corrupted. He knew that GOD plagued Pharaoh to force him to let the children of Israel leave Egypt[2] and plagued Israel over the golden calf.[3] He is persuaded by his observations that GOD had plagued him.

Asaph was present when the first attempt to bring the Ark of the Covenant to Mount Zion failed. He was the one to whom David handed the Psalm that he composed for the day the Ark of the Covenant was properly brought to the Tabernacle that David constructed to house it.[4] When the Ark of the Covenant is left in the new Tabernacle, Asaph was one of those in whose care it was placed.[5] Asaph knows what it means to be in fellowship or out of fellowship with the GOD of Heaven.

He is active in the worship of the nation. He is leading the music of that worship; even so, he feels that he is being plagued "all day long." The heaviness of soul is nearly overwhelming. He is surrounded with those who are praying and having prayers answered; but his prayers are perfunctory and answerless. He hears the praises that are offered from grateful lips, but there is no responding note of thanksgiving in his mouth. He is able to fulfill the technical responsibilities for the choirs and the instruments, but he has no melody in his heart.

While the sacrifices were still offered in the Tabernacle of Moses with the brazen altar and the Levitical priesthood at Gibeon, the Ark of the Covenant was on Mount Zion in the Tabernacle that David prepared. It was to this Tabernacle that the people came to pray and to rejoice. It was a place of worship without an altar for sacrifice. It that way, this Tabernacle may prefigure the New Testament church for that also is the place of worship without an altar for a sacrifice. The life of Asaph is centered in the Tabernacle of David.

Yet, Asaph is miserable. Surrounded by joy and all that he sees is the hypocrisy of those that come to the Tabernacle. He sees the wicked prospering. Perhaps, he sees successful men with abundant blessings, but without humility. Among those coming to the Tabernacle are some that use the prayers for gossip and abuse.[6]

He has tried to be right and to do right and he is plagued. Perhaps, even worse, he felt that he was being also being chastened. Asaph knew that in the Law, GOD had said that He would chasten the individual Israelites.

> Deuteronomy 8:5 Thou shalt also consider in thine heart, that, as a man chasteneth his son, *so* the LORD thy God chasteneth thee. 6 Therefore thou shalt keep the commandments of the LORD thy God, to walk in his ways, and to fear him.

123

He cleansed his heart and washed his hands. As best that he knew, Asaph had no unconfessed sin and he did not know of a violation of the Law. Yet, he assumes that GOD is chastising him. He does not understand why it would be so. While he is being chastised, he sees that the wicked hypocrite is blessed and has *no bands*, no constraints. Additionally, that unrighteous man has freedom to abundance; his lifestyle has no restraints. Asaph is perplexed as to how this could be and he is depressed that it is happening.

Then, Asaph takes notice that the ungodly are better off than he is. They do not even make a pretense of serving GOD and yet they *increase in riches*.

Asaph cannot not deny that "God *is* good to Israel, *even* to such as are of a clean heart." It is that GOD is not being good to him; and like Job, Asaph cannot understand why he was plagued and being chastened.[7]

Asaph finally puts his innermost thoughts into the stark words: "Verily I have cleansed my heart *in* vain, and washed my hands in innocency. For all the day long have I been plagued, and chastened every morning." I have tried to serve GOD by following His word but I still have not pleased Him. Everything that I have done is empty and worthless. I might as well never have done any of it. I wish I had not ... the thought itself would be *too painful* to continue."[8]

We may never arrive at a fully satisfactory answer to why the wicked do prosper and the children of GOD suffer. Moses evaluated the issues of life and eternity and made a determination. His testimony is properly considered in this context. Moses did not find an answer, he just continued to walk by faith.

Hebrews 11:24 By faith Moses, when he was come to years, refused to be called the son of Pharaoh's daughter; 25 **Choosing rather to suffer affliction with the people of God**, than to enjoy the pleasures of sin for a season; 26 **Esteeming the reproach of Christ** greater riches than the treasures in Egypt: for he had respect unto the recompence of the reward. 27 By faith he forsook Egypt, **not fearing the wrath of the king**: for he endured, as seeing him who is invisible.

It is right for the child of GOD to maintain our obedience and continue our profession in spite of the near certainty of perplexing difficulties, possible persecution, and even the potential eventuality of our death as a martyr. However, it is proper that we do not walk blindly with an expectation of an unfettered, unhindered, and unmolested journey between here and our eternal Home.

If you think the stories of the men and women that we have considered thus far are perplexing, where our study now takes us is to what is perhaps the most perplexing sentence found in all of Scripture. Many have quoted Martin Luther's reported cry of despair allegedly uttered after an extended meditation on these words that we now approach, "God forsaking God. Who can understand that?" Perhaps, that is the wrong question.

When we discuss mortal men and women, we are at one level of possibilities; but these words and this Person move us to an incomparable level. Those words "My God, my God, why hast thou forsaken me?" were uttered by the Son of GOD.

Those words spoken by that Person brings us to the most difficult statement of the word of GOD to grasp.

As we focus our attention on this sentence, I do not propose that I shall be able to present a full explanation where many giants of the faith have hesitated or stumbled. What I will attempt to do is to place this passage within the context of the whole of Scripture and, by doing so, show that certain teachings forced upon the passage are incorrect and that others derived from the passage are radically false.

While all Bereans[9] as a matter of firm conviction know that Scriptures are to be compared with one another and not to be set in conflict with each other, the application of that principle is sometimes forgotten or the potential conflict is not recognized.

Scriptures do not conflict and they never contradict. What was written first does not conflict with what was written after and that which was written after does not contradict what was written first.

Scriptures do compliment and do complete. What was written first compliments what was written after and that which was written after completes what was written first.

The two Testaments, the Old and the New, are one complete and composite whole: the word of GOD, that which we call the Bible. The unity of Scripture is stated repeatedly throughout the whole of Scripture. Notice how these texts show that the words of the LORD are the word of the LORD and that the word of the LORD is the words of the LORD.

> Numbers 11:23 And the LORD said unto Moses, Is the LORD'S hand waxed short? thou shalt see now whether my word shall come to pass unto thee or not. 24 And Moses went out, and told the people the words of the LORD, and gathered the seventy men of the elders of the people, and set them round about the tabernacle.

> 2 Chronicles 34:21 Go, inquire of the LORD for me, and for them that are left in Israel and

126

in Judah, concerning the words of the book that is found: for great is the wrath of the LORD that is poured out upon us, because our fathers have not kept the word of the LORD, to do after all that is written in this book.

Psalm 119:57 Thou art my portion, O LORD: I have said that I would keep thy words. 58 I intreated thy favour with my whole heart: be merciful unto me according to thy word. ... 101 I have refrained my feet from every evil way, that I might keep thy word. 102 I have not departed from thy judgments: for thou hast taught me. 103 How sweet are thy words unto my taste! yea, sweeter than honey to my mouth! 104 Through thy precepts I get understanding: therefore I hate every false way. 105 Thy word is a lamp unto my feet, and a light unto my path. ... 130 The entrance of thy words giveth light; it giveth understanding unto the simple. 131 I opened my mouth, and panted: for I longed for thy commandments. 132 Look thou upon me, and be merciful unto me, as thou usest to do unto those that love thy name. 133 Order my steps in thy word: and let not any iniquity have dominion over me. ... 139 My zeal hath consumed me, because mine enemies have forgotten thy words. 140 Thy word is very pure: therefore thy servant loveth it.

Jeremiah 15:16 Thy words were found, and I did eat them; and thy word was unto me the joy and rejoicing of mine heart: for I am called by thy name, O LORD God of hosts.

Amos 8:11 Behold, the days come, saith the Lord GOD, that I will send a famine in the land, not a famine of bread, nor a thirst for water, but of hearing the words of the LORD: 12 And they shall wander from sea to sea, and from the north even to the east, they shall run to and fro to seek the word of the LORD, and shall not find it.

John 12:48 He that rejecteth me, and receiveth not my words, hath one that judgeth him: the word that I have spoken, the same shall judge him in the last day.

John 14:23 Jesus answered and said unto him, If a man love me, he will keep my words: and my Father will love him, and we will come unto him, and make our abode with him. 24 He that loveth me not keepeth not my sayings: and the word which ye hear is not mine, but the Father's which sent me.

John 17:6 I have manifested thy name unto the men which thou gavest me out of the world: thine they were, and thou gavest them me; and they have kept thy word. 7 Now they have known that all things whatsoever thou hast given me are of thee. 8 For I have given unto them the words which thou gavest me; and they have received them, and have known surely that I came out from thee, and they have believed that thou didst send me.

The LORD Jesus speaks of the words of the LORD that collectively comprise the word of the LORD. The words of the word of GOD form a unified whole and cannot be divided into disjointed sections or discordant themes. The prophets were not in opposition; they were in concord. They were allies, not enemies. Though they were separated by time, and when not by time, by distance, they were nonetheless collaborators, colleagues, and coworkers in the composition of one Book.

2 Peter 1:20 Knowing this first, that no prophecy of the scripture is of any private interpretation. 21 For the prophecy came not in old time by the will of man: but holy men of God spake as they were moved by the Holy Ghost.

Since they wrote, "not in the words which man's wisdom teacheth," but "as they were moved by the Holy Ghost," there cannot be one word in the entirety of Scripture that is *out of tune* with any other word in the symphony of Scripture. The Book that we call the Bible had One Author. Not a single word is incompatible, inconsistent, in disagreement, or at variance with any other word in the whole of the rest of Scripture.

With that foundation as a solid anchorage, we may comfortably place Scripture alongside Scripture.

> 1 Corinthians 2:12 Now we have received, not the spirit of the world, but the spirit which is of God; that we might know the things that are freely given to us of God. 13 Which things also we speak, not in the words which man's wisdom teacheth, but which the Holy Ghost teacheth; comparing spiritual things with spiritual. 14 But the natural man receiveth not the things of the Spirit of God: for they are foolishness unto him: neither can he know them, because they are spiritually discerned.

Comparing Scripture with Scripture, we may search to see whether these things be so and we may do so with confidence and with contentment.

Let us apply that principle to this very difficult, **perhaps *the most* difficult** statement of all of Scripture. We first notice that it is found in the writings of three witnesses that the matter may be established.[10]

The statement, which is recorded five times, thrice in English and twice in Aramaic,[11] in three passages, is "My God, my God, why hast thou forsaken me?"

> Psalm 22:1 My God, my God, why hast thou forsaken me? why art thou so far from helping me, and from the words of my roaring?

> Matthew 27:46 And about the ninth hour Jesus cried with a loud voice, saying, Eli, Eli, lama sabachthani? that is to say, My God, my God, why hast thou forsaken me?

Mark 15:34 And at the ninth hour Jesus cried with a loud voice, saying, Eloi, Eloi, lama sabachthani? which is, being interpreted, My God, my God, why hast thou forsaken me?

We shall, as one should, begin with the first mention; establish the context in which the sentence is found; and then sit the other passages alongside, keeping them in their context, and as we do so, may we each ask the Holy Spirit to open our eyes, that we may behold wondrous things out of the word of GOD.[12]

While this listing is not exhaustive, the nine words of this statement have been most often *explained* by commentators and preachers by one of the following eight theories, including the following four foolish suggestions.

1. Jesus of Nazareth suddenly realized that he was actually going to die and that he had been deluded by manipulators or had deceived himself into believing that he was the Messiah.
2. Jesus of Nazareth was following a well-constructed script and, knowing that these words were thought by some to be messianic, he quoted them at this time in his plot to be recognized as the Messiah.
3. Jesus of Nazareth never said these words on the cross, but the apostles or later writers put them into his mouth to build the story that he was the Messiah.
4. The Christ left the man Jesus at this point and let him die, confused and alone.

It is rather easy to read these four propositions and to realize that they are not advanced nor are they accepted by anyone that believes in the deity of Jesus of Nazareth. It is not possible to reconcile any suggestion that (1) Jesus of Nazareth was a plotter manipulating Himself into being the Messiah or that (2) He was deceived by scheming men into believing that He could be the Messiah with the declaration that the Word was made flesh and dwelt among us. However, the first three are intellectually argued as fact by today's progressive Christian writers, formerly identified as liberal and as modernists before that, and the fourth is taught by some of the cults.

All that recognize and accept Jesus of Nazareth as GOD manifest in the flesh reject these first four proposals without further consideration. The errors that they express are self evident to all Bible believers.

The next four are defended by individuals identifying themselves as traditional evangelical Christians and are often proclaimed in some combination by individuals that identify themselves as conservative and even fundamentalistic in their doctrinal positions. I do not challenge their sincerity but I categorically reject these propositions and their devotion to them as also being an unwitting or unrecognized rejection of the deity of the LORD Jesus.

5. When the Son of GOD became a man in the Incarnation, He emptied Himself of His deity and the divine attributes and, having only the knowledge and capacities of a man came to know the horror of dying; then, as man, the fear of what He must face overwhelmed Him and He begged not to die.

6. Having emptied Himself of the divine attributes as He came to die, His humanity took control and He was afraid of death and in the anguish of the hour, He plead for deliverance.

7. As man, He was struggling with doing the will of GOD. These words are only His humanity speaking. As GOD (the other part or portion of Himself), He was willing, but the human feelings are reported so that we may know that He felt like us.

8. GOD made Jesus to become sin and as GOD He could not look upon His Son, Who was now made sin, and so He turned His back upon Jesus and the bond of unity was for those

131

three hours of darkness was broken. For that brief time, (What is three hours in the measurement of eternity?), the Son could not know any communion, feel any fellowship, or have any communication with the Father. For those three darkened hours, the unity of the TRINITY was broken. At the end of the three hours, the Son cries these words in fear and confusion for He had never known that isolation before. However, soon afterwards, with the debt paid, the fellowship would be restored.

These last four theories are constructed on the premise that for the Word of GOD to be made flesh required that He *empty* Himself of the prerogatives of Deity. The assumption forming the foundation of this idea is that, at a minimum, when the Son of GOD became the Son of David, He had to set aside His *omnipotence, omniscience, and omnipresence.* This thinking is primarily derived from one word in one verse: the Greek word εκενωσεν,[13] which lies behind the English words "made of no reputation" in verse seven of the second chapter of Philippians.

Philippians 2:5 Let this mind be in you, which was also in Christ Jesus: 6 Who, being in the form of God, thought it not robbery to be equal with God: 7 But made himself of no reputation, and took upon him the form of a servant, and was made in the likeness of men: 8 And being found in fashion as a man, he humbled himself, and became obedient unto death, even the death of the cross. 9 Wherefore God also hath highly exalted him, and given him a name which is above every name: 10 That at the name of Jesus every knee should bow, of things in heaven, and things in earth, and things under the earth; 11 And that every tongue should confess that Jesus Christ is Lord, to the glory of God the Father.

The translators of the Authorized Version, following Tyndale and Wycliffe, perfectly rendered the word in Philippians 2:7 with the phrase: "made himself of no reputation."[14] That phrase is sound in both the accuracy of translation and the fidelity of doctrine.

The Greek word εκενωσεν has been transliterated into English as *kenosis*. The English word *kenosis* is defined by the Merriam-Webster 11th Collegiate Dictionary as "the relinquishment of divine attributes by Jesus Christ in becoming human."[15]

However, a term used by theologians in a way that negates Biblical truth, even when that usage is adopted by the foremost English dictionary, cannot become the final authority for truth. **The word of GOD, and not a dictionary or a theology book, must always define Biblical truth.** Theology, at its very best, is nothing more than a human effort to codify the truths of Scripture. When a theologian or a system of theology is determined to be contrary to Scripture, both the theologian and the system must be rejected and they must be repudiated.

It is not possible for the Son of GOD to empty Himself, to remove from Himself, any portion, substance, part, aspect, attribute, or prerogative of deity. It is also not possible that another could do this to Him. To do so would require Him to be less than He was; and therefore, He would become something that he was not and thus He would not be GOD.

We may have challenges in explaining the Incarnation—*and we do*—but we have no justification in offering any explanation of the Incarnation that is built upon any premise that conflicts or contradicts the word of GOD.

To advocate that Jesus of Nazareth was less than God manifest in the flesh[16] is to follow the Arian[17] heresy that has been rejected by mainstream *and* Biblical Christianity since the fourth century.

To erect divisions between the humanity and the deity of Jesus of Nazareth is to follow the heresy of the Nestorians[18] that has been rejected by mainstream *and* Biblical Christianity since the fifth century.

The theory of kenosis is a more modern movement; generally traced[19] to an introduction in the late 1800s in Germany by Gottfried Thomasius (1802–1875), a Lutheran theologian. Theologians and preachers that promote the kenosis theory must utilize concepts derived from one or the other of the ancient heresies of Arianism or Nestorianism in order to support kenosis.

Kenosis requires that the Son of GOD must become less than the fullness of GOD (Arianism) or else the GOD-part and the man-part must be kept isolated with Jesus of Nazareth operating sometimes from the GOD-part and at other times from the man-part (Nestorianism). In either position, Jesus of Nazareth must become less than full deity on some occasion. For some advocates of kenosis, this occurs at the Incarnation; for others, the change transpires during the three hours of darkness. When is immaterial; if it occurred, then Jesus of Nazareth was not GOD for that occasion. It is impossible for GOD not to be GOD.

Since each of the last four intellectual schemes have an obvious conflict with definitive unambiguous statements of Scripture, I reject them without hesitation as without merit. I therefore conclude that there is at least one more additional understanding that does not violate the integrity of Scripture. *Confusion at Calvary* is my attempt to propose a solution that does not violate the Scriptures.

At about the ninth hour as He was suspended between Heaven and earth, it is unquestionably affirmed that Jesus of Nazareth cried with a loud voice saying, "Eli, Eli, lama sabachthani? that is to say, My God, my God, why hast thou forsaken me?"[20] The questions now laid before us are very direct and, yet, very simple. The order may be adjusted, but the following questions raised by that outcry are certainly definable.

1. Who made that cry? Did the Son of GOD ask that question or was it the Son of man that cried out?
2. Was the Christ spirit a separate entity from the man Jesus?
3. Had the GOD-part abandoned the man-part of Jesus of Nazareth?
4. Did Jesus of Nazareth not understand what was happening on the cross?
5. Was the actual dying a surprise to Jesus of Nazareth?
6. Whose blood was shed on the cross? Was it the blood of the Son of man or the blood of the Son of GOD?[21]
7. Who died on that cross? Was it the Son of GOD or the Son of man?
8. Did GOD the Father turn His back upon GOD the Son?

Those questions and others must be confronted straightforwardly and they must be resolved steadfastly. The resolution must be achieved without creating inconsistencies or contradictions with any other Scripture.

What actually happened between JEHOVAH the Father and JEHOVAH the Son? Was the Son of GOD forsaken?

¹ Asaph continues with an explanation of how he resolved the issue in his heart; but he does not answer the question as to the incongruity of the command to obey and the experience of the obedient. In effect, he becomes willing to leave the matter in the hands of God and to be content to serve the LORD.

Psalm 73:17 Until I went into the sanctuary of God; *then* understood I their end. 18 Surely thou didst set them in slippery places: thou castedst them down into destruction. 19 How are they *brought* into desolation, as in a moment! they are utterly consumed with terrors. 20 As a dream when *one* awaketh; *so*, O Lord, when thou awakest, thou shalt despise their image. 21 Thus my heart was grieved, and I was pricked in my reins. 22 So foolish *was* I, and ignorant: I was *as* a beast before thee. 23 Nevertheless I *am* continually with thee: thou hast holden *me* by my right hand. 24 Thou shalt guide me with thy counsel, and afterward receive me *to* glory. 25 Whom have I in heaven *but thee*? and *there is* none upon earth *that* I desire beside thee. 26 My flesh and my heart faileth: *but* God *is* the strength of my heart, and my portion for ever. 27 For, lo, they that are far from thee shall perish: thou hast destroyed all them that go a whoring from thee. 28 But *it is* good for me to draw near to God: I have put my trust in the Lord GOD, that I may declare all thy works.

² Genesis 12:17 And the LORD plagued Pharaoh and his house with great plagues because of Sarai Abram's wife.

Joshua 24:5 I sent Moses also and Aaron, and I plagued Egypt, according to that which I did among them: and afterward I brought you out.

³ Exodus 32:35 And the LORD plagued the people, because they made the calf, which Aaron made.

⁴ 1 Chronicles 16:7 Then on that day David delivered first *this psalm* to thank the LORD into the hand of Asaph and his brethren.

⁵ 1 Chronicles 16:37 So he left there before the ark of the covenant of the LORD Asaph and his brethren, to minister before the ark continually, as every day's work required:

⁶ It is perhaps worthy of notice that the only two times the phrase "not as other men are" is in this Psalm of Asaph and in the prayer of the Pharisee who used his prayer to gossip about the publican.

Luke 18:11 The Pharisee stood and prayed thus with himself, God, I thank thee, that I am not as other men *are*, extortioners, unjust, adulterers, or even as this publican. 12 I fast twice in the week, I give tithes of all that I possess. 13 And the publican, standing afar off, would not lift up so much as *his* eyes unto heaven, but smote upon his breast, saying, God be merciful to me a sinner. 14 I tell you, this man went down to his house justified *rather* than the other: for every one that exalteth himself shall be abased; and he that humbleth himself shall be exalted.

⁷ Job 6:24 Teach me, and I will hold my tongue: and cause me to understand wherein I have erred.

7:20 I have sinned; what shall I do unto thee, O thou preserver of men? why hast thou set me as a mark against thee, so that I am a burden to myself? 21 And why dost thou not pardon my transgression, and take away mine iniquity? for now shall I sleep in the dust; and thou shalt seek me in the morning, but I *shall* not *be*.

9:1 Then Job answered and said, 2 I know *it is* so of a truth: but how should man be just with God? 3 If he will contend with him, he cannot answer him one of a thousand. 4 *He is* wise in heart, and mighty in strength: who hath hardened *himself* against him, and hath prospered? 5 Which removeth the mountains, and they know not: which overturneth them in his anger. 6 Which shaketh the earth out of her place, and the pillars thereof tremble. 7 Which commandeth the sun, and it riseth not; and sealeth up the stars. 8 Which alone spreadeth out the heavens, and treadeth upon the waves of the sea. 9 Which maketh Arcturus, Orion, and Pleiades, and the chambers of the south. 10 Which doeth great things past finding out; yea, and wonders without number. 11 Lo, he goeth by me, and I see *him* not: he passeth on also, but I perceive him not. 12 Behold, he taketh away, who can hinder him? who will say unto him, What doest thou? 13 *If* God will not withdraw his anger, the proud helpers do stoop under him. 14 How much less shall I answer him, *and* choose out my words *to reason* with him? 15 Whom, though I were righteous, *yet* would I not answer, *but* I would make supplication to my judge. 16 If I had called, and he had answered me; *yet* would I not believe that he had hearkened unto my voice. 17 For he breaketh me with a tempest, and multiplieth my wounds without cause. 18 He will not suffer me to take my breath, but filleth me with bitterness. 19 If *I speak* of strength, lo, *he is* strong: and if of judgment, who shall set me a time *to plead?* 20 If I justify myself, mine own mouth shall condemn me: *if I say*, I *am* perfect, it shall also prove me perverse. 21 *Though* I *were* perfect, *yet* would I not know my soul: I would despise my life. 22 This *is* one *thing*, therefore I said *it*, He destroyeth the perfect and the wicked. 23 If the scourge slay suddenly, he will laugh at the trial of the innocent. 24 The earth is given into the hand of the wicked: he covereth the faces of the judges thereof; if not, where, *and* who *is* he? 25 Now my days are swifter than a post: they flee away, they see no good. 26 They are passed away as the swift ships: as the eagle *that* hasteth to the prey. 27 If I say, I will forget my complaint, I will leave off my heaviness, and comfort *myself.* 28 I am afraid of all my sorrows, I know that thou wilt not hold me innocent. 29 *If* I be wicked, why then labour I in vain? 30 If I wash myself with snow water, and make my hands never so clean; 31 Yet shalt thou plunge me in the ditch, and mine own clothes shall abhor me. 32 For *he is* not a man, as I *am, that* I should answer him, *and* we should come together in judgment. 33 Neither is there any daysman betwixt us, *that* might lay his hand upon us both. 34 Let him take his rod away from me, and let not his fear terrify me: 35 *Then* would I speak, and not fear him; but *it is* not so with me.

10:1 My soul is weary of my life; I will leave my complaint upon myself; I will speak in the bitterness of my soul. 2 I will say unto God, Do not condemn me; shew me wherefore thou contendest with me. 3 *Is it* good unto thee that thou shouldest oppress, that thou shouldest despise the work of thine hands, and shine upon the counsel of the wicked? 4 Hast thou eyes of flesh? or seest thou as man seeth? 5 *Are* thy days as the days of man? *are* thy years as man's days, 6 That thou inquirest after mine iniquity, and searchest after my sin? 7 Thou knowest that I am not wicked; and *there is* none that can deliver out of thine hand. 8 Thine hands have made me and fashioned me together round about; yet thou dost destroy me. 9 Remember, I beseech thee, that thou hast made me as the clay; and wilt thou bring me into dust again? 10 Hast thou not poured me out as milk, and curdled me like cheese? 11 Thou hast clothed me with skin and flesh, and hast fenced me with bones and sinews. 12 Thou hast granted me life and favour, and thy visitation hath preserved my spirit. 13 And these *things* hast thou hid in thine heart: I know that this *is* with thee. 14 If I sin, then thou markest me, and thou wilt not acquit me from mine iniquity. 15 If I be wicked, woe unto me; and *if* I be righteous, *yet* will I not lift up my head. *I am* full of confusion; therefore see thou mine affliction; 16 For it increaseth. Thou huntest me as a fierce lion: and again thou shewest thyself marvellous upon me. 17 Thou renewest thy witnesses against me, and increasest thine indignation upon me; changes and war *are* against me. 18 Wherefore then hast thou brought me forth out of the womb? Oh that I had given up the ghost, and no eye had seen me! 19 I should have been as though I had not been; I should have been carried from the womb to the grave. 20 *Are* not my days few? cease *then, and* let me alone, that I may take comfort a little, 21 Before I go *whence* I shall not return, *even* to the land of darkness and the shadow of death; 22 A land of darkness, as darkness *itself; and* of the shadow of death, without any order, and *where* the light *is* as darkness.

13:23 How many *are* mine iniquities and sins? make me to know my transgression and my sin. 24 Wherefore hidest thou thy face, and holdest me for thine enemy? 25 Wilt thou break a leaf driven to and fro? and wilt thou pursue the dry stubble? 26 For thou writest bitter things against me, and makest me to possess the iniquities of my youth. 27 Thou puttest my feet also in the stocks, and lookest narrowly unto all my paths; thou settest a print upon the heels of my feet.

16:11 God hath delivered me to the ungodly, and turned me over into the hands of the wicked. 12 I was at ease, but he hath broken me asunder: he hath also taken *me* by my neck, and shaken me to pieces, and set me up for his mark. 13 His archers compass me round about, he cleaveth my reins asunder, and doth not spare; he poureth out my gall upon the ground. 14 He breaketh me with breach upon breach, he runneth upon me like a giant. 15 I have sewed sackcloth upon my skin, and defiled my horn in the dust. 16 My face is foul with weeping, and on my eyelids *is* the shadow of death; 17 Not for *any* injustice in mine hands: also my prayer *is* pure. 18 O earth, cover not thou my blood, and let my cry have no place. 19 Also now, behold, my witness *is* in heaven, and my record *is* on high.

19:6 Know now that God hath overthrown me, and hath compassed me with his net. 7 Behold, I cry out of wrong, but I am not heard: I cry aloud, but *there is* no judgment. 8 He hath fenced up my way that I cannot pass, and he hath set darkness in my paths. 9 He hath stripped me of my glory, and taken the crown *from* my head. 10 He hath destroyed me on every side, and I am gone: and mine hope hath he removed like a tree. 11 He hath also kindled his wrath against me, and he counteth me unto him as *one of* his enemies. 12 His troops come together, and raise up their way against me, and encamp round about my tabernacle. 13 He hath put my brethren far from me, and mine acquaintance are verily estranged from me. 14 My kinsfolk have failed, and my familiar friends have forgotten me. 15 They that dwell in mine house, and my maids, count me for a stranger: I am an alien in their sight. 16 I called my servant, and he gave *me* no answer; I intreated him with my mouth. 17 My breath is strange to my wife, though I intreated for the children's *sake* of mine own body. 18 Yea, young children despised me; I arose, and they spake against me. 19 All my inward friends abhorred me: and they whom I loved are turned against me. 20 My bone cleaveth to my skin and to my flesh, and I am escaped with the skin of my teeth. 21 Have pity upon me, have pity upon me, O ye my friends; for the hand of God hath touched me.

23:2 Even to day *is* my complaint bitter: my stroke is heavier than my groaning. 3 Oh that I knew where I might find him! *that* I might come *even* to his seat! 4 I would order *my* cause before him, and fill my mouth with arguments. 5 I would know the words *which* he would answer me, and understand what he would say unto me. ... 23:8 Behold, I go forward, but he *is* not *there*; and backward, but I cannot perceive him: 9 On the left hand, where he doth work, but I cannot behold *him*: he hideth himself on the right hand, that I cannot see *him*:

27:2 *As* God liveth, *who* hath taken away my judgment; and the Almighty, *who* hath vexed my soul;

30:20 I cry unto thee, and thou dost not hear me: I stand up, and thou regardest me *not.* 21 Thou art become cruel to me: with thy strong hand thou opposest thyself against me. 22 Thou liftest me up to the wind; thou causest me to ride *upon it,* and dissolvest my substance. ... 30:26 When I looked for good, then evil came *unto me*: and when I waited for light, there came darkness.

8 In spite of his despair, Asaph instinctively finds himself drawn to the sanctuary of GOD. I wish to focus on the use of the word *sanctuary.*

Psalm 73:16 When I thought to know this, it *was* too painful for me; 17 Until I went into the sanctuary of God; *then* understood I their end.

That term *sanctuary* would not apply to the Tabernacle of David. It is a reference to the Tabernacle of Moses. The sacrifices were to be taken to the Tabernacle. Something about the atoning sacrifices touched Asaph in a way that the praises did not. It was the coming judgment on those "that speak wickedly *concerning* oppression: they speak loftily." I see in this phrase that is set off by a colon a reference to the fall of Lucifer.

> Isaiah 14:13 For thou hast said in thine heart, I will ascend into heaven, I will exalt my throne above the stars of God: I will sit also upon the mount of the congregation, in the sides of the north: 14 I will ascend above the heights of the clouds; I will be like the most High.

Asaph realized that the day would come when GOD is going to *settle the score.* The reason was, I think, the necessity of the blood atonement called to his mind *the end of the ungodly.* In my understanding, the atonement of the blood of the LORD Jesus is the argument for the eternal judgment of those that rise to set themselves above GOD. Though I have called attention to Asaph's final comments, I believe these are properly repeated here: 24 Thou shalt guide me with thy counsel, and afterward receive me *to* glory. 25 Whom have I in heaven *but thee*? and *there is* none upon earth *that* I desire beside thee. 26 My flesh and my heart faileth: *but* God *is* the strength of my heart, and my portion for ever.

9 The term has come to mean earnest Bible students based upon Acts 17:10. And the brethren immediately sent away Paul and Silas by night unto Berea: who coming *thither* went into the synagogue of the Jews. 11 These were more noble than those in Thessalonica, in that they received the word with all readiness

of mind, and searched the scriptures daily, whether those things were so.

10 Deuteronomy 19:15 One witness shall not rise up against a man for any iniquity, or for any sin, in any sin that he sinneth: at the mouth of two witnesses, or at the mouth of three witnesses, shall the matter be established.

Matthew 18:16 But if he will not hear *thee, then* take with thee one or two more, that in the mouth of two or three witnesses every word may be established.

2 Corinthians 13:1 This *is* the third *time* I am coming to you. In the mouth of two or three witnesses shall every word be established.

11 I bow to the scholars and use the term Aramaic, **though I must take notice that Pilate had Hebrew inscribed above the cross, John interpreted the Hebrew words for his Greek readers, and Paul spoke in Hebrew when he gave his defense from the stairs.** *Frankly, I would rather accept the testimony of the Scripture over the propositions of the scholars.* **If no one spoke Hebrew, it made no sense for Pilate to use that tongue; if the Jews did not speak it, it made no sense for Paul to use an unknown tongue! If the Hebrew tongue was unknown, I see no reason for John to reference it.**

1. The inscription over the cross was in Hebrew.

Luke 23:38 And a superscription also was written over him in letters of Greek, and Latin, and Hebrew, THIS IS THE KING OF THE JEWS.

2. John interprets Hebrews for his Greek readers.

John 5:2 Now there is at Jerusalem by the sheep *market* a pool, which is called in the Hebrew tongue Bethesda, having five porches. ... 19:13 When Pilate therefore heard that saying, he brought Jesus forth, and sat down in the judgment seat in a place that is called the Pavement, but in the Hebrew, Gabbatha. ... 19:17 And he bearing his cross went forth into a place called *the place* of a skull, which is called in the Hebrew Golgotha:

Revelation 9:11 And they had a king over them, *which is* the angel of the bottomless pit, whose name in the Hebrew tongue *is* Abaddon, but in the Greek tongue hath *his* name Apollyon. ... 16:16 And he gathered them together into a place called in the Hebrew tongue Armageddon.

3. Paul spoke in Hebrew to the Jews from the stairs.

Acts 21:40 And when he had given him licence, Paul stood on the stairs, and beckoned with the hand unto the people. And when there was made a great silence, he spake unto *them* in the Hebrew tongue, saying, ... 22:2 (And when they heard that he spake in the Hebrew tongue to them, they

141

kept the more silence: and he saith,) ... 26:14 And when we were all fallen to the earth, I heard a voice speaking unto me, and saying in the Hebrew tongue, Saul, Saul, why persecutest thou me? *it is* hard for thee to kick against the pricks.

[12] Psalm 119:18 Open thou mine eyes, that I may behold wondrous things out of thy law.

[13] Textus Receptus for Philippians 2:7: αλλ εαυτον εκενωσεν μορφην δουλου λαβων εν ομοιωματι ανθρωπων γενομενος

Wycliffe translated Philippians: 2:7 but he lowide hym silf, takinge the forme of a seruaunt, and was maad in to the licknesse of men, and in abite was foundun as a man.

Tyndale translated Philippians 2:7: Nevethelesse he made him silfe of no reputacion and toke on him the shape of a servaunte and became lyke vnto men

[14] None of the popular post-AV translations approaches the simplicity of translation and the doctrinal integrity of the King James Version.

New International Version (©1984): but made himself nothing, taking the very nature of a servant, being made in human likeness.

New Living Translation (©2007): *Instead, he gave up his divine privileges; he* took the humble position of a slave and was born as a human being. When he appeared in human form,

English Standard Version (©2001): but made himself nothing, taking the form of a servant, being born in the likeness of men.

New American Standard Bible (©1995): but emptied Himself, taking the form of a bond-servant, and being made in the likeness of men.

International Standard Version (©2008): Instead, poured out in emptiness, a servant's form did he possess, a mortal man becoming. In human form he chose to be,

GOD'S WORD® Translation (©1995): Instead, he emptied himself by taking on the form of a servant, by becoming like other humans, by having a human appearance.

American Standard Version (1901): but emptied himself, taking the form of a servant, being made in the likeness of men;

Douay-Rheims Bible: But emptied himself, taking the form of a servant, being made in the likeness of men, and in habit found as a man.

Darby Bible Translation: but emptied himself, taking a bond-man's form, taking his place in the likeness of men;

English Revised Version (1888): but emptied himself, taking the form of a servant, being made in the likeness of men;

Weymouth New Testament: Nay, He stripped Himself of His glory, and took on Him the nature of a bondservant by becoming a man like other men.

World English Bible: but emptied himself, taking the form of a servant, being made in the likeness of men.

Young's Literal Translation: but did empty himself, the form of a servant having taken, in the likeness of men having been made.

[15] This Greek word is found in five verses in the New Testament and never has a meaning of emptying of attributes. Merriam-Webster has given the English word the definition of certain theologians; thereby, making the word unusable for those defending the deity of Jesus of Nazareth.

Romans 4:14 For if they which are of the law *be* heirs, faith is made void (κενοω) and the promise made of none effect [This final phrase is the translation of a different Greek word.]:

1 Corinthians 1:17 For Christ sent me not to baptize, but to preach the gospel: not with wisdom of words, lest the cross of Christ should be made of none effect (κενοω.

1 Corinthians 9:15 But I have used none of these things: neither have I written these things, that it should be so done unto me: for it were better for me to die, than that any man should make (κενοω) my glorying void (κενοω).

2 Corinthians 9:3 Yet have I sent the brethren, lest our boasting of you should be in vain (κενοω) in this behalf; that, as I said, ye may be ready:

Philippians 2:7 But made (κενοω) himself of no reputation (κενοω) and took upon him the form of a servant, and was made in the likeness of men:

[16] Matthew 1:23 Behold, a virgin shall be with child, and shall bring forth a son, and they shall call his name Emmanuel, which being interpreted is, God with us.

1 Timothy 3:16 And without controversy great is the mystery of godliness: God was manifest in the flesh, justified in the Spirit, seen of angels, preached unto the Gentiles, believed on in the world, received up into glory.

Colossians 1:15 Who is the image of the invisible God, the firstborn of every creature:

Hebrews 1:3 Who being the brightness of *his* glory, and the express image of his person, and upholding all things by the word of his power, when he had by himself purged our sins, sat down on the right hand of the Majesty on high;

1 John 1:2 (For the life was manifested, and we have seen *it*, and bear witness, and shew unto you that eternal life, which was with the Father, and was manifested unto us;)

John 1:1-2 In the beginning was the Word, and the Word was with God, and the Word was God. 2 The same was in the beginning with God.

John 1:14 And the Word was made flesh, and dwelt among us, (and we beheld his glory, the glory as of the only begotten of the Father,) full of grace and truth.

[17] Merriam-Webster Dictionary: "of or relating to Arius or his doctrines especially that the Son is not of the same substance as the Father but was created as an agent for creating the world." Arius died in the middle of the fourth century.

[18] Merriam-Webster Dictionary: "of or relating to the doctrine ascribed to Nestorius ... that divine and human persons remained separate in the incarnate Christ." Nestorius died in the middle of the fifth century.

[19]http://www.blackwellreference.com/public/tocnode?id=g9781405135078_chunk_g978140513507849

[20] Mark 15:34 And at the ninth hour Jesus cried with a loud voice, saying, Eloi, Eloi, lama sabachthani? which is, being interpreted, My God, my God, why hast thou forsaken me?

[21] Hebrews 9:14 How much more shall the blood of Christ, who through the eternal Spirit offered himself without spot to God, purge your conscience from dead works to serve the living God?

Acts 20:28 Take heed therefore unto yourselves, and to all the flock, over the which the Holy Ghost hath made you overseers, to feed the church of God, which he hath purchased with his own blood.

1 Peter 1:2 Elect according to the foreknowledge of God the Father, through sanctification of the Spirit, unto obedience and sprinkling of the blood of Jesus Christ: Grace unto you, and peace, be multiplied.

Revelation 5:9 And they sung a new song, saying, Thou art worthy to take the book, and to open the seals thereof: for thou wast slain, and hast redeemed us to God by thy blood out of every kindred, and tongue, and people, and nation;

Hebrews 10:19 Having therefore, brethren, boldness to enter into the holiest by the blood of Jesus ... 13:12 Wherefore Jesus also, that he might sanctify the people with his own blood, suffered without the gate.

1 John 1:7 But if we walk in the light, as he is in the light, we have fellowship one with another, and the blood of Jesus Christ his Son cleanseth us from all sin.

CHAPTER 12

WAS JESUS OF NAZARETH FORSAKEN?

PSALM 22

To the chief Musician upon Aijeleth Shahar,

A Psalm of David.

The heading of the 22nd Psalm identifies this Psalm as among the fifty-five Psalms that are assigned to the watchcare or that were committed to the performance of Asaph, the Chief Musician. Since we are taught by scholarship to consider these headings to be uninspired additions of well-intended individuals, we tend to ignore[1] the headings of the Psalms and the transliterated Hebrew words those headings contain; but in doing so, we miss great truths or even misunderstand the setting of the Psalm.

Those headings are found in the most ancient of documentary evidence for the text of the Scriptures. We Gentile believers, unfamiliar with the Hebrew of the Old Testament, also fail to realize that the Hebrew Scriptures do not separate those headings from the text of the Psalms; and that, consequently, even the modern Hebrew Bibles have those headings as the first verse or a portion of the first verse of the Psalm.

It has been advanced by scholars that these *additions*, if they are indeed additions, may have been placed there by Ezra, who is credited by many with the collecting of most of the Old Testament canon. Only the guesses of the textual scholars attempt to date the first appearance of any of the headings. The mere antiquity of the headings garners respect and the information conveyed in those headings is worth the reading. We may need a dictionary to decipher the words, but that meager effort is well expended.

The marginal notes in the Cambridge edition of the Authorized Version call to our attention that the transliterated Hebrew "Aijeleth Shahar" has the meaning of "the hind (h·i·n·d, rhymes with kind) of the morning." The hind is the female red deer, which is only mentioned ten times in Scripture. The hart (h·a·r·t, rhymes with dart) is the male red deer and is mentioned but eleven times. The most remembered occurrence is Psalm 42:1: As the hart panteth after the water brooks, so panteth my soul after thee, O God.

The phrase "the hart of the morning" as used in this heading has three probable explanations and all three have a wondrous relationship to each other.

1. The term signifies a particular musical instrument used by the Jews for times of mourning.

2. "The Morning Hind" was the name for those Levites that sang for the morning watch in the Tabernacle and Temple. From the days of David, there was always singing and instrumental music in the Tabernac-

le. When the Temple was finished, the music continued.[2]

1 Chronicles 6:31 And these are they whom David set over the service of song in the house of the LORD, after that the ark had rest. 32 And they ministered before the dwelling place of the tabernacle of the congregation with singing, until Solomon had built the house of the LORD in Jerusalem: and then they waited on their office according to their order.

1 Chronicles 9:33 And these *are* the singers, chief of the fathers of the Levites, *who* remaining in the chambers *were* free: for they were employed in *that* work day and night.

These Levites were continually near the Tabernacle or the Temple where they "waited on their office." They fulfilled the responsibility according to their order in the assignment given to them.

There is a most intriguing insertion of information in verse 22 of this ninth chapter.

All these *which were* chosen to be porters in the gates *were* two hundred and twelve. These were reckoned by their genealogy in their villages, whom David and Samuel the seer did ordain in their set office.

The inference may certainly be that, with the placement of the Tabernacle in a permanent setting waiting for the construction of the Temple, the responsibilities of the Levities in relation to the transportation of the Tabernacle no longer having any useful purpose so these new assignments were delegated and that these new tasks would continue with the Temple worship. The intriguing aspect is that Samuel and David made these assignments *before* David was on the throne of Israel. Samuel died before the death of Saul and the ascension of David. These two men, both identified as prophets in Scripture, did this in prophetic anticipation of both the kingship of David and the construction of the Temple.[3]

These Levites were instructed to remain in their chambers "free"; that is, they had no other obligation or responsibility. Their task was to provide the instrumental and vocal music for the Tabernacle and the Temple *all day and all night.* They were not to be diverted from that task. The Levites were divided into three groups or shifts under the direction of Heman, Asaph, and Ethan. The music in the Tabernacle of David and in the Temple never ceased.

> 1 Chronicles 15:16 And David spake to the chief of the Levites to appoint their brethren *to be* the singers with instruments of musick, psalteries and harps and cymbals, sounding, by lifting up the voice with joy. 17 So the Levites appointed Heman the son of Joel; and of his brethren, Asaph the son of Berechiah; and of the sons of Merari their brethren, Ethan the son of Kushaiah;

Of these three men, Asaph was the Chief Musician.

> 1 Chronicles 16:5 Asaph the chief, and next to him Zechariah, Jeiel, and Shemiramoth, and Jehiel, and Mattithiah, and Eliab, and Benaiah, and Obededom: and Jeiel with psalteries and with harps; but Asaph made a sound with cymbals; ... 7 Then on that day David delivered first this psalm to thank the LORD into the hand of Asaph and his brethren. ... 37 So he left there before the ark of the covenant of the LORD Asaph and his

brethren, to minister before the ark continually, as every day's work required:

3. The image conveyed in this Psalm is
   - (a). that of a hind having been chased all
     night by the hunters; and, as the
     morning sky breaks, the defenseless
     red deer has been flushed by dogs
     and men from the forest; and, with no
     place left to run, stands exhausted,
     waiting for death. This image is that
     same image, which is conveyed by the
     mournful musical instrument. That
     picture of the hunted deer is surely an
     illustrative picture of the LORD Jesus
     in His journey from the Garden even
     until His death on the cross; or
   - (b). that of the female deer at the break of
     dawn, having fed through the night
     while surviving all the dangers of the
     dark hours on the open meadows,
     readies herself to return to the safety
     and shelter of the forest. That image
     could be applied to the choir as it wel-
     comes the fresh day. This too could be
     a picture of the LORD Jesus as His
     time has come to "go to the Father."[4]

All three of these Jewish suggestions speak of
types of the LORD Jesus. In fact, until the devel-
opment of rabbinical Judaism in the Second and
Third Centuries, Jewish teachers nearly univer-
sally would seem to have taught that this was a
Messianic Psalm.

Many of the old Jewish rabbis, according to
the commentator John Gill,[5] held that this
"Aijeleth Shahar" was a title for the morning
sacrifice and that other rabbis taught that it was
a title for the morning star. Gill also identifies still
other rabbis that held it described the personal
glory of GOD: the Shekinah.[6]

149

More recent rabbis, for obvious self-serving reasons, have tried to disassociate this Psalm from the Messiah and to associate this Psalm with Esther in her trial against Haman *or* to Israel as a nation as she experienced the wars and exiles associated with the Assyrian, Babylonian, and Roman empires *or* even with the holocaust practiced by the Nazis. Their bias betrays them.

However, the fervent attempts of both the ancient and modern rabbis to find something outside the life of David to fit Psalm 22 is significant. **It is the proper recognition that this Psalm does not correspond with any time or event in the life of David. Psalm 22 is not about David.**

Yet, it is unquestioned that the Psalm is identified as a Psalm of David. No conservative scholar of any persuasion assigns this Psalm to anyone but David. The Psalm is most detailed and very specific regarding definite events and times. The particulars are intriguing, however, in that they do not describe any event or any time in the life of David. To say it another way, the Twenty-second Psalm would take wild hyperbole to find any connection to the experience of David.

As we read the Psalm, think of the life of David and take notice in the the text how it is clear that it cannot refer to David.

The Psalm seems naturally to divide into three sections of verses: 1-10; 11-21; 22-31. The first division speaks of the reputation, the character, of GOD the Father. The second presents the sufferings, the condition, of the Son of GOD, and the third proclaims His future glorification, His coronation.

Verses 1, 8, 18, and 22 are cited in the New Testament[7] almost as if they were being read from a script. This is indeed what the critics of the deity of Jesus of Nazareth actually allege. The

150

circumstances to the contrary prove that these correlations were prophesied and were not programmed. The quotations are so familiar that you will identify them immediately.

> 1 My God, my God, why hast thou forsaken me? *why art thou so* far from helping me, *and from* the words of my roaring? 2 O my God, I cry in the daytime, but thou hearest not; and in the night season, and am not silent. 3 But thou *art* holy, *O thou* that inhabitest the praises of Israel. 4 Our fathers trusted in thee: they trusted, and thou didst deliver them. 5 They cried unto thee, and were delivered: they trusted in thee, and were not confounded. 6 But I *am* a worm, and no man; a reproach of men, and despised of the people. 7 All they that see me laugh me to scorn: they shoot out the lip, they shake the head, *saying,* 8 He trusted on the LORD *that* he would deliver him: let him deliver him, seeing he delighted in him. 9 But thou *art* he that took me out of the womb: thou didst make me hope *when I was* upon my mother's breasts. 10 I was cast upon thee from the womb: thou *art* my God from my mother's belly.

Notice the change in emphasis in this second division from the character of the Father to the condition of the Son as He is hanging on that cross of Calvary.

> 11 Be not far from me; for trouble *is* near; for *there is* none to help. 12 Many bulls have compassed me: strong *bulls* of Bashan have beset me round. 13 They gaped upon me *with* their mouths, *as* a ravening and a roaring lion. 14 I am poured out like water, and all my bones are out of joint: my heart is like wax; it is melted in the midst of my bowels. 15 My strength is dried up like a potsherd; and my tongue cleaveth to my jaws; and thou hast brought me into the dust of death. 16 For dogs have compassed me: the assembly of the

wicked have inclosed me: they pierced my hands and my feet. 17 I may tell all my bones: they look *and* stare upon me. 18 They part my garments among them, and cast lots upon my vesture. 19 But be not thou far from me, O LORD: O my strength, haste thee to help me. 20 Deliver my soul from the sword; my darling from the power of the dog. 21 Save me from the lion's mouth: for thou hast heard me from the horns of the unicorns.

Note now how the emphasis in this third section now shifts to the future condition of an exalted Son, even speaking of His kingdom.

22 I will declare thy name unto my brethren: in the midst of the congregation will I praise thee. 23 Ye that fear the LORD, praise him; all ye the seed of Jacob, glorify him; and fear him, all ye the seed of Israel. 24 For he hath not despised nor abhorred the affliction of the afflicted; neither hath he hid his face from him; but when he cried unto him, he heard. 25 My praise *shall be* of thee in the great congregation: I will pay my vows before them that fear him. 26 The meek shall eat and be satisfied: they shall praise the LORD that seek him: your heart shall live for ever. 27 All the ends of the world shall remember and turn unto the LORD: and all the kindreds of the nations shall worship before thee. 28 For the kingdom *is* the LORD'S: and he *is* the governor among the nations. 29 All *they that be* fat upon earth shall eat and worship: all they that go down to the dust shall bow before him: and none can keep alive his own soul. 30 A seed shall serve him; it shall be accounted to the Lord for a generation. 31 They shall come, and shall declare his righteousness unto a people that shall be born, that he hath done *this*.

That last phrase has a special interest. In the Hebrew, the word for "hath done" would be equal to the Greek for "finished." The blessed old translators of the Authorized Version have properly supplied the word *this* to call our attention to what has been finished. You recall the shout from the cross: "It is finished."[8] Verse 31 is "he hath done this—he finished this." The *this* is salvation.

The LORD Jesus finished salvation—there is no more work to be done. It is all His work. Salvation is a gift to us.

This Psalm is prophetic; and, specifically, it is Messianic in its prophecy. This Psalm fits *no* person in *no* place at *no* time *except* that day at the place of the skull outside the city of Jerusalem as the LORD Jesus died on that old rugged cross. This Psalm speaks of no one other than Jesus of Nazareth, the Son of GOD.

There is simply no single event, series of events, or even an era in the life of David that fits the description of this Psalm. Look back on the Psalm with me at how specific this Psalm is. The *only* time and the *only* place when the events of this Psalm were ever fulfilled in all of time will be found on a hill called Calvary just outside the gate of Jerusalem and only then when the LORD Jesus was crucified. This Psalm is a very time-specific and event-detailed prophecy.

1 My God, my God, why hast thou forsaken me?

That phrase is more familiar as one of the seven words from the cross. Here in the Psalm, it is more of an introductory statement, a descriptive title for the Psalm.

The Psalms, according to the Old Testament scholars, were identified by the first sentence of the Psalm. It identifies this Psalm as the answer to the question of why the LORD Jesus is on the cross. To all those looking on that scene at Golgotha that day and to all appearances for those who hear or read of the crucifixion at Calvary, the

LORD Jesus *is deserted by His friends and for-saken by His GOD.* However, the question raised in our minds is **"Did GOD forsake Him as He hangs upon that tree?"**

That perplexing problem is answered—it is settled by this Psalm. This Psalm describes *no* other time, *no* other place, *no* other event, and *no* other person, other than when the LORD Jesus suffers, bleeds, and dies on that awful hill of crucifixion.

Does it also describe a time when the Son of GOD was forsaken by GOD the Father? It is our task to take the Psalm as it stands written and as it stands positioned in the context of Scripture.

It is a common teaching that "GOD the Father turned His back upon GOD the Son as He was made to be sin for us, because GOD cannot look upon sin." Two particular texts are lifted from the context, combined, and then, used to promote this argument:

1. Habakkuk 1:13 Thou art of purer eyes than to behold evil, and canst not look on iniquity: wherefore lookest thou upon them that deal treacherously, and holdest thy tongue when the wicked devoureth the man that is more righteous than he?

2. 2 Corinthians 5:21 For he hath made him to be sin for us, who knew no sin; that we might be made the righteousness of God in him.

The question is whether these two verses say what some allege that they say. A search of a Bible concordance will show immediately that no verse or passage in Scripture reads "GOD cannot look upon sin" or "GOD turned His back on His Son." The text from Habakkuk speaks of GOD not beholding or looking on evil and iniquity,[9] which is a sin, but a full colon follows the statement. A full colon is a special mark of punctuation in the English language. It has been described as a *mark of expectation* with its function to call attention to that which follows. The clause following the colon will emphasize and/or explain what came before. In Habakkuk 1:13, the statement before the colon is contrasted with the statement that follows.

The attentive reader observes and understands that the affirmation "LORD, You do not behold evil or look on iniquity" is followed with the interrogation "Then, why are You looking on "them that deal treacherously" and why are You holding Your tongue "when the wicked devours the man that is more righteous than he"?

The beholding and the looking is not the act of visually observing, because the connected statement affirms that GOD is observing upon what is being done. The two connected statements do not conflict with or contradict one another. Habakkuk is perplexed that the Chaldeans, Babylonians, with all of their wickedness and idolatry, are going to be used by the holy God of Heaven to chasten the people of GOD.[10]

Therefore, in order to use this verse as proof that GOD *must* forsake the LORD Jesus Christ as He is dying as the sacrifice for our sins, the verse must be wrested from the context in which the statement is found and made to stand alone divorced from all the rest of Scripture. The verse simply does not say what those who advocate that "the Father turned His back upon the Son" want it to say.

The second passage does not involve a constitutional change in the LORD Jesus.

> 2 Corinthians 5:21 For he hath made him to be sin for us, who knew no sin; that we might be made the righteousness of God in him.

During days of His flesh,[11] the LORD Jesus never was less than GOD. That is an absolute. That cannot be surrendered.

How will it be explained that while the Father as GOD cannot look upon sin, the Incarnate Son not only looked upon sin,[12] but he even ate with sinners?[13] The inconsistency of that argument is amazing to consider.

Is not the LORD Jesus GOD manifest in the flesh as He walked the hills of Galilee, the streets of Jerusalem, or sat in Levi's house with publicans and sinners? Is He not the Word made flesh as He drives the moneychangers from the Temple? Is He not the only begotten of the Father as He rebukes the Pharisees for their sins? Was He not very GOD of very GOD when He was dying upon the cross? How could He ever be less than GOD at any time or in any place and still be GOD in some other time and some other place?

There is a grave danger of a serious error should we begin to provide a time, when He was not GOD manifest in the flesh, *even for the three hours of darkness—yea, even for 3 milliseconds.* Any limitation as to His deity is bordering on heresy, if indeed it does not cross that line, even unintentionally.

There was no time and no place from the conception[14] until His yielding up the ghost and placing His spirit into the Father's hands that Jesus of Nazareth was not "without sin,"[15] "holy ... separate from sinners,"[16] and the Lamb of GOD[17] without blemish and without spot.[18]

As we come to 2 Corinthians 5:21, I suggest that we focus on the key words: "made *to be* sin." The words "to be" are provided to us in italics showing that the translators have, properly and rightly, supplied them to complete the thought.

In order to help us understand the particular grammatical construction of this verse, I call attention to two verses that have a similar construction, which is emphasized to catch our attention.

> Romans 8:3 For what the law could not do, in that it was weak through the flesh, God sending his own Son in the likeness of sinful flesh, **and for sin**, condemned sin in the flesh:

> Hebrews 10:6 In burnt offerings **and *sacrifices* for sin** thou hast had no pleasure.

Notice the phrase "for sin" in Romans 8:3 and "*sacrifices* for sin" in Hebrews 10:6. In the Greek language, these are the same words; it is the context that determines the meaning, whether the sin, the sin offering, or both. The word *sin* in Romans 8:3 has a dual purpose—it represents both *sin* and *sacrifices for sin*. The sin offering is identified with the sin because the sin is imputed to the sin offering. This imputation is clearly portrayed in the Fifty-third chapter of Isaiah.

> Isaiah 53:4 Surely he hath borne our griefs, and carried our sorrows: yet we did esteem him stricken, smitten of God, and afflicted. 5 But he was wounded for our transgressions, he was bruised for our iniquities: the chastisement of our peace was upon him; and with his stripes we are healed. 6 All we like sheep have gone astray; we have turned every one to his own way; and the LORD hath laid on him the iniquity of us all. 7 He was oppressed, and he was afflicted, yet he opened not his mouth: he is brought as a lamb to the slaughter, and as a sheep before her shearers is dumb, so he openeth not his mouth. 8 He was taken from prison and from judgment: and who shall declare his generation? for he was cut off out of the land of the living: for the transgression of my people was he stricken. 9 And he made his grave with the wicked, and with the rich in his death; because he had done no violence, nei-

157

ther was any deceit in his mouth. 10 Yet it pleased the LORD to bruise him; he hath put him to grief: when thou shalt make his soul an offering for sin, he shall see his seed, he shall prolong his days, and the pleasure of the LORD shall prosper in his hand. 11 He shall see of the travail of his soul, and shall be satisfied: by his knowledge shall my righteous servant justify many; for he shall bear their iniquities. 12 Therefore will I divide him a portion with the great, and he shall divide the spoil with the strong; because he hath poured out his soul unto death: and he was numbered with the transgressors; and he bare the sin of many, and made intercession for the transgressors.

This doctrine of imputation is the subject of the apostle Paul in 2 Corinthians chapter 5 where the verse in question, verse 21 is found. The verb "to impute" means "to lay the responsibility for," "to credit to, to put to the account of." Left to stand in its context, verse 21 is emphatic in showing that our sins were imputed to the LORD Jesus and His righteousness is imputed to us. The one who believes in the LORD Jesus has put to his credit the righteousness of Christ.

14 For the love of Christ constraineth us; because we thus judge, that if one died for all, then were all dead: 15 And that he died for all, that they which live should not henceforth live unto themselves, but unto him which died for them, and rose again. 16 Wherefore henceforth know we no man after the flesh: yea, though we have known Christ after the flesh, yet now henceforth know we him no more. 17 Therefore if any man be in Christ, he is a new creature: old things are passed away; behold, all things are become new. 18 And all things are of God, who hath reconciled us to himself by Jesus Christ, and hath given to us the ministry of reconciliation; 19 To wit, that God

was in Christ, reconciling the world unto himself, not imputing their trespasses unto them; and hath committed unto us the word of reconciliation. 20 Now then we are ambassadors for Christ, as though God did beseech you by us: we pray you in Christ's stead, be ye reconciled to God. 21 For he hath made him to be sin for us, who knew no sin; that we might be made the righteousness of God in him.

Clearly, **it is not the intent** of the verse to teach that:

(1) the LORD Jesus literally was made sin; or that,

(2) the LORD Jesus was made a sinner; or that

(3) the LORD Jesus was guilty as a transgressor of the law. [19]

The LORD Jesus did not become sin in the sense that there was a change in His nature—in either the divine essence or the human nature. To have done so would have made Him less than GOD. Surely, most of those who would make the argument that the LORD Jesus became sin must never have thought through the implications of the teaching.

The verse reveals that our sins were *charged against* the LORD Jesus so that His righteousness might be *credited to* us. The Son of GOD was made responsible for our sins so that we might receive the imputation of righteousness. He paid our debt; He redeemed us from our indebtedness.

In the clearest of language, the Psalm **does not** convey a picture of GOD the Father turning His back upon the Son of GOD. It is not that the Father does not see the Son or does not hear the Son. The depiction of the Father in this Psalm is that of One Who is near and Who not only hears, but is actively involved and answers.

Psalm 22:24 **For he hath not despised nor abhorred the affliction of the afflicted; neither hath he hid his face from him; but when he cried unto him, he heard.**

How is it possible that this verse is not applied to that time on the cross but the other parallels in the same Psalm are? Only a pre-established reason explains that failure.

This is the same portrayal that is given in the Gospels.

After the LORD Jesus has had His prayer heard and was saved from death,[20] *after* the mob, led by Judas, has entered the garden, *after* the kiss by the betrayer, *after* Peter has used his sword, the Son of GOD states that He does not have to go to the cross because of the pressure of the mob or circumstances and that He is not forced to the cross by the capricious will of the Father.

Matthew 26:52 Then said Jesus unto him, Put up again thy sword into his place: for all they that take the sword shall perish with the sword. 53 Thinkest thou that I cannot now pray to my Father, and he shall presently give me more than twelve legions of angels? 54 But how then shall the scriptures be fulfilled, that thus it must be?

Twelve legions[21] of angels easily could have dispelled a mob composed of the entire population of the world; even so, there is something far more important to our discussion in that statement: if the Father would provide twelve legions of angels if asked; then He was, most obviously, not forcing His Son to go to the cross against the will of the Son.

I do not pretend to understand or to be able to reconcile all that is involved in the apparent conflict between those legions and the fulfillment of the Scriptures. The lack of the ability to do either does not preclude the acceptance of those verses exactly as they are written. Faith accepts what GOD has recorded solely because GOD has recorded it; and, not because what is recorded is explainable, reconcilable, *or comfortable.*

There is something far different[22] than the despair of being forsaken in these prophetic words of Psalm 22 ,"My God, my God, why hast thou forsaken me?" and in the words spoken by the LORD Jesus with a loud voice at the ninth hour of that day as He hung upon that cross.

In one sense, in Psalm 23, it is as though the Saviour is putting into words the thoughts of those who are looking upon that scene.

1 "My God, my God, why hast thou forsaken me?"*why art thou so* far from helping me, *and from* the words of my roaring? 2 O my God, I cry in the daytime, but thou hearest not; and in the night season, and am not silent.

This would not be the only time in Scripture that the Son of GOD asks a question to which He knows the answer.[23] Notice that immediately upon voicing the question that the LORD turns confidently to the unchangeable character of GOD.

3 But thou *art* holy, *O thou* that inhabitest the praises of Israel.

There is no fault or blame assigned to the Father. He is holy. He has not departed, forsaking His Son; for He *inhabitest* the praises of Israel. The Son is praying to the Father; the Father has not forsaken the Son, because He is close enough to hear His prayer. The Son speaks to a Father that cares and that is listening; moreover, the Father not only listens, He answers.

While the declaration that the Father answered the Son is not made until verse 24, the confidence of the LORD Jesus is apparent through the entire Psalm.

> 4 Our fathers trusted in thee: they trusted, and thou didst deliver them. 5 They cried unto thee, and were delivered: they trusted in thee, and were not confounded.

The next verses quite apparently never occurred on any occasion in the life of David. This Psalm is not autobiographical of David with a secondary application to Jesus of Nazareth; the Psalm is Messianic prophecy from the first verse to the last.

> 6 But I *am* a worm, and no man; a reproach of men, and despised of the people. 7 All they that see me laugh me to scorn: they shoot out the lip, they shake the head, *saying,* 8 He trusted on the LORD *that* he would deliver him: let him deliver him, seeing he delighted in him.

The following verses also do not appear to relate an event from the life of David.

> 11 Be not far from me; for trouble *is* near; for *there is* none to help. 12 Many bulls have compassed me: strong *bulls* of Bashan have beset me round. 13 They gaped upon me *with* their mouths, *as* a ravening and a roaring lion.

This wording could certainly be descriptive of a personal attack by Satanic forces.

> 14 I am poured out like water, and all my bones are out of joint: my heart is like wax; it is melted in the midst of my bowels. 15 My strength is dried up like a potsherd; and my tongue cleaveth to my jaws; and thou hast brought me into the dust of death. 16 For dogs have compassed me: the assembly of the wicked have inclosed me: they pierced my hands and my feet. 17 I may tell all my bones: they look *and* stare upon me. 18 They part my

162

garments among them, and cast lots upon my vesture.

David's hands and his feet were never pierced. The garments of David were never distributed by the casting of lots. He never endured any of the physical sufferings as described in this Psalm.

Indeed, physicians have written that these verses are a medically correct description of what a person endures in crucifixion.[24] David certainly was not crucified; in fact, crucifixion was not known in the land of Judea until centuries after David.[25]

20 Deliver my soul from the sword; my darling from the power of the dog. 21 Save me from the lion's mouth: for thou hast heard me from the horns of the unicorns.

The "lion's mouth" might even suggest a personal appearance of Satan—perhaps in the Garden or during the darkness. There was an appearance of Satan at the close of the forty days of temptation; Satan, at that time, left Him "for a season."[26] The LORD Jesus "resisted unto blood, striving against sin"[27] during the hours in the Garden of Gethsemane. The text does not identify Satan as being present: therefore, I would not be dogmatic, but the phrasing of the Gospel of Luke, Hebrews, and this Psalm certainly opens that possibility. Satan certainly tempted David;[28] however, David did not resist, but succumbed.

It is also true of the rest of the Psalm: these enumerated things never happened to David. This is a Psalm of prophecy not a Psalm describing a type from the life of David that would be fulfilled in Christ as the antitype.

The Psalm has reference to none but Jesus of Nazareth and to the events on that day at Golgotha. This Psalm is prophetic and Messianic exactly as is Isaiah 53. Isaiah 53 did not occur to

Isaiah or to anyone else—it is prophetic of what will occur. It is Messianic in that it refers only to Jesus of Nazareth and to no one else. Further, it refers to Him only when He was on the cross on that hill called Calvary and Golgotha.

That introductory statement—My God, my God, why hast thou forsaken me?—is worthy of our attention.

Few phrases have been more misused and abused than this verse.

1. Those words are used to accuse GOD the Father of child abuse. That is the printed argument of that group that identifies themselves as the new atheists.
2. Those words are used to show that Jesus of Nazareth and the Christ are two separate entities and that the Christ spirit left the man Jesus to die on the cross.
3. Those words are used to suggest that Jesus of Nazareth had doubts in the garden and fear on the cross because the GOD-part of Him was suppressed by the human part.
4. In a milder form of this latter concept, those words are used to show that Jesus set aside all of His deity and lived on earth only as a human being, a man.

All of these are pathetic attempts to deny the unity of GOD and man in Jesus. To end the struggle to explain this commonly named *the fourth of the seven words from the cross*, let us set the statement in its full and proper Scriptural context.

Indeed, those are the precise words that the LORD Jesus spoke at about the ninth hour as the darkness lifted. It is debated among Biblical scholars and students as to the reason that these words passed the lips of Jesus of Nazareth.

1. Did He say this in fear and wonderment because of what He was enduring at that time?

2. Are these words uttered because He did not understand why He was dying?

3. Was He asking to gain information or to reveal information?

4. Was He quoting these words to call attention to the Twenty-second Psalm?

Jesus of Nazareth was not a man following a programmed script in order to create a Messiah for Israel. However, His life was clearly prophesied in minute detail in the Old Testament—all of the Old Testament—and He was aware of those prophecies.

> Luke 24:44 And he said unto them, These are the words which I spake unto you, while I was yet with you, that all things must be fulfilled, which were written in the law of Moses, and in the prophets, and in the psalms, concerning me.

One passage, in particular, seems to me that it might indicate a single instance where the LORD Jesus might have said something to fulfill Scripture. I call attention to this instance because it also has a direct link to Psalm 22.

> John 19:28 After this, Jesus knowing that all things were now accomplished, that the scripture might be fulfilled, saith, I thirst.

> Psalm 22:15 My strength is dried up like a potsherd; and my tongue cleaveth to my jaws; and thou hast brought me into the dust of death. ... 69:21 They gave me also gall for my meat; and in my thirst they gave me vinegar to drink.

The statement "My God, my God, why hast thou forsaken me?" is quoted verbatim by the LORD Jesus as He was on the cross and the event is provided twice for us so that at the mouth of two witnesses the very words are established:

> Matthew 27:46 And about the ninth hour Jesus cried with a loud voice, saying, Eli, Eli, lama sabachthani? that is to say, **My God, my God, why hast thou forsaken me?**

> Mark 15:34 And at the ninth hour Jesus cried with a loud voice, saying, Eloi, Eloi, lama sabachthani? which is, being interpreted, **My God, my God, why hast thou forsaken me?**

There is no question of the words; but, if we are to comprehend the words, then we must establish the **Scriptural context** of those words: **My God, my God, why hast thou forsaken me?**

One of the definitions that the Merriam-Webster 11th Collegiate Dictionary provides for context is especially fitting for our inquiry: "the parts of a discourse that surround a word or passage and can throw light on its meaning ... the interrelated conditions in which something exists or occurs." In the search for the understanding for any portion of Scripture, it is essential to know all the parts of the "discourse" that surrounds the passage. Words are never isolated; there is always a context of the discourse.

Merriam-Webster provides several definitions of the word *discourse*; the one that helps us most in our pursuit is "a linguistic unit (as a conversation or a story) larger than a sentence." This impels us to place a word in a sentence and the sentence in a paragraph and the paragraph in the conversation and the conversation in the life. [parenthesis in the original]

We know the words that were said.

We know the Person that spoke the words.

We know the place where the words were spoken.

We know the time that the words were spoken.

We know the events occurring when the words were spoken.

However, the context is more than the answers to the questions of who, what, when, and where; the context also includes the why.

The last, the why, is the one part of the statement that is the difficult question to answer. We have at least one instance where the LORD Jesus spoke to the Father in what appears to be a prayer when *the why of the prayer* was for the purpose of helping (instructing, teaching, training) those who heard Him to understand that the Father "sent" the LORD Jesus.

> John 11:41 Then they took away the stone from the place where the dead was laid. And Jesus lifted up his eyes, and said, Father, I thank thee that thou hast heard me. 42 And I knew that thou hearest me always: **but because of the people which stand by I said it**, that they may believe that thou hast sent me.

Matthew Poole wrote in explanation of this statement:

> "I know that thou always willest those things which I will; and I will nothing but what thou willest, and hast sent me to do in the world; so as in these things it is impossible but that thou shouldest always be ready to grant what I ask of thee; nay, there is no need of my asking. I only give thee thanks for the people's sake, who here stand by; who believe thee to be the true God, and to have an Almighty power; but will not as yet believe that I am thy Son, by thee sent into the world, and that I do the works which I do in thee and from thee."[29]

Neither Matthew Poole nor I suggest that this prayer was less than a prayer. It is to call attention to the reality that the words were said publically for the singular purpose of having the people hear them. The words had a purpose beyond the prayer or in addition to the prayer.

We must consider this as a possibility as we examine the why of this prayer in its context.

---

[1] Many printed editions of the Psalm no longer include the traditional headings. It is as though those publishers are not content to have the headings considered as being *uninspired,* but desire to have them also judged as *uninformative* and *unimportant.* Certain commentators argue that these titles and descriptions belong to the previous Psalm and are misplaced in the "traditional texts." It is less than compelling to have one scholar (or a dozen more) discover that the 47 scholars that gave us the Authorized Version and the hundreds of other Jewish and Christian scholars over the centuries that honored these headings were so blind or ignorant as to miss this confusion of the placement of the headings, which ought to be endings. The facts are that contemporary textual critics present no different arguments than did their predecessors in the past and genuine Bible believers considered and rejected the proposals. I walk in good company when I let the headings of the Psalm instruct me. Were those headings placed there by the inspiration of God? I do not know. They offer no doctrine, but do provide information as to setting and purpose. Nothing is lost in using them, and, by doing so, much is gained.

[2] 1 Chronicles 15:16 And David spake to the chief of the Levites to appoint their brethren *to be* the singers with instruments of musick, psalteries and harps and cymbals, sounding, by lifting up the voice with joy. 17 So the Levites appointed Heman the son of Joel; and of his brethren, Asaph the son of Berechiah; and of the sons of Merari their brethren, Ethan the son of Kushaiah; 18 And with them their brethren of the second *degree,* Zechariah, Ben, and Jaaziel, and Shemiramoth, and Jehiel, and Unni, Eliab, and Benaiah, and Maaseiah, and Mattithiah, and Elipheleh, and Mikneiah, and Obededom, and Jeiel, the porters. 19 So the singers, Heman, Asaph, and Ethan, *were appointed* to sound with cymbals of brass; 20 And Zechariah, and Aziel, and Shemiramoth, and Jehiel, and Unni, and Eliab, and Maaseiah, and Benaiah, with psalteries on Alamoth; 21 And Mattithiah, and Elipheleh, and Mikneiah, and Obededom, and Jeiel, and Azaziah, with harps on the Sheminith to excel. 22 And Chenaniah, chief of the Levites, *was* for song: he instructed about the song, because he *was* skilful. 23 And Berechiah and Elkanah *were* doorkeepers for the ark. 24 And Shebaniah, and Jehoshaphat, and Nethaneel, and Amasai, and Zechariah, and Benaiah, and Eliezer, the priests, did blow with the trumpets before the ark of God: and Obededom and Jehiah *were* doorkeepers for the ark.

1 Chronicles 25:1 Moreover David and the captains of the host separated to the service of the sons of Asaph, and of Heman, and of Jeduthun, who should prophesy with harps, with psalteries, and with cymbals: and the number of the workmen

according to their service was: 2 Of the sons of Asaph; Zaccur, and Joseph, and Nethaniah, and Asarelah, the sons of Asaph under the hands of Asaph, which prophesied according to the order of the king. 3 Of Jeduthun: the sons of Jeduthun; Gedaliah, and Zeri, and Jeshaiah, Hashabiah, and Mattithiah, six, under the hands of their father Jeduthun, who prophesied with a harp, to give thanks and to praise the LORD. 4 Of Heman: the sons of Heman; Bukkiah, Mattaniah, Uzziel, Shebuel, and Jerimoth, Hananiah, Hanani, Eliathah, Giddalti, and Romamtiezer, Joshbekashah, Mallothi, Hothir, *and* Mahazioth: 5 All these *were* the sons of Heman the king's seer in the words of God, to lift up the horn. And God gave to Heman fourteen sons and three daughters. 6 All these *were* under the hands of their father for song *in* the house of the LORD, with cymbals, psalteries, and harps, for the service of the house of God, according to the king's order to Asaph, Jeduthun, and Heman.

3 Music, vocal and instrumental, was so important to worship that it was established as an unceasing essential component of the Tabernacle and the Temple. Some professing to be a church that honors Christ refuse to have instruments in their worship service.

Others have brought the music of the world into the alleged worshipping music—could anyone imagine the music of the Egyptians, Canaanites, Hittites, Amorites, Perizzites, Hivites, Jebusites, Girgashites, Philistines, Sidonians , Ashdodites, Arabians, or even that of the Ammonites or the Moabites being played or sung in the Tabernacle while Moses was alive? Who could conceive of David or Solomon allowing these musical atrocities to enter the Tabernacle or the Temple? Ezra 9:1 is a complaint that the people of the remnant "have not separated themselves from the people of the lands, *doing* according to their abominations, *even* of the Canaanites, the Hittites, the Perizzites, the Jebusites, the Ammonites, the Moabites, the Egyptians, and the Amorites. The music of paganism is an abomination still.

Some within Christianity seem to use the music only as a transition from one segment to the next with little or no forethought of planning to use the music as worship, instruction, or praise. Too often, the music and the message are "on different pages." Planning is not formalism. Coordination is not fleshly. A unity of music and message is the better choice. The Holy Spirit is fully able to direct a week in advance as well as on the spot; after all, the text of the message will be 2000 years old or older.

While there is no Biblical mandate or even example of any assignment of perpetual music for the church, there is no prohibition; and Matthew 26:30, Mark 14:26, 1 Corinthians

14:26, Ephesians 5:19, and Colossians 3:16 surely show that music was involved in the worship of the early churches.

> Matthew 26:30 And when they had sung an hymn, they went out into the mount of Olives.

> Mark 14:26 And when they had sung an hymn, they went out into the mount of Olives.

> 1 Corinthians 14:26 How is it then, brethren? when ye come together, every one of you hath a psalm, hath a doctrine, hath a tongue, hath a revelation, hath an interpretation. Let all things be done unto edifying.

> Ephesians 5:19 Speaking to yourselves in psalms and hymns and spiritual songs, singing and making melody in your heart to the Lord;

> Colossians 3:16 Let the word of Christ dwell in you richly in all wisdom; teaching and admonishing one another in psalms and hymns and spiritual songs, singing with grace in your hearts to the Lord.

We also know that singing songs will take place in Heaven, Revelation 5:9; 14:3; and 15:3.

> Revelation 5:9 And they sung a new song, saying, Thou art worthy to take the book, and to open the seals thereof: for thou wast slain, and hast redeemed us to God by thy blood out of every kindred, and tongue, and people, and nation;

> Revelation 14:3 And they sung as it were a new song before the throne, and before the four beasts, and the elders: and no man could learn that song but the hundred *and* forty *and* four thousand, which were redeemed from the earth.

> Revelation 15:3 And they sing the song of Moses the servant of God, and the song of the Lamb, saying, Great and marvellous *are* thy works, Lord God Almighty; just and true *are* thy ways, thou King of saints.

[4] John 16:16 A little while, and ye shall not see me: and again, a little while, and ye shall see me, because I go to the Father. 17 Then said *some* of his disciples among themselves, What is this that he saith unto us, A little while, and ye shall not see me: and again, a little while, and ye shall see me: and, Because I go to the Father? ... 28 I came forth from the Father, and am come into the world: again, I leave the world, and go to the Father.

[5] The English Baptist John Gill (November 23, 1697-October 14, 1771) was a biblical scholar and a Calvinist. He pastored for fifty-one years the Baptist church that Benjamin Keach had pastored. This same church would be pastored by Charles Spurgeon. He is identified as the first writing theologian. The University of Aberdeen conveyed the Doctor of Divinity in 1748 in recognition of his scholarship, which likely will never

be matched. His volume of work is amazing. Setting aside his Calvinistic leanings, there are no richer volumes available.

His more important writings are:

The Doctrine of the Trinity Stated and Vindicated London, 1731.

The Cause of God and Truth 4 parts, 1735-8.

An Exposition of the New Testament 3 volumes, 1746-8.

The Exposition of the Old Testament 6 volumes, 1748-63.

Together, these Expositions contain over ten million words and provide access to the gleanings from works no longer accessible.

A Dissertation on the Antiquity of the Hebrew Language, 1767.

A Body of Doctrinal Divinity, 1767.

A Body of Practical Divinity, 1770.

6 *SwordSearcher: John Gill's Exposition of the Entire Bible,* Psalm 22.

7 The specific citations are as follows.

Verse 1: Matthew 27:46 And about the ninth hour Jesus cried with a loud voice, saying, Eli, Eli, lama sabachthani? that is to say, My God, my God, why hast thou forsaken me?

Mark 15:34 And at the ninth hour Jesus cried with a loud voice, saying, Eloi, Eloi, lama sabachthani? which is, being interpreted, My God, my God, why hast thou forsaken me?

Verse 8: Matthew 27:42 He saved others; himself he cannot save. If he be the King of Israel, let him now come down from the cross, and we will believe him. 43 He trusted in God; let him deliver him now, if he will have him: for he said, I am the Son of God.

Mark 15:30 Save thyself, and come down from the cross. 31 Likewise also the chief priests mocking said among themselves with the scribes, He saved others; himself he cannot save. 32 Let Christ the King of Israel descend now from the cross, that we may see and believe. And they that were crucified with him reviled him.

Luke 23:35 And the people stood beholding. And the rulers also with them derided *him,* saying, He saved others; let him save himself, if he be Christ, the chosen of God.

Verse 18: Matthew 27:35 And they crucified him, and parted his garments, casting lots: that it might be fulfilled which was spoken by the prophet, They parted my garments among them, and upon my vesture did they cast lots.

Mark 15:24 And when they had crucified him, they parted his garments, casting lots upon them, what every man should take.

Luke 23:34 Then said Jesus, Father, forgive them; for they know not what they do. And they parted his raiment, and cast lots.

172

John 19:23 Then the soldiers, when they had crucified Jesus, took his garments, and made four parts, to every soldier a part; and also *his* coat: now the coat was without seam, woven from the top throughout. 24 They said therefore among themselves, Let us not rend it, but cast lots for it, whose it shall be: that the scripture might be fulfilled, which saith, They parted my raiment among them, and for my vesture they did cast lots. These things therefore the soldiers did.

Verse 22: Hebrews 2:11 For both he that sanctifieth and they who are sanctified *are* all of one: for which cause he is not ashamed to call them brethren, 12 Saying, I will declare thy name unto my brethren, in the midst of the church will I sing praise unto thee. [Matthew 26:30 And when they had sung an hymn, they went out into the mount of Olives.]

8 Certain of the Puritan writers held that the passage beginning from verse 1 of Psalm 22 and continuing to verse 5 of Psalm 31 was spoken by the LORD Jesus while on the cross. That portion certainly makes interesting reading with that perception in mind. Psalm 31:5 Into thine hand I commit my spirit: thou hast redeemed me, O LORD God of truth.

9 Iniquity is scripturally defined as performing religious or spiritual counterfeits.

Matthew 7:21 Not every one that saith unto me, Lord, Lord, shall enter into the kingdom of heaven; but he that doeth the will of my Father which is in heaven. 22 **Many will say to me in that day, Lord, Lord, have we not prophesied in thy name? and in thy name have cast out devils? and in thy name done many wonderful works?** 23 And then will I profess unto them, I never knew you: depart from me, ye that **work iniquity**. 24 Therefore whosoever heareth these sayings of mine, and doeth them, I will liken him unto a wise man, which built his house upon a rock: 25 And the rain descended, and the floods came, and the winds blew, and beat upon that house; and it fell not: for it was founded upon a rock. 26 And every one that heareth these sayings of mine, and doeth them not, shall be likened unto a foolish man, which built his house upon the sand: 27 And the rain descended, and the floods came, and the winds blew, and beat upon that house; and it fell: and great was the fall of it.

10 This is very similar to the perplexity that Asaph presents in Psalm 73: "Why do the wicked seem to thrive while the people of God suffer."

Habakkuk 1:6 For, lo, I raise up the Chaldeans, *that* bitter and hasty nation, which shall march through the breadth of the land, to possess the dwellingplaces *that are* not theirs. 7 They *are* terrible and dreadful: their judgment and their dignity shall proceed of themselves. 8 Their horses also are swifter than the leopards, and are more fierce than the evening wolves: and their horsemen shall spread themselves, and their horsemen shall come from far; they shall fly as the eagle *that* hasteth to eat. 9 They shall come all for violence: their faces shall sup up *as* the east wind, and they shall gather the captivity as the sand.

Habakkuk 1:12 *Art* thou not from everlasting, O LORD my God, mine Holy One? we shall not die. O LORD, thou hast ordained them for judgment; and, O mighty God, thou hast established them for correction.

11 Hebrews 5:7 Who in the days of his flesh, when he had offered up prayers and supplications with strong crying and tears unto him that was able to save him from death, and was heard in that he feared;

12 The LORD Jesus lived among humanity and observed all that men do. Within His vision came sinners and their sins of every possible imagination

13 Mark 2:16 And when the scribes and Pharisees saw him eat with publicans and sinners, they said unto his disciples, How is it that he eateth and drinketh with publicans and sinners?

14 Luke 1:31 And, behold, thou shalt conceive in thy womb, and bring forth a son, and shalt call his name JESUS. 32 He shall be great, and shall be called the Son of the Highest: ... 35 ... The Holy Ghost shall come upon thee, and the power of the Highest shall overshadow thee: therefore also that holy thing which shall be born of thee shall be called the Son of GOD.

15 Hebrews 4:15 For we have not an high priest which cannot be touched with the feeling of our infirmities; but was in all points tempted like as we are, yet without sin.

16 Hebrews 7:26 For such an high priest became us, who is holy, harmless, undefiled, separate from sinners, and made higher than the heavens;

17 John 1:29 The next day John seeth Jesus coming unto him, and saith, Behold the Lamb of God, which taketh away the sin of the world.

18 1 Peter 1:19 But with the precious blood of Christ, as of a lamb without blemish and without spot:

19 Hebrews 4:15 For we have not an high priest which cannot be touched with the feeling of our infirmities; but was in all points tempted like as we are, yet without sin. ... 7:26 For such an high priest became us, who is holy, harmless, undefiled, separate from sinners, and made higher than the heavens;

1 Peter 1:19 But with the precious blood of Christ, as of a lamb without blemish and without spot: ... 22 Who did no sin, neither was guile found in his mouth: 23 Who, when he was reviled, reviled not again; when he suffered, he threatened not; but committed himself to him that judgeth righteously: 24 Who his own self bare our sins in his own body on the tree, that we,

being dead to sins, should live unto righteousness: by whose stripes ye were healed.

1 John 3:5 And ye know that he was manifested to take away our sins; and in him is no sin.

[20] Hebrews 5:7 Who in the days of his flesh, when he had offered up prayers and supplications with strong crying and tears unto him that was able to save him from death, and was heard in that he feared;

Luke 22:42 Saying, Father, if thou be willing, remove this cup from me: nevertheless not my will, but thine, be done. 43 And there appeared an angel unto him from heaven, strengthening him. 44 And being in an agony he prayed more earnestly: and his sweat was as it were great drops of blood falling down to the ground.

[21] A Romans legion numbered a minimum of 10,000 soldiers.

[22] For another example of a statement having a meaning beyond the words and requiring careful reading of the entire context, consider Matthew 15:23-28: But he answered her not a word. And his disciples came and besought him, saying, Send her away; for she crieth after us. 24 But he answered and said, I am not sent but unto the lost sheep of the house of Israel. 25 Then came she and worshipped him, saying, Lord, help me. 26 But he answered and said, It is not meet to take the children's bread, and to cast *it* to dogs. [Mark 7:27 But Jesus said unto her, Let the children first be filled: for it is not meet to take the children's bread, and to cast *it* unto the dogs.] 27 And she said, Truth, Lord: yet the dogs eat of the crumbs which fall from their masters' table. 28 Then Jesus answered and said unto her, O woman, great *is* thy faith: be it unto thee even as thou wilt. And her daughter was made whole from that very hour.

[23] Among the many possible references illustrating this, consider Luke 24:38 And he said unto them, Why are ye troubled? and why do thoughts arise in your hearts?

[24] http://www.frugalsites.net/jesus/crucifixion.htm
The Physical Death of Jesus Christ, a Study by Mayo Clinic

[25] According to historians, crucifixion was devised by the Persians, adopted by Alexander the Great, and "perfected" by the Romans.

According to an internet search, crucifixion remains a legal form of execution in the Sudan based upon Sharia law.

http://www.frugalsites.net/jesus/crucifixion.htm

[26] Luke 4:13 And when the devil had ended all the temptation, he departed from him for a season.

[27] Hebrews 12:4 Ye have not yet resisted unto blood, striving against sin.

[28] 1 Chronicles 21:1 And Satan stood up against Israel, and provoked David to number Israel.

[29] *SwordSearcher: Matthew Poole's Commentary on the Holy Bible:* John 11:41-42

CHAPTER 13
CONTEXT OF THE CROSS

Consider how and where these words fit into the context of His ministry. The hour did not slip up on the LORD Jesus. He was not taken unawares. He clearly states that He was prepared for the hour and that it was the purpose for which He came into the world. He knew what time it was. Jesus of Nazareth knew that He was going to be crucified and He knew when that crucifixion would occur.[1]

John 12:23 And Jesus answered them, saying, The hour is come, that the Son of man should be glorified. ... 27 Now is my soul troubled; and what shall I say? Father, save me from this hour: but for this cause came I unto this hour.

16:32 Behold, the hour cometh, yea, is now come, that ye shall be scattered, every man to his own, and shall leave me alone: and yet I am not alone, because the Father is with me.

17:1 These words spake Jesus, and lifted up his eyes to heaven, and said, Father, the hour is come; glorify thy Son, that thy Son also may glorify thee:

18:11 Then said Jesus unto Peter, Put up thy sword into the sheath: the cup which my Father hath given me, shall I not drink it?

The LORD Jesus says, "I am not alone, because the Father is with me." However, He says much more than that. He qualifies the time and the conditions when this would occur and does so with details that enable us to identify the very place when the Father would not abandon Him.

The texts state that the Father would not abandon Jesus of Nazareth when the disciples fled from His presence.

The texts state that the Father would not abandon Jesus of Nazareth when *His hour* came.

1. That hour was the hour that He was to be glorified.

2. That hour was the hour for which He came into the world.

3. That hour was the hour from which He did not ask the Father to save Him.

There has been only one time and only one place when those conditions existed. That was on the hill called Calvary when Jesus of Nazareth was crucified.

The LORD Jesus affirms by those statements the prophecy that David was moved to record in Psalm 22.

24 For he hath not despised nor abhorred the affliction of the afflicted; **neither hath he hid his face from him; but when he cried unto him, he heard.**

The prophet Isaiah also foresaw and described with exquisite details *the hour* which the LORD Jesus described.

Isaiah 50:6 I gave my back to the smiters, and my cheeks to them that plucked off the hair: I hid not my face from shame and spitting. 7 **For the Lord GOD will help me**; therefore shall I not be confounded: therefore have I set my face like a flint, and I know that I shall not be ashamed. 8 **He is near that justifieth me;** who will contend with me? **let us stand together**: who *is* mine adversary? let him come near to me. 9 **Behold, the Lord GOD will help me;** who *is* he *that* shall condemn me? lo, they all shall wax old as a garment; the moth shall eat them up.

Since verse six was fulfilled,[2] why would it not be expected that verses seven, eight, and nine would also be fulfilled? Those verses affirm that the Lord GOD would not forsake the One Whose back was given to the smiters and was spit upon.

The use of the English words Lord GOD in Isaiah 50:7 identifies GOD the Father as being near and helping the smitten One. The passage is calling attention to the Father's active presence with the Son during the time of the crucifixion.

The translators of the Authorized Version used capitals to identify in the English the distinction clearly in the Hebrew between GOD the Father and GOD the Son.[3] One of the passages where this planned assistance is easy for English readers to discern is in Isaiah chapter 48.

16 Come ye near unto me, hear ye this; I have not spoken in secret from the beginning; from the time that it was, there *am* I: and now the Lord GOD, and his Spirit, hath sent me. 17 Thus saith the LORD, thy Redeemer, the Holy One of Israel; I *am* the LORD thy God which teacheth thee to profit, which leadeth thee by the way *that* thou shouldest go.

The English words Lord GOD are used to represent the Hebrew words Adonai JEHOVAH and that is the name of GOD the Father. When the reader sees Lord GOD in the Bible text of the Authorized Version, he may be assured that it is the Father that is speaking, doing, or being addressed.

The English words LORD God are used to represent the Hebrew words JEHOVAH Elohim and that is the name of GOD the Son. When the reader sees LORD God in the Bible text of the Authorized Version, he may be assured that it is the Son that is speaking, doing, or being addressed.

With that knowledge, revisit with me Isaiah 50:6-9. Verse six establishes the time of fulfillment.

> Isaiah 50:6 I gave my back to the smiters, and my cheeks to them that plucked off the hair: I hid not my face from shame and spitting. 7 **For the Lord GOD will help me**; therefore shall I not be confounded: therefore have I set my face like a flint, and I know that I shall not be ashamed. 8 *He is* **near that justifieth me;** who will contend with me? **let us stand together**: who *is* mine adversary? let him come near to me. 9 **Behold, the Lord GOD will help me;** who *is* he *that* shall condemn me? lo, they all shall wax old as a garment; the moth shall eat them up.

The description is that of the time *after* the Garden and *during* the interrogations. Through all of the pre-crucifixion abuse, the Father is present and will help the Son. Therefore, the Son of GOD is confident that He shall not be ashamed and He sets His face as a flint to go to the cross. This prophecy seems to be the subject of the declaration in the Gospel of Luke regarding His determination to go to Jerusalem for these very hours of our concern.

> Luke 9:51 And it came to pass, when the time was come that he should be received up, he stedfastly set his face to go to Jerusalem,

Twice in these verses from Isaiah chapter fifty, the Son of GOD declares that the Lord GOD, the Father, will help him.

As the LORD Jesus spoke to His disciples as recorded in John chapter sixteen, He is affirming the prophecies of Psalm Twenty-two and Isaiah Fifty. He tells His disciples that when they are scattered and leave Him alone that He will not be alone *because the Father will be with Him.*

> Behold, the hour cometh, yea, is now come, that ye shall be scattered, every man to his own, and shall leave me alone: and yet I am not alone, because the Father is with me.

If these verses are accurately recorded and translated *and they are,* and if the words are to be understood as having the commonly accepted definitions that they bear *and they are,* then it must be conceded that from the day of His baptism through the meal in the Upper Room, Jesus of Nazareth was committed to the death upon the cross. There is no alternative, except unbelief.

While it is diametrically in opposition to the affirmations of the LORD Jesus, a sizeable number of Christians are seemingly convinced that Jesus of Nazareth tried to renege on taking the cup in the Garden, *which cup they define as the death of the cross;* and they are also seemingly convinced that Jesus of Nazareth was forsaken by GOD on the cross.

The journey to Golgotha began in Bethlehem[4] and the protecting presence of the Father with the Son is apparent every day and with each step from the manger to the cross. Three times, the Father speaks from Heaven to validate the character and the Person of His Son.

The records of the answers to prayer are abundant within the Gospels. There is not the glimmer of any discord or the hint of any distance between the Father and the Son in all of the ministry of Jesus of Nazareth. It is not until the Garden of Gethsemane where the first appearance of discordance is alleged to have surfaced and that is supposedly found in the prayer of Christ.

> Mark 14:36 And he said, **Abba, Father, all things *are* possible unto thee; take away this cup from me: nevertheless not what I will, but what thou wilt.**

Some Christians insist that this is evidence that it was not until the Garden that the full realization of what He must do to provide the atonement settled upon the mind of Jesus of Nazareth. According to this theory, the terror of that sudden comprehension caused Him to reconsider and to seek desperately some way to avoid the cross. It is the wording of the prayer that He prayed while in the Garden that is used to fuel this speculation. The conjecture focuses especially on the *cup* that is mentioned in His prayer.

When He knelt in the Garden, He does indeed pray specifically for "this cup"—a particular cup— to be taken from Him. By the use of the adjective *this*, the LORD Jesus is identifying a specific *cup* that is "present or near in place, time."[5] It is "this *cup*" that He is facing in the Garden that is His thoughts and speech and not a future *cup* that will confront Him.

> Matthew 26:36 Then cometh Jesus with them unto a place called Gethsemane, and saith unto the disciples, Sit ye here, while I go and pray yonder. 37 And he took with him Peter and the two sons of Zebedee, and began to be sorrowful and very heavy. 38 Then saith he unto them, My soul is exceeding sorrowful, even unto death: tarry ye here, and watch with me. 39 And he went a little further, and fell on his face, and prayed, saying, **O my Father, if it be possible, let this cup pass from me: nevertheless not as I will, but as thou *wilt*.** 40 And he cometh unto the disciples, and findeth them asleep, and saith unto Peter, What, could ye not watch with me one

182

hour? 41 Watch and pray, that ye enter not into temptation: the spirit indeed *is* willing, but the flesh *is* weak. 42 He went away again the second time, and prayed, saying, **O my Father, if this cup may not pass away from me, except I drink it, thy will be done.** 43 And he came and found them asleep again: for their eyes were heavy. 44 And he left them, and went away again, and prayed the third time, **saying the same words.**

That "this cup," which He seeks to avoid, cannot be the cup for which He came into the world to drink and that He said He would accept.

John 18:11 Then said Jesus unto Peter, Put up thy sword into the sheath: **the cup which my Father hath given me, shall I not drink it**?

He will unhesitatingly and willingly drink the cup that He came to drink. While John 18:11 is spoken *after* the time of prayer in Gethsemane, the words restate what the LORD had said previously.

Hebrews 12:2 Looking unto Jesus the author and finisher of *our* faith; who for **the joy that was set before him** endured the cross, despising the shame, and is set down at the right hand of the throne of God.

The prophecy in Psalm 16 is interpreted by the Holy Spirit as speaking of the death, burial, and resurrection of Jesus of Nazareth.

Psalm 16:8 I have set the LORD always before me: because *he is* at my right hand, I shall not be moved. 9 Therefore my heart is glad, and my glory rejoiceth: my flesh also shall rest in hope. 10 For thou wilt not leave my soul in hell; neither wilt thou suffer thine Holy One to see corruption. 11 Thou wilt shew me the path of life: in thy presence *is* fulness of joy; at thy right hand *there are* pleasures for evermore.

The apostle Peter is used to connect the passage from Psalms and the Holy Spirit had it recorded by Luke for us in the second chapter of Acts.[6]

22 Ye men of Israel, hear these words; Jesus of Nazareth, a man approved of God among you by miracles and wonders and signs, which God did by him in the midst of you, as ye yourselves also know: 23 Him, being delivered by the determinate counsel and foreknowledge of God, ye have taken, and by wicked hands have crucified and slain: 24 Whom God hath raised up, having loosed the pains of death: because it was not possible that he should be holden of it. 25 For David speaketh concerning him, I foresaw the Lord always before my face, for he is on my right hand, that I should not be moved: 26 Therefore did my heart rejoice, and my tongue was glad; moreover also my flesh shall rest in hope: 27 Because thou wilt not leave my soul in hell, neither wilt thou suffer thine Holy One to see corruption. 28 Thou hast made known to me the ways of life; thou shalt make me full of joy with thy countenance. 29 Men *and* brethren, let me freely speak unto you of the patriarch David, that he is both dead and buried, and his sepulchre is with us unto this day. 30 Therefore being a prophet, and knowing that God had sworn with an oath to him, that of the fruit of his loins, according to the flesh, he would raise up Christ to sit on his throne; 31 He seeing this before spake of the resurrection of Christ, that his soul was not left in hell, neither his flesh did see corruption. 32 This Jesus hath God raised up, whereof we all are witnesses. 33 Therefore being by the right hand of God exalted, and having received of the Father the promise of the Holy Ghost, he hath shed forth this, which ye now see and hear. 34 For David is not ascended into the heavens: but he saith himself,

The LORD said unto my Lord, Sit thou on my right hand, 35 Until I make thy foes thy foot-stool. 36 Therefore let all the house of Israel know assuredly, that God hath made that same Jesus, whom ye have crucified, both Lord and Christ.

Surely, the phrasing in the Psalm beyond that speaking of the burial and resurrection must be familiar to those who know the record of the death of Jesus of Nazareth. If the passage speaks of the death, the burial, and the resurrection of Christ, *and it does,* it is assuredly not a wresting of the Scriptures to see that these other statements are also referencing the relationship between GOD the Father and GOD the Son during the crucifixion, *as well as* the ascension of Jesus of Nazareth.

David speaketh concerning him ... foresaw the Lord always before my face ... I should not be moved ... Therefore did my heart rejoice, and my tongue was glad ... my flesh shall rest in hope ... thou shalt make me full of joy with thy countenance ... by the right hand of God exalted ... Sit thou on my right hand.

The Sixteenth Psalm, therefore, corroborates the Twenty-second Psalm and the Isaiah Fifty passage as to the unceasing union and commun-ion of GOD the Father and GOD the Son during the crucifixion.

The alleged controversy centers on the content of the "this cup" that the LORD Jesus in His prayer asks to be taken from Him. I maintain that the "this cup" **was taken** from Him. I believe that we are not left to speculate regarding the contents of "this cup." That particular cup to which the Saviour referred is identified for us by Paul in the Book of Hebrews.

Hebrews 5:7 Who in the days of his flesh, when he had offered up prayers and supplica-tions with strong crying and tears unto him that was able to save him from death, **and**

was heard in that he feared; 8 Though he were a Son, yet learned he obedience by the things which he suffered;

It is declared that His prayer was heard. He prayed for the "this cup", which is defined for us in Hebrews 5:7 as death, to be removed and His prayer was heard. I repeat, **the Son of man asked to be saved from death and He was heard**.[7] The result of that answer is that He was delivered from death. No discussion is necessary to show that *it was not* the death of the cross from which He was delivered. It could not be that death, because He went to the cross and there He died; deliverance from that death was not the answer to His prayer.

Some other death is death in that Garden cup. That death was a death to prevent Him from going to the cross. The death in "this cup" was not the death of the cross; it was a death in the Garden. That cup was not a cup that the Father was attempting to have the Son take. The Father is assuredly not trying to kill the LORD Jesus in the Garden. Such a blasphemous concept is not in the text.

It is not GOD the Father trying to force that cup upon Jesus of Nazareth. Satan desired to kill Him in the Garden, but Jesus of Nazareth desired to live and to go to the cross to die. He survived the Garden; **that was the answer to His prayer**.

Luke 22:41 And he was withdrawn from them about a stone's cast, and kneeled down, and prayed, 42 Saying, Father, if thou be willing, remove this cup from me: nevertheless not my will, but thine, be done. 43 **And there appeared an angel unto him from heaven, strengthening him.** 44 And being in an agony he prayed more earnestly: and his sweat was as it were great drops of blood falling down to the ground.

If "this cup" were from the Father, why would the Father send the angel to strengthen Him? The angel came before the final session of praying. The struggle in the Garden continued past the arrival of the angel. An avenging angel would be no comfort. An angel bringing condemnation or judgment would be no strengthening. The angel came to comfort.

Again, the emphasis that is given in the prayer is to a *cup* that is identified as "this cup" in distinction to all other cups.

> Luke 22:41 And he was withdrawn from them about a stone's cast, and kneeled down, and prayed, 42 Saying, Father, if thou be willing, **remove this cup from me:** nevertheless not my will, but thine, be done. 43 And there appeared an angel unto him from heaven, strengthening him. 44 And being in an agony he prayed more earnestly: and his sweat was as it were great drops of blood falling down to the ground.

His prayer was not to avoid the cup that He *would receive* from the Father, but to have the cup in the Garden removed from Him. His prayer was that He might live in order that He could drink the cup that He came to drink. Even so, He asked to be delivered from that Garden cup because to do so would be the will of the Father and not because it was His Own separate independent will. That distinction is important to observe.

Using terminology that describes and identifies human emotions and actions to describe the TRINITY always carries the potential of misleading or misdirecting. Adamic humanity can never be more than an approximation of deity. Our experiences as well as our vocabulary is limited to humanity. One day we shall know as we are known[8] and we will then have a far better understanding of our GOD. Until then, we are only able to know in part.

This is especially apparent when we consider the submission to the will of the Father by the Son of GOD during His days on this earth. The relationship between the Father and the Son during the earthly sojourn of Jesus of Nazareth is explained to us in the Epistle of Paul to the Philippians.

> 2:5 Let this mind be in you, which was also in Christ Jesus: 6 Who, being in the form of God, thought it not robbery to be equal with God: 7 But made himself of no reputation, and took upon him the form of a servant, and was made in the likeness of men: 8 And being found in fashion as a man, he humbled himself, and became obedient unto death, even the death of the cross. 9 Wherefore God also hath highly exalted him, and given him a name which is above every name: 10 That at the name of Jesus every knee should bow, of *things* in heaven, and *things* in earth, and *things* under the earth; 11 And *that* every tongue should confess that Jesus Christ *is* Lord, to the glory of God the Father.

While I do not understand all that is involved, what I do understand is that without becoming less than the fullness of the GODHEAD bodily[9] the Son of GOD became flesh and dwelt among us.

> Colossians 2:9 For in him dwelleth all the fulness of the Godhead bodily.

Scripture does not explain the *mechanics* of the Incarnation. The closest to an explanation is the declaration "And without controversy great is the mystery of godliness: God was manifest in the flesh."[10] That which the GOD of Heaven does not chose to explain ought not to become the speculation of believers; it is to be received by faith.

It is important to understand that the word GODHEAD is not strictly a synonym for the word TRINITY; it is primarily a term for the essence of deity—that which makes GOD to be GOD.[11] The mystery of the TRINITY is not to be explained; it is either accepted or it is rejected.

The cultists delight in depicting the GODHEAD as a three-headed gargoyle-styled monstrosity. Their ignorance is exposed in that the word does not define as a Triune Deity, but as the essence of Deity.[12]

GOD the Son took upon Him the form of a servant and became obedient; but in doing so, He did not become less than Deity. He was fully GOD before the Incarnation and He is fully GOD afterwards. He did not empty Himself of His deity—not even the *prerogatives* of deity. During His ministry, Jesus of Nazareth exercised all of the prerogatives of deity.[13]

Even so, He always conducted Himself as One in submission to the Father. The phrasings "made himself of no reputation, and took upon him the form of a servant" and" he humbled himself, and became obedient" are perhaps best explained by the apostle Paul in Hebrews chapter five, a passage to which we have already referred.

> 7 Who in the days of his flesh, when he had offered up prayers and supplications with strong crying and tears unto him that was able to save him from death, and was heard in that he feared; 8 Though he were a Son, yet learned he obedience by the things which he suffered; 9 And being made perfect, he became the author of eternal salvation unto all them that obey him; 10 Called of God an high priest after the order of Melchisedec.

"Though he were a Son"—He was the Son of GOD before the Incarnation and He was the Son of GOD in the Garden. Jesus of Nazareth is never less than the Son of GOD. "[Y]et learned he obedience by the things which he suffered"—this is not a learning that increases knowledge. It is the learning that comes through experiencing. Perhaps Albert Barnes explained it as well as we humans are capable.

> Verse 8. *Though he were a Son.* Though the Son of God. Though he sustained this exalted rank, and was conscious of it, yet he was willing to learn experimentally what is meant by obedience in the midst of sufferings.
>
> *Yet learned he obedience.* That is, he learned experimentally and practically. It cannot be supposed that he did not know what obedience was; or that he was *indisposed* to obey God before he suffered; or that he had, as we have, perversities of nature, leading to rebellion, which required to be subdued by suffering;--but that he was willing *to test* the power of obedience in sufferings; to become personally and practically acquainted with the nature of such obedience in the midst of protracted woes. The *object* here is, to show how well fitted the Lord Jesus was to be a Saviour for man-kind *[sic]*; and the argument is, that he has set us an example, and has shown that the most perfect obedience may be manifested in the deepest sorrows of the body and the soul.[14]

The Son of GOD lived on earth as a man.[15] He subjected Himself to hunger[16] and to thirst.[17] He exposed Himself to such weariness[18] of the flesh that exhausted, He slept amidst a terrible storm of wind and waves.[19] He knew what it was to have disappointment.[20] He experienced suffering.[21] He prayed[22] and left the issues of life in the hands of the Father rather than speak whatever He desired into being.[23] His entire life on earth was lived in submission to the Father.

All of this was done that the Son of GOD might identify with humanity. Job posed the question that explains the reason and purpose of the Incarnation very succinctly as recorded for us in chapter ten, verse 4.

> Hast thou eyes of flesh? or seest thou as man seeth? 5 *Are* thy days as the days of man? *are* thy years as man's days,

The Incarnation is the answer to the question of Job.

> Hebrews 2:14 Forasmuch then as the children are partakers of flesh and blood, he also himself likewise took part of the same; that through death he might destroy him that had the power of death, that is, the devil; 15 And deliver them who through fear of death were all their lifetime subject to bondage. 16 For verily he took not on *him the nature of* angels; but he took on *him* the seed of Abraham. 17 Wherefore in all things it behoved him to be made like unto *his* brethren, that he might be a merciful and faithful high priest in things *pertaining* to God, to make reconciliation for the sins of the people. 18 For in that he himself hath suffered being tempted, he is able to succour them that are tempted.

The LORD Jesus became "in all thing ... made like unto" you and me and in doing so He provided us the example as to how we are to live. Indeed, He showed us that it is possible to live so as to please GOD; He gave us an example.

> John 13:15 For I have given you an example, that ye should do as I have done to you.

> 1 Peter 2:21 For even hereunto were ye called: because Christ also suffered for us, leaving us an example, that ye should follow his steps: 22 Who did no sin, neither was guile found in his mouth: 23 Who, when he was reviled, reviled not again; when he suffered, he threatened not; but committed *himself* to him that

judgeth righteously: 24 Who his own self bare our sins in his own body on the tree, that we, being dead to sins, should live unto righteousness: by whose stripes ye were healed.

Therefore, this prayer is not *out of character* for Jesus of Nazareth. His life has been a life of prayer for every event along the way to the cross. He will not stop praying when He arrives in the Garden. There is no resistance arisen in His heart or mind to taking the cup that the Father will give Him. He is asking that the "this cup," *the particular cup in the Garden,* be removed.

The LORD Jesus was not trying to avoid the cross. A day or so before this prayer in Gethsemane, the LORD Jesus asked rhetorically as to whether He should ask the Father to save Him from this hour. He answered His question Himself with an emphatic response and that answer received the affirmation of the Father.

John 12:27 Now is my soul troubled; and what shall I say? Father, save me from this hour: but for this cause came I unto this hour. 28 Father, glorify thy name. Then came there a voice from heaven, *saying,* I have both glorified *it*, and will glorify *it* again.

To construct a scenario where the LORD would change His mind almost overnight and sweat great drops of blood trying to persuade the Father to save Him from that hour, which was the purpose of His coming, is to create a image of a Christ with a false bravado that betrays Him and causes Him to appear cowardly and overcome by fear. I submit that such an image borders on blasphemy. It is not a Biblical concept and it distorts the prayer of Christ in Gethsemane.

The prayer was not spoken in a vacuum; it has a specific context. Notice that the words are recorded for us. This is worth special consideration. The three nearest apostles were asleep as were those further away; no disciple heard the prayers that Christ prayed in the Garden. For us to have these words means that the Holy Spirit gave the words to Matthew, Mark, and Luke.

This destroys the common critical view that Matthew wrote from the memory of what he saw or was told by the other witnesses; Mark largely received his information from Peter; and Luke gleaned his material from interviews. The concept itself is an attack on the inspiration of Scripture. To hear or read evangelical conservatives repeat the overshadowing superintending of the research is evidence of the strong influence of the critical scholars and commentaries.

The content and context of the three separate prayers of the LORD Jesus does not support the concept that Jesus of Nazareth had second thoughts and attempted to renege on His covenant to be the Lamb of GOD. I do not propose that we have every word that the LORD Jesus spoke in His prayers, but I do assert that we have every word that the GOD of Heaven intended for us to have and to hold.

The full passage from Matthew that provides us the three times of prayer does not present a picture of a wavering fearful Messiah. Nor do the accounts of Mark or Luke convey anything to suggest that the Son of GOD was seeking to avoid the purpose for which He came into the world.

> Matthew 26:36 Then cometh Jesus with them unto a place called Gethsemane, and saith unto the disciples, Sit ye here, while I go and pray yonder. 37 And he took with him Peter and the two sons of Zebedee, and began to be sorrowful and very heavy. 38 Then saith he unto them, My soul is exceeding sorrowful, even unto death: tarry ye here, and watch with me. 39 And he went a little further, and fell on his face, and prayed, saying, **O my Fa-**

193

ther, if it be possible, let this cup pass from me: nevertheless not as I will, but as thou *wilt*. 40 And he cometh unto the disciples, and findeth them asleep, and saith unto Peter, What, could ye not watch with me one hour? 41 Watch and pray, that ye enter not into temptation: the spirit indeed *is* willing, but the flesh *is* weak. 42 He went away again the second time, and prayed, saying, **O my Father, if this cup may not pass away from me, except I drink it, thy will be done.** 43 And he came and found them asleep again: for their eyes were heavy. 44 And he left them, and went away again, and prayed the third time, **saying the same words.**

Mark 14:36 And he said, **Abba, Father, all things *are* possible unto thee; take away this cup from me: nevertheless not what I will, but what thou wilt.**

Luke 22:41 And he was withdrawn from them about a stone's cast, and kneeled down, and prayed, 42 Saying, **Father, if thou be willing, remove this cup from me: nevertheless not my will, but thine, be done.** 43 And there appeared an angel unto him from heaven, strengthening him. 44 And being in an agony he prayed more earnestly: and his sweat was as it were great drops of blood falling down to the ground. 45 And when he rose up from prayer, and was come to his disciples, he found them sleeping for sorrow, 46 And said unto them, Why sleep ye? rise and pray, lest ye enter into temptation.

The image that is established is one of the Messiah having engaged in a battle and having obtained the victory is fully in charge of His emotions, His mind, and His life. This image continues in all that follows the Garden; He is shown to be in control in the houses of Annas and Caiaphas, when He stands before Pilate or Herod or again before Pilate. He is in full control as He hangs on that cross and He dismisses His spirit. Nothing portrays a Messiah that is hesitant or One that is being forced to comply.

The LORD Jesus came from Heaven and eternity for the purpose of drinking the cup that the Father would give Him. He did not come to drink that *other* cup that was being thrust upon Him in the Garden that night.

Where is the origin of this cup in the Garden? Who orchestrated its appearance in Gethsemane? What was that cup?

That cup was death. We know this. It is not a matter of uncertainty, because His prayer was heard and He was delivered from death. Thus, the question is "Who wanted Jesus of Nazareth to die in the Garden and not to live so that He could die on the cross?"

It seems to me to be clear that as Satan had attempted from the time of Herod's butchery of the infants and continuing through the entire earthly sojourn of the Son of GOD, that great red dragon, the old serpent, called the Devil and Satan, was trying to kill Jesus of Nazareth in the Garden. I believe that this is shown in these passages of Scripture.

Luke 4:13 And when **the devil** had ended all the temptation, he **departed from him for a season**.

John 12:31 Now is the judgment of this world: now shall **the prince of this world** be cast out.

John 16:11 Of judgment, because **the prince of this world** is judged.

John 14:30 Hereafter I will not talk much with you: for **the prince of this world** cometh, and hath nothing in me.

Luke 22:53 When I was daily with you in the temple, ye stretched forth no hands against me: but this is your hour, **and the power of darkness**.

Hebrews 12:4 **Ye have not yet resisted unto blood, striving against sin.**

Luke 22:41 And he was withdrawn from them about a stone's cast, and kneeled down, and prayed, 42 Saying, Father, if thou be willing, **remove this cup from me**: nevertheless not my will, but thine, be done. 43 And there appeared an angel unto him from heaven, strengthening him. 44 And being in an agony he prayed more earnestly: and **his sweat was as it were great drops of blood falling down to the ground.**

Matthew 26:36 Then cometh Jesus with them unto a place called Gethsemane, and saith unto the disciples, Sit ye here, while I go and pray yonder. 37 And he took with him Peter and the two sons of Zebedee, and began to be sorrowful and very heavy. 38 Then saith he unto them, **My soul is exceeding sorrowful, even unto death**: tarry ye here, and watch with me.

Based on these passages, I believe that we should understand that Satan was present in Jerusalem. While I do not understand all of the implications of the statement, I believe the passages inform us that Satan was in the Garden and that the agony of the LORD Jesus in the Garden was due to the spiritual conflict that brought Him to say, "My soul is exceeding sorrowful, even unto death." I understand that to mean that the devil was motivated by a desire to keep Jesus of Nazareth from the death of the cross and that the Saviour was resisting not as GOD in the flesh, but as the Son living entirely dependent upon the Father.

It is not a matter of being devoid of His prerogative of deity or being emptied of His attributes; it is the Son humbling Himself and learning obedience as He left us an example that we should follow.[24]

Were the LORD to have died at any other time, in any other place, or in any other manner, *there would have been no atonement.* Were He to have died with those babies of Bethlehem, there would be no salvation purchased.[25] Were He to have been thrown from the brow of the hill, there would be no redemption.[26] Were He to have been stoned, He would not have provided the blood of reconciliation.[27] Had He drowned, there would have been no pardon for sins.[28] Had He been killed in mob violence, there would be no basis for forgiveness of sins.[29] Had He died of starvation or thirst, the death would have been meaningless. There at Calvary was the only place, the only time, and the only method that enabled salvation.

The prayers of the Son of GOD were heard and He did not die—He was saved "from death." He comes out of the Garden alive. Having His prayer answered and having been spared death in the Garden, He is now headed to drink the cup for which He came into the world, that cup which the Father has for Him to drink. There is no hesitation within Him.

Before He leaves the Garden, the LORD Jesus declares His determination. He does this even as He also affirms that He could avoid the cross if He so determined.

> John 18:11 Then said Jesus unto Peter, Put up thy sword into the sheath: the cup which my Father hath given me, shall I not drink it?
>
> Matthew 26:52 Then said Jesus unto him, Put up again thy sword into his place: for all they that take the sword shall perish with the sword. 53 Thinkest thou that I cannot now pray to my Father, and he shall presently give me more than twelve legions of angels? 54 But

how then shall the scriptures be fulfilled, that thus it must be?

I do not understand this statement to suggest that the LORD Jesus was contemplating seeking to avoid the coming hours. I understand that He is telling Peter that He does not need Peter to defend Him. He is explaining to Peter that if He were to desire defensive measures, He would ask the Father and He would send angels to come to His aid. He would not deliver Himself; He is in submission to the Father.

I believe that when the LORD Jesus asks the rhetorical question "But how then shall the scriptures be fulfilled, that thus it must be?" that He is not speaking from a fatalistic mindset; but that He is saying that He is going to fulfill the commitment that He made in the Scriptures. I understand it not as a statement of resignation, but as a proclamation of dedication.

Following this declaration in the Garden over the next several hours, the LORD Jesus accepts the cup from the Father. That cup and its contents are described in several passages, such as:

Psalm 75:8 For in the hand of the LORD there is a cup, and the wine is red; it is full of mixture; and he poureth out of the same: but the dregs thereof, all the wicked of the earth shall wring them out, and drink them.

Psalm 11:6 Upon the wicked he shall rain snares, fire and brimstone, and an horrible tempest: this shall be the portion of their cup.

That cup, which He willingly accepts, is the wrath of GOD, which is the second death. The Son of GOD tasted the second death[30] so that we will never have to do so. Those that refuse to accept the salvation that is provided by and in the death of the LORD Jesus will find the dregs of that cup is the Lake of Fire.

From the Garden through the various interrogations with all the abuse, the Son of GOD continues steadfastly[31] into the cup that the Father has given to Him. About the time of the morning sacrifice, during the third hour of the day, the LORD Jesus lay down on the cross and was fastened to that instrument of death. The nails were driven through the flesh of His hands and His feet into that wooden cross. He plainly said, "Therefore doth my Father love me, because I lay down my life, that I might take it again. No man taketh it from me, but I lay it down of myself. I have power to lay it down, and I have power to take it again. This commandment have I received of my Father."[32]

The LORD Jesus was not a reluctant Saviour. He was not a hesitant Redeemer. He was not a resisting Sacrifice. He was not dragged struggling to the cross; He was not forced to stretch His arms. He went to the slaughter as does a lamb.[33] He laid down His life willingly, knowing that He had power to take His life up again. He went to the cross for "the joy that was sent before Him."[34]

At the sixth hour, the sun was darkened; the heavens refused to shine, and silence reigned for three hours. During those curtained off hours, the Saviour endured the darkness of eternal damnation that should have been our portion.

At the ninth hour, the darkness lifted and the Son of GOD spoke with a loud voice—that itself was miraculous. How any ability to form words or to make sounds existed after the agony of those hours is inexplicable. Yet, He is in command of not only his own physical and mental faculties. The LORD Jesus controls the events themselves.

We have the record that seven times during those six hours, the Son of GOD spoke from the cross. These statements have been traditionally given the name *the seven words from the cross.* The particular statement which concerns us comes exactly in the middle of the seven words and near the end of His time on the cross.

At the 3rd hour, He is crucified.[35]

1st Word: Then said Jesus, Father, forgive them; for they know not what they do. And they parted his raiment, and cast lots. Luke 23:34

2nd Word: And Jesus said unto him, Verily I say unto thee, To day shalt thou be with me in paradise. Luke 23:43

3rd Word: When Jesus therefore saw his mother, and the disciple standing by, whom he loved, he saith unto his mother, Woman, behold thy son! Then saith he to the disciple, Behold thy mother! And from that hour that disciple took her unto his own home. John 19:26-27

At the 6th hour, darkness covered the earth. The LORD Jesus does not speak during the three hours.

At the 9th hour, the darkness was lifted. After six hours on the cross and immediately following these three hours of darkness, the LORD Jesus breaks the silence with His loud voice.

4th Word: And at the ninth hour Jesus cried with a loud voice, saying, Eloi, Eloi, lama sabachthani? which is, being interpreted, My God, my God, why hast thou forsaken me? Mark 15:34

Does He suddenly believe that the Father has forgotten and forsaken Him? Is it that the LORD Jesus as He hangs on the cross forgets why He is there? Has His courage failed Him?

His next words do not indicate a sense of despair or failure. No bitterness is present. Instead, we observe a Saviour that is in charge of all that is being done.

> 5th Word: After this, Jesus knowing that all things were now accomplished, that the scripture might be fulfilled, saith, I thirst. John 19:28

It is His decision as to the time of death and not the choice of the chief priests or the high priest. Pilate did not signal His death. The attending soldiers did not cause His death. Satan did not force a cup upon the Saviour. The Son of GOD was in full control. As the time of the evening sacrifice arrived, the Son of GOD made the declaration of completion and then dismissed His spirit into the hands of the Father.

> 6th Word: When Jesus therefore had received the vinegar, he said, It is finished. John 19:30

> 7th Word And when Jesus had cried with a loud voice, he said, Father, into thy hands I commend my spirit: and having said thus, he gave up the ghost. Luke 23:46[36]

We now have settled the context of the time—the words were spoken in the very middle of the seven words and at the ninth hour on the cross, very near to the moment of His death. Then, with confidence and without hesitation, the LORD Jesus dismisses His spirit into the hands of the Father as One Who is fully in charge of all that is transpiring. The context of the statement as relates to His ministry is one of unqualified, unrestricted confidence in the Father and in His Own personal competence.

When the record of Scripture is that Jesus of Nazareth went willingly and stedfastly[37] to the cross, it becomes an attack upon the character of GOD the Son—nay, upon His nature, His deity—

to propose that Jesus of Nazareth tried to avoid the cross in the Garden or that He had regrets upon the cross.

It is an attack upon the GOD the Father to suggest that He sent His Son to die alone and forsaken, when the Scriptures of both Testaments record that He never left His Son and was His abiding help.

¹ The sheer volume of the passages that record the pronouncements of the LORD Jesus as to the manner of His death, the attendant circumstances, the participants, and the timing is impossible to justify other than with one of two explanations. Either Jesus of Nazareth said these precise statements at the time and places indicated in the text or the apostles or some other editors living within the first two centuries after the apostolic era fabricated the statements and manufactured the text. It is one or the other; there is no other alternative.

The authenticity and integrity of Jesus of Nazareth hinges on which of those options is true. Mine eternal destiny and that of my readers depends upon which of the two possibilities we decide individually to accept.

John 20:30 And many other signs truly did Jesus in the presence of his disciples, which are not written in this book: 31 But these are written, that ye might believe that Jesus is the Christ, the Son of God; and that believing ye might have life through his name.

1 John 5:12 He that hath the Son hath life; and he that hath not the Son of God hath not life. 13 These things have I written unto you that believe on the name of the Son of God; that ye may know that ye have eternal life, and that ye may believe on the name of the Son of God.

Matthew 16:21 From that time forth began Jesus to shew unto his disciples, how that he must go unto Jerusalem, and suffer many things of the elders and chief priests and scribes, and be killed, and be raised again the third day. ... 17:12 But I say unto you, That Elias is come already, and they knew him not, but have done unto him whatsoever they listed. Likewise shall also the Son of man suffer of them. ... 17:22 And while they abode in Galilee, Jesus said unto them, The Son of man shall be betrayed into the hands of men: 23 And they shall kill him, and the third day he shall be raised again. And they were exceeding sorry. ... 20:17 And Jesus going up to Jerusalem took the twelve disciples apart in the way, and said unto them, 18 Behold, we go up to Jerusalem; and the Son of man shall be betrayed unto the chief priests and unto the scribes, and they shall condemn him to death, 19 And shall deliver him to the Gentiles to mock, and to scourge, and to crucify *him*: and the third day he shall rise again. ... 20:28 Even as the Son of man came not to be ministered unto, but to minister, and to give his life a ransom for many. ... 26:1 And it came to pass, when Jesus had finished all these sayings, he said unto his disciples, 2 Ye know that after two days is *the feast of* the passover, and the Son of man is betrayed to be crucified. ... 26:19 And the disciples did as Jesus had appointed them; and they made ready the passover. 20 Now when the even was come, he sat down with the twelve. 21 And as they did eat, he said, Verily I say unto you, that one of you shall betray me. 22 And they were exceeding sorrowful, and began every one of them to say unto him, Lord, is it I? 23 And he answered and said, He that dippeth *his* hand with me in the dish, the same shall betray me. 24 The Son of man goeth as it is written of him: but woe unto that man by whom the Son of man is betrayed! it had been good for that man if he had not been born. 25 Then Judas, which betrayed him, answered and said, Master, is it I? He said unto him, Thou hast said. 26 And as they were eating, Jesus took bread, and blessed *it*, and brake *it*, and gave *it* to the disciples, and said, Take, eat; this is my body. 27 And he took the cup, and gave thanks, and gave *it* to them, saying, Drink ye all of it; 28 For this is my blood of the new testament, which is shed for many for the remission of sins. 29 But I say unto you, I will not drink henceforth of this fruit of the vine, until that day when I drink it new with you in my Father's kingdom. 30 And when they had sung an hymn, they went out into the mount of Olives. 31 Then saith Jesus unto them, All ye shall be offended because of me this night: for it is written, I will smite the shepherd, and the sheep of the flock shall be scattered abroad. 32 But after I am risen again, I will go before you into Galilee. ... 26:52 Then said Jesus unto him, Put up again thy sword into his place: for all they that take the sword shall perish with the sword. 53 Thinkest thou that I cannot now pray to my Father, and he shall presently give me more than twelve legions of angels? 54 But how then shall the scriptures be fulfilled, that thus it must be?

Mark 8:31 And he began to teach them, that the Son of man must suffer many things, and be rejected of the elders, and *of* the chief priests, and scribes, and be killed, and after three days rise again. ... 9:31 For he taught his disciples, and said unto them, The Son of man is delivered into the hands of men, and they shall kill him; and after that he is killed, he shall rise the third day. 32 But they understood not that saying, and were afraid to ask him. ... 10:32 And they were in the way going up to Jerusalem; and Jesus went before them: and they were amazed; and as they followed, they were afraid. And he took again the twelve, and began to tell them what things should happen unto him, 33 *Saying*, Behold, we go up to Jerusalem; and the Son of man shall be delivered unto the chief priests, and unto the scribes; and they shall condemn him to death, and shall deliver him to the Gentiles: 34 And they shall mock him, and shall scourge him, and shall spit upon him, and shall kill him: and the third day he shall rise again. ...

Luke 9:21 And he straitly charged them, and commanded *them* to tell no man that thing; 22 Saying, The Son of man must suffer many things, and be rejected of the elders and chief priests and scribes, and be slain, and be raised the third day. ... 9:28 And it came to pass about an eight days after these sayings, he took Peter and John and James, and went up into a mountain to pray. 29 And as he prayed, the fashion of his countenance was altered, and his raiment *was* white *and* glistering. 30 And, behold, there talked with him two men, which were Moses and Elias: 31 Who appeared in glory, and spake of his decease which he should accomplish at Jerusalem. ... 9:21 And he straitly charged them, and commanded *them* to tell no man that thing; 22 Saying, The Son of man must suffer many things, and be rejected of the elders and chief priests and scribes, and be slain, and be raised the third day. 23 And he said to *them* all, If any *man* will come after me, let him deny himself, and take up his cross daily, and follow me. 24 For whosoever will save his life shall lose it: but whosoever will lose his life for my sake, the same shall save it. 25 For what is a man advantaged, if he gain the whole world, and lose himself, or be cast away? ... 9:43 And they were all amazed at the mighty power of God. But while they wondered every one at all things which Jesus did, he said unto his disciples, 44 Let these sayings sink down into your ears: for the Son of man shall be delivered into the hands of men. 45 But they understood not this saying, and it was hid from them, that they perceived it not: and they feared to ask him of that saying. ... 12:50 But I have a baptism to be baptized with; and how am I straitened till it be accomplished! ... 18:31 Then he took *unto him* the twelve, and said unto them, Behold, we go up to Jerusalem, and all things that are written by the prophets concerning the Son of man shall be accomplished. 32 For he shall be delivered unto the Gentiles, and shall be mocked, and spitefully entreated, and spitted on: 33 And they shall scourge *him*, and put him to death: and the third day he shall rise again. 34 And they understood none of these things: and this saying was hid from them, neither knew they the things which were spoken.

John 2:18 Then answered the Jews and said unto him, What sign shewest thou unto us, seeing that thou doest these things? 19 Jesus answered and said unto them, Destroy this temple, and in three days I will raise it up. 20 Then said the Jews, Forty and six years was this temple in building, and wilt thou rear it up in three days? 21 But he spake of the temple of his body. 22 When therefore he was risen from the dead, his disciples remembered that he had said this unto them; and they believed the scripture, and the word which Jesus had said. ... 3:14 And as Moses lifted up the serpent in the wilderness, even so must the Son of man be lifted up: ... 4:34 Jesus saith unto them, My meat is to do the will of him that sent me, and to finish his work. ... 7:6 Then Jesus said unto them, My time is not yet come: but your time is alway ready. 7 The world cannot hate you; but me it hateth, because I testify of it, that the works thereof are evil. 8 Go ye up unto this feast: I go not up yet unto this feast; for my time is not yet full come. ... 7:10 But when his brethren were gone up, then went he also up unto the feast, not openly, but as it were in secret. ... 10:15 As the Father knoweth me, even so know I the Father: and I lay down my life for the sheep. ... 10:17 Therefore doth my Father love me, because I lay down my life, that I might take it again. 18 No man taketh it from me, but I lay it down of myself. I have power to lay it down, and I have power to take it again. This commandment have I received of my Father. ... 12:23 And Jesus answered them, saying, The hour is come, that the Son of man should be glorified. 24 Verily, verily, I say unto you, Except a corn of wheat fall into the ground and die, it abideth alone: but if it die, it bringeth forth much fruit. 25 He that loveth his life shall lose it; and he that hateth his life in this world shall keep it unto life eternal. 26 If any man serve me, let him follow me; and where I am, there shall also my servant be: if any man serve me, him will *my* Father honour. 27 Now is my soul troubled; and what shall I say? Father, save me from this hour: but for this cause came I unto this hour. 28 Father, glorify thy name. Then came there a voice from heaven, *saying*, I have both glorified *it*, and will glorify *it* again. ... 12:31 Now is the judgment of this world: now shall the prince of this world be cast out. 32 And I, if I be lifted up from the earth, will draw all *men* unto me. ... 13:31 Therefore, when he was gone out, Jesus said, Now is the Son of man glorified, and God is glorified in him. 32 If God be glorified in him, God shall also glorify him in himself, and shall straightway glorify him. ... 16:28 I came forth from the Father, and am come into the world: again, I leave the world, and go to the Father. ... 17:1 These words spake Jesus, and lifted up his eyes to heaven, and said, Father, the hour is come; glorify thy Son, that thy Son also may glorify thee: ... 17:11 And now I am no more in the world, but these are in the world, and I come to thee. Holy Father, keep through thine own name those whom thou hast given me, that they may be one, as we *are*. ... 17:18 As thou hast sent me into the world, even so have I also sent them into the world. ... 18:11 Then said Jesus unto Peter, Put up thy sword into the sheath: the cup which my Father hath given me, shall I not drink it?

2 Matthew 27:26 Then released he Barabbas unto them: and when he had scourged Jesus, he delivered *him* to be crucified. ... 29 And when they had platted a crown of thorns, they put *it* upon his head, and a reed in his right hand: and they bowed the knee before him, and mocked him, saying, Hail, King of the Jews! 30 And they spit upon him, and took the reed, and smote him on the head. ... 67 Then did they spit in his face, and buffeted him; and others smote *him* with the palms of their hands, 68 Saying, Prophesy unto us, thou Christ, Who is he that smote thee?

Mark 14:65 And some began to spit on him, and to cover his face, and to buffet him, and to say unto him, Prophesy: and the

206

servants did strike him with the palms of their hands. ... 15:19 And they smote him on the head with a reed, and did spit upon him, and bowing *their* knees worshipped him.

Luke 22:63 And the men that held Jesus mocked him, and smote *him*. 64 And when they had blindfolded him, they struck him on the face, and asked him, saying, Prophesy, who is it that smote thee?

John 18:22 And when he had thus spoken, one of the officers which stood by struck Jesus with the palm of his hand, saying, Answerest thou the high priest so? ... 19:1 Then Pilate therefore took Jesus, and scourged *him*. 2 And the soldiers platted a crown of thorns, and put *it* on his head, and they put on him a purple robe, 3 And said, Hail, King of the Jews! and they smote him with their hands.

3 The translators assigned by King James made distinctions in the translation to convey to the common man who had no knowledge of Hebrew or Greek certain riches that a simple literal translation would not convey.

This is the explanation for the use of "thee, thou. thine, thy, and thyself" for the singular second person pronoun and "ye, you, your, and yourselves" for the plural second person pronoun.

4 I agree that the journey began before the foundation of the world; however in combating the error of kenosis, one is limited in discussing actions of Jesus of Nazareth during the time of His earthly life.

John 17:24 Father, I will that they also, whom thou hast given me, be with me where I am; that they may behold my glory, which thou hast given me: for thou lovedst me before the foundation of the world.

1 Peter 1:20 Who verily was foreordained before the foundation of the world, but was manifest in these last times for you,

Revelation 13:8 And all that dwell upon the earth shall worship him, whose names are not written in the book of life of the Lamb slain from the foundation of the world.

5 Merriam-Webster 11th Collegiate Dictionary entry for the word *this.*

6 The apostle Paul was also moved by the Holy Spirit to apply the sixteenth Psalm to the death, burial, and resurrection of Jesus of Nazareth.

Acts 13:32 And we declare unto you glad tidings, how that the promise which was made unto the fathers, 33 God hath fulfilled the same unto us their children, in that he hath raised up Jesus again; as it is also written in the second psalm, Thou art my Son, this day have I begotten thee. 34 And as concerning that he raised him up from the dead, *now* no more to return to corruption, he said on this wise, I will give you the sure mercies of David. 35 Wherefore he saith also in another *psalm,* Thou shalt not suffer thine Holy One to see corruption. 36 For David, after he had served his own generation by the will of God, fell on sleep, and was laid unto his fathers, and saw corruption: 37 But he, whom God raised again, saw no corruption. 38 Be it known unto you therefore, men *and* brethren, that through this man is preached unto you the forgiveness of sins:

7 John 11:42 And I knew that thou hearest me always: but because of the people which stand by I said it, that they may believe that thou hast sent me.

8 1 Corinthians 13:12 For now we see through a glass, darkly; but then face to face: now I know in part; but then shall I know even as also I am known.

9 Colossians 1:19 For it pleased *the Father* that in him should all fulness dwell;

10 1 Timothy 3:16 And without controversy great is the mystery of godliness: God was manifest in the flesh, justified in the Spirit, seen of angels, preached unto the Gentiles, believed on in the world, received up into glory.

11 Acts 17:29 Forasmuch then as we are the offspring of God, we ought not to think that the Godhead is like unto gold, or silver, or stone, graven by art and man's device.

Romans 1:20 For the invisible things of him from the creation of the world are clearly seen, being understood by the things that are made, *even* his eternal power and Godhead; so that they are without excuse:

Colossians 2:9 For in him dwelleth all the fulness of the Godhead bodily.

12 Merriam-Webster 11th Collegiate Dictionary defines GODHEAD thusly: 1: divine nature or essence: DIVINITY; 2 capitalized a: GOD; b : the nature of God especially as existing in three persons"

13 It is certain that Jesus of Nazareth claimed to be GOD incarnate. **He asserted that He was the Son of GOD.**

John 9:35 Jesus heard that they had cast him out; and when he had found him, he said unto him, Dost thou believe on the Son of God? 36 He answered and said, Who is he, Lord, that I might believe on him? 37 And Jesus said unto him, Thou hast both seen him, and it is he that talketh with thee.

John 10:36 Say ye of him, whom the Father hath sanctified, and sent into the world, Thou blasphemest; because I said, I am the Son of God?

He identified Himself as the Son of man, and did so repeatedly—thirty times in the Gospel of Matthew.

Matthew 8:20 And Jesus saith unto him, The foxes have holes, and the birds of the air *have* nests; but the Son of man hath not where to lay *his* head. ... 9:6 But that ye may know that the Son of man hath power on earth to forgive sins, (then saith he to the sick of the palsy,) Arise, take up thy bed, and go unto thine house. ... 10:23 But when they persecute you in this city, flee ye into another: for verily I say unto you, Ye shall not have gone over the cities of Israel, till the Son of man be come. ... 11:19 The Son of man came eating and drinking, and they say, Behold a man gluttonous, and a winebibber, a friend of publicans and sinners. But wisdom is justified of her children. ... 12:8 For the Son of man is Lord even of the sabbath day. ... 12:32 And whosoever speaketh a word against the Son of man, it shall be forgiven him: but whosoever speaketh against the Holy Ghost, it shall not be forgiven him, neither in this world, neither in the *world* to come. ... 12:40 For as Jonas was three days and three nights in the whale's belly; so shall the Son of man be three days and three nights in the heart of the earth. ... 13:37 He answered and said unto them, He that soweth the good seed is the Son of man; ... 13:41 The Son of man shall send forth his angels, and they shall gather out of his kingdom all things that offend, and them which do iniquity; ... 16:13 When Jesus came into the coasts of Caesarea Philippi, he asked his disciples, saying, Whom do men say that I the Son of man am? ... 16:27 For the Son of man shall come in the glory of his Father with his angels; and then he shall reward every man according to his works. ... 16:28 Verily I say unto you, There be some standing here, which shall not taste of death, till they see the Son of man coming in his kingdom. ... 17:9 And as they came down from the mountain, Jesus charged them, saying, Tell the vision to no man, until the Son of man be risen again from the dead. ... 17:12 But I say unto you, That Elias is come already, and they knew him not, but have done unto him whatsoever they listed. Likewise shall also the Son of man suffer of them. ... 17:22 And while they abode in Galilee, Jesus said unto them, The Son of man shall be betrayed into the hands of men: ... 18:11 For the Son of man is come to save that which was lost. ... 19:28 And Jesus said unto them, Verily I say unto you, That ye which have followed me, in the regeneration when the Son of man shall sit in the throne of his glory, ye also shall sit upon twelve thrones, judging the twelve tribes of Israel. ... 20:18 Behold, we go up to Jerusalem; and the Son of man shall be betrayed unto the chief priests and unto the scribes, and they shall condemn him to death, ... 20:28 Even as the Son of man came not to be ministered unto, but to minister, and to give his life a ransom for many. ... 24:27 For as the lightning cometh out of the east, and shineth even unto the west; so shall also the coming of the Son of man be. ... 24:30 And then shall appear the sign of the Son of man in heaven: and then shall all the tribes of the earth mourn, and they shall see the Son of man coming in the clouds of heaven with power and great glory. ... 24:37 But as the days of Noe *were*, so shall also the coming of the Son of man be. ... 24:39 And knew not until the flood came, and took them all away; so shall also the coming of the Son of man be. ... 24:44 Therefore be ye also ready: for in such an hour as ye think not the Son of man cometh. ... 25:13 Watch therefore, for ye know neither the day nor the hour wherein the Son of man cometh. ... 25:31 When the Son of man shall come in his glory, and all the holy angels with him, then shall he sit upon the throne of his glory: ... 26:2 Ye know that after two days is *the feast of* the passover, and the Son of man is betrayed to be crucified. ... 26:24 The Son of man goeth as it is written of him: but woe unto that man by whom the Son of man is betrayed! it had been good for that man if he had not been born. ... 26:45 Then cometh he to his disciples, and saith unto them, Sleep on now, and take *your* rest: behold, the hour is at hand, and the Son of man is betrayed into the hands of sinners. ... 26:64 Jesus saith unto him, Thou hast said: nevertheless I say unto you, Hereafter shall ye see the Son of man sitting on the right hand of power, and coming in the clouds of heaven.

This title was understood by the Jews to be Messianic and a claim of equality to the title Son of GOD, a claim of being GOD in the flesh.

Matthew 26:59 Now the chief priests, and elders, and all the council, sought false witness against Jesus, to put him to death; 60 But found none: yea, though many false witnesses came, *yet* found they none. At the last came two false witnesses, 61 And said, This *fellow* said, I am able to destroy the temple of God, and to build it in three days. 62 And the high priest arose, and said unto him, Answerest thou nothing? what *is it which* these witness against thee? 63 But Jesus held his peace. And the high priest answered and said unto him, I adjure thee by the living God, that thou tell us whether thou be the Christ, the Son of God. 64 Jesus saith unto him, Thou hast said: nevertheless I say unto you, Hereafter shall ye see the

Son of man sitting on the right hand of power, and coming in the clouds of heaven. 65 Then the high priest rent his clothes, saying, He hath spoken blasphemy; what further need have we of witnesses? behold, now ye have heard his blasphemy. 66 What think ye? They answered and said, He is guilty of death. 67 Then did they spit in his face, and buffeted him; and others smote *him* with the palms of their hands, 68 Saying, Prophesy unto us, thou Christ, Who is he that smote thee?

He made Himself equal with the Father.

John 5:17 But Jesus answered them, My Father worketh hitherto, and I work. 18 Therefore the Jews sought the more to kill him, because he not only had broken the sabbath, but said also that God was his Father, making himself equal with God.

John 10:30 I and my Father are one.

The issue is not really His claims, but rather the matter rests on whether He demonstrated that He was GOD by exercising the prerogatives that only GOD could accomplish. While this listing is not intended to be exhaustive, it is sufficient to sustain the premise that Jesus of Nazareth did do those things that only GOD could do.

He performed creative acts.

John 2:6 And there were set there six waterpots of stone, after the manner of the purifying of the Jews, containing two or three firkins apiece. 7 Jesus saith unto them, Fill the waterpots with water. And they filled them up to the brim. 8 And he saith unto them, Draw out now, and bear unto the governor of the feast. And they bare *it*. 9 When the ruler of the feast had tasted the water that was made wine, and knew not whence it was: (but the servants which drew the water knew;) the governor of the feast called the bridegroom, 10 And saith unto him, Every man at the beginning doth set forth good wine; and when men have well drunk, then that which is worse: *but* thou hast kept the good wine until now. 11 This beginning of miracles did Jesus in Cana of Galilee, and manifested forth his glory; and his disciples believed on him.

Matthew 12:10 And, behold, there was a man which had *his* hand withered. And they asked him, saying, Is it lawful to heal on the sabbath days? that they might accuse him. 11 And he said unto them, What man shall there be among you, that shall have one sheep, and if it fall into a pit on the sabbath day, will he not lay hold on it, and lift *it* out? 12 How much then is a man better than a sheep? Wherefore it is lawful to do well on the sabbath days. 13 Then saith he to the man, Stretch forth thine hand. And he stretched *it* forth; and it was restored whole, like as the other.

He forgave sins.

Mark 2:1 And again he entered into Capernaum, after *some* days; and it was noised that he was in the house. 2 And straightway many were gathered together, insomuch that there was no room to receive *them*, no, not so much as about the door: and he preached the word unto them. 3 And they come unto him, bringing one sick of the palsy, which was borne of four. 4 And when they could not come nigh unto him for the press, they uncovered the roof where he was: and when they had broken *it* up, they let down the bed wherein the sick of the palsy lay. 5 When Jesus saw their faith, he said unto the sick of the palsy, Son, thy sins be forgiven thee. 6 But there were certain of the scribes sitting there, and reasoning in their hearts, 7 Why doth this *man* thus speak blasphemies? who can forgive sins but God only? 8 And immediately when Jesus perceived in his spirit that they so reasoned within themselves, he said unto them, Why reason ye these things in your hearts? 9 Whether is it easier to say to the sick of the palsy, *Thy* sins be forgiven thee; or to say, Arise, and take up thy bed, and walk? 10 But that ye may know that the Son of man hath power on earth to forgive sins, (he saith to the sick of the palsy,) 11 I say unto thee, Arise, and take up thy bed, and go thy way into thine house. 12 And immediately he arose, took up the bed, and went forth before them all; insomuch that they were all amazed, and glorified God, saying, We never saw it on this fashion.

He pronounced judgment.

Matthew 21:19 And when he saw a fig tree in the way, he came to it, and found nothing thereon, but leaves only, and said unto it, Let no fruit grow on thee henceforward for ever. And presently the fig tree withered away.

He controlled creation.

Mark 4:36 And when they had sent away the multitude, they took him even as he was in the ship. And there were also with him other little ships. 37 And there arose a great storm of wind, and the waves beat into the ship, so that it was now full. 38 And he was in the hinder part of the ship, asleep on a pillow: and they awake him, and say unto him, Master, carest thou not that we perish? 39 And he arose, and rebuked the wind, and said unto the sea, Peace, be still. And the wind ceased, and there was a great calm. 40 And he said unto them, Why are ye so fearful? how is it that ye have no faith? 41 And they feared exceedingly, and said one to another, What manner of man is this, that even the wind and the sea obey him?

Matthew 17:24 And when they were come to Capernaum, they that received tribute *money* came to Peter, and said, Doth not your master pay tribute? 25 He saith, Yes. And when he was come into the house, Jesus prevented him, saying, What thinkest thou, Simon? of whom do the kings of the earth take custom or tribute? of their own children, or of strangers? 26 Peter saith unto him, Of strangers. Jesus saith unto him, Then are the children free. 27 Notwithstanding, lest we should offend them, go thou to the sea, and cast an hook, and take up the fish that first cometh up; and when thou hast opened his mouth, thou shalt find a piece of money: that take, and give unto them for me and thee.

John 21:3 Simon Peter saith unto them, I go a fishing. They say unto him, We also go with thee. They went forth, and entered into a ship immediately; and that night they caught nothing. 4 But when the morning was now come, Jesus stood on the shore: but the disciples knew not that it was Jesus. 5 Then Jesus saith unto them, Children, have ye any meat? They answered him, No. 6 And he said unto them, Cast the net on the right side of the ship, and ye shall find. They cast therefore, and now they were not able to draw it for the multitude of fishes.

He accepted worship (before the Resurrection).

Matthew 8:2 And, behold, there came a leper and worshipped him, saying, Lord, if thou wilt, thou canst make me clean. ... 9:18 While he spake these things unto them, behold, there came a certain ruler, and worshipped him, saying, My daughter is even now dead: but come and lay thy hand upon her, and she shall live. ... 14:33 Then they that were in the ship came and worshipped him, saying, Of a truth thou art the Son of God. ... 15:25 Then came she and worshipped him, saying, Lord, help me. ... 18:26 The servant therefore fell down, and worshipped him, saying, Lord, have patience with me, and I will pay thee all.

Mark 5:6 But when he saw Jesus afar off, he ran and worshipped him,

John 9:38 And he said, Lord, I believe. And he worshipped him.

[14] *SwordSearcher: Albert Barnes Notes on the Bible;* Hebrews 5:8

[15] Luke 2:52 And Jesus increased in wisdom and stature, and in favour with God and man.

[16] Mark 11:11 And Jesus entered into Jerusalem, and into the temple: and when he had looked round about upon all things, and now the eventide was come, he went out unto Bethany with the twelve. 12 And on the morrow, when they were come from Bethany, he was hungry:

[17] John 19:28 After this, Jesus knowing that all things were now accomplished, that the scripture might be fulfilled, saith, I thirst.

[18] John 4:6 Now Jacob's well was there. Jesus therefore, being wearied with *his* journey, sat thus on the well: *and* it was about the sixth hour.

[19] Mark 4:37 And there arose a great storm of wind, and the waves beat into the ship, so that it was now full. 38 And he was in the hinder part of the ship, asleep on a pillow: and they awake him, and say unto him, Master, carest thou not that we perish?

[20] Mark 10:21 Then Jesus beholding him loved him, and said unto him, One thing thou lackest: go thy way, sell whatsoever thou hast, and give to the poor, and thou shalt have treasure in heaven: and come, take up the cross, and follow me. 22 And he was sad at that saying, and went away grieved: for he had great possessions. 23 And Jesus looked round about, and saith unto his disciples, How hardly shall they that have riches enter into the kingdom of God!

[21] Hebrews 2:18 For in that he himself hath suffered being tempted, he is able to succour them that are tempted.

Hebrews 5:8 Though he were a Son, yet learned he obedience by the things which he suffered;

[22] Luke 3:21 Now when all the people were baptized, it came to pass, that Jesus also being baptized, and praying, the heaven was opened, ... 5:16 And he withdrew himself into the wilderness, and prayed. ... 6:12 And it came to pass in those days, that he went out into a mountain to pray, and continued all night in prayer to God. ... 9:18 And it came to pass, as he was alone praying, his disciples were with him: and he asked them, saying, Whom say the people that I am? ... 9:28 And it came to pass about an eight days after these sayings, he took Peter and John and James, and went up into a mountain to pray. 29 And as he prayed, the fashion of his countenance was

altered, and his raiment *was* white *and* glistering. ... 11:1 And it came to pass, that, as he was praying in a certain place, when he ceased, one of his disciples said unto him, Lord, teach us to pray, as John also taught his disciples. ... 22:32 But I have prayed for thee, that thy faith fail not: and when thou art converted, strengthen thy brethren. ... 22:41 And he was withdrawn from them about a stone's cast, and kneeled down, and prayed, ... 22:44 And being in an agony he prayed more earnestly: and his sweat was as it were great drops of blood falling down to the ground. ... 22:45 And when he rose up from prayer, and was come to his disciples, he found them sleeping for sorrow,

John 14:16 And I will pray the Father, and he shall give you another Comforter, that he may abide with you for ever; ... 16:26 At that day ye shall ask in my name: and I say not unto you, that I will pray the Father for you: ... 17:9 I pray for them: I pray not for the world, but for them which thou hast given me; for they are thine. ... 17:15 I pray not that thou shouldest take them out of the world, but that thou shouldest keep them from the evil. ... 17:20 Neither pray I for these alone, but for them also which shall believe on me through their word;, building up yourselves on your most holy faith, praying in the Holy Ghost,

23 This in and of itself ought to forever reveal the fallacy of the false doctrines of the ministries that teach Positive Confession, the Prosperity Gospel, Name It—Claim It, and "you are little gods or little christs."

24 Philippians 2:2-11; Hebrews 5:7-9; 1 Peter 2:21.

25 Matthew 2:16 Then Herod, when he saw that he was mocked of the wise men, was exceeding wroth, and sent forth, and slew all the children that were in Bethlehem, and in all the coasts thereof, from two years old and under, according to the time which he had diligently inquired of the wise men. 17 Then was fulfilled that which was spoken by Jeremy the prophet, saying, 18 In Rama was there a voice heard, lamentation, and weeping, and great mourning, Rachel weeping *for* her children, and would not be comforted, because they are not.

26 Luke 4:28 And all they in the synagogue, when they heard these things, were filled with wrath, 29 And rose up, and thrust him out of the city, and led him unto the brow of the hill whereon their city was built, that they might cast him down headlong. 30 But he passing through the midst of them went his way, 31 And came down to Capernaum, a city of Galilee, and taught them on the sabbath days.

27 John 8:59 Then took they up stones to cast at him: but Jesus hid himself, and went out of the temple, going through the midst of them, and so passed by.

John 10:31 Then the Jews took up stones again to stone him.

[28] Matthew 8:23 And when he was entered into a ship, his disciples followed him. 24 And, behold, there arose a great tempest in the sea, insomuch that the ship was covered with the waves: but he was asleep.

Luke 8:22 Now it came to pass on a certain day, that he went into a ship with his disciples: and he said unto them, Let us go over unto the other side of the lake. And they launched forth. 23 But as they sailed he fell asleep: and there came down a storm of wind on the lake; and they were filled *with water,* and were in jeopardy.

[29] John 5:18 Therefore the Jews sought the more to kill him, because he not only had broken the sabbath, but said also that God was his Father, making himself equal with God.

John 10:39 Therefore they sought again to take him: but he escaped out of their hand,

[30] Hebrews 2:9 But we see Jesus, who was made a little lower than the angels for the suffering of death, crowned with glory and honour; that he by the grace of God should taste death for every man.

Matthew 16:28 Verily I say unto you, There be some standing here, which shall not taste of death, till they see the Son of man coming in his kingdom.

Mark 9:1 And he said unto them, Verily I say unto you, That there be some of them that stand here, which shall not taste of death, till they have seen the kingdom of God come with power.

Luke 9:27 But I tell you of a truth, there be some standing here, which shall not taste of death, till they see the kingdom of God.

John 8:52 Then said the Jews unto him, Now we know that thou hast a devil. Abraham is dead, and the prophets; and thou sayest, If a man keep my saying, he shall never taste of death.

Revelation 2:11 He that hath an ear, let him hear what the Spirit saith unto the churches; He that overcometh shall not be hurt of the second death.

Revelation 20:6 Blessed and holy is he that hath part in the first resurrection: on such the second death hath no power, but they shall be priests of God and of Christ, and shall reign with him a thousand years.

Revelation 20:14 And death and hell were cast into the lake of fire. This is the second death.

Revelation 21:8 But the fearful, and unbelieving, and the abominable, and murderers, and whoremongers, and sorcerers, and idolaters, and all liars, shall have their part in the lake which burneth with fire and brimstone: which is the second death.

Hebrews 2:9 But we see Jesus, who was made a little lower than the angels for the suffering of death, crowned with glory and honour; that he by the grace of God should taste death for every man.

31 Luke 9:51 And it came to pass, when the time was come that he should be received up, he stedfastly set his face to go to Jerusalem,

32 John 10:17 Therefore doth my Father love me, because I lay down my life, that I might take it again. 18 No man taketh it from me, but I lay it down of myself. I have power to lay it down, and I have power to take it again. This commandment have I received of my Father.

33 Isaiah 53:7 He was oppressed, and he was afflicted, yet he opened not his mouth: he is brought as a lamb to the slaughter, and as a sheep before her shearers is dumb, so he openeth not his mouth.

34 Hebrews 12:2 Looking unto Jesus the author and finisher of *our* faith; who for the joy that was set before him endured the cross, despising the shame, and is set down at the right hand of the throne of God.

35 *SwordSearcher John Gill's Exposition of the Entire Bible*: John 19:14.

And about the sixth hour; to which agrees the account in Matthew 27:45 and Luke 27:45 but Mark 15:25 says that "it was the third hour, and they crucified him"; and Beza says, he found it so written in one copy; and so read Peter of Alexandria, Beza's ancient copy, and some others, and Nonnus: but the copies in general agree in, and confirm the common reading, and which is differently accounted for; some by the different computations of the Jews and Romans; others by observing that the day was divided into four parts, each part containing three hours, and were called the third, the sixth, the ninth, and the twelfth hours; and not only that time, when one of these hours came, was called by that name, but also from that all the space of the three hours, till the next came, was called by the name of the former: for instance, all the space from nine o'clock till twelve was called "the third hour"; and all from twelve till three in the afternoon "the sixth hour": hence the time of Christ's crucifixion being supposed to be somewhat before, but yet near our twelve of the clock, it may be truly here said that it was about the sixth hour; and as truly by Mark the third hour; that space, which was called by the name of the third hour, being not yet passed, though it drew toward an end. This way go Godwin and Hammond, whose words I have expressed, and bids fair for the true solution of the difficulty: though it should be observed, that Mark 15:33 agrees with the other evangelists about the darkness which was at the sixth hour, the time of Christ's crucifixion, and it is to be remarked, that he does not say that it was the third hour "when" they crucified him, or that they crucified him at the third hour; but it was the third hour, "and" they crucified him, as Dr. Lightfoot observes. It was the time of day when they should have been at the daily sacrifice, and preparing for the solemnity of that day particularly, which was their Chagigah, or grand feast; but instead of this they were prosecuting his crucifixion, which they brought about by the sixth hour.

36 Psalm 31:1 In thee, O LORD, do I put my trust; let me never be ashamed: deliver me in thy righteousness. 2 Bow down thine ear to me; deliver me speedily: be thou my strong rock, for an house of defence to save me. 3 For thou *art* my rock and my fortress; therefore for thy name's sake lead me, and guide me. 4 Pull me out of the net that they have laid privily for me: for thou *art* my strength. 5 Into thine hand I commit my spirit: thou hast redeemed me, O LORD God of truth.

37 Luke 9:51 And it came to pass, when the time was come that he should be received up, he stedfastly set his face to go to Jerusalem,

CHAPTER 14

CONTEXT OF HIS RESURRECTION

As we return to Psalm Twenty-two, notice the consistent use of the future tense. The Psalm is one of expectation of ultimate victory. We know on this side of the event that the victory was the resurrection. The anticipation of the deliverance by the Father is all through the Psalm.

In the Psalm, the LORD Jesus proclaims that the Father is holy. He insists that the Incarnation was on purpose and with purpose. The expression of settled faith is constant. The Father is not far distant; He is very present.

> 3 But thou *art* holy, *O thou* that inhabitest the praises of Israel. ... 9 But thou *art* he that took me out of the womb: thou didst make me hope *when I was* upon my mother's breasts. 10 I was cast upon thee from the womb: thou *art* my God from my mother's belly.

> 11 Be not far from me; for trouble *is* near; for *there is* none to help. ... 19 But be not thou far from me, O LORD: O my strength, haste thee to help me. 20 Deliver my soul from the

sword; my darling from the power of the dog.
21 Save me from the lion's mouth:

Consider the forcefulness of the declaration:

for thou hast heard me from the horns of the
unicorns.

The shout of victory is very evident.

22 I will declare thy name unto my brethren:
in the midst of the congregation will I praise
thee.

The Son of GOD invites us to join Him in
praise.

23 Ye that fear the LORD, praise him; all ye
the seed of Jacob, glorify him; and fear him,
all ye the seed of Israel.

How does anyone misconstrue the words that
follow the phrases just cited that are so clearly
connected with the Person and Ministry of the
LORD Jesus in particular with His crucifixion and
resurrection? These words are emphatic and in
direct and irreconcilable conflict with any idea
that the Father hid His face from the Son as He
was on that cross.

24 For he hath not despised nor abhorred the
affliction of the afflicted; neither hath he hid
his face from him; but when he cried unto
him, he heard.

The words are spoken in the context of the assured deliverance of the resurrection. By quoting
from this Psalm while He was on the cross, the
LORD Jesus is calling attention to the entire
Psalm—a Psalm of valor, a Psalm of vindication, a
Psalm of victory. These words do not come as a
whining complaint; all that follows that statement
("My God, my God, why hast thou forsaken me?")
give those words a setting of praise. Read the
victory described in verse 24 and 25.

For he hath not despised nor abhorred the affliction of the afflicted; neither hath he hid his

face from him; but when he cried unto him, he heard. My praise shall be of thee in the great congregation: I will pay my vows before them that fear him.

The Lamb of GOD never had a hesitation about dying the death of the cross.

Matthew 16:21 From that time forth began Jesus to shew unto his disciples, how that he must go unto Jerusalem, and suffer many things of the elders and chief priests and scribes, and be killed, and be raised again the third day.

Matthew 20:18 Behold, we go up to Jerusalem; and the Son of man shall be betrayed unto the chief priests and unto the scribes, and they shall condemn him to death, 19 And shall deliver him to the Gentiles to mock, and to scourge, and to crucify him: and the third day he shall rise again.

John 12:27 Now is my soul troubled; and what shall I say? Father, save me from this hour: but for this cause came I unto this hour. 28 Father, glorify thy name. Then came there a voice from heaven, saying, I have both glorified it, and will glorify it again.

Hebrews 12:2 Looking unto Jesus the author and finisher of our faith; who for the joy that was set before him endured the cross, despising the shame, and is set down at the right hand of the throne of God.

Philippians 2:8 And being found in fashion as a man, he humbled himself, and became obedient unto death, even the death of the cross. 9 Wherefore God also hath highly exalted him, and given him a name which is above every name: 10 That at the name of Jesus every knee should bow, of things in heaven, and things in earth, and things under the earth; 11 And that every tongue should confess that Jesus Christ is Lord, to the glory of God the Father.

Psalm 16:9 Therefore my heart is glad, and my glory rejoiceth: my flesh also shall rest in hope. 10 For thou wilt not leave my soul in hell; neither wilt thou suffer thine Holy One to see corruption. 11 Thou wilt shew me the path of life: in thy presence is fulness of joy; at thy right hand there are pleasures for evermore.

Isaiah 53:10 Yet it pleased the LORD to bruise him; he hath put him to grief: when thou shalt make his soul an offering for sin, he shall see his seed, he shall prolong his days, and the pleasure of the LORD shall prosper in his hand. 11 He shall see of the travail of his soul, and shall be satisfied: by his knowledge shall my righteous servant justify many; for he shall bear their iniquities. 12 Therefore will I divide him a portion with the great, and he shall divide the spoil with the strong; because he hath poured out his soul unto death: and he was numbered with the transgressors; and he bare the sin of many, and made intercession for the transgressors.

Luke 24:25 Then he said unto them, O fools, and slow of heart to believe all that the prophets have spoken: 26 Ought not Christ to have suffered these things, and to enter into his glory? 27 And beginning at Moses and all the prophets, he expounded unto them in all the scriptures the things concerning himself.

Luke 24:39 Behold my hands and my feet, that it is I myself: handle me, and see; for a spirit hath not flesh and bones, as ye see me have. 40 And when he had thus spoken, he shewed them his hands and his feet. ... 44 And he said unto them, These are the words which I spake unto you, while I was yet with you, that all things must be fulfilled, which were written in the law of Moses, and in the prophets, and in the psalms, concerning me. 45 Then opened he their understanding, that they might understand the scriptures, 46 And said unto them, Thus it is written, and thus it behoved Christ to suffer, and to rise from the dead the third day: 47 And that repentance and remission of sins should be preached in his name among all nations, beginning at Jerusalem.

John 12:24 Verily, verily, I say unto you, Except a corn of wheat fall into the ground and die, it abideth alone: but if it die, it bringeth forth much fruit. ... 32 And I, if I be lifted up from the earth, will draw all men unto me.

John 17:1 These words spake Jesus, and lifted up his eyes to heaven, and said, Father, the hour is come; glorify thy Son, that thy Son also may glorify thee: 2 As thou hast given him power over all flesh, that he should give eternal life to as many as thou hast given him. 3 And this is life eternal, that they might know thee the only true God, and Jesus Christ, whom thou hast sent. 4 I have glorified thee on the earth: I have finished the work which thou gavest me to do.

The weight of the testimony of Scripture is an unmistakable emphasis that the LORD Jesus, the Son of GOD, willing and knowingly,[1] went to the cross without hesitation or faltering. As it were, He marched with determination to the cross.

Luke 9:51 And it came to pass, when the time was come that he should be received up, he stedfastly set his face to go to Jerusalem,

Luke 12:50 But I have a baptism to be baptized with; and how am I straitened till it be accomplished!

Isaiah 50:5 The Lord GOD hath opened mine ear, and I was not rebellious, neither turned away back. 6 I gave my back to the smiters, and my cheeks to them that plucked off the hair: I hid not my face from shame and spitting. 7 For the Lord GOD will help me; therefore shall I not be confounded: therefore have

I set my face like a flint, and I know that I shall not be ashamed.

As I prepared this material, I came to a passage that stirred my heart to realize that the LORD Jesus was given by the Father *all things*. These *all things* must, by definition include the Incarnation and all that accompanied His being made flesh to dwell among us that we might behold His glory, the glory as of the only begotten of the Father. Because the *all things* included the Incarnation, then *the death of the cross*[2] was included. Notice the words: "the Father had given all things into His hands."

> John 13:3 Jesus knowing that **the Father had given all things into his hands**, and that he was come from God, and went to God; ... 31 Therefore, when he was gone out, Jesus said, Now is the Son of man glorified, and God is glorified in him. 32 If God be glorified in him, God shall also glorify him in himself, and shall straightway glorify him.

I almost physically shudder (to use a human expression) to describe this relationship, because human terminology will always fall short. The Son was given full autonomy by the Father in "all things"; therefore, and, again I am speaking in human terminology, the Son, if He should desire to do so, could have avoided the events of the garden of Gethsemane, those actions of His enemies from the garden to the cross, even the entire time at Calvary, or He could have left the cross at any time. **The death of the cross was in His hands.**

Mere nails could not hold Him to that rugged tree. The power of Rome and her vaunted legions did not hold Him on that cross. The bitter hatred of the Jewish leadership did not bind Him to the cross. Once again, I speak in human terms: it was also not the anger or the wrath of GOD the Father that kept Him on the cross.

Two verses touching this theme force their way into the mind and heart.

The first:

> John 13:1 Now before the feast of the passover, when Jesus knew that his hour was come that he should depart out of this world unto the Father, having loved his own which were in the world, he loved them unto the end.

This is the wondrous truth so forcefully placed in Revelation 1:5: ... Unto him that loved us, and washed us from our sins in his own blood,

The second:

> Hebrews 12:2 Looking unto Jesus the author and finisher of our faith; who for the joy that was set before him endured the cross, despising the shame, and is set down at the right hand of the throne of God.

Perhaps, I am in the minority, but I do not see "the joy that was set before Him" as the resurrection or even the ascension; instead, I believe it to speak of the joy He had in providing redemption, reconciliation, and eternal life for those who will receive Him as Saviour. This is not to discount or to minimize the joy of the resurrection and that of the ascension; those were glorious and joyous. However, the cross is that which was set before Him; it was the cross that He endured.

I find in Psalm 16:9 that the gladness and the rejoicing are there before the death!

> Therefore my heart is glad, and my glory rejoiceth: my flesh also shall rest in hope.

I do not understand and I cannot explain, but it seems to me that the Lamb of GOD found joy in being the atoning sacrifice.

It is apparent to those that consult only the Scriptures that no level of friction existed between the Father and the Son. The declaration of the Son of GOD that "I and my Father are one"[3] was true before the creation of the world; it was true at the cross; and it remains true today as He sits at the right hand of the Father. They have never been disassociated, the Son from the Father or the Father from the Son, in essence or in purpose. They are ever of the same mind.

The resurrection speaks of that unity between the Father and the Son. It is emphasized (no less than eighteen times) that it is the Father that raised the Jesus of Nazareth from the dead.[4] That is not to be overlooked or minimized. I believe that one of the reasons why so many verses affirm this truth is to cement the understanding that there was no breach between the Father and the Son.

Jesus of Nazareth was raised to sit at the right hand of the Father. Three times during His earthly ministry, the Father had proclaimed that He was pleased with the Son. The seat of honor at the right hand is the ultimate declaration that the Father is pleased.

Having presented the atoning blood and thereby obtaining redemption,[5] the LORD Jesus sits now at the right hand of the Majesty on high as the Great High Priest.

Hebrews 1:1 God, who at sundry times and in divers manners spake in time past unto the fathers by the prophets, 2 Hath in these last days spoken unto us by *his* Son, whom he hath appointed heir of all things, by whom also he made the worlds; 3 Who being the brightness of *his* glory, and the express image of his person, and upholding all things by the word of his power, when he had by himself purged our sins, sat down on the right hand of the Majesty on high; 4 Being made so much better than the angels, as he hath by inheritance obtained a more excellent name than they.

Hebrews 8:1 Now of the things which we have spoken *this is* the sum: We have such an high priest, who is set on the right hand of the throne of the Majesty in the heavens; 2 A minister of the sanctuary, and of the true tabernacle, which the Lord pitched, and not man.

I wish to proceed carefully and cautiously. The resurrection is important to our salvation.

Romans 4:24 But for us also, to whom it shall be imputed, **if we believe on him that raised up Jesus our Lord from the dead**; 25 Who was delivered for our offences, and was raised again for our justification.

Romans 10:9 That if thou shalt confess with thy mouth the Lord Jesus, **and shalt believe in thine heart that God hath raised him from the dead**, thou shalt be saved.

I understand these verses to state that a belief in the resurrection is necessary for salvation. A person that denies the literal physical resurrection of the body of Jesus of Nazareth is not a Biblical Christian.

1 Corinthians 15:14 And if Christ be not risen, then is our preaching vain, and your faith is also vain. ... 17 And if Christ be not raised, your faith is vain; ye are yet in your sins. 18 Then they also which are fallen asleep in Christ are perished. 19 If in this life only we have hope in Christ, we are of all men most miserable.

I believe that Hebrews 10:19-20 places a level of importance on the resurrected body of the LORD Jesus that needs to be recognized. "Having therefore, brethren, **boldness to enter** into the holiest by the blood of Jesus, 20 By a new and living way, which he hath consecrated for us, **through the veil, that is to say, his flesh**." That seems to be to be a very clear statement that the flesh, the body, of the LORD Jesus is vitally connected with our salvation and will be so connected throughout eternity.

Every descriptive passage presenting the presence of the LORD Jesus since the resurrection and including into the eternal state after the new heaven and the new earth presents Him in a recognizable bodily form. I do not find any reason in Scripture to believe that the resurrected body in which He was seen for the forty days between the Resurrection and the Ascending was a temporary expediency.

In John 20:27, Thomas was told that he might "Reach hither thy finger, and behold my hands; and reach hither thy hand, and thrust *it* into my side: and be not faithless, but believing." While our natural mind might shrink at the prospect of doing so, the Son of GOD is not associated with the grotesque, the gruesome, the macabre, or the ghoulish. The act, if Thomas did it, would not have been repulsive. Jesus, the Son of GOD, would not have introduced the subject or offered the opportunity if it were ghoulish or improper.

That these evidences of the consequences of the crucifixion are present in eternity is at least implied in three specific statements.

1. The "same Jesus" that ascended will be the same Jesus that returns.

In Acts 1:11, the two men in white apparel addressed the disciples as they were watching where the LORD Jesus had ascended, "Ye men of Galilee, why stand ye gazing up into heaven? this same Jesus, which is taken up from you into heaven, shall so come in like manner as ye have seen him go into heaven." This same Jesus implies that when He returns, He will

228

be in the same body as when He ascended.

This same Jesus returns to resurrect "the dead in Christ" and to catch up those living believers:

> 1 Thessalonians 4:13 But I would not have you to be ignorant, brethren, concerning them which are asleep, that ye sorrow not, even as others which have no hope. 14 For if we believe that Jesus died and rose again, even so them also which sleep in Jesus will God bring with him. 15 For this we say unto you by the word of the Lord, that we which are alive and remain unto the coming of the Lord shall not prevent them which are asleep. 16 For the Lord himself shall descend from heaven with a shout, with the voice of the archangel, and with the trump of God: and the dead in Christ shall rise first: 17 Then we which are alive and remain shall be caught up together with them in the clouds, to meet the Lord in the air: and so shall we ever be with the Lord. 18 Wherefore comfort one another with these words.

This same Jesus returns at the conclusion of the Great Tribulation to bring judgment on the unrepentant world:

> 2 Thessalonians 1:7 And to you who are troubled rest with us, when the Lord Jesus shall be revealed from heaven with his mighty angels, 8 In flaming fire taking vengeance on them that know not God, and that obey not the gospel of our Lord Jesus Christ: 9 Who shall be punished with everlasting destruction from the presence of the Lord, and from the

glory of his power; 10 When he shall come to be glorified in his saints, and to be admired in all them that believe (because our testimony among you was believed) in that day. 11 Wherefore also we pray always for you, that our God would count you worthy of this calling, and fulfil all the good pleasure of his goodness, and the work of faith with power: 12 That the name of our Lord Jesus Christ may be glorified in you, and ye in him, according to the grace of our God and the Lord Jesus Christ.

This same Jesus is the light of the New Jerusalem in eternity.

Revelation 21:23 And the city had no need of the sun, neither of the moon, to shine in it: for the glory of God did lighten it, and the Lamb *is* the light thereof.

2. The Messiah that is pierced is recognized by those that pierced Him through the evidence of those piercings.

David, in Psalm 22:16, speaks prophetically of the Messiah being pierced in His hands and His feet: "For dogs have compassed me: the assembly of the wicked have inclosed me: they pierced my hands and my feet." This was fulfilled by the nails of the crucifixion.

The prophet Zechariah gives two distinctly Messianic prophecies that involve a piercing and wounds in the hands, but which had only a partial fulfillment at the crucifixion.

12:10 And I will pour upon the house of David, and upon the inhabitants of

> Jerusalem, the spirit of grace and of supplications: and they shall look upon me whom they have pierced, and they shall mourn for him, as one mourneth for *his* only *son,* and shall be in bitterness for him, as one that is in bitterness for *his* firstborn.
>
> 13:6 And *one* shall say unto him, What *are* these wounds in thine hands? Then he shall answer, *Those* with which I was wounded *in* the house of my friends.

Zechariah 12:10 is referenced as fulfilled in John 19:34–37.

> But one of the soldiers with a spear pierced his side, and forthwith came there out blood and water. And he that saw *it* bare record, and his record is true: and he knoweth that he saith true, that ye might believe. For these things were done, that the scripture should be fulfilled, A bone of him shall not be broken. And again another scripture saith, They shall look on him whom they pierced."
>
> However, that piercing is into His side, not His hands or His feet.

John in Revelation 1:7 connects the viewing of the marks of the piercings with the return of the Messiah. This would be the fulfillment of the second prophecy of Zechariah 13:6.

> Behold, he cometh with clouds; and every eye shall see him, and they *also* which pierced him: and all kindreds of the earth shall wail because of him. Even so, Amen."

3. **The LORD Jesus is described in terms that reference the crucifixion even in eternity.**

231

Revelation 5:6 And I beheld, and, lo, in the midst of the throne and of the four beasts, and in the midst of the elders, stood a Lamb as it had been slain, having seven horns and seven eyes, which are the seven Spirits of God sent forth into all the earth. ... 5:12 Saying with a loud voice, Worthy is the Lamb that was slain to receive power, and riches, and wisdom, and strength, and honour, and glory, and blessing. ... 13:8 And all that dwell upon the earth shall worship him, whose names are not written in the book of life of the Lamb slain from the foundation of the world.

Spurgeon offers a reasonable answer to the question as to why the wounds would be borne by the LORD Jesus in eternity and one that does no damage to Scripture.[6]

Lo, in the midst of the throne . . . stood a Lamb as it had been slain." Revelation 5:6

Why should our exalted Lord appear in His wounds in glory? The wounds of Jesus are His glories, His jewels, His sacred ornaments. To the eye of the believer, Jesus is passing fair because He is "white and ruddy" white with innocence, and ruddy with His own blood. We see Him as the lily of matchless purity, and as the rose crimsoned with His own gore. Christ is lovely upon Olivet and Tabor, and by the sea, but oh! there never was such a matchless Christ as He that did hang upon the cross. There we beheld all His beauties in perfection, all His attributes developed, all His love drawn out, all His character expressed. Beloved, the wounds of Jesus are far more fair in our eyes than all the splendour and pomp of kings. The thorny crown is more than an imperial diadem. It is true that He bears not now the sceptre of reed, but there was a glory in it that never flashed from sceptre of gold. Jesus

232

wears the appearance of a slain Lamb as His court dress in which He wooed our souls, and redeemed them by His complete atonement. Nor are these only the ornaments of Christ: they are the *trophies* of His love and of His victory. He has divided the spoil with the strong. He has redeemed for Himself a great multitude whom no man can number, and these scars are the memorials of the fight. Ah! if Christ thus loves to retain the thought of His sufferings for His people, *how precious should his wounds be to us*!

"Behold how every wound of His
A precious balm distils,
Which heals the scars that sin had made,
And cures all mortal ills.
"Those wounds are mouths
that preach His grace;
The ensigns of His love;
The seals of our expected bliss
In paradise above."

The resurrection is the ultimate testimony of the approval of the Father on the conduct of the Son. Among the multiple references that declare the involvement of GOD the Father in the resurrection of the lord Jesus are fifteen times when it is directly reported that God raised His Son. [7]

The Father raised Him and exalted Him.

Philippians 2:9 Wherefore God also hath highly exalted him, and given him a name which is above every name: 10 That at the name of Jesus every knee should bow, of *things* in heaven, and *things* in earth, and *things* under the earth; 11 And *that* every tongue should confess that Jesus Christ *is* Lord, to the glory of God the Father.

Ephesians 1:20 Which he wrought in Christ, when he raised him from the dead, and set *him* at his own right hand in the heavenly *places*, 21 Far above all principality, and power, and might, and dominion, and every name that is named, not only in this world, but also in that which is to come: 22 And hath put all *things* under his feet, and gave him *to be* the head over all *things* to the church, 23 Which is his body, the fulness of him that filleth all in all.

The LORD Jesus would seem to reference His submission and obedience as He spoke the letter to the church of the Laodiceans.

Revelation 3:21 To him that overcometh will I grant to sit with me in my throne, even as I also overcame, and am set down with my Father in his throne.

---

[1] How strange even to have to use these terms in describing the omnipotent, omniscience, eternal Son of GOD during His Incarnation. The subject should never come up!

[2] Philippians 2:5 Let this mind be in you, which was also in Christ Jesus: 6 Who, being in the form of God, thought it not robbery to be equal with God: 7 But made himself of no reputation, and took upon him the form of a servant, and was made in the likeness of men: 8 And being found in fashion as a man, he humbled himself, and became obedient unto death, even the death of the cross.

[3] John 10:30

[4] Acts 2:24 Whom God hath raised up, having loosed the pains of death: because it was not possible that he should be holden of it. ... 2:32 This Jesus hath God raised up, whereof we all are witnesses. ... 3:15 And killed the Prince of life, whom God hath raised from the dead; whereof we are witnesses. ... 3:26 Unto you first God, having raised up his Son Jesus, sent him to bless you, in turning away every one of you from his iniquities. ... 4:10 Be it known unto you all, and to all the people of Israel, that by the name of Jesus Christ of Nazareth, whom ye crucified, whom God raised from the dead, even by him doth this man stand here before you whole. ... 5:30 The God of our fathers raised up Jesus, whom ye slew and hanged on a tree. ... 10:40 Him God raised up the third day, and shewed him openly; ... 13:23 Of this man's seed hath God according to his promise raised unto Israel a Saviour, Jesus: ... 13:30 But God raised him from the dead: ... 13:33 God hath fulfilled the same unto us their children, in that he hath raised up Jesus again; as it is also written in the second psalm, Thou art my Son, this day have I begotten thee. ... 13:37 But he, whom God raised again, saw no corruption.

Romans 8:11 But if the Spirit of him that raised up Jesus from the dead dwell in you, he that raised up Christ from the dead shall also quicken your mortal bodies by his Spirit that dwelleth in you. ... 10:9 That if thou shalt confess with thy mouth the Lord Jesus, and shalt believe in thine heart that God hath raised him from the dead, thou shalt be saved.

1 Corinthians 6:14 And God hath both raised up the Lord, and will also raise up us by his own power. ... 15:15 Yea, and we are found false witnesses of God; because we have testified of God that he raised up Christ: whom he raised not up, if so be that the dead rise not.

Galatians 1:1 Paul, an apostle, (not of men, neither by man, but by Jesus Christ, and God the Father, who raised him from the dead;)

Colossians 2:12 Buried with him in baptism, wherein also ye are risen with him through the faith of the operation of God, who hath raised him from the dead.

1 Peter 1:21 Who by him do believe in God, that raised him up from the dead, and gave him glory; that your faith and hope might be in God.

5 Hebrews 9:11 But Christ being come an high priest of good things to come, by a greater and more perfect tabernacle, not made with hands, that is to say, not of this building; 12 Neither by the blood of goats and calves, but by his own blood he entered in once into the holy place, having obtained eternal redemption *for us.*

6 *SwordSearcher: Spurgeon's Morning and Evening Devotional.* Revelation 5:6 for April 23.

7 Acts 2:24 Whom God hath raised up, having loosed the pains of death: because it was not possible that he should be holden of it.

Acts 2:32 This Jesus hath God raised up, whereof we all are witnesses.

Acts 3:15 And killed the Prince of life, whom God hath raised from the dead; whereof we are witnesses.

Acts 3:26 Unto you first God, having raised up his Son Jesus, sent him to bless you, in turning away every one of you from his iniquities.

Acts 4:10 Be it known unto you all, and to all the people of Israel, that by the name of Jesus Christ of Nazareth, whom ye crucified, whom God raised from the dead, *even* by him doth this man stand here before you whole.

Acts 5:30 The God of our fathers raised up Jesus, whom ye slew and hanged on a tree.

Acts 10:40 Him God raised up the third day, and shewed him openly;

Acts 13:30 But God raised him from the dead:

Acts 13:33 God hath fulfilled the same unto us their children, in that he hath raised up Jesus again; as it is also written in the second psalm, Thou art my Son, this day have I begotten thee.

Acts 13:37 But he, whom God raised again, saw no corruption.

Romans 10:9 That if thou shalt confess with thy mouth the Lord Jesus, and shalt believe in thine heart that God hath raised him from the dead, thou shalt be saved.

1 Corinthians 6:14 And God hath both raised up the Lord, and will also raise up us by his own power.

Galatians 1:1 Paul, an apostle, (not of men, neither by man, but by Jesus Christ, and God the Father, who raised him from the dead;)

Colossians 2:12 Buried with him in baptism, wherein also ye are risen with *him* through the faith of the operation of God, who hath raised him from the dead.

1 Peter 1:21 Who by him do believe in God, that raised him up from the dead, and gave him glory; that your faith and hope might be in God.

CHAPTER 15

CONTEXT OF THE TRINITY

GOD the Father is not the vengeful GOD of justice and judgment while GOD the Son is the GOD of love and mercy. The LORD Jesus is not protecting us from the wrath of the Father as He intercedes for us now nor did He go to the cross in opposition to the Father then. The LORD Jesus endured the cross, not because He was forsaken by the Father, but because of the joy of His love for us.

It is an attack upon the TRINITY to suggest a breach between the Father and the Son. Not all of those proposing that such a rupture or breach of fellowship existed between the Father and the Son understand the effect of that which they teach. Perhaps those individuals have never been exposed to any other view. Perhaps they have never thought through what they think that they believe.

The following statements are typical of those declarations that are used to advocate this concept of utter separation.

It is said that Jesus "was made to be sin"; therefore, the Father had to turn His back, because He cannot look upon sin.

It is said when Jesus was on the cross, the Father poured His wrath upon Him.

It is said that the Father hid His face from the Son and abandoned Him to die the sinner's death.

It is said that sin separated the Son from the Father and the Father had to reject Him and had to refuse to deliver Him from the cross.

It is said that the eternal communion between the Father and the Son was broken during the darkness that day as the Father separated Himself from the Son.

I have heard all of those and other similar statements made in sermons by good men. I have no question of their sincerity or of their love for the LORD. I do not impugn their heart. I do believe that they are wrong.

Sadly, sometimes, well-intentioned sermonic illustrations have become doctrine. Preachers have often said something like the following in an attempt to portray the truth of the imputation of the righteousness of Christ to the believer:

You are standing before the GOD of Heaven and the books are opened and your sins are all listed. GOD is ready to pronounce judgment and send you into the eternity in hell that you so richly deserve; but Jesus stands and says, "Put that person's sins on my account. I shed My blood and paid the price of those sins." GOD then must say, "You are forgiven. You may enter Heaven."

The details of the illustrations will vary from sermon to sermon, but the general theme is certainly there: "the Father would send the soul to hell if the Son did not intervene." The idea conveyed is that "the only way that GOD can love us is because Jesus died for us."

A pause to consider the facts represented in the well-intended illustration quickly reveals how far from biblical doctrine the illustration actually is.

1. No believer ever stands before GOD while the books are opened and his sins are rehearsed and he is condemned.
   a. The picture presented is that of the Great White Throne when only the unsaved are present before the Throne for judgment.
   b. At the Judgment Seat of Christ, Christians are not judged out of the Books for salvation. The issue is that of receiving rewards or of the loss of rewards.
2. Salvation is determined before one steps into eternity.
3. No believer is ever in danger of being sent to hell, having passed from death unto life. [1]
4. Salvation is the new birth, not an intervention after judgment.

The truth that the LORD Jesus did pay the debt of our sins is presented in this illustration, but the reality is obscured by the illustration.

Sadly, sermonic illustrations are often more remembered than the Biblical truth. At the very best, illustrations are only human attempts to demonstrate Biblical truth. The danger is that they are considered *to be* Biblical truth so that illustrations too often become doctrine.

A passage that has been misunderstood—perhaps by the illustrations used to demonstrate it—is 2 Corinthians 5:21 For he hath made him *to be* sin for us, who knew no sin; that we might be made the righteousness of God in him.

The verse does not suggest or require a constitutional change in the LORD Jesus; that is, He was not changed from holy in nature to sin in nature.

1. He did not become a sinner when He was on the cross.
2. He did not become sin in substance, composition, character, or nature while He was on the cross.

The Son of GOD is never less than GOD while He is on that cross; were He ever to become less than GOD, He would not be GOD. That ought to be so obvious that the statement brings a smile of condescension for having written it. However, that is precisely what is being conveyed by this concept of Christ being made to become sin.

The Son of GOD was not changed. GOD is unchangeable; the theological term is immutable.

Malachi 3:6 For I am the LORD, I change not; therefore ye sons of Jacob are not consumed.

James 1:17 Every good gift and every perfect gift is from above, and cometh down from the Father of lights, with whom is no variableness, neither shadow of turning.

Psalm 102:24 I said, O my God, take me not away in the midst of my days: thy years are throughout all generations. 25 Of old hast thou laid the foundation of the earth: and the heavens are the work of thy hands. 26 They shall perish, but thou shalt endure: yea, all of them shall wax old like a garment; as a vesture shalt thou change them, and they shall be changed: 27 But thou art the same, and thy years shall have no end.

Hebrews 1:10 And, Thou, Lord, in the beginning hast laid the foundation of the earth; and

the heavens are the works of thine hands: 11
They shall perish; but thou remainest; and
they all shall wax old as doth a garment; 12
And as a vesture shalt thou fold them up, and
they shall be changed: but thou art the same,
and thy years shall not fail.

Hebrews 13:8 Jesus Christ the same yesterday, and to day, and for ever.

His perfection is eternal; His essence is unal-
terable; His sameness is perpetual. GOD is perfection and nothing is added or removed from perfection without destroying perfection. Of the LORD
Jesus it is declared, "For it pleased the Father
that in him should all fulness dwell; ... For in him
dwelleth all the fulness of the Godhead bodily."[2]

There is no possibility that even for a instant
that the LORD Jesus was not fully GOD. The
LORD Jesus did not change while He was on the
cross. During the hours of darkness, He did not
become *at any time* some entity other than "God
manifest in the flesh,"[3] "who is holy, harmless,
undefiled, separate from sinners, and made
higher than the heavens."[4]

The apostle is referencing the prophet Isaiah's
Messianic prophecies of chapter Fifty-three. The
language is unmistakable: the LORD Jesus was
made to be our sin offering in fulfillment of the
Old Testament types.

1 Who hath believed our report? and to whom
is the arm of the LORD revealed? 2 For he
shall grow up before him as a tender plant,
and as a root out of a dry ground: he hath no
form nor comeliness; and when we shall see
him, there is no beauty that we should desire
him. 3 He is despised and rejected of men; a
man of sorrows, and acquainted with grief:
and we hid as it were our faces from him; he
was despised, and we esteemed him not. 4
Surely he hath borne our griefs, and carried
our sorrows: yet we did esteem him stricken,

smitten of God, and afflicted. 5 But he was wounded for our transgressions, he was bruised for our iniquities: the chastisement of our peace was upon him; and with his stripes we are healed. 6 All we like sheep have gone astray; we have turned every one to his own way; and the LORD hath laid on him the iniquity of us all. 7 He was oppressed, and he was afflicted, yet he opened not his mouth: he is brought as a lamb to the slaughter, and as a sheep before her shearers is dumb, so he openeth not his mouth. 8 He was taken from prison and from judgment: and who shall declare his generation? for he was cut off out of the land of the living: for the transgression of my people was he stricken. 9 And he made his grave with the wicked, and with the rich in his death; because he had done no violence, neither was any deceit in his mouth. 10 Yet it pleased the LORD to bruise him; he hath put him to grief: when **thou shalt make his soul an offering for sin**, he shall see *his* seed, he shall prolong *his* days, and the pleasure of the LORD shall prosper in his hand. 11 He shall see of the travail of his soul, *and* shall be satisfied: by his knowledge shall my righteous servant justify many; for **he shall bear their iniquities**. 12 Therefore will I divide him *a portion* with the great, and he shall divide the spoil with the strong; because he hath poured out his soul unto death: and **he was numbered with the transgressors**; and **he bare the sin of many, and made intercession for the transgressors**.

The LORD Jesus became our sin offering; our sin was imputed to Him that His righteousness might be imputed to us. He became our Passover;[5] yet He did not become a literal Passover lamb. He is the Lamb of GOD, but He did not change into a lamb.

No lamb in any sacrifice in the Old Testament was changed into sin, but every lamb was made to be sin for the sacrifice offering. Sin was imputed to the lamb and the lamb died for the atonement of the imputed sin and not for its own sin or as becoming sin.

In this passage from Leviticus chapter 4, the words for sin and sin offering are either the same words or derivates of the same word. The identification of the one with the other is inescapable and yet each remains distinct.

> 3 If the priest that is anointed do sin according to the sin of the people; then let him bring for his sin, which he hath sinned, a young bullock without blemish unto the LORD for a sin offering. ... 27 And if any one of the common people sin through ignorance, while he doeth somewhat against any of the commandments of the LORD concerning things which ought not to be done, and be guilty; 28 Or if his sin, which he hath sinned, come to his knowledge: then he shall bring his offering, a kid of the goats, a female without blemish, for his sin which he hath sinned. 29 And he shall lay his hand upon the head of the sin offering, and slay the sin offering in the place of the burnt offering. 30 And the priest shall take of the blood thereof with his finger, and put it upon the horns of the altar of burnt offering, and shall pour out all the blood thereof at the bottom of the altar. 31 And he shall take away all the fat thereof, as the fat is taken away from off the sacrifice of peace offerings; and the priest shall burn it upon the altar for a sweet savour unto the LORD; and the priest shall make an atonement for him, and it shall be forgiven him. 32 And if he bring a lamb for a sin offering, he shall bring it a female without blemish. 33 And he shall lay his hand upon the head of the sin offering, and slay it for a sin offering in the place where they kill the burnt offering. 34 And the priest shall take of the blood of the sin offering with his finger, and put it upon the horns of the altar of burnt offering, and shall pour out all the blood thereof at the bottom of the altar: 35 And he shall take away all the fat thereof, as the fat of the

lamb is taken away from the sacrifice of the peace offerings; and the priest shall burn them upon the altar, according to the offerings made by fire unto the LORD: and the priest shall make an atonement for his sin that he hath committed, and it shall be forgiven him.

This precise truth is conveyed in the following verses:

Ephesians 5:2 And walk in love, as Christ also hath loved us, and hath given himself for us an offering and a sacrifice to God for a sweetsmelling savour.

Galatians 1:4 Who gave himself for our sins, that he might deliver us from this present evil world, according to the will of God and our Father:

Hebrews 10:10-11 By the which will we are sanctified through the offering of the body of Jesus Christ once *for all.* 11 And every priest standeth daily ministering and offering oftentimes the same sacrifices, which can never take away sins:

This returns us to those powerful words: My God, my God, why hast thou forsaken me? *why art thou so* far from helping me, *and from* the words of my roaring?

Those words are contextually united with His death. His death is described as being forsaken by GOD. In the simplest of truths, the LORD Jesus died. The Father let the Son die. That is the forsaking, the abandoning.

A somewhat similar relationship is conveyed in a passage from the Book of Hebrews:

Hebrews 11:32-40 And what shall I more say? for the time would fail me to tell of Gedeon, and *of* Barak, and *of* Samson, and *of* Jephthae; *of* David also, and Samuel, and *of* the prophets: 33 Who through faith subdued kingdoms, wrought righteousness, obtained promises, stopped the mouths of lions, 34

Quenched the violence of fire, escaped the edge of the sword, out of weakness were made strong, waxed valiant in fight, turned to flight the armies of the aliens. 35 Women received their dead raised to life again: and others were tortured, not accepting deliverance; that they might obtain a better resurrection: 36 And others had trial of *cruel* mockings and scourgings, yea, moreover of bonds and imprisonment: 37 They were stoned, they were sawn asunder, were tempted, were slain with the sword: they wandered about in sheepskins and goatskins; being destitute, afflicted, tormented; 38 (Of whom the world was not worthy:) they wandered in deserts, and *in* mountains, and *in* dens and caves of the earth. 39 And these all, having obtained a good report through faith, received not the promise: 40 God having provided some better thing for us, that they without us should not be made perfect.

Notice the colon at the end of verse 35 and consider it as the introduction for verse 36. Until verse 36, all those mentioned had experienced great events and marvelous, even supernatural, deliverances; however, verse 36 introduces those who did not receive deliverance, but who were, in a real and observable sense, forsaken by GOD— they were allowed to suffer and even to die.

These who are identified as *others* were no less men and women of faith. They could have been spared the trials, sufferings, and death; but they were allowed to suffer and to die. From all appearances and from the apparent reality of the facts, they were forsaken by GOD.

We know that GOD did not turn His back upon them, He did not despise them, and He did not curse them. The verses that follow this passage make this abundantly clear: "these all received a good report";[6] and they will receive the "better resurrection." They were not forsaken *even though* it might appear that they were.

This appearance of being forsaken is precisely the picture that day as the LORD Jesus is forsaken on the cross. He is not abandoned; He is allowed to die. The Son laid down His life; the Father agreed to permit Him to die. There is no disunity, no disharmony, and no disagreement between the Father and the Son. I may go farther and assert that there was perfect unity of the TRINITY in the death of the LORD Jesus.

He laid down His Own life.

John 10:15 As the Father knoweth me, even so know I the Father: and I lay down my life for the sheep. ... 17 Therefore doth my Father love me, because I lay down my life, that I might take it again.

Hebrews 10:12 But this man, after he had offered one sacrifice for sins for ever, sat down on the right hand of God;

He was offered through the Holy Spirit.

Hebrews 9:14 How much more shall the blood of Christ, who through the eternal Spirit offered himself without spot to God, purge your conscience from dead works to serve the living God?

1 Peter 3:18 For Christ also hath once suffered for sins, the just for the unjust, that he might bring us to God, being put to death in the flesh, but quickened by the Spirit ...

He was offered by the Father.

Romans 8:3 For what the law could not do, in that it was weak through the flesh, God sending his own Son in the likeness of sinful flesh, and for sin, condemned sin in the flesh: ... 32 He that spared not his own Son, but delivered him up for us all, how shall he not with him also freely give us all things?

Remember the sacrifice of the lambs in the Old Testament. When the lamb was sacrificed, did GOD turn His back on the sacrifice? The exact opposite took place; GOD saw the sacrifice and accepted the offering that was presented to make an atonement.

> Leviticus 4:27 And if any one of the common people **sin** through ignorance, while he doeth *somewhat against* any of the commandments of the LORD *concerning things* which ought not to be done, and be guilty; 28 Or if his **sin, which he hath sinned**, come to his knowledge: then he shall bring his offering, a kid of the goats, a female without blemish, for his sin **which he hath sinned**. 29 And he shall lay his hand upon the head of **the sin offering**, and slay **the sin offering** in the place of the burnt offering. 30 And the priest shall take of the blood thereof with his finger, and put *it* upon the horns of the altar of burnt offering, and shall pour out all the blood thereof at the bottom of the altar. 31 And he shall take away all the fat thereof, as the fat is taken away from off the sacrifice of peace offerings; **and the priest shall burn *it* upon the altar for a sweet savour unto the LORD; and the priest shall make an atonement for him, and it shall be forgiven him.**

The offering of the LORD Jesus was *a sweet savour* unto the LORD. The LORD was pleased—this was not a sadistic pleasure taken in the unspeakable sufferings endured, but it was the pleasure of satisfaction, agreement, approval, and fulfillment.

> Isaiah 53:10 Yet it pleased the LORD to bruise him; he hath put him to grief: when thou shalt make his soul an offering for sin [Margin: his soul shall make an offering], he shall see his seed, he shall prolong his days, and the pleasure of the LORD shall prosper in his hand.

Even as the Father was pleased, the LORD Jesus endured the cross for the joy set before Him.

> Hebrews 12:1 Wherefore seeing we also are compassed about with so great a cloud of witnesses, let us lay aside every weight, and the sin which doth so easily beset us, and let us run with patience the race that is set before us, 2 Looking unto Jesus the author and finisher of our faith; **who for the joy that was set before him endured the cross**, despising the shame, and is set down at the right hand of the throne of God. 3 For consider him that endured such contradiction of sinners against himself, lest ye be wearied and faint in your minds. 4 Ye have not yet resisted unto blood, striving against sin.

This joy is also found in the prophetic words of the Psalmist that are applied to the LORD Jesus by the apostle Peter.

> Psalm 16:9 **Therefore my heart is glad, and my glory rejoiceth: my flesh also shall rest in hope.** 10 For thou wilt not leave my soul in hell; neither wilt thou suffer thine Holy One to see corruption. 11 Thou wilt shew me the path of life: in thy presence *is* fulness of joy; at thy right hand *there are* pleasures for evermore.

It is impossible to read the multiple prophecies of the suffering Servant and believe that the death of the LORD Jesus on the cross was *an unexpected turn of events that just happened to catch unawares* the Son of GOD. GOD the Son was not blindsided by GOD the Father with the sudden obscuring of the light of the sun and an unexpected oppression of that darkness.

Though I cannot explain the fullness of the truth, the Scriptures abundantly and emphatically make it a matter of record that the LORD Jesus was headed to the cross of Calvary from before the foundation of the world.

Ephesians 1:4 According as he hath chosen us in him before the foundation of the world, that we should be holy and without blame before him in love:

Hebrews 4:3 For we which have believed do enter into rest, as he said, As I have sworn in my wrath, if they shall enter into my rest: although the works were finished from the foundation of the world.

Hebrews 9:26 For then must he often have suffered since the foundation of the world: but now once in the end of the world hath he appeared to put away sin by the sacrifice of himself.

1 Peter 1:20 Who verily was foreordained before the foundation of the world, but was manifest in these last times for you,

Revelation 13:8 And all that dwell upon the earth shall worship him, whose names are not written in the book of life of the Lamb slain from the foundation of the world.

The evening before He went to the cross, the Son of GOD affirmed His confidence in the love of His Father for Him.

John 17:24 Father, I will that they also, whom thou hast given me, be with me where I am; that they may behold my glory, which thou hast given me: for thou lovedst me before the foundation of the world.

There is no Biblical evidence of a breach among the TRINITY at any time or among any circumstances. Contrariwise, the Scriptures preclude any possibility of such a division.

Though the textual critics deny inspiration to the verse, the testimony of 1 John 5:7 is a strong witness to the eternal unity of the TRINITY.[7]

1 John 5:7 For there are three that bear record in heaven, the Father, the Word, and the Holy Ghost: and these three are one.

The use of the word one declares the unity of the Father, the Son, and the Holy Ghost. No discordance could have ever existed among the GODHEAD concerning the crucifixion.

The divine perfection of the GODHEAD does not permit disharmony or disunity. For a difference to exist would destroy that perfection. Such is not a possibility.

Degrees of perfection do not exist. Nothing could be added to perfection; perfection is complete. Nothing could be removed from perfection; the result would be less than perfection.

Had there ever been one instance with any disharmony, disagreement, displeasure, disconnection, disapproval, disruption, or distance and there would have brought disunity. The possibility of disunity does not exist.

No discordance could have ever existed among the GODHEAD concerning the crucifixion.

---

[1] John 5:24 Verily, verily, I say unto you, He that heareth my word, and believeth on him that sent me, hath everlasting life, and shall not come into condemnation; but is passed from death unto life.

John 5:24 Verily, verily, I say unto you, He that heareth my word, and believeth on him that sent me, hath everlasting life, and shall not come into condemnation; but is passed from death unto life.

[2] Colossians 1:19 and 2:19

[3] 1 Timothy 3:16 And without controversy great is the mystery of godliness: God was manifest in the flesh, justified in the Spirit, seen of angels, preached unto the Gentiles, believed on in the world, received up into glory.

[4] Hebrews 7:26 For such an high priest became us, *who is* holy, harmless, undefiled, separate from sinners, and made higher than the heavens;

[5] 1 Corinthians 5:7 Purge out therefore the old leaven, that ye may be a new lump, as ye are unleavened. For even Christ our passover is sacrificed for us:

[6] Matthew 25:21 His lord said unto him, Well done, *thou* good and faithful servant: thou hast been faithful over a few things, I will make thee ruler over many things: enter thou into the joy of thy lord. ... 23 His lord said unto him, Well done, good and faithful servant; thou hast been faithful over a few things, I will make thee ruler over many things: enter thou into the joy of thy lord.

Luke 19:17 And he said unto him, Well, thou good servant: because thou hast been faithful in a very little, have thou authority over ten cities.

[7] I deny authority to the textual critics to determine the word of GOD and I give their rantings no credibility.

CHAPTER 16
CONTEXT OF ADAM

Who is the one man that has the most guilt of all the sinners that have ever lived or that will ever live? I understand that the apostle Paul said that he was the chief of sinners—this is recorded as part of the inspired word of GOD, so I accept that statement as accurate. I also take note that Paul is the only person recorded as "touching the righteousness which is in the law, blameless."[1]

Paul is the chief of sinners; that is not the answer to my question—who has the greatest *guilt*?

It seems to me that the sinner with the greatest of guilt would be Adam; therefore, would he not be described as the greatest sinner? The indictment brought against Adam by Scripture is heavy and condemning. It begins with the charge that Adam was not deceived, he knew what he was doing.

1 Timothy 2:14 Adam was not deceived ...

The indictment continues by charging that Adam covered his transgressions (plural) and hid his iniquity.

> Job 31:33 If I covered my transgressions as Adam, by hiding mine iniquity in my bosom:

The next charge is that by his sin, Adam incurred death for all.

> 1 Corinthians 15:22 ... in Adam all die ...
>
> Romans 5:12 Wherefore, as by one man sin entered into the world, and death by sin; and so death passed upon all men, for that all have sinned:... 15 But not as the offence, so also is the free gift. For if through the offence of one many be dead, much more the grace of God, and the gift by grace, which is by one man, Jesus Christ, hath abounded unto many. ... 17 For if by one man's offence death reigned by one; much more they which receive abundance of grace and of the gift of righteousness shall reign in life by one, Jesus Christ.) ... 5:19 For as by one man's disobedience many were made sinners, so by the obedience of one shall many be made righteous.

Adam did all of this deliberately and knowingly; Scripture is clear that he was not deceived. Adam knew that he was violating the direct commandment of the LORD God and did so without hesitation. While some individuals have tried to find a way to give a noble motivation to Adam, such as forcing GOD to save Eve,[2] Scripture does not allow that interpretation. No good motive can be ascribed to deliberate sin.

Adam had transgressions—not one simple violation, but multiple acts of *going beyond boundaries*[3] that His Creator and GOD had established. Adam covered his sin and practiced iniquity, spiritual counterfeiting.[4]

256

Every the consequence of sin that have plagues the human race for these 6000 years since the Fall in the Garden of Eden flows directly from Adam and his willful sin. Surely, those terrible results are apparent without the necessity of a lengthy vivid description. All of the human and animal suffering and all of the wrongs of the past centuries are the direct result of the sin of Adam.

When Adam sinned, exactly how did GOD treat him? Did GOD forsake him? Did He abandon Him? Did He turn His back to him? You know that GOD did not do those things. While Adam was driven from the Garden and while GOD placed the cherubim and the flaming sword at the entrance of the Garden of Eden to prevent Adam from returning to the Tree of Life, GOD did not forsake Adam or Eve.

The story of how GOD dealt with Adam is told in a simple way by the woman that Joab employed to use as a ploy to reunite Absalom with his father David as related in 2 Samuel, chapter 14. Give special attention to verse 14.

> 4 And when the woman of Tekoah spake to the king, she fell on her face to the ground, and did obeisance, and said, Help, O king. 5 And the king said unto her, What aileth thee? And she answered, I am indeed a widow woman, and mine husband is dead. 6 And thy handmaid had two sons, and they two strove together in the field, and there was none to part them, but the one smote the other, and slew him. 7 And, behold, the whole family is risen against thine handmaid, and they said, Deliver him that smote his brother, that we may kill him, for the life of his brother whom he slew; and we will destroy the heir also: and so they shall quench my coal which is left, and shall not leave to my husband neither name nor remainder upon the earth. 8 And

the king said unto the woman, Go to thine house, and I will give charge concerning thee. 9 And the woman of Tekoah said unto the king, My lord, O king, the iniquity be on me, and on my father's house: and the king and his throne be guiltless. 10 And the king said, Whosoever saith ought unto thee, bring him to me, and he shall not touch thee any more. 11 Then said she, I pray thee, let the king remember the LORD thy God, that thou wouldest not suffer the revengers of blood to destroy any more, lest they destroy my son. And he said, As the LORD liveth, there shall not one hair of thy son fall to the earth. 12 Then the woman said, Let thine handmaid, I pray thee, speak one word unto my lord the king. And he said, Say on. 13 And the woman said, Wherefore then hast thou thought such a thing against the people of God? for the king doth speak this thing as one which is faulty, in that the king doth not fetch home again his banished. 14 For we must needs die, and are as water spilt on the ground, which cannot be gathered up again; neither doth God respect any person: yet doth he devise means, that his banished be not expelled from him.

Adam was **banished** from the garden, but he was not **expelled** from GOD. There was a means devised to "fetch him home again." GOD did not stop the consequences of his sin, but He provided Adam and Eve "coats of skins and clothed them."[5] A lamb or lambs were slain to provide those skins; a sacrifice was made. Along with that provision for atonement and temporal clothing, the LORD God gave the promise that culminated in the death on the cross that day at Calvary.[6]

As we consider our question, "Would GOD forsake Jesus of Nazareth the Son of Adam," let us be reminded that GOD did not abandon Adam. GOD did not turn His back upon the first man, Adam. GOD did not abandon that first man.

The Scriptures state that Adam was in some way "a figure of him that was to come"—the LORD Jesus.

> 1 Corinthians 15:22 For as in Adam all die, even so in Christ shall all be made alive.

> 1 Corinthians 15:45 And so it is written, The first man Adam was made a living soul; the last Adam *was made* a quickening spirit. ... 46 Howbeit that *was* not first which is spiritual, but that which is natural; and afterward that which is spiritual. 47 The first man *is* of the earth, earthy: the second man *is* the Lord from heaven.

> Romans 5:14 Nevertheless death reigned from Adam to Moses, even over them that had not sinned after the similitude of Adam's transgression, who is the figure of him that was to come.

Jesus of Nazareth is (1) the Second Man—the head of the new creation, (2) the Last Adam—there will be no more Adams, and (3) the One of Whom Adam was a figure as described in Romans 5:14.

Adam was a figure or type in that as the sin of Adam came upon all that are born of the flesh[7] so the righteousness of Christ comes upon all that are born of the Spirit.

> Romans 5:12 Wherefore, as by one man sin entered into the world, and death by sin; and so death passed upon all men, for that all have sinned: 13 (For until the law sin was in the world: but sin is not imputed when there is no law. 14 Nevertheless death reigned from Adam to Moses, even over them that had not sinned after the similitude of Adam's transgression, who is the figure of him that was to come. 15 But not as the offence, so also *is* the free gift. For if through the offence of one many be dead, much more the grace of God, and the gift by grace, *which is* by one man,

259

Jesus Christ, hath abounded unto many. 16 And not as *it was* by one that sinned, *so is* the gift: for the judgment *was* by one to condemnation, but the free gift *is* of many offences unto justification. 17 For if by one man's offence death reigned by one; much more they which receive abundance of grace and of the gift of righteousness shall reign in life by one, Jesus Christ.) 18 Therefore as by the offence of one *judgment came* upon all men to condemnation; even so by the righteousness of one *the free gift came* upon all men unto justification of life. 19 For as by one man's disobedience many were made sinners, so by the obedience of one shall many be made righteous. 20 Moreover the law entered, that the offence might abound. But where sin abounded, grace did much more abound: 21 That as sin hath reigned unto death, even so might grace reign through righteousness unto eternal life by Jesus Christ our Lord.

The first Adam is also a figure in that as he was not forsaken by GOD, even so the Father certainly did not forsake the Last Adam, the Son of man and the Son of GOD: GOD manifest in the flesh.

[1] Philippians 3:4 Though I might also have confidence in the flesh. If any other man thinketh that he hath whereof he might trust in the flesh, I more: 5 Circumcised the eighth day, of the stock of Israel, *of* the tribe of Benjamin, an Hebrew of the Hebrews; as touching the law, a Pharisee; 6 Concerning zeal, persecuting the church; touching the righteousness which is in the law, blameless.

[2] The reasoning seems to be that Adam knew GOD had a purpose in having created him. Since Eve had violated the prohibition, she would have to die. Because Adam loved Eve, Adam ate then determined to eat the fruit, thereby forcing GOD to do something to save him from the penalty and also to save Eve. This is certainly wisdom gleaned somewhere beyond Scripture and deserves to be cast aside as specious.

[3] Merriam-Webster 11th Collegiate Dictionary definition of transgression.

[4] See footnote 8, page 148 for why I define iniquity as a spiritual counterfeit.

[5] Genesis 4:21 And his brother's name *was* Jubal: he was the father of all such as handle the harp and organ.

[6] Genesis 3:15 And I will put enmity between thee and the woman, and between thy seed and her seed; it shall bruise thy head, and thou shalt bruise his heel.

[7] John 3:3 Jesus answered and said unto him, Verily, verily, I say unto thee, Except a man be born again, he cannot see the kingdom of God. 4 Nicodemus saith unto him, How can a man be born when he is old? can he enter the second time into his mother's womb, and be born? 5 Jesus answered, Verily, verily, I say unto thee, Except a man be born of water and *of* the Spirit, he cannot enter into the kingdom of God. 6 That which is born of the flesh is flesh; and that which is born of the Spirit is spirit.

CHAPTER 17

CONTEXT OF THE ATONEMENT

It is often presented that the words "My God, my God, why hast thou forsaken me?" were spoken only *after* the atonement was accomplished in those dreadful three hours of darkness and that the lifting of the darkness with its restoration of light was only possible because the atonement had been made and the unity of the TRINITY could then be reestablished.

While the individual advancing this concept may or may not realize the ramifications of this proposal, *the entire concept seriously conflicts with Scripture's clarity.*

I would not desire to minimize the indescribable awfulness of the darkness that shrouded the earth[1] between the sixth and the ninth hours that day when the LORD Jesus was crucified. Those three hours were the segment of time of which it truly may be said that hell was on earth. Uncountable numbers of Adam's children have experienced a terrible awesome time and have labeled it as being *hell.* However, it is only during those three hours of darkness as the LORD Jesus was veiled from human view when He tasted

263

death for every man[2] that we might speak of *hell on earth*. The death that He tasted during those three hours was "the second death."[3]

However, it must be acknowledged that the LORD Jesus did not physically die during those three hours. Moreover, when He did die, He did not die from wounds sustained on the way to the cross, or from those wounds inflicted through the act of nailing Him to the cross, or from the loss of blood from the multiple lacerations of His flesh and His five wounds, or from infection, or from enduring the punishment for our sins. The death of Jesus of Nazareth, GOD Incarnate, **came only when He Himself gave permission for the spirit and the soul to depart from the body, which then died**.

> John 10:18 No man taketh it from me, but I lay it down of myself. I have power to lay it down, and I have power to take it again. This commandment have I received of my Father.
>
> Matthew 27:50 Jesus, when he had cried again with a loud voice, yielded up the ghost.
>
> Mark 15:37 And Jesus cried with a loud voice, and gave up the ghost. ... 39 And when the centurion, which stood over against him, saw that he so cried out, and gave up the ghost, he said, Truly this man was the Son of GOD.
>
> Luke 23:46 And when Jesus had cried with a loud voice, he said, Father, into thy hands I commend my spirit: and having said thus, he gave up the ghost.
>
> John 19:30 When Jesus therefore had received the vinegar, he said, It is finished: and he bowed his head, and gave up the ghost.

Physical death[4] is the separation of the soul and spirit from the body,[5] but it affects only the body. When we speak of His death, we are speaking of the death of the body, which was prepared for Him.[6] The physical death of the LORD Jesus is required for our atonement.[7] Until He died, He could not yet have **made** the atonement. Atonement must be made; for an atonement to be made there must be death.[8]

The English word *atonement* is found eighty-two times in Scripture. The single occurrence in the New Testament[9] "by whom we have now received the atonement" speaks of the believer having no part in the atonement except that of receiving the atonement. In one occurrence in the Old Testament, the word atonement is found in the descriptive phrase "beside the sin offering of atonement."[10] In the other eighty instances where the word *atonement* is found, the word is connected with the verb *to make*.

Atonement is **made**; having been made, atonement may then be **received.**

Having an understanding of the making of the atonement will help in our study. Though these chapters from the Book of Hebrews form a lengthy passage, they present the Holy Spirit given exposition of the atonement.

> Hebrews 7:1 For this Melchisedec, king of Salem, priest of the most high God, who met Abraham returning from the slaughter of the kings, and blessed him; 2 To whom also Abraham gave a tenth part of all; first being by interpretation King of righteousness, and after that also King of Salem, which is, King of peace; 3 Without father, without mother, without descent, having neither beginning of days, nor end of life; but made like unto the Son of GOD; abideth a priest continually. 4 Now consider how great this man was, unto whom even the patriarch Abraham gave the tenth of the spoils. 5 And verily they that are of the sons of Levi, who receive the office of the priesthood, have a commandment to take tithes of the people according to the law, that is, of their brethren, though they come out of

the loins of Abraham: 6 But he whose descent is not counted from them received tithes of Abraham, and blessed him that had the promises. 7 And without all contradiction the less is blessed of the better. 8 And here men that die receive tithes; but there he receiveth them, of whom it is witnessed that he liveth. 9 And as I may so say, Levi also, who receiveth tithes, payed tithes in Abraham. 10 For he was yet in the loins of his father, when Melchisedec met him. 11 If therefore perfection were by the Levitical priesthood, (for under it the people received the law,) what further need was there that another priest should rise after the order of Melchisedec, and not be called after the order of Aaron? 12 For the priesthood being changed, there is made of necessity a change also of the law. 13 For he of whom these things are spoken pertaineth to another tribe, of which no man gave attendance at the altar. 14 For it is evident that our Lord sprang out of Juda; of which tribe Moses spake nothing concerning priesthood. 15 And it is yet far more evident: for that after the similitude of Melchisedec there ariseth another priest, 16 Who is made, not after the law of a carnal commandment, but after the power of an endless life.

The Holy Spirit through the apostle Paul focuses on the LORD Jesus with two descriptive identifications. One is what He is not and the other is what He is.

(1) He is not from the priestly tribe, Levi, but from the tribe of Judah, and

(2) His priesthood is anchored to the power of an endless life.

17 For he testifieth, Thou art a priest for ever after the order of Melchisedec. 18 For there is verily a disannulling of the commandment going before for the weakness and unprofitableness thereof. 19 For the law made nothing

perfect, but **the bringing in of a better hope did**; by the which we draw nigh unto God. 20 And inasmuch as not without an oath he was made priest: 21 (For those priests were made without an oath; but this with an oath by him that said unto him, The Lord sware and will not repent, Thou art a priest for ever after the order of Melchisedec:) 22 **By so much was Jesus made a surety of a better testament**.

He was made a surety of "a better testament" through the Incarnation. Merriam-Webster gives us definitions of the English word *surety* that highlight this truth "a formal engagement (as a pledge) given for the fulfillment of an undertaking," "a basis of confidence or security," and "one who has become legally liable for the debt, default, or failure in duty of another." The Epistle of 1 John focuses on the propitiation as the purpose of the Incarnation:

8 He that loveth not knoweth not God; for God is love. 9 In this was manifested the love of God toward us, because that God sent his only begotten Son into the world, that we might live through him. 10 Herein is love, not that we loved God, but that he loved us, and sent his Son *to be* the propitiation for our sins.

Years ago, a friend in the ministry named Karl Gehrig, placed a strong emphasis on this word *propitiation*. He was burdened that the word was not used by preachers and was, therefore, not understood by the Christians in the pew. His stressing of that word made an indelible impression on me. The word propitiation is only found three times within the Scriptures. [11] However, the concept of propitiation is the very message of all of Scripture. Sadly, the word propitiation is no longer being used by the modern translations.

Romans 3:21 But now the righteousness of God without the law is manifested, being witnessed by the law and the prophets; 22 Even the righteousness of God *which is* by faith of Jesus Christ unto all and upon all them that believe: for there is no difference: 23 For all have sinned, and come short of the glory of God; 24 Being justified freely by his grace through the redemption that is in Christ Jesus: 25 Whom God hath set forth *to be* a **propitiation** through faith in his blood, to declare his righteousness for the remission of sins that are past, through the forbearance of God; 26 To declare, *I say*, at this time his righteousness: that he might be just, and the justifier of him which believeth in Jesus. 27 Where *is* boasting then? It is excluded. By what law? of works? Nay: but by the law of faith.

The word[12] translated for us as propitiation in verse 25 is also given to us as the compound word mercyseat in Hebrews chapter nine, verse 5. In the Old Testament, the words are separated and we find *mercy seat*. In the New Testament, the words are joined and we read *mercyseat.*[13]

3 And after the second veil, the tabernacle which is called the Holiest of all; 4 Which had the golden censer, and the ark of the covenant overlaid round about with gold, wherein *was* the golden pot that had manna, and Aaron's rod that budded, and the tables of the covenant; 5 And over it the cherubims of glory shadowing the **mercyseat;** of which we cannot now speak particularly.

That is the very picture that is involved in the word *propitiation*. The LORD Jesus is the our mercyseat where GOD will meet with us. There is no other meeting place between GOD and humanity except the Great White Throne.[14]

Exodus 25:17 And thou shalt make a **mercy seat** *of* pure gold: two cubits and a half *shall be* the length thereof, and a cubit and a half the breadth thereof. 18 And thou shalt make two cherubims *of* gold, *of* beaten work shalt thou make them, in the two ends of the **mer-**

cy seat. 19 And make one cherub on the one end, and the other cherub on the other end: *even* of the **mercy seat** shall ye make the cherubims on the two ends thereof. 20 And the cherubims shall stretch forth *their* wings on high, covering the **mercy seat** with their wings, and their faces *shall look* one to another; toward the **mercy seat** shall the faces of the cherubims be. 21 And thou shalt put the **mercy seat** above upon the ark; and in the ark thou shalt put the testimony that I shall give thee. 22 And **there I will meet with thee, and I will commune with thee** from above the **mercy seat**, from between the two cherubims which *are* upon the ark of the testimony, of all *things* which I will give thee in commandment unto the children of Israel.

The cross is where the LORD Jesus made the atonement to purchase our redemption. At His resurrection, He entered the within the veil and obtained eternal redemption "for us."

Hebrews 6:17 Wherein God, willing more abundantly to shew unto the heirs of promise the immutability of his counsel, confirmed *it* by an oath: 18 That by two immutable things, in which *it was* impossible for God to lie, we might have a strong consolation, who have fled for refuge to lay hold upon the hope set before us: 19 Which *hope* we have as an anchor of the soul, both sure and stedfast, and which entereth into that **within the veil; 20 Whither the forerunner is for us entered,** *even* **Jesus,** made an high priest for ever after the order of Melchisedec.

Hebrews 9:11 But Christ being come an high priest of good things to come, by a greater and more perfect tabernacle, not made with hands, that is to say, not of this building; 12 Neither by the blood of goats and calves, but **by his own blood he entered in once into the holy place, having obtained eternal redemption** *for us.*

I view these verses as intended to be understood as they are written. I do not believe that these passages are allegorical.

> Hebrews 9:24 For Christ is not entered into the holy places made with hands, *which are* the figures of the true but into heaven itself, now to appear in the presence of God for us: 25 Nor yet that he should offer himself often, as the high priest entereth into the holy place every year with blood of others; 26 For then must he often have suffered since the foundation of the world: but now once in the end of the world hath he appeared to put away sin by the sacrifice of himself. 27 And as it is appointed unto men once to die, but after this the judgment: 28 So Christ was once offered to bear the sins of many; and unto them that look for him shall he appear the second time without sin unto salvation.

Our High Priest will continue to be our High Priest *ever*. There will never be a time when the LORD Jesus is not our High Priest. His High Priesthood is of paramount importance. However, too many believers have serious misconceptions regarding the High Priesthood of the LORD Jesus or they have no concept of that High Priesthood at all.

> Hebrews 7:23 And they truly were many priests, because they were not suffered to continue by reason of death: 24 But this man, because he continueth ever, hath an unchangeable priesthood. 25 Wherefore he is able also to save them to the uttermost that come unto God by him, seeing he ever liveth to make intercession for them.

The efficacy of the priesthood of the LORD Jesus is dependent (as it were) on His endless life (verse 16)—"because He continueth ever" ... "He ever liveth." The strong consistent emphasis on the continuation of the life of the LORD Jesus presented in the passage explaining the atonement is vital to our understanding of the making of the atonement.

> 26 **For such an high priest became us, who is holy, harmless, undefiled, separate from sinners, and made higher than the heavens**;

The LORD Jesus was "holy, harmless, undefiled separate from sinners." This, I think, is a reference to His uniqueness as the Son of GOD: (1) shown in His virgin birth, [15] and (2) shown in His sinlessness. [16]

> 27 **Who needeth not daily, as those high priests, to offer up sacrifice, first for his own sins, and then for the people's: for this he did once, when he offered up himself**.

The LORD Jesus "offered up Himself." While this comprehends the whole of the earthly sojourn of the LORD Jesus, the primary reference is to His actions as the Great High Priest. [17]

> 28 For the law maketh men high priests which have infirmity; but **the word of the oath, which was since the law, maketh the Son, who is consecrated for evermore.**

> Hebrews 8:1 Now of the things which we have spoken *this is* the sum: **We have such an high priest, who is set on the right hand of the throne of the Majesty in the heavens;**

We speak of the High Priestly prayer being in John chapter seventeen. That prayer is indeed a foreshadowing of His High Priestly work; however, the LORD Jesus did not enter His work as the Great High Priest until His resurrection. Notice in verse four that His priesthood has to do with Heaven and not earth.

> 2 A minister of the sanctuary, and of the true tabernacle, which the Lord pitched, and not man. 3 For every high priest is ordained to offer gifts and sacrifices: wherefore *it is* of ne-

271

cessity that this man have somewhat also to offer. 4 **For if he were on earth, he should not be a priest**, seeing that there are priests that offer gifts according to the law: 5 Who serve unto the example and shadow of heavenly things, as Moses was admonished of God when he was about to make the tabernacle: for, See, saith he, *that* thou make all things according to the pattern shewed to thee in the mount. 6 **But now hath he obtained a more excellent ministry, by how much also he is the mediator of a better covenant, which was established upon better promises**. 7 For if that first *covenant* had been faultless, then should no place have been sought for the second. 8 For finding fault with them, he saith, Behold, the days come, saith the Lord, when I will make a new covenant with the house of Israel and with the house of Judah: 9 Not according to the covenant that I made with their fathers in the day when I took them by the hand to lead them out of the land of Egypt; because they continued not in my covenant, and I regarded them not, saith the Lord. 10 For this *is* the covenant that I will make with the house of Israel after those days, saith the Lord; I will put my laws into their mind, and write them in their hearts: and I will be to them a God, and they shall be to me a people: 11 And they shall not teach every man his neighbour, and every man his brother, saying, Know the Lord: for all shall know me, from the least to the greatest. 12 **For I will be merciful to their unrighteousness, and their sins and their iniquities will I remember no more**. 13 In that he saith, A new *covenant*, he hath made the first old. Now that which decayeth and waxeth old *is* ready to vanish away.

Hebrews 9:1 Then verily the first *covenant* had also ordinances of divine service, and a worldly sanctuary. 2 For there was a tabernacle made; the first, wherein *was* the candlestick, and the table, and the shewbread; which is called the sanctuary. 3 And after the second veil, the tabernacle which is called the Holiest of all; 4 Which had the golden censer, and the ark of the covenant overlaid round about with gold, wherein *was* the golden pot that had manna, and Aaron's rod that budded, and the tables of the covenant; 5 And over it the cherubims of glory shadowing the mercyseat; of which we cannot now speak particularly. 6 Now when these things were thus ordained, the priests went always into the first tabernacle, accomplishing the service *of God*. 7 But into the second *went* the high priest alone once every year, not without blood, which he offered for himself, and *for* the errors of the people: 8 The Holy Ghost this signifying, that the way into the holiest of all was not yet made manifest, while as the first tabernacle was yet standing: 9 Which *was* a figure for the time then present, in which were offered both gifts and sacrifices, that could not make him that did the service perfect, as pertaining to the conscience; 10 *Which stood* only in meats and drinks, and divers washings, and carnal ordinances, imposed *on them* until the time of reformation. 11 **But Christ being come an high priest of good things to come, by a greater and more perfect tabernacle, not made with hands, that is to say, not of this building; 12 Neither by the blood of goats and calves, but by his own blood he entered in once into the holy place, having obtained eternal redemption *for us*.**

Having obtained redemption, which I understand as the pouring out of His soul, the shedding of His blood, in His death,[18] He then made the atonement. The text does not read that He entered the hours of darkness, but that He entered into *the holy place not made with hands*. He entered within *the holy place* to offer "His Own blood."

13 For if the blood of bulls and of goats, and the ashes of an heifer sprinkling the unclean, sanctifieth to the purifying of the flesh: 14 **How much more shall the blood of Christ, who through the eternal Spirit offered himself without spot to God, purge your conscience from dead works to serve the living God? 15 And for this cause he is the mediator of the new testament, that by means of death, for the redemption of the transgressions** *that were* **under the first testament, they which are called might receive the promise of eternal inheritance.** 16 For where a testament *is*, there must also of necessity be the death of the testator. 17 For a testament *is* of force after men are dead: otherwise it is of no strength at all while the testator liveth. 18 **Whereupon neither the first** *testament* **was dedicated without blood.** 19 For when Moses had spoken every precept to all the people according to the law, he took the blood of calves and of goats, with water, and scarlet wool, and hyssop, and sprinkled both the book, and all the people, 20 Saying, This *is* the blood of the testament which God hath enjoined unto you. 21 Moreover he sprinkled with blood both the tabernacle, and all the vessels of the ministry. 22 And almost all things are by the law purged with blood; and without shedding of blood is no remission. 23 *It was* **therefore necessary that the patterns of things in the heavens should be purified with these; but the heavenly things themselves with better sacrifices than these.**

I understand this purification of the "heavenly things" to be as literal and as real as when those "patterns of things in the heavens" were purified by Moses when the Tabernacle was dedicated on the plains near Mount Sinai. I further believe that the blood[19] of the LORD Jesus is in Heaven. I am convinced that *all* nine of the entities identified in

Hebrews 12:22-24 are to be understood as literal entities and not as figurative representations. "But ye are come unto

(1) mount Sion, and unto

(2) the city of the living God, the heavenly Jerusalem, and

(3) to an innumerable company of angels,

(4) to the general assembly and

(5) church of the firstborn, which are written in heaven, and

(6) to God the Judge of all, and

(7) to the spirits of just men made perfect, and

(8) to Jesus the mediator of the new covenant, and

(9) to the blood of sprinkling, that speaketh better things than that of Abel."

If the city is literal, if GOD is literal, and if Jesus is literal, then why would the last entity in the list suddenly become figurative in contradistinction to the rest of the entities? That unidentified alteration would be confusion.

24 For **Christ is not entered into the holy places made with hands,** *which are* **the figures of the true; but into heaven itself, now to appear in the presence of God for us**: 25 Nor yet that he should offer himself often, as the high priest entereth into the holy place every year with blood of others; 26 For then must he often have suffered since the foundation of the world: but now once in the end of the world hath he appeared to put away sin by **the sacrifice of himself.** 27 And as it is appointed unto men once to die, but after this the judgment: 28 **So Christ was once offered to bear the sins of many**; and unto them that look for him shall he appear the second time without sin unto salvation.

The atonement was not made until the blood was poured or sprinkled on the altar: "For the life of the flesh *is* in the blood: and I have given it to you upon the altar to make an atonement for your souls: for it *is* the blood *that* maketh an atonement for the soul." (Leviticus 17:11) Once the priest had presented the blood from an acceptable sacrifice, there was an atonement for sin.

Atonement is made with blood—*not just the death.* Those teachers[20] that remove the blood on the altar from the atonement by redefining *blood* as *death* are also removing the efficacy of the atonement. Their intellect has clouded their minds. I believe that these teachers are entirely wrong in their teaching.

Sadly, these views are being accepted as a sound commentary by many Baptists and other conservative, fundamental Christians. Translations[21] that replace the word *blood"* with such terms as *costly sacrifice* and *sacrificial death* follow the same premise as these teachers.

With the invention of the "emerging church," these denials of the Biblical affirmation of the essential connection of the blood of the LORD Jesus with the atonement. Brian McLaren said in an interview with Leif Hansen on Hansen's *Bleeding Purple Podcast* "The cross isn't the center then. The cross is almost a distraction and false advertising for GOD."[22] I do not understand those words coming from anyone claiming to be a Christian.

Others step away from the blood atonement and deny that the blood of Jesus of Nazareth has any part in the role that Jesus played in the plan of GOD: "The material blood of Jesus was no more efficacious to cleanse from sin when it was shed on 'the accursed tree,' than when it was flowing in his veins as he went daily about his Father's business."[23]

> Hebrews 10:1 For the law having a shadow of good things to come, *and* not the very image of the things, can never with those sacrifices which they offered year by year continually make the comers thereunto perfect. 2 For then would they not have ceased to be offered? because that the worshippers once purged should have had no more conscience of sins. 3 But in those *sacrifices there is* a remembrance again *made* of sins every year. 4 For *it is* not possible that the blood of bulls and of goats should take away sins. 5 **Wherefore when he cometh into the world, he saith, Sacrifice and offering thou wouldest not, but a body hast thou prepared me**: 6 **In burnt offerings and *sacrifices* for sin thou hast had no pleasure**. 7 Then said I, Lo, I come (in the volume of the book it is written of me,) to do thy will, O God. 8 Above when he said, Sacrifice and offering and burnt offerings and *offering* for sin thou wouldest not, neither hadst pleasure *therein*; which are offered by the law; 9 Then said he, Lo, I come to do thy will, O God. He taketh away the first, that he may establish the second. 10 **By the which will we are sanctified through the offering of the body of Jesus Christ once *for all*.** 11 And every priest standeth daily ministering and offering oftentimes the same sacrifices, which can never take away sins: 12 **But this man, after he had offered one sacrifice for sins for ever, sat down on the right hand of God**;

The physical body of the LORD Jesus is vitally involved with the atonement.

> 1 Peter 2:24 **Who his own self bare our sins in his own body** on the tree, that we, being dead to sins, should live unto righteousness: by whose stripes ye were healed.

However, the bearing in His body of our sins involved more than the six hours[24] upon the cross. The Holy Spirit by His Interpretation in Matthew 8:17 of Isaiah 53:4 reveals that the entire earthly life of the LORD Jesus was involved in the offering of His body.[25]

> Matthew 8:17 That it might be fulfilled which was spoken by Esaias the prophet, saying, Himself took our infirmities, and bare *our* sicknesses.

> Isaiah 53:4 Surely he hath borne our griefs, and carried our sorrows: yet we did esteem him stricken, smitten of God, and afflicted.

His life in that physical body[26] is connected inseparably, unalterably, immutably with our **righteousness**.

The Merriam-Webster 11th Collegiate Dictionary defines the word *righteousness* as "acting in accord with divine or moral law: free from guilt or sin." Noah Webster in his *American Dictionary of the English Language,* published in 1828, is more extensive and more biblically orientated in his effort at defining the word:

1. Purity of heart and rectitude of life; conformity of heart and life to the divine law. Righteousness, as used in Scripture and theology, in which it is chiefly used, is nearly equivalent to holiness, comprehending holy principles and affections of heart, and conformity of life to the divine law. It includes all we call justice, honesty and virtue, with holy affections; in short, it is true religion.

2. Applied to God, the perfection or holiness of his nature; exact rectitude; faithfulness.

3. The active and passive obedience of Christ, by which the law of God is fulfilled. Daniel 9.

4. Justice; equity between man and man. Luke 1.

5. The cause of our justification. The Lord our righteousness. Jer. *[sic]* 23.

Deuteronomy 6:25 defines righteousness as obedience to the law of GOD: "And it shall be our righteousness, if we observe to do all these commandments before the LORD our God, as he hath commanded us."

Righteousness requires the observance of *all* of the commandments given by GOD and that observance is done *before the LORD* and that obedience is to be done *as* the LORD *commanded.* Since we are sometimes oblivious to the obvious, I call specific attention to the reality that *righteousness is obtained through works*: "And it shall be our righteousness, if we observe to do."

From Adam until the present hour, only one Son of Adam[27] has fulfilled that definition. Of all the descendents of Adam, only Jesus of Nazareth has entered this world through the womb of a woman and lived a sinless life.[28] Not one man or woman out of the other billions[29] born has been sinless—not even one.[30] His sinless life becomes our righteousness by imputation.

The Holy Spirit moves the apostle Paul to explain how we achieve righteousness through the life of the LORD Jesus.[31] The Book of Romans rings with the word righteousness thirty-three times in chapters 1 through 14; the heart of the exposition of how the righteousness of the LORD Jesus is involved with the atonement is found in chapter 5.

> Romans 5:12 Wherefore, as by one man sin entered into the world, and death by sin; and so death passed upon all men, for that all have sinned: 13 (For until the law sin was in the world: but sin is not imputed when there is no law. 14 Nevertheless death reigned from Adam to Moses, even over them that had not sinned after the similitude of Adam's transgression, who is the figure of him that was to come. 15 But not as the offence, so also *is* the

free gift. For if through the offence of one many be dead, much more the grace of God, and the gift by grace, *which is* by one man, Jesus Christ, hath abounded unto many. 16 And not as *it was* by one that sinned, *so is* the gift: for the judgment *was* by one to condemnation, but the free gift *is* of many offences unto justification. 17 For if by one man's offence death reigned by one; much more **they which receive abundance of grace and of the gift of righteousness** shall reign in life by one, Jesus Christ.) 18 Therefore as by the offence of one *judgment came* upon all men to condemnation; **even so by the righteousness of one** *the free gift came* **upon all men** unto justification of life. 19 For as by one man's disobedience many were made sinners, so **by the obedience of one shall many be made righteous**. 20 Moreover the law entered, that the offence might abound. But where sin abounded, grace did much more abound: 21 That as sin hath reigned unto death, even so might grace reign through righteousness unto eternal life by Jesus Christ our Lord.

What we are unable to accomplish, we obtain through the life of the LORD Jesus. The believer is *made* righteousness because the righteousness of Christ is imputed to the believer:

Romans 4:11 And he received the sign of circumcision, a seal of the righteousness of the faith which he had yet being uncircumcised: that he might be the father of **all them that believe**, though they be not circumcised; that **righteousness might be imputed** unto them also: ... 16 Therefore **it is of faith, that it might be by grace**;[32] to the end the promise might be sure to all the seed; not to that only which is of the law, but to that also which is of the faith of Abraham; who is the father of us all, ... 22 And therefore **it was imputed to him for righteousness**. 23 Now it was not written for his sake alone, that **it was imput-**

ed to him; 24 But for us also, to whom **it shall be imputed**, if we believe on him that raised up Jesus our Lord from the dead;

James 2:23 And the scripture was fulfilled which saith, Abraham believed God, and **it was imputed unto him for righteousness**: and he was called the Friend of God.

Thus, it may be written, Romans 10:4, that "Christ is the end of the law for righteousness to everyone that believeth."

5 For Moses describeth the righteousness which is of the law, That the man which doeth those things shall live by them. 6 But **the righteousness which is of faith** speaketh on this wise, Say not in thine heart, Who shall ascend into heaven? (that is, to bring Christ down from above:) 7 Or, Who shall descend into the deep? (that is, to bring up Christ again from the dead.) 8 But what saith it? **The word is nigh thee, even in thy mouth, and in thy heart: that is, the word of faith, which we preach**; 9 That if thou shalt confess with thy mouth the Lord Jesus, and shalt believe in thine heart that God hath raised him from the dead, thou shalt be saved. 10 **For with the heart man believeth unto righteousness**; and with the mouth confession is made unto salvation. 11 For the scripture saith, Whosoever believeth on him shall not be ashamed. 12 For there is no difference between the Jew and the Greek: for the same Lord over all is rich unto all that call upon him. 13 **For whosoever shall call upon the name of the Lord shall be saved. 14 How then shall they call on him in whom they have not believed? and how shall they believe in him of whom they have not heard? and how shall they hear without a preacher?** 15 And how shall they preach, except they be sent? as it is written, How beautiful are the feet of them that preach the gospel of peace, and bring glad tidings of good things! 16 But

they have not all obeyed the gospel. For Esaias saith, Lord, who hath believed our report? 17 **So then faith** *cometh* **by hearing, and hearing by the word of GOD**.

The body of Jesus Christ indeed was offered[33] on the cross—it was there that He died. The body was placed into a borrowed tomb where it remained for the three days. The dead body was never offered in the holy place in Heaven.

After the resurrection of that body, the LORD Jesus as the High Priest entered the holy place in Heaven and offered His Own blood as the atonement. The sacrifice for sins that was taken into the heavenly Temple was the blood of Christ. It is after He offered His blood that He sat down on the right hand of the Father. He then sat down on the right hand of GOD having made the atonement.

This brings us back to Hebrews 10, where the text continues to call attention to the physical body of the Son of GOD; not as the primary message, but as a message that cannot be ignored without damaging both Scripture and the Person of the LORD Jesus.

13 From henceforth expecting till his enemies be made his footstool. 14 **For by one offering he hath perfected for ever them that are sanctified**. 15 *Whereof* the Holy Ghost also is a witness to us: for after that he had said before, 16 This *is* the covenant that I will make with them after those days, saith the Lord, I will put my laws into their hearts, and in their minds will I write them; 17 And their sins and iniquities will I remember no more. 18 Now where remission of these *is, there is* no more offering for sin. 19 **Having therefore, brethren, boldness to enter into the holiest by the blood of Jesus**, 20 **By a new and living way, which he hath consecrated for us, through the veil, that is to say, his flesh**;[34]

We are not to minimize the body of the LORD Jesus—His flesh. He Himself calls our specific attention to His body, His flesh, in the communion service:[35]

> 1 Corinthians 11:2 ... keep the ordinances, as I delivered *them* to you. ... 23 For I have received of the Lord that which also I delivered unto you, That the Lord Jesus the *same* night in which he was betrayed took bread: 24 And when he had given thanks, he brake *it*, and said, Take, eat: this is my body, which is broken for you: this do in remembrance of me. ... 26 For as often as ye eat this bread, ... 27 Wherefore whosoever shall eat this bread, ... shall be guilty of the body ... of the Lord. 28 But let a man examine himself, and so let him eat of *that* bread, ... 29 For he that eateth ... unworthily, eateth ... damnation to himself, not discerning the Lord's body. ... 33 ... when ye come together to eat, [36]

Though the theme is rarely examined in sermon or book, the physical body of the LORD Jesus is plainly and often connected to our atonement.

> Colossians 1:20 And, having made peace through the blood of his cross, by him to reconcile all things unto himself; by him, *I say*, whether *they be* things in earth, or things in heaven. 21 And you, that were sometime alienated and enemies in *your* mind by wicked works, yet now hath he reconciled 22 **In the body of his flesh through death**, to present you holy and unblameable and unreproveable in his sight:

> Ephesians 2:13 But now in Christ Jesus ye who sometimes were far off are made nigh by the blood of Christ. 14 For he is our peace, who hath made both one, and hath broken down the middle wall of partition between us; 15 Having abolished **in his flesh** the enmity, even the law of commandments contained in

ordinances; for to make in himself of twain one new man, so making peace; 16 And that he might reconcile both unto God in one body by the cross, having slain the enmity thereby: 17 And came and preached peace to you which were afar off, and to them that were nigh.

Not only is the body a vessel for the person of the LORD Jesus, the entire body is united intimately with the atonement. Earlier, I wrote, "The physical body of the LORD Jesus is vitally involved with the atonement. ... His life in that physical body is connected inseparably, unalterably, immutably with our righteousness." His hands, His feet, His Head, His cheeks, His hair, His face, His back, His heart—the entirety of His physical body was involved in our atonement. This should give us a new alertness to passages such as:

Hebrews 10:5 Wherefore when he cometh into the world, he saith, Sacrifice and offering thou wouldest not, but a body hast thou prepared me: ... 10 By the which will we are sanctified through **the offering of the body of Jesus Christ** once for all.

John 2:19 Jesus answered and said unto them, Destroy this temple, and in three days I will raise it up. 20 Then said the Jews, Forty and six years was this temple in building, and wilt thou rear it up in three days? 21 But he spake of the temple of his body.

Consider these exquisitely[37] descriptive verses of the way His physical body *served* us:

Isaiah 50:4 The Lord GOD hath given me the tongue of the learned, that I should know how to speak a word in season to him that is weary: he wakeneth morning by morning, he wakeneth mine ear to hear as the learned. 5 The Lord GOD hath opened mine ear, and I was not rebellious, neither turned away back.

284

6 **I gave my back to the smiters, and my cheeks to them that plucked off the hair: I hid not my face from shame and spitting.** 7 For the Lord GOD will help me; therefore shall I not be confounded: therefore have I set my face like a flint, and I know that I shall not be ashamed. 8 He is near that justifieth me; who will contend with me? let us stand together: who is mine adversary? let him come near to me. 9 Behold, the Lord GOD will help me; who is he that shall condemn me? lo, they all shall wax old as a garment; the moth shall eat them up.

Isaiah 53:1 ... he hath **no form nor comeliness**; and when we shall see him, there is **no beauty that we should desire him**. 3 ... **a man of sorrows, and acquainted with grief: and we hid as it were our faces from him**; ... 4 Surely he hath **borne our griefs, and carried our sorrows: yet we did esteem him stricken, smitten of God, and afflicted.** 5 But he was **wounded for our transgressions**, he was **bruised for our iniquities: the chastisement of our peace was upon him; and with his stripes we are healed** ... 7 He was **oppressed, and** he was **afflicted**, yet he **opened not his mouth**: he is **brought as a lamb to the slaughter, and as a sheep before her shearers is dumb**, so he **openeth not his mouth**. 8 He was taken from **prison** and from judgment: and who shall declare his generation? for he was **cut off out of the land of the living**: for the transgression of my people was he **stricken** ... 10 Yet it pleased the LORD to **bruise him**; he hath put him to **grief**: when thou shalt make his soul an offering for sin, ... 11 He shall see of **the travail of his soul**, ... 12 ... he hath **poured out his soul unto death**: and he was **numbered with the transgressors**; ...

Matthew 21:18 Now in the morning as he returned into the city, **he hungered**.

John 4:6 Now Jacob's well was there. Jesus therefore, being **wearied** with *his* journey, sat thus on the well: *and* it was about the sixth hour.

John 19:28 After this, Jesus knowing that all things were now accomplished, that the scripture might be fulfilled, saith, **I thirst**.

Luke 22:44 And being in an agony he prayed more earnestly: and **his sweat was as it were great drops of blood falling down to the ground**.

Matthew 26:36 ... began to be **sorrowful and very heavy**. 38 ... My soul is **exceeding sorrowful, even unto deat**h ... 50 ... Then came they, and **laid hands on Jesus, and took him**. ... 56 ... all the disciples **forsook him**, and fled. 57 And they that had **laid hold** on Jesus **led *him* away** to Caiaphas the high priest, where the scribes and the elders were assembled ... 67 Then did they **spit in his face**, and **buffeted him**; and **others smote *him*** **with the palms of their hands** ...

Matthew 27:2 And when they had **bound him**, they **led *him* away**, and **delivered him** to Pontius Pilate the governor ... 26 ... and when he had **scourged** Jesus, he **delivered** *him* to be crucified ... 28 And they **stripped him**, and put on him a scarlet robe. 29 And when they had **platted a crown of thorns**, they **put *it* upon his head**, and a reed in his right hand: and they bowed the knee before him, and **mocked him,** saying, Hail, King of the Jews! 30 And they **spit upon him**, and **took the reed**, and **smote him on the head**. 31 And after that they had **mocked him**, they **took the robe off from him**, and put his own raiment on him, and **led him away** to crucify *him* ... 34 They gave him **vinegar to drink** mingled with gall: and when he had tasted *thereof,* **he would not drink**. 35 And they **crucified him**, and **parted his garments** ... 36 And sitting down they watched him thee ...

39 And they that passed by **reviled him, wagging their heads**, 40 And saying, Thou that destroyest the temple, and buildest *it* in three days, save thyself. If thou be the Son of GOD, come down from the cross. 41 Likewise also the chief priests **mocking** *him*, with the scribes and elders, said, 42 He saved others; himself he cannot save. If he be the King of Israel, let him now come down from the cross, and we will believe him. 43 He trusted in God; let him deliver him now, if he will have him: for he said, I am the Son of GOD. 44 The thieves also, which were crucified with him, **cast the same in his teeth** ... 48 And straightway one of them ran, and took a spunge, and **filled *it* with vinegar**, and put *it* on a reed, and **gave him to drink**.

Mark 14:33 ... **began to be sore amazed, and to be very heavy**; 34 ... My soul is **exceeding sorrowful unto death** ... 43 a great multitude with swords and staves ... 46 And **they laid their hands on him**, and **took him** ... 53 And they **led Jesus away** to the high ... 65 And some began to **spit on him**, and to **cover his face**, and to **buffet him**, and to say unto him, Prophesy: and the servants **did strike him with the palms of their hands**.

Mark 15:1 ... and **bound** Jesus, and **carried *him* away, and delivered *him*** to Pilate ... 15 And *so* Pilate ... **delivered Jesus**, when he had **scourged *him***, to be crucified. 16 And the soldiers **led him away** into the hall, called Praetorium; and they call together the whole band. 17 And they **clothed him with purple, and platted a crown of thorns, and put it about his *head***, 18 And began to salute him, Hail, King of the Jews! 19 And they **smote him on the head with a reed, and did spit upon him**, and bowing *their* knees worshipped him. 20 And when they had **mocked him**, they **took off the purple from him**, and put his own clothes on him, and **led him out**

to crucify him ... 23 And they gave him to drink **wine mingled with myrrh: but he received** *it* **not**. 24 And when they had **crucified him, they parted his garments** ... 25 And it was the third hour, and **they crucified him** ... 29 And they that passed by **railed on him**, wagging their heads, and saying, Ah, thou that destroyest the temple, and buildest *it* in three days, 30 Save thyself, and come down from the cross. 31 Likewise also the chief priests **mocking** said among themselves with the scribes, He saved others; himself he cannot save. 32 Let Christ the King of Israel descend now from the cross, that we may see and believe. And they that were crucified with him **reviled him** ... 36 And one ran and filled a spunge full of vinegar, and put *it* on a reed, and gave him to drink, saying, Let alone; let us see whether Elias will come to take him down.

Luke 22:44 And **being in an agony** he prayed more earnestly: and **his sweat was as it were great drops of blood falling down to the ground** ... 54 Then **took they him, and led** *him,* **and brought him** into the high priest's house ... 63 And the men that held Jesus **mocked** him, and **smote** *him.* 64 And when they had **blindfolded** him, they **struck him on the face**, and asked him, saying, Prophesy, who is it that **smote** thee? 65 And many other things blasphemously spake they against him. 66 And as soon as it was day ... **led him** into their council ...

Luke 23:1 And the whole multitude of them arose, and **led him** unto Pilate. 2 And they began to **accuse him** ... 5 And they were the more **fierce** ... 7 ... he **sent him** to Herod ... 10 And the chief priests and scribes stood and vehemently accused him. 11 And Herod with his men of war **set him at nought, and mocked** *him,* and arrayed him in a gorgeous robe, and **sent him again** to Pilate ... 24 And

Pilate gave sentence that it should be as they required. 25 ... he **delivered** Jesus to their will ... 33 And when they were come to the place, which is called Calvary, there **they crucified him** ... 34 ... And they **parted his raiment**, and cast lots. 35 ... And the rulers also with them **derided** *him*, saying, He saved others; let him save himself, if he be Christ, the chosen of God. 36 And the soldiers also **mocked** him, coming to him, and offering him vinegar ...

John 18:12 Then the band and the captain and officers of the Jews **took Jesus, and bound him**, 13 And **led him away** to Annas first ... 22 ... one of the officers which stood by **struck Jesus with the palm of his hand** ... 24 Now Annas had sent him bound unto Caiaphas the high priest ... 28 Then **led** they Jesus from Caiaphas unto the hall of judgment

John 19:1 Then Pilate therefore **took Jesus, and scourged** *him*. 2 And the soldiers **platted a crown of thorns, and put** *it* **on his head**, and they put on him a purple robe, 3 And said, Hail, King of the Jews! and they **smote him with their hands**. 4 Pilate therefore went forth again, and saith unto them, Behold, I bring him forth to you, that ye may know that I find no fault in him. 5 Then came Jesus forth, wearing the crown of thorns, and the purple robe. And *Pilate* saith unto them, Behold the man! ... 16 Then **delivered** he him ... And they **took Jesus, and led** *him* **away**. 17 And he **bearing his cross** went ... 18 Where **they crucified him** ... 23 Then the soldiers, when they had **crucified Jesus, took his garments**, and made four parts, to every soldier a part; and also *his* coat: now the coat was without seam, woven from the top throughout ... 28 After this, Jesus knowing that all things were now accomplished, that the scripture might be fulfilled, saith, **I thirst**. 29 Now there was set a vessel full of vinegar:

and they filled a spunge with vinegar, and put *it* upon hyssop, and put *it* to his mouth. 30 When Jesus therefore had received the vinegar, he said, It is finished: and he bowed his head, and gave up the ghost ... 33 But when they came to Jesus, and saw that he was dead already, they brake not his legs: 34 But one of the soldiers with a spear **pierced his side, and forthwith came there out blood and water** ...

John 20 ... 27 Then saith he to Thomas, Reach hither thy finger, and behold my hands; and reach hither thy hand, and thrust *it* into my side ...

Matthew 8:17, That it might be fulfilled which was spoken by Esaias the prophet, saying, Himself took our infirmities, and bare our sicknesses.

Isaiah 53:4 and Matthew 8:17 may suggest a context for the unusual comment of the LORD Jesus "And he said unto them, Ye will surely say unto me this proverb, **Physician, heal thyself**: whatsoever we have heard done in Capernaum, do also here in thy country." Luke 4:23

The statement raises the question of what did He have a need to be healed? He was "afflicted," bore our "griefs," carried our "sorrows," took our "infirmities," and bare our "sicknesses." Is there some possibility of this being a literal healing of which He stood in need.

The LORD Jesus had "no form nor comeliness ... no beauty that we should desire him." A group of Jews made a twenty-year mistake in His age;[38] was that mistake because of His physical appearance: did the pressures of living have an impact on His physical body? Was He, in our terminology, appearing older than His years? However, that may be, the whole of His body was committed to our atonement.

Paul, the speaker of the sermon[39] that we know as the Epistle to the Hebrews, now continues by emphasizing the assurance that we may have in the atonement.

> 21 And *having* an high priest over the house of God; 22 Let us draw near with a true heart in full assurance of faith, having our hearts sprinkled from an evil conscience, and our bodies washed with pure water. 23 Let us hold fast the profession of *our* faith without wavering; (for he *is* faithful that promised;)

Our faith is in the person and work of the LORD Jesus. He is our hope of righteousness.

> 24 And let us consider one another to provoke unto love and to good works: 25 Not forsaking the assembling of ourselves together, as the manner of some *is*; but exhorting *one another:* and so much the more, as ye see the day approaching. 26 For if we sin wilfully after that we have received the knowledge of the truth, there remaineth no more sacrifice for sins, 27 But a certain fearful looking for of judgment and fiery indignation, which shall devour the adversaries. 28 He that despised Moses' law died without mercy under two or three witnesses: 29 Of how much sorer punishment, suppose ye, shall he be thought worthy, who hath trodden under foot the Son of GOD, and hath counted the blood of the covenant, wherewith he was sanctified, an unholy thing, and hath done despite unto the Spirit of grace? 30 For we know him that hath said, Vengeance *belongeth* unto me, I will recompense, saith the Lord. And again, The Lord shall judge his people. 31 *It is* a fearful thing to fall into the hands of the living God. 32 But call to remembrance the former days, in which, after ye were illuminated, ye endured a great fight of afflictions; 33 Partly, whilst ye were made a gazingstock both by reproaches and afflictions; and partly, whilst ye became companions of them that were so used. 34 For

ye had compassion of me in my bonds, and took joyfully the spoiling of your goods, knowing in yourselves that ye have in heaven a better and an enduring substance. 35 Cast not away therefore your confidence, which hath great recompence of reward. 36 For ye have need of patience, that, after ye have done the will of God, ye might receive the promise. 37 For yet a little while, and he that shall come will come, and will not tarry. 38 Now the just shall live by faith: but if *any man* draw back, my soul shall have no pleasure in him. 39 But we are not of them who draw back unto perdition; but of **them that believe to the saving of the soul**.

I return to the pivot point in the Book of Hebrews, chapter 8 and verse 1: "Now of the things which we have spoken this is the sum: We have such an high priest, who is set on the right hand of the throne of the Majesty in the heavens."

The LORD Jesus is our High Priest. He is High Priest because He is righteous in action as well as by nature. All that comes before in Hebrews comes to validate that Jesus of Nazareth is sinless and that He is qualified and that He is accepted by GOD as our High Priest. He could not have been *made* sin and have been able to *make* the atonement.

In fact, it is easily verified in Scripture that no offering ever *became* sin in the sense of a constitutional change. He was *made to be sin for us* in the same way that we *might be made the righteousness of God*—both are by imputation.

The familiar verse of 1 Corinthians 15:3 has more in view than the fulfillment of prophecies concerning the crucifixion. That phrase "according to the scriptures" carries the fullness of the doctrine of imputation. Our sins were placed upon Him and His righteousness is placed upon us.

1 Corinthians 15:3 For I delivered unto you first of all that which I also received, how that Christ died for our sins according to the scriptures;

Our sin was imputed to Him so that His righteousness might be imputed to us. The sin remains ours—it never became His.

John Bunyan, writer of *The Pilgrim's Progress*, put the truth in simple English words: "Our sins, when laid upon Christ, were yet personally ours, not his; so his righteousness, when put upon us, is yet personally his, not ours."[40]

There is no basis in Scripture for Jesus of Nazareth having His holiness removed to be replaced with sin.

Hebrews 9:29 says that He was offered to bear our sins; but no verse says that our sins became a part of Him.

Isaiah 53:3 declares that He was "despised and rejected of men"; but no verse says that He was despised or rejected by GOD.

Isaiah 53:3 says that we hid (as it were) our faces from Him, but no verse says that GOD hid His face from the LORD Jesus.

Isaiah 53:3 says that we did not esteem Him; but no verse says that GOD did not esteem Him.

Isaiah 53:5 says that He was wounded for our transgressions and bruised for our iniquities; but no verse says that our transgressions and iniquities became His transgressions and His iniquities.

Isaiah 53:6 says that the LORD laid our iniquities upon Him; but no verse says that our iniquities were made His.

Isaiah 53:12 says that He was numbered with the transgressors; but no verse says that He was ever a transgressor—not for three dark hours—not even for a single moment during those three hours or any other time. How sad it is that so many seem not to continue reading Verse 12 to find that the verse declares that as He was numbered with transgressors that He made intercession for transgressors. He could not have made intercession for transgressors if He were a transgressor Himself.

> **I repeat: Jesus of Nazareth
> could not have made intercession
> for the transgressors,
> with whom He was numbered,
> if He became a transgressor Himself.**

Calvary confuses the worldlings.[41] The individual that is engrossed with the things of this present world, whether that person is a believer or a Christ-rejecter, does not have a mindset that understands spiritual concepts.

> 1 Corinthians 2:14 But the natural man receiveth not the things of the Spirit of God: for they are foolishness unto him: neither can he know *them*, because they are spiritually discerned.

When a child of GOD approaches Scripture allowing his natural reasoning to control his thinking by depending upon the tools of human wisdom and the guidance of human philosophy, the result cannot be anything other than confusion. He might not consider the words of Scripture to be foolishness as the Christ-rejecter does, but he most assuredly will not understand them. The Bible is the revelation of GOD; therefore, it differs from every other collection of words ever assembled in the history of the world.

The Bible is not true because it has been confirmed by humanity's experience or has been validated by man's reasoning; it is true because it was spoken by GOD Who is true. The LORD Jesus said, "... thy word is truth."[42] The revelation of

GOD is called "the word of truth" five separate times[43] and once it is called "the Scripture of truth."[44] The Bible is not submitted to mankind for approval; it is to be declared as "Thus saith the LORD."[45]

The unbeliever views Biblical truth as foolishness, especially so does he value the Gospel.[46] He rejects the miraculous without hesitation because it contradicts his range of experience and his level of knowledge. Like those of whom the apostle Paul wrote the Philippians in 3:19 "whose God is their belly," the unbeliever has understanding only of a God that fits with his appetites and lifestyle. He cannot conceive of anything remotely like the vicarious substitutional atoning death of the Son of GOD. It appears to him to be irrational, even perverse.

Calvary has confused and will continue to confuse the scoffer and the mocker. They will never understand what the TRINITY was doing at Calvary. They cannot comprehend the words of Jesus of Nazareth; they will never understand the actions of GOD the Father. The darkness of Calvary clouds their minds and they refuse the light of the Scriptures, so they stumble over Calvary. Their questions rise as the ridiculous and always border on and sometimes cross into blasphemous accusations.

Calvary has also puzzled multiple believers. How would it have been possible for GOD the Father to forsake GOD the Son? Did the Son of GOD desire to avoid the cross because He feared death? Was Jesus of Nazareth only a man when He was on the cross? Was there confusion at Calvary within the TRINITY? Some among believers have raised all and more of these questions and have offered proposals to solve all of these propositions; the issue is whether they are needed.

To begin with, Biblical revelation must be accepted by faith; it can never be explained by human reasoning. The revelation of GOD rests at a far higher level than humanity can reach by means of a humanly constructed intellectual or experiential ladder. A measure of understanding is attainable by the comparison of Scripture with Scripture, but even Daniel[47] had to confess that he heard the words of GOD, but "understood not" and Peter[48] acknowledged that Paul wrote some things that were "hard to be understood." Neither man questioned the words nor doubted the GOD that spoke them; both accepted all of the words and did so without doubt and certainly without mockery.

In writing this material, I make no claim to possessing a special key that unlocks mysteries where others have failed; I have only attempted to lay Scripture alongside Scripture and to allow the words of GOD to speak for GOD.

Whether you accept my understanding of the events during those hours of darkness at Calvary and of the words of the LORD Jesus from the cross, you should agree that GOD the Father was not confused, that GOD the Son was not confused, and that GOD the Spirit was not confused.

You and I may not understand Calvary; you or I might even have elements of confusion in our thinking regarding Calvary, but it is impossible for there to have been confusion at Calvary within the TRINITY. The suggestion itself is a slander against the TRINITY.

[1]Matthew 27:45 Now from the sixth hour there was darkness over all the land unto the ninth hour.

Mark 15:33-34 And when the sixth hour was come, there was darkness over the whole land until the ninth hour. 34 And at the ninth hour Jesus cried with a loud voice, saying, Eloi, Eloi, lama sabachthani? which is, being interpreted, My God, my God, why hast thou forsaken me?

Luke 23:44-46 And it was about the sixth hour, and there was a darkness over all the earth until the ninth hour. 45 And the sun was darkened, and the veil of the temple was rent in the midst. 46 And when Jesus had cried with a loud voice, he said, Father, into thy hands I commend my spirit: and having said thus, he gave up the ghost.

[2] Matthew 16:28 Verily I say unto you, There be some standing here, which shall not taste of death, till they see the Son of man coming in his kingdom.

Mark 9:1 And he said unto them, Verily I say unto you, That there be some of them that stand here, which shall not taste of death, till they have seen the kingdom of God come with power.

Luke 9:27 But I tell you of a truth, there be some standing here, which shall not taste of death, till they see the kingdom of God.

John 8:52 Then said the Jews unto him, Now we know that thou hast a devil. Abraham is dead, and the prophets; and thou sayest, If a man keep my saying, he shall never taste of death.

Hebrews 2:9 But we see Jesus, who was made a little lower than the angels for the suffering of death, crowned with glory and honour; that he by the grace of God should taste death for every man.

[3] Revelation 2:11 He that hath an ear, let him hear what the Spirit saith unto the churches; He that overcometh shall not be hurt of the second death.

Revelation 20:6 Blessed and holy *is* he that hath part in the first resurrection: on such the second death hath no power, but they shall be priests of God and of Christ, and shall reign with him a thousand years.

Revelation 20:14 And death and hell were cast into the lake of fire. This is the second death.

Revelation 21:8 But the fearful, and unbelieving, and the abominable, and murderers, and whoremongers, and sorcerers, and idolaters, and all liars, shall have their part in the lake which burneth with fire and brimstone: which is the second death.

[4] As I understand the Scriptures, physical death may be defined in two ways: by definition and by evidence.

(1) When the soul leaves the body, the body dies.

Genesis 35:18 And it came to pass, as her soul was in depart-ing, (for she died) that she called his name Benoni: but his father called him Benjamin.

1 Kings 17:21 And he stretched himself upon the child three times, and cried unto the LORD, and said, O LORD my God, I pray thee, let this child's soul come into him again. 22 And the LORD heard the voice of Elijah; and the soul of the child came into him again, and he revived.

(2) The physical evidences of death are two.

(a)When the breath leaves the body, there is death. When the blood ceases to flow there is death.

Genesis 2:7 And the LORD God formed man *of* the dust of the ground, and breathed into his nostrils the breath of life; and man became a living soul.

(b) When the blood ceases to flow there is death.

Genesis 9:4 But flesh with the life thereof, *which is* the blood thereof, shall ye not eat.

Leviticus 17:11 For the life of the flesh *is* in the blood: and I have given it to you upon the altar to make an atonement for your souls: for it *is* the blood *that* maketh an atonement for the soul.

Leviticus 17:14 For *it is* the life of all flesh; the blood of it *is* for the life thereof: therefore I said unto the children of Israel, Ye shall eat the blood of no manner of flesh: for the life of all flesh *is* the blood thereof: whosoever eateth it shall be cut off.

Deuteronomy 12:23 Only be sure that thou eat not the blood: for the blood *is* the life; and thou mayest not eat the life with the flesh.

(c) The heart is connected with the flow of blood.

Proverbs 14:30 A sound heart *is* the life of the flesh: but envy the rottenness of the bones.

5 Genesis 35:18 And it came to pass, as her soul was in departing, (for she died) that she called his name Benoni: but his father called him Benjamin.

1 Kings 17:22 And the LORD heard the voice of Elijah; and the soul of the child came into him again, and he revived.

Luke 8:53-55 And they laughed him to scorn, knowing that she was dead. 54 And he put them all out, and took her by the hand, and called, saying, Maid, arise. 55 And her spirit came again, and she arose straightway: and he commanded to give her meat.

6 Hebrews 10:5 Wherefore when he cometh into the world, he saith, Sacrifice and offering thou wouldest not, but a body hast thou prepared me: ... 10 By the which will we are sancti-fied through the offering of the body of Jesus Christ once *for all.*

7 Hebrews 2: 9 But we see Jesus, who was made a little lower than the angels for the suffering of death, crowned with glory and honour; that he by the grace of God should taste death for every man. ... 14 Forasmuch then as the children are partakers of flesh and blood, he also himself likewise took part of the same; that through death he might destroy him that had the power of death, that is, the devil;

Hebrews 9:15 And for this cause he is the mediator of the new testament, that by means of death, for the redemption of the transgressions that were under the first testament, they which are called might receive the promise of eternal inheritance. 16 For where a testament is, there must also of necessity be the death of the testator.

Genesis 3:15 And I will put enmity between thee and the woman, and between thy seed and her seed; it shall bruise thy head, and thou shalt bruise his heel.

John 12:27 Now is my soul troubled; and what shall I say? Father, save me from this hour: but for this cause came I unto this hour.

Romans 5:6 For when we were yet without strength, in due time Christ died for the ungodly.

Romans 5:8 But God commendeth his love toward us, in that, while we were yet sinners, Christ died for us.

Romans 14:15 But if thy brother be grieved with thy meat, now walkest thou not charitably. Destroy not him with thy meat, for whom Christ died.

1 Corinthians 8:11 And through thy knowledge shall the weak brother perish, for whom Christ died?

1 Corinthians 15:3 For I delivered unto you first of all that which I also received, how that Christ died for our sins according to the scriptures;

8 Romans 5:16 For when we were yet without strength, in due time Christ died for the ungodly. 7 For scarcely for a righteous man will one die: yet peradventure for a good man some would even dare to die. 8 But God commendeth his love toward us, in that, while we were yet sinners, Christ died for us. 9 Much more then, being now justified by his blood, we shall be saved from wrath through him. 10 For if, when we were enemies, we were reconciled to God by the death of his Son, much more, being reconciled, we shall be saved by his life. 11 And not only so, but we also joy in God through our Lord Jesus Christ, by whom we have now received the atonement. 12 Wherefore, as by one man sin entered into the world, and death by sin; and so death passed upon all men, for that all have sinned: 13 (For until the law sin was in the world: but sin is not imputed when there is no law. 14 Nevertheless death reigned from Adam to Moses, even over them that had not sinned after the similitude

of Adam's transgression, who is the figure of him that was to come. 15 But not as the offence, so also *is* the free gift. For if through the offence of one many be dead, much more the grace of God, and the gift by grace, *which is* by one man, Jesus Christ, hath abounded unto many. 16 And not as *it was* by one that sinned, *so is* the gift: for the judgment *was* by one to condemnation, but the free gift *is* of many offences unto justification. 17 For if by one man's offence death reigned by one; much more they which receive abundance of grace and of the gift of righteousness shall reign in life by one, Jesus Christ.) 18 Therefore as by the offence of one *judgment came* upon all men to condemnation; even so by the righteousness of one *the free gift came* upon all men unto justification of life. 19 For as by one man's disobedience many were made sinners, so by the obedience of one shall many be made righteous. 20 Moreover the law entered, that the offence might abound. But where sin abounded, grace did much more abound: 21 That as sin hath reigned unto death, even so might grace reign through right-eousness unto eternal life by Jesus Christ our Lord.

Romans 6:9 Knowing that Christ being raised from the dead dieth no more; death hath no more dominion over him. 10 For in that he died, he died unto sin once: but in that he liveth, he liveth unto God.

⁹ Romans 5:11 And not only *so*, but we also joy in God through our Lord Jesus Christ, by whom we have now received the atonement.

¹⁰ Numbers 29:11 One kid of the goats *for* a sin offering; beside the sin offering of atonement, and the continual burnt offering, and the meat offering of it, and their drink offerings.

¹¹ 1 John 2:1 My little children, these things write I unto you, that ye sin not. And if any man sin, we have an advocate with the Father, Jesus Christ the righteous: 2 And he is the propitiation for our sins: and not for ours only, but also for *the sins of* the whole world.

1 John 4:9 In this was manifested the love of God toward us, because that God sent his only begotten Son into the world, that we might live through him. 10 Herein is love, not that we loved God, but that he loved us, and sent his Son *to be* the propitiation for our sins.

¹² *SwordSearcher: Strong's Greek Dictionary*

2435. ιλαστηριον hilasterion; neuter of a derivative of 2433; an expiatory (place or thing), i.e. (concretely) an atoning victim, or (specially) the lid of the Ark (in the Temple):—mercyseat, propitiation.

¹³ This was an intentional action on the part of the transla-tors of the Authorized Version even as they did other formatting

devices to convey the distinctions between the to Testaments; such as the differences in names as in Zion and Sion.

[14] Revelation 20:11 And I saw a great white throne, and him that sat on it, from whose face the earth and the heaven fled away; and there was found no place for them. 12 And I saw the dead, small and great, stand before God; and the books were opened: and another book was opened, which is *the book* of life: and the dead were judged out of those things which were written in the books, according to their works. 13 And the sea gave up the dead which were in it; and death and hell delivered up the dead which were in them: and they were judged every man according to their works. 14 And death and hell were cast into the lake of fire. This is the second death. 15 And whosoever was not found written in the book of life was cast into the lake of fire.

[15] Luke 1:35 And the angel answered and said unto her, The Holy Ghost shall come upon thee, and the power of the Highest shall overshadow thee: therefore also that holy thing which shall be born of thee shall be called the Son of GOD.

[16] 2 Corinthians 5:21 For he hath made him to be sin for us, who knew no sin; that we might be made the righteousness of God in him.

John 14:30 Hereafter I will not talk much with you: for the prince of this world cometh, and hath nothing in me.

Hebrews 9:14 How much more shall the blood of Christ, who through the eternal Spirit offered himself without spot to God, purge your conscience from dead works to serve the living God?

1 Peter 1:19 But with the precious blood of Christ, as of a lamb without blemish and without spot: ... 2:22 Who did no sin, neither was guile found in his mouth

[17] Hebrews 4:14 Seeing then that we have a great high priest, that is passed into the heavens, Jesus the Son of God, let us hold fast *our* profession.

[18] Isaiah 53:12 Therefore will I divide him *a portion* with the great, and he shall divide the spoil with the strong; because he hath poured out his soul unto death: and he was numbered with the transgressors; and he bare the sin of many, and made intercession for the transgressors.

Leviticus 17:11 For the life of the flesh *is* in the blood: and I have given it to you upon the altar to make an atonement for your souls: for it *is* the blood *that* maketh an atonement for the soul.

Hebrews 9:15 And for this cause he is the mediator of the new testament, that by means of death, for the redemption of the transgressions *that were* under the first testament, they which are called might receive the promise of eternal inheritance.

19 I understand that men, who are far more intelligent than I, deride this statement with passionate mockery. I have been questioned over how the blood would be preserved for these centuries. I accept as irrefutable truth that "with God nothing is impossible"; I do not need to explain how God might keep the blood. The question assumes that there is the possibility of corruption either in Heaven itself or in the blood of Jesus. Both assumptions are absurd babblings from science (knowledge) falsely so called. If Hebrews 12:22-24 is to be understood literally, then the incorruptible blood of Christ (Hebrews 9:14; Acts 20:28) is in Heaven.

20 On page 237 of his commentary on Hebrews, MacArthur states that it is "not Jesus' physical blood that saves us, but His dying on our behalf." In a letter to Mr. Tim Weidlich, dated April 4, 1986, MacArthur writes, "Obviously, it was not the blood of Jesus that saves or He could have bled for us without dying. ... Yes, the blood of Christ is precious - but as precious as it is - it could not save." MacArthur reduces the blood of Christ to a mere symbol of death. In this same letter of Mr. Weidlich. He writes, "I admit that because of some traditional hymns there is an emotional attachment to the blood - but that should not pose problem when one is dealing with theological or textual specificity. I can sing hymns about the blood and rejoice with them - but I understand that reference to be a metonym for His death." I have copies of these documents and personal correspondence with Dr. John MacArthur.

21 "... it was the costly sacrifice of Christ, who was like a lamb without defect or flaw..." "and from Jesus Christ, the faithful witness, the first to be raised from death and who is also the ruler of the kings of the world. He loves us, and by his sacrificial death he has freed us from our sins." 1 Peter 1:19 and Revelation 1:5 as found in the Good News Translation, copyright by the American Bible Society.

22 http://reformednazarene.wordpress.com/emergent-church-what-is-it/brian-mclaren-the-cross-as-false-advertising/

23 Mary Baker Eddy, Science and Health With Key to the Scriptures, page 25.

24 Mark 15:25 And it was the third hour, and they crucified him.
Luke 23:44 And it was about the sixth hour, and there was a darkness over all the earth until the ninth hour. 45 And the sun was darkened, and the veil of the temple was rent in the midst. 46 And when Jesus had cried with a loud voice, he said, Father, into thy hands I commend my spirit: and having said thus, he gave up the ghost.

25 Matthew 8:17, That it might be fulfilled which was spoken by Esaias the prophet, saying, Himself took our infirmities, and bare our sicknesses.

302

Isaiah 53:4 Surely he hath borne our griefs, and carried our sorrows: yet we did esteem him stricken, smitten of God, and afflicted.

26 As we will explore later, it is the whole of the physical body that is connected to our atonement. The body is involved not just as a "container" for the person of Jesus of Nazareth.

27 Luke 3:38 Which was *the son* of Enos, which was *the son* of Seth, which was *the son* of Adam, which was *the son* of God.

28 Hebrews 4:15 For we have not an high priest which cannot be touched with the feeling of our infirmities; but was in all points tempted like as *we are, yet* without sin.

2 Corinthians 5:21 For he hath made him *to be* sin for us, who knew no sin; that we might be made the righteousness of God in him.

1 Peter 2:22 Who did no sin, neither was guile found in his mouth:

1 John 3:5 And ye know that he was manifested to take away our sins; and in him is no sin.

29 Population estimate for the U.S. is 313,487,941 and for the World is 7,011,418,664; dated 14:41 UTC (EST+5) May 05, 2012. http://www.census.gov/population/international/

30 Romans 3:10 As it is written, There is none righteous, no, not one: ... 23 For all have sinned, and come short of the glory of God;

Job 15:14 What *is* man, that he should be clean? and *he which is* born of a woman, that he should be righteous?

Psalm 14:1 The fool hath said in his heart, *There is* no God. They are corrupt, they have done abominable works, *there is* none that doeth good. 2 The LORD looked down from heaven upon the children of men, to see if there were any that did understand, *and* seek God. 3 They are all gone aside, they are *all* together become filthy: *there is* none that doeth good, no, not one..... 53:1 The fool hath said in his heart, *There is* no God. Corrupt are they, and have done abominable iniquity: *there is* none that doeth good. 2 God looked down from heaven upon the children of men, to see if there were *any* that did understand, that did seek God. 3 Every one of them is gone back: they are altogether become filthy; *there is* none that doeth good, no, not one.

31 Romans 3:22 Even the righteousness of God *which is* by faith of Jesus Christ unto all and upon all them that believe: for there is no difference: ... 10:4 For Christ is the end of the law for righteousness to every one that believeth.

32 This phrase would seem to destroy the premise of the Calvinist: the entrance into the grace of God is through the avenue of faith and not by sovereign decree. Yet, Dr. Gill writes "which is done, 'that it might be by grace'; appear to be of the

free grace and favour of God, as each of these blessings are: forasmuch as every blessing is received by faith, it is manifest it must be by grace; since faith itself is a gift of God's grace." Thereby reconstructing that phrase in the verse to read "it is *by the gift of God's grace* of faith, that it might be by grace." Dr. Gill, whose writings remain among the best of the efforts of man to exposit the Scriptures has accomplished a most confusing redundancy by his insertion of a non-Biblical definition for faith. His manipulation (common to all Calvinists) would cause Romans to be even more bewildering.."By whom also we have access by faith into this grace wherein we stand, and rejoice in hope of the glory of God." is contorted into "By whom also we have access by *the gift of grace*, faith, into this grace wherein we stand ..."

33 Hebrews 10:10 By the which will we are sanctified through the offering of the body of Jesus Christ once *for all*.

34 I believe that this verse places an importance on the body of the LORD Jesus that is not considered by most believers.

35 Matthew 26:26-30 And as they were eating, Jesus took bread, and blessed *it*, and brake *it*, and gave *it* to the disciples, and said, Take, eat; this is my body. 27 And he took the cup, and gave thanks, and gave *it* to them, saying, Drink ye all of it; 28 For this is my blood of the new testament, which is shed for many for the remission of sins. 29 But I say unto you, I will not drink henceforth of this fruit of the vine, until that day when I drink it new with you in my Father's kingdom. 30 And when they had sung an hymn, they went out into the mount of Olives.

Mark 14:22-26 And as they did eat, Jesus took bread, and blessed, and brake *it*, and gave to them, and said, Take, eat: this is my body. 23 And he took the cup, and when he had given thanks, he gave *it* to them: and they all drank of it. 24 And he said unto them, This is my blood of the new testament, which is shed for many. 25 Verily I say unto you, I will drink no more of the fruit of the vine, until that day that I drink it new in the kingdom of God. 26 And when they had sung an hymn, they went out into the mount of Olives.

Luke 22:19-20 And he took bread, and gave thanks, and brake *it*, and gave unto them, saying, This is my body which is given for you: this do in remembrance of me. 20 Likewise also the cup after supper, saying, This cup *is* the new testament in my blood, which is shed for you. 1 Corinthians 10:16 The cup of blessing which we bless, is it not the communion of the blood of Christ? The bread which we break, is it not the communion of the body of Christ? ... 11:27 Wherefore whosoever shall eat this bread, and drink *this* cup of the Lord, unworthily, shall be guilty of the body and blood of the Lord.

[36] The full text of the chapter is given for ease of reference. 1 Corinthians 11:1 Be ye followers of me, even as I also *am* of Christ. 2 Now I praise you, brethren, that ye remember me in all things, and keep the ordinances, as I delivered *them* to you. ... 17 Now in this that I declare *unto you* I praise *you* not, that ye come together not for the better, but for the worse. 18 For first of all, when ye come together in the church, I hear that there be divisions among you; and I partly believe it. 19 For there must be also heresies among you, that they which are approved may be made manifest among you. 20 When ye come together therefore into one place, *this* is not to eat the Lord's supper. 21 For in eating every one taketh before *other* his own supper: and one is hungry, and another is drunken. 22 What? have ye not houses to eat and to drink in? or despise ye the church of God, and shame them that have not? What shall I say to you? shall I praise you in this? I praise *you* not. 23 For I have received of the Lord that which also I delivered unto you, That the Lord Jesus the *same* night in which he was betrayed took bread: 24 And when he had given thanks, he brake *it*, and said, Take, eat: this is my body, which is broken for you: this do in remembrance of me. 25 After the same manner also *he took* the cup, when he had supped, saying, This cup is the new testament in my blood: this do ye, as oft as ye drink *it*, in remembrance of me. 26 For as often as ye eat this bread, and drink this cup, ye do shew the Lord's death till he come. 27 Wherefore whosoever shall eat this bread, and drink *this* cup of the Lord, unworthily, shall be guilty of the body and blood of the Lord. 28 But let a man examine himself, and so let him eat of *that* bread, and drink of *that* cup. 29 For he that eateth and drinketh unworthily, eateth and drinketh damnation to himself, not discerning the Lord's body. 30 For this cause many *are* weak and sickly among you, and many sleep. 31 For if we would judge ourselves, we should not be judged. 32 But when we are judged, we are chastened of the Lord, that we should not be condemned with the world. 33 Wherefore, my brethren, when ye come together to eat, tarry one for another. 34 And if any man hunger, let him eat at home; that ye come not together unto condemnation. And the rest will I set in order when I come.

[37] Merriam-Webster: "... carefully selected ... marked by ... deep sensitivity ..."

[38] John 8:57 Then said the Jews unto him, Thou art not yet fifty years old, and hast thou seen Abraham?

[39] (I believe the Book was a sermon of the apostle that Timothy wrote down—see the subscription following the last verse of the Book of Hebrews.)

[40] Page 302, The works of that eminent servant of Christ, John Bunyan, Volume 2

[41] Merriam-Webster Dictionary: "a person engrossed in the concerns of this present world."

[42] John 17:17 Sanctify them through thy truth: thy word is truth.

[43] Psalm 119:43 And take not the word of truth utterly out of my mouth; for I have hoped in thy judgments.

2 Corinthians 6:7 By the word of truth, by the power of God, by the armour of righteousness on the right hand and on the left,

Ephesians 1:13 In whom ye also *trusted*, after that ye heard the word of truth, the gospel of your salvation: in whom also after that ye believed, ye were sealed with that holy Spirit of promise,

2 Timothy 2:15 Study to shew thyself approved unto God, a workman that needeth not to be ashamed, rightly dividing the word of truth.

James 1:18 Of his own will begat he us with the word of truth, that we should be a kind of firstfruits of his creatures.

[44] Daniel 10:21 But I will shew thee that which is noted in the scripture of truth: and *there is* none that holdeth with me in these things, but Michael your prince.

[45] At least 815 times "saith the LORD."

[46] 1 Corinthians 1:18 For the preaching of the cross is to them that perish foolishness; but unto us which are saved it is the power of God.

[47] Daniel 12:4 But thou, O Daniel, shut up the words, and seal the book, *even* to the time of the end: many shall run to and fro, and knowledge shall be increased. 5 Then I Daniel looked, and, behold, there stood other two, the one on this side of the bank of the river, and the other on that side of the bank of the river. 6 And *one* said to the man clothed in linen, which *was* upon the waters of the river, How long *shall it be to* the end of these wonders? 7 And I heard the man clothed in linen, which *was* upon the waters of the river, when he held up his right hand and his left hand unto heaven, and sware by him that liveth for ever that *it shall be* for a time, times, and an half; and when he shall have accomplished to scatter the power of the holy people, all these *things* shall be finished. 8 And I heard, but I understood not: then said I, O my Lord, what *shall be* the end of these *things*? 9 And he said, Go thy way, Daniel: for the words *are* closed up and sealed till the time of the end.

[48] 2 Peter 3:15 And account *that* the longsuffering of our Lord *is* salvation; even as our beloved brother Paul also according to the wisdom given unto him hath written unto you; 16 As also in all his epistles, speaking in them of these things; in which are some things hard to be understood, which they that are unlearned and unstable wrest, as *they do* also the other scriptures, unto their own destruction.

CHAPTER 18

THE FAITHFULNESS OF JEHOVAH

Scripture records multiple promises that are made to individuals, both believers and unbelievers, and to collective groups. Among the promises are some that specifically are Messianic—promises that apply to the Son of GOD during His earthly sojourn. Within these, I suggest that the following pertain to the time on the cross and have a particular application to the hours of darkness and immediately thereafter. They have a direct obvious bearing on the issue of whether or not the Son of GOD was forsaken by GOD the Father.

Psalm 9:10 And they that know thy name will put their trust in thee: for thou, LORD, hast not forsaken them that seek thee.

Psalm 20:6 Now know I that the LORD saveth his anointed; he will hear him from his holy heaven with the saving strength of his right hand.

Psalm 91:1 He that dwelleth in the secret place of the most High shall abide under the shadow of the Almighty. 2 I will say of the LORD, *He is* my refuge and my fortress: my God; in him will I trust. 3 Surely he shall deliver thee from the snare of the fowler, *and* from the noisome pestilence. 4 He shall cover thee with his feathers, and under his wings shalt thou trust: his truth *shall be thy* shield and buckler. 5 Thou shalt not be afraid for the terror by night; *nor* for the arrow *that* flieth by day; 6 *Nor* for the pestilence *that* walketh in darkness; *nor* for the destruction *that* wasteth at noonday. 7 A thousand shall fall at thy side, and ten thousand at thy right hand; *but* it shall not come nigh thee. 8 Only with thine eyes shalt thou behold and see the reward of the wicked. 9 Because thou hast made the LORD, *which is* my refuge, *even* the most High, thy habitation; 10 There shall no evil befall thee, neither shall any plague come nigh thy dwelling. *[Satan seemed to understand that this Psalm is Messianic.]* 11 For he shall give his angels charge over thee, to keep thee in all thy ways. 12 They shall bear thee up in *their* hands, lest thou dash thy foot against a stone. 13 Thou shalt tread upon the lion and adder: the young lion and the dragon shalt thou trample under feet. 14 Because he hath set his love upon me, therefore will I deliver him: I will set him on high, because he hath known my name. 15 He shall call upon me, and I will answer him: I *will be* with him in trouble; I will deliver him, and honour him. 16 With long life will I satisfy him, and shew him my salvation.

Isaiah 41:17 *When* the poor and needy seek water, and *there is* none, *and* their tongue faileth for thirst, I the LORD will hear them, *I* the God of Israel will not forsake them.

Psalm 22:24 For he hath not despised nor abhorred the affliction of the afflicted; neither hath he hid his face from him; but when he cried unto him, he heard.

The Bible is the Book of Prophecy. Every believer knows that; but, what we believers often fail to appreciate is that some of those prophecies that are indicative of the large events that will happen to the world in the future are also predictive (to declare in advance) of what appears to be small almost insignificant things that will and did occur in the life of the Messiah. Among those are these events that pertain to the time when the Lamb of GOD was hanging on the cross. They speak directly to the question of whether or not GOD the Father forsook GOD the Son.

> Isaiah 50:6 I gave my back to the smiters, and my cheeks to them that plucked off the hair: I hid not my face from shame and spitting. 7 For the Lord GOD will help me; therefore shall I not be confounded: therefore have I set my face like a flint, and I know that I shall not be ashamed. 8 He is near that justifieth me; who will contend with me? let us stand together: who is mine adversary? let him come near to me. 9 Behold, the Lord GOD will help me; who is he that shall condemn me? lo, they all shall wax old as a garment; the moth shall eat them up.

> Psalm 35:10 All my bones shall say, LORD, who is like unto thee, which deliverest the poor from him that is too strong for him, yea, the poor and the needy from him that spoileth him?

> Psalm 116:3 The sorrows of death compassed me, and the pains of hell gat hold upon me: I found trouble and sorrow. 4 Then called I upon the name of the LORD; O LORD, I beseech thee, deliver my soul. 5 Gracious is the LORD, and righteous; yea, our God is merciful. 6 The LORD preserveth the simple: I was brought low, and he helped me.

These promises and prophecies confirm that GOD the Father did not reject, abandon, or forsake the Son of GOD at any time while the Son was on the cross. They also confirm that GOD the Son had no desire, and made no attempt, to avoid the cross.

The events that transpired in the Garden of Gethsemane and between the Garden and the empty tomb are the singular record of promises and prophecies. The promises were made and those promises were kept. The prophecies were given and those prophecies were fulfilled.

The apostle Paul reminded the congregation gathered in the synagogue in Antioch of the comprehensive execution of the promises of GOD. He then used the record of the integrity of the GOD of Heaven in discharging His promises to remind the hearers that GOD would continue to honor His word.

> Acts 13:26 Men *and* brethren, children of the stock of Abraham, and whosoever among you feareth God, to you is the word of this salvation sent. 27 For they that dwell at Jerusalem, and their rulers, because they knew him not, nor yet the voices of the prophets which are read every sabbath day, they have fulfilled *them* in condemning *him.* 28 And though they found no cause of death *in him,* yet desired they Pilate that he should be slain. 29 And when they had fulfilled all that was written of him, they took *him* down from the tree, and laid *him* in a sepulchre. 30 But God raised him from the dead: 31 And he was seen many days of them which came up with him from Galilee to Jerusalem, who are his witnesses unto the people. 32 And we declare unto you glad tidings, how that the promise which was made unto the fathers, 33 God hath fulfilled the same unto us their children, in that he hath raised up Jesus again; as it is also written in the second psalm, Thou art my Son, this day have I begotten thee. 34 And as concerning that he raised him up from the dead, *now* no more to return to corruption, he said on this wise, I will give you the sure mercies of David. 35 Wherefore he saith also in another *psalm,* Thou shalt not suffer thine Holy One to

see corruption. 36 For David, after he had served his own generation by the will of God, fell on sleep, and was laid unto his fathers, and saw corruption: 37 But he, whom God raised again, saw no corruption. 38 Be it known unto you therefore, men *and* brethren, that through this man is preached unto you the forgiveness of sins: 39 And by him all that believe are justified from all things, from which ye could not be justified by the law of Moses. 40 Beware therefore, lest that come upon you, which is spoken of in the prophets; 41 Behold, ye despisers, and wonder, and perish: for I work a work in your days, a work which ye shall in no wise believe, though a man declare it unto you.

The *beware therefore* is a caution that ought to encourage the faithful believer and to caution every unfaithful believer, even as it warns the unbeliever, that GOD will keep every one of His promises and fulfill all His prophecies, not the least of which are the promise of eternal life for the believer and that of eternal death for the unbeliever.

It is beyond question that the GOD of Heaven kept His promises and fulfilled His prophecies to His only begotten Son. A discussion to the contrary is absurd to contemplate.

The Son of GOD was not forsaken.

CHAPTER 19

ADDITIONAL TYPES AND TERMINOLOGY

The Levitical offerings of the Old Testament were types[1] of the LORD Jesus. Due to the failure of many commentators to accept the typology of the Old Testament as having validity as a tool in the understanding and the interpretation of Scripture, the Levitical offerings are not studied for correlation with the offering of the LORD Jesus. However, as we have already observed, this is precisely what the Holy Spirit does in the Book of Hebrews. The Old Testament types are used to teach what the sacrifice of the LORD Jesus was and how that sacrifice was offered.

Even the cursory reading of the passages describing the Passover lamb will reveal that the lamb that was offered in the sacrifice was not changed by the offering as the sacrifice from being "without blemish" into a tainted lamb. The lamb did not become defiled.

The Passover lamb did not become an unclean animal. The evidence is obvious; the Passover lamb was eaten by the family. There was no change in the lamb. The lamb was without blemish before the offering, continued unblemished during the offering, and remained unblemished after the offering.

> Exodus 12:1 And the LORD spake unto Moses and Aaron in the land of Egypt, saying, 2 This month *shall be* unto you the beginning of months: it *shall be* the first month of the year to you. 3 Speak ye unto all the congregation of Israel, saying, In the tenth *day* of this month they shall take to them every man a lamb, according to the house of *their* fathers, a lamb for an house: 4 And if the household be too little for the lamb, let him and his neighbour next unto his house take *it* according to the number of the souls; every man according to his eating shall make your count for the lamb. 5 Your lamb shall be **without blemish**, a male of the first year: ye shall take *it* out from the sheep, or from the goats: 6 And ye shall keep it up until the fourteenth day of the same month: and the whole assembly of the congregation of Israel shall kill it in the evening. 7 And they shall take of the blood, and strike *it* on the two side posts and on the upper door post of the houses, wherein they shall eat it. 8 And they shall eat the flesh in that night, roast with fire, and unleavened bread; *and* with bitter *herbs* they shall eat it. 9 Eat not of it raw, nor sodden at all with water, but roast *with* fire; his head with his legs, and with the purtenance thereof. 10 And ye shall let nothing of it remain until the morning; and that which remaineth of it until the morning ye shall burn with fire. 11 And thus shall ye eat it; *with* your loins girded, your shoes on your feet, and your staff in your hand; and ye shall eat it in haste: it *is* the LORD'S passover. 12 For I will pass through the land of Egypt this night, and will smite all the firstborn in the land of Egypt, both man and beast; and against all the gods of Egypt I will execute judgment: I *am* the LORD. 13 And

the blood shall be to you for a token upon the houses where ye *are*: and when I see the blood, I will pass over you, and the plague shall not be upon you to destroy *you*, when I smite the land of Egypt. 14 And this day shall be unto you for a memorial; and ye shall keep it a feast to the LORD throughout your generations; ye shall keep it a feast by an ordinance for ever. 15 Seven days shall ye eat unleavened bread; even the first day ye shall put away leaven out of your houses: for whosoever eateth leavened bread from the first day until the seventh day, that soul shall be cut off from Israel. 16 And in the first day *there shall be* an holy convocation, and in the seventh day there shall be an holy convocation to you; no manner of work shall be done in them, save *that* which every man must eat, that only may be done of you. 17 And ye shall observe *the feast of* unleavened bread; for in this selfsame day have I brought your armies out of the land of Egypt: therefore shall ye observe this day in your generations by an ordinance for ever. 18 In the first *month*, on the fourteenth day of the month at even, ye shall eat unleavened bread, until the one and twentieth day of the month at even. 19 Seven days shall there be no leaven found in your houses: for whosoever eateth that which is leavened, even that soul shall be cut off from the congregation of Israel, whether he be a stranger, or born in the land. 20 Ye shall eat nothing leavened; in all your habitations shall ye eat unleavened bread. 21 Then Moses called for all the elders of Israel, and said unto them, Draw out and take you a lamb according to your families, and kill the passover. 22 And ye shall take a bunch of hyssop, and dip *it* in the blood that *is* in the bason, and strike the lintel and the two side posts with the blood that *is* in the bason; and none of you shall go out at the door of his house until the morning. 23 For the LORD will pass through to smite the

Egyptians; and when he seeth the blood upon the lintel, and on the two side posts, the LORD will pass over the door, and will not suffer the destroyer to come in unto your houses to smite *you*. 24 And ye shall observe this thing for an ordinance to thee and to thy sons for ever. 25 And it shall come to pass, when ye be come to the land which the LORD will give you, according as he hath promised, that ye shall keep this service. 26 And it shall come to pass, when your children shall say unto you, What mean ye by this service? 27 That ye shall say, It *is* the sacrifice of the LORD'S passover, who passed over the houses of the children of Israel in Egypt, when he smote the Egyptians, and delivered our houses. And the people bowed the head and worshipped. 28 And the children of Israel went away, and did as the LORD had commanded Moses and Aaron, so did they. ...

43 And the LORD said unto Moses and Aaron, This *is* the ordinance of the passover: There shall no stranger eat thereof: 44 But every man's servant that is bought for money, when thou hast circumcised him, then shall he eat thereof. 45 A foreigner and an hired servant shall not eat thereof. 46 In one house shall it be eaten; thou shalt not carry forth ought of the flesh abroad out of the house; neither shall ye break a bone thereof. 47 All the congregation of Israel shall keep it. 48 And when a stranger shall sojourn with thee, and will keep the passover to the LORD, let all his males be circumcised, and then let him come near and keep it; and he shall be as one that is born in the land: for no uncircumcised person shall eat thereof. 49 One law shall be to him that is homeborn, and unto the stranger that sojourneth among you. 50 Thus did all the children of Israel; as the LORD commanded Moses and Aaron, so did they. 51 And it came to pass the selfsame day, *that* the LORD

316

did bring the children of Israel out of the land of Egypt by their armies.

The Lamb of GOD, the LORD Jesus, was "a lamb without blemish and without spot" before the cross and He was not changed by the cross into a lamb with blemish and with spot. Using His Own words, I may write safely, accurately, and reverently that *He was still eatable after the cross*:

> John 6:53 Then Jesus said unto them, Verily, verily, I say unto you, Except ye eat the flesh of the Son of man, and drink his blood, ye have no life in you. 54 Whoso eateth my flesh, and drinketh my blood, hath eternal life; and I will raise him up at the last day. 55 For my flesh is meat indeed, and my blood is drink indeed. 56 He that eateth my flesh, and drinketh my blood, dwelleth in me, and I in him. 57 As the living Father hath sent me, and I live by the Father: so he that eateth me, even he shall live by me.

Perhaps even more striking, the sacrifice for the trespass offering was eaten after it was offered. Not only was it *permitted* to be eaten; it was *required* to be eaten. The sacrifice was given to the priests for them to eat and it would be a sin for them not to eat that sacrifice.

> Leviticus 7:1 Likewise this *is* the law of the trespass offering: it *is* most holy. 2 In the place where they kill the burnt offering shall they kill the trespass offering: and the blood thereof shall he sprinkle round about upon the altar. 3 And he shall offer of it all the fat thereof; the rump, and the fat that covereth the inwards, 4 And the two kidneys, and the fat that *is* on them, which *is* by the flanks, and the caul *that is* above the liver, with the kidneys, it shall he take away: 5 And the priest shall burn them upon the altar *for* an offering made by fire unto the LORD: it *is* a trespass offering. 6 **Every male among the priests shall eat thereof: it shall be eaten**

317

in the holy place: it *is* **most holy.** 7 As the sin offering *is*, so *is* the trespass offering: *there is* one law for them: the priest that maketh atonement therewith shall have *it*. 8 **And the priest that offereth any man's burnt offering,** *even* **the priest shall have to himself the skin of the burnt offering which he hath offered.** 9 **And all the meat offering that is baken in the oven, and all that is dressed in the fryingpan, and in the pan, shall be the priest's that offereth it.** 10 **And every meat offering, mingled with oil, and dry, shall all the sons of Aaron have, one** *as much* **as another.** 11 And this *is* the law of the sacrifice of peace offerings, which he shall offer unto the LORD. 12 If he offer it for a thanksgiving, then he shall offer with the sacrifice of thanksgiving unleavened cakes mingled with oil, and unleavened wafers anointed with oil, and cakes mingled with oil, of fine flour, fried. 13 Besides the cakes, he shall offer *for* his offering leavened bread with the sacrifice of thanksgiving of his peace offerings. 14 And of it he shall offer one out of the whole oblation *for* an heave offering unto the LORD, **and it shall be the priest**'s that sprinkleth the blood of the peace offerings. 15 **And the flesh of the sacrifice of his peace offerings for thanksgiving shall be eaten the same day that it is offered; he shall not leave any of it until the morning.** 16 **But if the sacrifice of his offering** *be* **a vow, or a voluntary offering, it shall be eaten the same day that he offereth his sacrifice: and on the morrow also the remainder of it shall be eaten:** 17 But the remainder of the flesh of the sacrifice on the third day shall be burnt with fire. 18 And if *any* of the flesh of the sacrifice of his peace offerings be eaten at all on the third day, it shall not be accepted, neither shall it be imputed unto him that offereth it: it shall be an abomination, and the soul that eateth of it shall bear his iniquity.

19 And **the flesh that toucheth any unclean *thing* shall not be eaten**; it shall be burnt with fire: and as for the flesh, all that be clean shall eat thereof. 20 But the soul that eateth *of* the flesh of the sacrifice of peace offerings, that *pertain* unto the LORD, having his uncleanness upon him, even that soul shall be cut off from his people. 21 Moreover the soul that shall touch any unclean *thing, as* the uncleanness of man, or *any* unclean beast, or any abominable unclean *thing*, and eat of the flesh of the sacrifice of peace offerings, which *pertain* unto the LORD, even that soul shall be cut off from his people. ... 28 And the LORD spake unto Moses, saying, 29 Speak unto the children of Israel, saying, He that offereth the sacrifice of his peace offerings unto the LORD shall bring his oblation unto the LORD of the sacrifice of his peace offerings. 30 His own hands shall bring the offerings of the LORD made by fire, the fat with the breast, it shall he bring, that the breast may be waved *for* a wave offering before the LORD. 31 And the priest shall burn the fat upon the altar: **but the breast shall be Aaron's and his sons'.** 32 And **the right shoulder shall ye give unto the priest** *for* an heave offering of the sacrifices of your peace offerings. 33 He among the sons of Aaron, that offereth the blood of the peace offerings, and the fat, **shall have the right shoulder for *his* part.** 34 **For the wave breast and the heave shoulder** have I taken of the children of Israel from off the sacrifices of their peace offerings, and **have given them unto Aaron the priest and unto his sons by a statute for ever** from among the children of Israel. 35 This *is the portion* of the anointing of Aaron, and of the anointing of his sons, out of the offerings of the LORD made by fire, in the day *when* he presented them to minister unto the LORD in the priest's office; 36 **Which the LORD commanded to be given them of the children of**

Israel, in the day that he anointed them, *by* **a statute for ever throughout their generations.** 37 This *is* the law of the burnt offering, of the meat offering, and of the sin offering, and of the trespass offering, and of the consecrations, and of the sacrifice of the peace offerings; 38 Which the LORD commanded Moses in mount Sinai, in the day that he commanded the children of Israel to offer their oblations unto the LORD, in the wilderness of Sinai.

It was not only this particular offering that was to be eaten. Other offerings were to be eaten. Moreover, if those offering were not eaten, the priests would be disobeying. The sacrifices were not changed by the act of sacrifice. The sacrifices did not become sin or sinful.

Leviticus 10:12 And Moses spake unto Aaron, and unto Eleazar and unto Ithamar, his sons that were left, Take the meat offering that remaineth of the offerings of the LORD made by fire, and eat it without leaven beside the altar: for it *is* most holy: 13 And ye shall eat it in the holy place, because it *is* thy due, and thy sons' due, of the sacrifices of the LORD made by fire: for so I am commanded. 14 And the wave breast and heave shoulder shall ye eat in a clean place; thou, and thy sons, and thy daughters with thee: for *they be* thy due, and thy sons' due, *which* are given out of the sacrifices of peace offerings of the children of Israel. 15 The heave shoulder and the wave breast shall they bring with the offerings made by fire of the fat, to wave *it for* a wave offering before the LORD; and it shall be thine, and thy sons' with thee, by a statute for ever; as the LORD hath commanded. 16 And Moses diligently sought the goat of the sin offering, and, behold, it was burnt: and he was angry with Eleazar and Ithamar, the sons of Aaron *which were* left *alive*, saying, 17 Wherefore have ye not eaten the sin offering in the holy place, seeing it *is* most holy, and *God* hath given it you to bear the iniquity of the congregation, to make atonement for them before the LORD? 18 Behold, the blood of it was not brought in within the holy *place*: ye should indeed have eaten it in the holy *place*, as I commanded. 19 And Aaron said unto Moses, Behold, this day have they offered their sin offering and their burnt offering before the LORD; and such things have befallen me: and *if* I had eaten the sin offering to day, should it have been accepted in the sight of the LORD? 20 And when Moses heard *that*, he was content.

The sheep, the goats, the bullocks, the heifers, the birds, etc.[2] of the Old Testament sacrifices were not changed by the altar. They were what they were before, during, and after being sacrificed on the altar.

The Antitype, Jesus of Nazareth, could not become something less than the type, the sacrifices of the Old Testament. The Lamb of GOD as the Sacrifice was as pure after the altar of the cross as He was before He lay down on the altar of the cross.

Every type in Scripture touches a particular aspect of the antitype and when compared to the antitype opens a better understanding of the antitype. I accept that it is possible to exaggerate typology and to promote weirdness in the place of Biblical truth. Typology must not be used to turn the Biblical language into ubiquitous allegory. However, the failure to understand the Biblical presence of types results in a great loss. GOD placed those types in His word for a purpose; the purpose of instruction.

1 Corinthians 10:11 Now all these things happened unto them for ensamples: and they are **written for** our admonition, upon whom the ends of the world are come.

1 Corinthians 10:6 Now these things were our examples, **to the intent** we should not lust after evil things, as they also lusted.

Romans 15:4 For whatsoever things were written aforetime were **written for** our learning, that we through patience and comfort of the scriptures might have hope.

While types ought to be acknowledged and studied, there are principles that should not be violated in the use of types.

1. The type does not originate doctrine; the type illustrates doctrine.
2. The type never contains the fullness of the antitype.
3. The type never replaces a literal meaning for a given passage.
4. The link between the type and the antitype must be clearly Biblically demonstrative and not subject to the imaginative whim and fancy of the interpreter to supply any meaning he wishes.
5. Shyness in the pursuit of types must not be replaced with zealous quest of types.

Perhaps, the most important caution is that the type is always a divinely purposed illustration of some truth; a valid type never requires forcing, it naturally flows from the Scripture. Types might be found in any of the following categories:[3]

1. A person: Romans 5:14 Nevertheless death reigned from Adam to Moses, even over them that had not sinned after the similitude of Adam's transgression, who is the figure of him that was to come.

2. An event: 1 Corinthians 10:11 Now all these things happened unto them for ensamples: and they are written for our admonition, upon whom the ends of the world are come.

3. An item: Hebrews 10:20 By a new and living way, which he hath consecrated for us, through the veil, that is to say, his flesh;

4. An office (priest, High Priest, judge, etc.): Hebrews 9:11 But Christ being come an high priest of good things to come, by a greater and more perfect tabernacle, not made with hands, that is to say, not of this building;

5. An offering, a feast, a ceremony: 1 Corinthians 5:7 Purge out therefore the old leaven, that ye may be a new lump, as ye are unleavened. For even Christ our passover is sacrificed for us.

In the *Reference Bible* bearing his name, C. I. Scofield wrote, "Types occur most frequently in the Pentateuch, but are found, more sparingly, elsewhere. The antitype, or fulfillment of the type, is found, usually, in the New Testament." In his statement, he reveals that he was infected with one of the diseases of aberrant typology as he opens the door for finding types that are not fulfilled in the New Testament—"fulfillment ... is found, **usually**, in the New Testament."

Scofield was wrong; if the antitype is not in the New Testament, then the proposed type is not a legitimate type.

There are multiple passages within the text of Scripture that may be legitimate types or that may simply be a valid illustrative picture that demonstrates a Biblical truth. I submit the following as such an example. Recently, in rereading the following passage, I took notice, for what I believe to be the first time in a new context, that the *earthen vessel* in which the sin offering is sodden[4] is to be *broken*. As I read, I recalled the words of the LORD Jesus: "And when he had given thanks, he brake it, and said, Take, eat: this is my body, which is broken for you: this do in remembrance of me." (1 Corinthians 11:24) I wondered if the LORD Jesus might have referenced the broken earthen vessel as He spoke.

Since the apostle will later refer to the physical body as an "earthen vessel,"[5] the analogy is proper. His physical body was, as is ours, a container to hold the soul and the spirit. His earthen vessel was broken for us.

> Leviticus 6:24 And the LORD spake unto Moses, saying, 25 Speak unto Aaron and to his sons, saying, This *is* the law of the sin offering: In the place where the burnt offering is killed shall the sin offering be killed before the LORD: it *is* most holy. 26 The priest that offereth it for sin shall eat it: in the holy place shall it be eaten, in the court of the tabernacle of the congregation. 27 Whatsoever shall touch the flesh thereof shall be holy: and when there is sprinkled of the blood thereof upon any garment, thou shalt wash that whereon it was sprinkled in the holy place. 28 But the earthen vessel wherein it is sodden shall be broken: and if it be sodden in a brasen pot, it shall be both scoured, and rinsed in water. 29 All the males among the priests shall eat thereof: it *is* most holy.

Whether it should or even could be identified as a type or should be understood as a passage useful for illustrative purpose is immaterial to the picture displayed: the atoning sacrifice was held as it endured the fire in an earthen vessel. That earthen vessel was to be broken.

However, the earthen vessel was not broken because of having become contaminated by contact with something unclean (as is the reason in Leviticus 11:23 and 15:12).[6] That which was sodden in the earthen vessel (verse 28) is clearly described as "most holy" in the next verse. Moreover, verse 27 explained that "[w]hatsoever shall touch the flesh thereof shall be holy."

The earthen vessels used in these Levitical sacrifices were made holy because of the sacrifice. The vessel and the sacrifice were both considered holy. Contemporary commentaries generally suggest that the vessels were destroyed because of the potential of contamination from the blood and flesh of the sacrifice because the earthen vessel being made of clay would absorb some of the liquids placed within. It seems to me that this conflicts with the clarity of the passage. The text describes the vessel as being made holy, not as being made contaminated.

For me, this single passage is sufficient to show that *no part* of the LORD Jesus could have been made sin. Those who attempt in their doctrine to have the *humanity* of Jesus of Nazareth to be made sin during the crucifixion have a serious problem. He was not GOD *and* man; the Word was made flesh; Jesus of Nazareth was GOD manifest in the flesh.

The sacrifice **itself was holy before, during, and after the sacrifice**. That no portion of the offering became sin is evident in that the sacrifice itself must be eaten and the earthen vessel that contained the offering for a brief time must be broken.

The offering for the sin offering made that common earthen vessel holy. That earthen vessel has become so identified with that sacrifice during the time of the offering of the sacrifice that the earthen vessel is broken so that the particular sacrifice cannot be repeated.

The antitype, the LORD Jesus, fulfills the type completely, entirely, and perfectly. The Son of GOD, Jesus of Nazareth, was holy in His soul, His spirit, and His body. He was holy in conception;[7] He was holy in His life; He was holy in His death.

Immediately upon death, the physical body begins to decompose; the Biblical term is "see corruption." The word of GOD, however, is very careful to make us understand that the body of Jesus of Nazareth *never saw corruption.*

> Psalm 16:10 For thou wilt not leave my soul in hell; **neither wilt thou suffer thine Holy One to see corruption**.

> Acts 2:26 Therefore did my heart rejoice, and my tongue was glad; moreover also **my flesh shall rest in hope**: 27 Because thou wilt not leave my soul in hell, **neither wilt thou suffer thine Holy One to see corruption**. ... 31 **He seeing this before spake of the resurrection of Christ, that his soul was not left in hell, neither his flesh did see corruption**.

> Acts 13:35 Wherefore he saith also in another psalm, **Thou shalt not suffer thine Holy One to see corruption**. ... 37 But **he, whom God raised again, saw no corruption**.

I believe that this six-fold emphasis that His body never saw corruption is to make us recognize that the earthen vessel of the Jesus of Nazareth, His physical body, was holy before, during, and after the crucifixion. If He became corruptible sin while on the cross, there be no significance or reason in recording that He saw no corruption in the grave.

He never became sin; He was never made unholy, in part or in whole. His body was never made unholy; His spirit was never made unholy; His soul was never made unholy. The very thought that He *could be made* unholy is repugnant.

The impeccability of the LORD Jesus, His inability to sin, is essential to His deity. Deity cannot sin.[8] The LORD Jesus, the Son of GOD and the Son of man, is incapable of sinning.[9]

He could not be made sin in the sense of changing Him into something that He is not. Holiness is essential to His deity; GOD is holy.[10] The LORD Jesus is holy or He is not GOD. This doctrinal position cannot be weakened through linguistic compromise or surrendered through libertine cowardice.

Noah Webster in 1828 wrote, "Applied to the Supreme Being, holy signifies perfectly pure, immaculate, and complete in moral character." Though the LORD Jesus endured the penalty of our sinfulness and of our sin, He never was contaminated with either our sinfulness or our sins. He was "perfectly pure, immaculate, and complete in moral character" before He the Incarnation, during the crucifixion, and throughout the three days when His body was in the grave,[11] His soul was with the saints in Paradise,[12] and His spirit was in the hands of the Father.[13]

The word of GOD states unequivocally the continuous sinlessness of Jesus of Nazareth. He made the declaration Himself.

> John 14:30 Hereafter I will not talk much with you: for the prince of this world cometh, and hath nothing in me.

His sinlessness is defended by the Holy Spirit through Paul, Peter, and John. Paul using the phrase "separate from sinners"; Peter identifies Him as "without blemish and without spot" and declares that He "did no sin"; John explains that "in him is no sin."

> Hebrews 4:15 For we have not an high priest which cannot be touched with the feeling of our infirmities; but was in all points tempted like as we are, yet without sin.

Hebrews 7:26 For such an high priest became us, who is holy, harmless, undefiled, separate from sinners, and made higher than the heavens; 27 Who needeth not daily, as those high priests, to offer up sacrifice, first for his own sins, and then for the people's: for this he did once, when he offered up himself.

1 Peter 1:18 Forasmuch as ye know that ye were not redeemed with corruptible things, as silver and gold, from your vain conversation received by tradition from your fathers; 19 But with the precious blood of Christ, as of a lamb without blemish and without spot:

1 Peter 2:22 Who did no sin, neither was guile found in his mouth: 23 Who, when he was reviled, reviled not again; when he suffered, he threatened not; but committed himself to him that judgeth righteously: 24 Who his own self bare our sins in his own body on the tree, that we, being dead to sins, should live unto righteousness: by whose stripes ye were healed.

1 John 3:5 And ye know that he was manifested to take away our sins; and in him is no sin.

I call attention in particular to the statement in 1 John 3:5 that is emphatic in asserting that in Jesus of Nazareth "is no sin." At no time and under no circumstances was sin present in Jesus Christ. He did not partake of sin; He did not ingest sin; He did not become sin. This is a line of separation between truth and error that cannot be breached.

Error is much like gossip; it morphs as it is retold. Slight departure from the truth will soon become complete rejection. That Jesus was substantiality and constitutionally changed so as to be made a sinner with a sinful nature is taught by certain cults. Others have espoused the concept that He was literally made sin. This supposed transformation has been identified as having occurred while He was in the Garden or when He was on the cross. That is not supported by any text or any type in Scripture. I know of no reason to soften the statement. To propose that the Incarnate Son of GOD had sin in Him is a grievous error that can only be described as untrue.

I do not know when these misconceptions entered Christendom. I have found evidence of the teaching as early as the Reformer Martin Luther who wrote the following strangeness regarding Galatians 3:13.

> But Christ took all our sins and died for them on the Cross. "He was numbered with the transgressors; and he bare the sin of many, and made intercession for the transgressors" (Isaiah 53:12). **All the prophets of old said that Christ should be the greatest transgressor, murderer, adulterer, thief, blasphemer that ever was or ever could be on earth. When He took the sins of the whole world upon Himself, Christ was no longer an innocent person. He was a sinner burdened with the sins of a Paul who was a blasphemer; burdened with the sins of a Peter who denied Christ; burdened with the sins of a David who committed adultery and murder, and gave the heathen occasion to laugh at the Lord. In short, Christ was charged with the sins of all men, that He should pay for them with His own blood.** The curse struck Him. The Law found Him among sinners. He was not only in the company of sinners. He had gone so far as to invest Himself with the flesh and blood of sinners. So the Law judged and hanged Him for a sinner. ...
>
> In separating Christ from us sinners and holding Him up as a holy exemplar, errorists rob us of our best comfort. They misrepresent Him as a threatening tyrant who is ready to slaughter us at the slightest provocation. **I am**

told that it is preposterous and wicked to call the Son of God a cursed sinner. I answer: If you deny that He is a condemned sinner, you are forced to deny that Christ died. It is not less preposterous to say, the Son of God died, than to say, the Son of God was a sinner. ...

John the Baptist called Him "the lamb of God, which taketh away the sin of the world." Being the unspotted Lamb of God, Christ was personally innocent. But because He took the sins of the world, **His sinlessness was defiled with the sinfulness of the world. Whatever sins I, you, all of us have committed or shall commit, they are Christ's sins as if He had committed them Himself.** Our sins have to be Christ's sins or we shall perish forever. Isaiah declares of Christ: "The Lord hath laid on him the iniquity of us all." We have no right to minimize the force of this declaration. God does not amuse Himself with words. What a relief for a Christian to know that Christ is covered all over with my sins, your sins, and the sins of the whole world. ...

The sins of the whole world, past, present, and future, fastened themselves upon Christ and condemned Him. But because Christ is God, He had an everlasting and unconquerable righteousness. These two, the sin of the world and the righteousness of God, met in a death struggle. Furiously the sin of the world assailed the righteousness of God. Righteousness is immortal and invincible. On the other hand, sin is a mighty tyrant who subdues all men. This tyrant pounces on Christ. But Christ's righteousness is unconquerable. The result is inevitable. Sin is defeated and righteousness triumphs and reigns forever. ...

In II Corinthians 5:21 Paul writes: "For he (God) hath made him (Christ) to be sin for us, who knew no sin; that we might be made the righteousness of God in him." Although this and similar passages may be properly explained by saying that Christ was made a sacrifice for the curse and for sin, yet in my judgment it is better to leave these passages stand as they read: **Christ was made sin itself; Christ was made the curse itself.**[14]

The impeccability of the Son of man cannot be amended, abridged, or abrogated. At the same time, the Scriptures clearly reveal that Jesus of Nazareth endured the penalty of our sin; He was treated *as if* He sinned. He was the sinless Substitute.

> 2 Corinthians 5:18 And all things are of God, who hath reconciled us to himself by Jesus Christ, and hath given to us the ministry of reconciliation; 19 To wit, that God was in Christ, reconciling the world unto himself, not imputing their trespasses unto them; and hath committed unto us the word of reconciliation. 20 Now then we are ambassadors for Christ, as though God did beseech you by us: we pray you in Christ's stead, be ye reconciled to God. 21 For he hath made him to be sin for us, who knew no sin; that we might be made the righteousness of God in him.

The text of 2 Corinthians chapter five, verse 21 certainly does state that GOD "hath made him [Christ] *to be* sin for us." In the immediate context, the statement is found "who knew no sin." The LORD Jesus was made sin, but He knew no sin. The first declaration cannot contradict the second declaration.

The question is "How are we to understand "made him *to be* sin."

The Old Testament sacrifices were *types* of the sacrifice of the LORD Jesus. Not a single sacrifice was ever considered a defiled thing after the offering.

The LORD Jesus is identified as the Lamb of GOD, in particular He is recognized as the Passover Lamb.

> John 1:29 The next day John seeth Jesus coming unto him, and saith, Behold the Lamb of God, which taketh away the sin of the world. ... 36 And looking upon Jesus as he walked, he saith, Behold the Lamb of God!
>
> 1 Corinthians 5:7 ... For even Christ our passover is sacrificed for us:

The Passover Lamb was not defiled by being made a sacrifice. That lamb was not changed from an unblemished lamb into a lamb with blemishes by being a sacrifice. In actual practice, the lamb was eaten as part of a delicious meal. The lamb was not an unholy thing because of the offering. The LORD Jesus and His disciples observed the Passover in which a Passover lamb was eaten. The text surely leaves open the possibility that the Son of GOD ate of that Passover lamb.

> Luke 22:14 And when the hour was come, he sat down, and the twelve apostles with him. 15 And he said unto them, With desire **I have desired to eat** this passover with you before I suffer:

When the Passover was first introduced, the stipulation was that the lamb was to be eaten. The composition, the essence, the substance of the lamb did not change

> Exodus 12:1 And the LORD spake unto Moses and Aaron in the land of Egypt, saying, 2 This month *shall be* unto you the beginning of months: it *shall be* the first month of the year to you. 3 Speak ye unto all the congregation of Israel, saying, In the tenth *day* of this month they shall take to them every man a lamb, according to the house of *their* fathers, a lamb for an house: 4 And if the household be too little for the lamb, let him and his neighbour next unto his house take *it* according to the

number of the souls; every man according to his eating shall make your count for the lamb. ... 8 And they shall eat the flesh in that night, roast with fire, and unleavened bread; *and* with bitter *herbs* they shall eat it. 9 Eat not of it raw, nor sodden at all with water, but roast *with* fire; his head with his legs, and with the purtenance thereof. 10 And ye shall let nothing of it remain until the morning; and that which remaineth of it until the morning ye shall burn with fire. 11 And thus shall ye eat it; *with* your loins girded, your shoes on your feet, and your staff in your hand; and ye shall eat it in haste: it *is* the LORD'S passover.

The lamb died *for, on the behalf of, in place of, vicariously as a substitute for* the firstborn. While the lamb was identified with the firstborn, the lamb did not become the firstborn. The lamb died *instead of* the firstborn. This is the doctrine of imputation, which is repeatedly connected with the death of Jesus of Nazareth in the Scriptures.

2 Corinthians 5:14 For the love of Christ constraineth us; because we thus judge, that if **one died for all**, then were all dead: 15 And *that* **he died for all**, that they which live should not henceforth live unto themselves, but unto him which died for them, and rose again. 16 Wherefore henceforth know we no man after the flesh: yea, though we have known Christ after the flesh, yet now henceforth know we *him* no more. 17 Therefore if any man *be* in Christ, *he is* a new creature: old things are passed away; behold, all things are become new. 18 And all things *are* of God, who hath reconciled us to himself by Jesus Christ, and hath given to us the ministry of reconciliation; 19 To wit, that **God was in Christ**, reconciling the world unto himself, **not imputing their trespasses unto them**; and hath committed unto us the word of reconciliation. 20 Now then we are ambassadors for Christ, as though God did beseech *you* by

us: we pray *you* in Christ's stead, be ye reconciled to God. 21 For **he hath made him** *to be* sin for us, who knew no sin; **that we might be made** the righteousness of God in him. 6:1 We then, *as* workers together *with him,* beseech *you* also that ye receive not the grace of God in vain. 2 (For he saith, I have heard thee in a time accepted, and in the day of salvation have I succoured thee: behold, now *is* the accepted time; behold, now *is* the day of salvation.)

Romans 4:1 What shall we say then that Abraham our father, as pertaining to the flesh, hath found? 2 For if Abraham were justified by works, he hath *whereof* to glory; but not before God. 3 For what saith the scripture? Abraham believed God, and it was **counted unto him** for righteousness. 4 Now to him that worketh is the reward not **reckoned** of grace, but of debt. 5 But to him that worketh not, but believeth on him that justifieth the ungodly, his faith is **counted for** righteousness. 6 Even as David also describeth the blessedness of the man, unto whom God **imputeth** righteousness without works, 7 *Saying,* Blessed *are* they whose iniquities are forgiven, and whose sins are covered. 8 Blessed *is* the man to whom the Lord will not **impute** sin. 9 *Cometh* this blessedness then upon the circumcision *only,* or upon the uncircumcision also? for we say that faith was **reckoned** to Abraham for righteousness. 10 How was it then **reckoned**? when he was in circumcision, or in uncircumcision? Not in circumcision, but in uncircumcision. 11 And he received the sign of circumcision, a seal of the righteousness of the faith which *he had yet* being uncircumcised: that he might be the father of all them that believe, though they be not circumcised; that righteousness might be **imputed** unto them also: 12 And the father of circumcision to them who are not of the circumcision only, but who also walk in the steps of that faith of our father Abraham, which *he had* being *yet* uncircumcised. 13 For the promise, that he should be the heir of the world, *was* not to Abraham, or to his seed, through the law, but through the righteousness of faith. 14 For if they which are of the law *be* heirs, faith is made void, and the promise made of none effect: 15 Because the law worketh wrath: for where no law is, *there is* no transgression. 16 Therefore *it is* of faith, that *it might be* by grace; to the end the promise might be sure to all the seed; not to that only which is of the law, but to that also which is of the faith of Abraham; who is the father of us all, 17 (As it is written, I have made thee a father of many nations,) before him whom he believed, *even* God, who quickeneth the dead, and **calleth those things which be not as though they were**. 18 Who against hope believed in hope, that he might become the father of many nations; according to that which was spoken, So shall thy seed be. 19 And being not weak in faith, he considered not his own body now dead, when he was about an hundred years old, neither yet the deadness of Sara's womb: 20 He staggered not at the promise of God through unbelief; but was strong in faith, giving glory to God; 21 And being fully persuaded that, what he had promised, he was able also to perform. 22 And therefore it was **imputed** to him for righteousness. 23 Now it was not written for his sake alone, that it was **imputed** to him; 24 But for us also, to whom it shall be **imputed**, if we believe on him that raised up Jesus our Lord from the dead; 25 Who was delivered for our offences, and was raised again for our justification.

Isaiah 53:5 But he *was* wounded for our transgressions, *he was* bruised for our iniquities: the chastisement of our peace *was* **upon him**; and with his stripes we are healed. 6 All we like sheep have gone astray; we have turned every one to his own way; and **the LORD hath laid on him the iniquity of us all.**

Isaiah 53:10 Yet it pleased the LORD to bruise him; he hath put *him* to grief: when thou shalt make his soul an offering for sin, he shall see *his* seed, he shall prolong *his* days, and the pleasure of the LORD shall prosper in his hand. 11 He shall see of the travail of his soul, *and* shall be satisfied: by his knowledge shall my righteous servant justify many; for **he shall bear their iniquities.** 12 Therefore will I divide him *a portion* with the great, and he shall divide the spoil with the strong; because he hath poured out his soul unto death: and he was numbered with the transgressors; and **he bare the sin of many**, and **made intercession** for the transgressors.

Hebrews 9:28 So **Christ was once offered to bear the sins of many**; and unto them that look for him shall he appear the second time without sin unto salvation.

1 Peter 2:21 For even hereunto were ye called: because **Christ also suffered for us**, leaving us an example, that ye should follow his steps: 22 Who did no sin, neither was guile found in his mouth: 23 Who, when he was reviled, reviled not again; when he suffered, he threatened not; but committed himself to him that judgeth righteously: 24 **Who his own self bare our sins in his own body on the tree,** that we, being dead to sins, should live unto righteousness: by whose stripes ye were healed.

This doctrine of imputation was expressed in and taught by the hymns of Isaac Watts. The old hymns of the faith were intended to teach doctrine in distinction to contemporary *songs* that seem to be designed more for making the hearers feel good than for instructing them.

This first hymn by Watts is not as well known as the second. [15] However it is very rich and ought to become familiar.

Not all the blood of beasts
On Jewish altars slain
Could give the guilty conscience peace
Or wash away the stain.

But Christ, the heav'nly Lamb,
Takes all our sins away;
A sacrifice of nobler name
And richer blood than they.

My faith would lay her hand
On that dear head of Thine,
While, like a penitent, I stand,
And there confess my sin.

My soul looks back to see
The burdens Thou didst bear
When hanging on the cursèd tree,
And hopes her guilt was there.

Believing, we rejoice
To see the curse remove;
We bless the Lamb with cheerful voice,
And sing His bleeding love.

Alas, and did my Savior bleed,
And did my Sov'reign die?
Would He devote that sacred head
For such a worm as I?

Thy body slain, sweet Jesus, thine,
And bathed in its own blood,
While all exposed to wrath divine
The glorious Suff'rer stood!

Was it for crimes that I had done
He groaned upon the tree?
Amazing pity! grace unknown!
And love beyond degree!

Well might the sun in darkness hide,
And shut his glories in,
When God, the mighty Maker, died
For man, the creature's sin.

Thus might I hide my blushing face
While his dear cross appears,
Dissolve my heart in thankfulness,
And melt mine eyes to tears.

But drops of grief can ne'er repay
The debt of love I owe;
Here, Lord, I give myself away,
'Tis all that I can do.

Perhaps the simplest presentation of the doctrine of imputation is to be found in Romans 5:8 and the use of the phrase "for us."

But God commendeth his love toward us, in that, while we were yet sinners, Christ died for us.

The doctrine of imputation is repeatedly affirmed by the use of the phrase *for us* in relation to the death of the LORD Jesus.

Romans 8:32 He that spared not his own Son, but delivered him up for us all, how shall he not with him also freely give us all things?

1 Corinthians 5:7 Purge out therefore the old leaven, that ye may be a new lump, as ye are unleavened. For even Christ our passover is sacrificed for us:

2 Corinthians 5:21 For he hath made him *to be* sin for us, who knew no sin; that we might be made the righteousness of God in him.

Galatians 3:13 Christ hath redeemed us from the curse of the law, being made a curse for us: for it is written, Cursed *is* every one that hangeth on a tree:

Ephesians 5:2 And walk in love, as Christ also hath loved us, and hath given himself for us an offering and a sacrifice to God for a sweetsmelling savour.

1 Thessalonians 5:10 Who died for us, that, whether we wake or sleep, we should live together with him.

Titus 2:14 Who gave himself for us, that he might redeem us from all iniquity, and purify unto himself a peculiar people, zealous of good works.

Hebrews 9:12 Neither by the blood of goats and calves, but by his own blood he entered in once into the holy place, having obtained eternal redemption *for us.*

Hebrews 10:20 By a new and living way, which he hath consecrated for us, through the veil, that is to say, his flesh;

1 Peter 2:21 For even hereunto were ye called: because Christ also suffered for us, leaving us an example, that ye should follow his steps:

1 Peter 4:1 Forasmuch then as Christ hath suffered for us in the flesh, arm yourselves likewise with the same mind: for he that hath suffered in the flesh hath ceased from sin;

1 John 3:16 Hereby perceive we the love *of God*, because he laid down his life for us: and we ought to lay down *our* lives for the brethren.

Jesus of Nazareth did not die *as* us.

The Son of GOD died *for* us.

---

[1] Merriam-Webster: a person or thing (as in the Old Testament) believed to foreshadow another (as in the New Testament) *American Dictionary of the English Language,* published in 1828: A sign; a symbol; a figure of something to come; as, Abraham's sacrifice and the paschal lamb, were types of Christ. To this word is opposed antitype. Christ, in this case, is the antitype.

[2] In addition to the animals of the Levitical sacrifices, Noah offered an acceptable sacrifice composed of individuals from every clean animal and fowl family.
Genesis 7:1 And the LORD said unto Noah, Come thou and all thy house into the ark; for thee have I seen righteous before me in this generation. 2 Of every clean beast thou shalt take to thee by sevens, the male and his female: and of beasts that *are* not clean by two, the male and his female. 3 Of fowls also of the air by sevens, the male and the female; to keep seed alive upon the face of all the earth. ... 8:20 And Noah builded an altar unto the LORD; and took of every clean beast, and of every clean fowl, and offered burnt offerings on the altar. 21 And the LORD smelled a sweet savour; and the LORD said in his heart, I will not again curse the ground any more for man's sake; for the imagination of man's heart *is* evil from his youth; neither will I again smite any more every thing living, as I have done. 22 While the earth remaineth, seedtime and harvest, and cold and heat, and summer and winter, and day and night shall not cease.

[3] Adapted from the notes in the Scofield Reference Bible 1917 edition.

[4] Leviticus 6:28 But the earthen vessel wherein it is sodden shall be broken: and if it be sodden in a brasen pot, it shall be both scoured, and rinsed in water. *SwordSearcher.* Strong's Hebrew Dictionary 1310. בָּשַׁל bashal; a primitive root; properly, to boil up; hence, to be done in cooking; figuratively to ripen:—bake, boil, bring forth, roast, seethe, sod (be sodden).

[5] 2 Corinthians 4:7 But we have this treasure in earthen vessels, that the excellency of the power may be of God, and not of us.

[6] Leviticus 11:23 But all *other* flying creeping things, which have four feet, *shall be* an abomination unto you.
Leviticus 15:12 And the vessel of earth, that he toucheth which hath the issue, shall be broken: and every vessel of wood shall be rinsed in water.

[7] Luke 1:35 And the angel answered and said unto her, The Holy Ghost shall come upon thee, and the power of the Highest shall overshadow thee: therefore also that holy thing which shall be born of thee shall be called the Son of God.

8 James 1:13 Let no man say when he is tempted, I am tempted of God: for God cannot be tempted with evil, neither tempteth he any man: 14 But every man is tempted, when he is drawn away of his own lust, and enticed. 15 Then when lust hath conceived, it bringeth forth sin: and sin, when it is finished, bringeth forth death.

9 The doctrine is defended in an article titled *The Impeccability of Christ*, written by Arthur W. Pink and found in *Studies in the Scriptures*, dated September 1932.

We are living in a world of sin, and the fearful havoc it has wrought is evident on every side. How refreshing, then, to fix our gaze upon One who is immaculately holy, and who passed through this scene unspoilt by its evil. Such was the Lord Jesus Christ, the Son of God incarnate. For thirty-three years He was in immediate contact with sin, yet He was never, to the slightest degree, contaminated. He touched the leper, yet was not defiled, even ceremonially. Just as the rays of the sun shine upon a stagnant pool without being sullied thereby, so Christ was unaffected by the iniquity which surrounded Him. He 'did no sin' (1 Pet. 2:22), 'in Him is no sin' (1 John 3:5 and contrast 1:8), He 'knew no sin' (2 Cor. 5:21), He was 'without sin' (Heb. 4:15). He was 'holy, harmless, undefiled, separate from sinners' (Heb. 7:26).

But not only was Christ sinless, He was impeccable, that is, incapable of sinning. No attempt to set forth the doctrine of His wondrous and peerless person would be complete, without considering this blessed perfection. Sad indeed is it to behold the widespread ignorance thereon today, and sadder still to hear and read this precious truth denied. The last Adam differed from the first Adam in His impeccability. Christ was not only able to overcome temptation, but He was unable to be overcome by it. Necessarily so, for He was 'the Almighty' (Rev. 1:8). True, Christ was man, but He was the God-man, and as such, absolute Master and Lord of all things. Being Master of all things—as His dominion over the winds and waves, diseases and death, clearly demonstrated—it was impossible that anything should master Him.

The immutability of Christ proves His impeccability, or incapability of sinning: 'Jesus Christ the same yesterday, and today, and forever' (Heb. 13:8). Because He was not susceptible to any change, it was impossible for the incarnate Son of God to sin. Herein we behold again His uniqueness. Sinless angels fell, sinless Adam fell: they were but creatures, and creaturehood and mutability are, really, correlative terms. But was not the manhood of Christ created? Yes, but it was never placed on probation, it never had a separate existence. From the very first moment of its conception in the virgin's womb, the humanity of Christ was taken into union with His Deity; and therefore could not sin.

The omnipotence of Christ proves His impeccability. That the Lord Jesus, even during the days of His humiliation, was possessed of omnipotence, is clear from many passages of Scripture. 'What things so ever He (the Father) doeth, these also doeth the Son likewise....For as the Father raiseth up the dead, and quickeneth, even so the Son quickeneth whom He will' (John 5:19, 21). When we say that Christ possessed omnipotence during His earthly sojourn, we do not mean that He was so endowed by the Holy Spirit, but that He was essentially, inherently, personally, omnipotent. Now to speak of an omnipotent person yielding to sin, is a contradiction in terms. All temptation to sin must proceed from a created being, and hence it is a finite power; but impossible is it for a finite power to overcome omnipotency.

The constitution of Christ's person proves His impeccability. In Him were united (in a manner altogether incomprehensible to created intelligence) the Divine and the human natures. Now 'God cannot be tempted with evil' (James 1:13); 'it is impossible for God to lie' (Heb. 6:18). And Christ was 'God manifest in flesh' (1 Tim. 3:16); 'Immanuel'—God with us (Matt. 1:23). Personality centered not in His humanity. Christ was a Divine person, who had been 'made in the likeness of men' (Phil. 2:7). Utterly impossible was it, then, for the God-man to sin. To affirm the contrary, is to be guilty of the most awful blasphemy. It is irreverent speculation to discuss what the human nature of Christ might have done if it had been alone. It never was alone; it never had a separate existence; from the first moment of its being it was united to a Divine person.

It is objected to the truth of Christ's impeccability that it is inconsistent with His temptability. A person who cannot sin, it is argued, cannot be tempted to sin. As well might one reason that because an army cannot be defeated, it cannot be attacked.

> "Temptability depends upon the constitutional susceptibility, while impeccability depends upon the will. So far as His natu-

342

ral susceptibility, both physical and mental, was concerned, Jesus Christ was open to all forms of human temptation, excepting those that spring out of lust, or corruption of nature. But His peccability, or the possibility of being overcome by these temptations, would depend upon the amount of voluntary resistance which He was able to bring to bear against them. Those temptations were very strong, but if the self-determination of His holy will was stronger than they, then they could not induce Him to sin, and He would be impeccable. And yet plainly He would be temptable" (W.G.T. Shedd, 1889).

Probably there were many reasons why God ordained that His incarnate Son should be tempted by men, by the Devil, by circumstances. *One of these was to demonstrate His impeccability.* Throw a lighted match into a barrel of gunpowder, and there will be an explosion; throw it into a barrel of water, and the match will be quenched. This, in a very crude way, may be taken to illustrate the difference between Satan's tempting us and his tempting of the God-man. In us, there is that which is susceptible to his 'fiery darts'; but the Holy One could say, 'The prince of this world cometh and hath nothing in Me' (John 14:30). The Lord Jesus was exposed to a far more severe testing and trying than the first Adam was, in order to make manifest His mighty power of resistance.

We have not an high priest which cannot be touched with the feeling of our infirmities; but was in all points tempted like as we are, without sin' (Heb. 4:15). 'This text teaches that the temptations of Christ were 'without sin' in their source and nature, and not merely, as the passage is sometimes explained, that they were 'without sin' in their result. The meaning is not, that our Lord was tempted in every respect exactly as fallen man is-by inward lust, as well as by other temptations—only He did not outwardly yield to any temptation; but that He was tempted in every way that man is, excepting by that class of temptations that are sinful, because originating in evil and forbidden desire.

"The fact that Christ was almighty and victorious in His resistance does not unfit Him to be an example for imitation to a weak and sorely-tempted believer. Because our

343

Lord overcame His temptations, it does not follow that His conflict and success was an easy one for Him. His victory cost Him tears and blood. 'His visage was so marred more than any man' (Isa. 52:14). There was the 'travail of His soul' (Isa. 52:14). In the struggle He cried, 'O My Father, if it be possible let this cup pass from Me' (Matt. 26:39). Because an army is victorious, it by no means follows that the victory was a cheap one" (W.G.T. Shedd).

One other objection may, perhaps, be noted, though we hesitate to defile these pages by even transcribing the filthy exhalations of the carnal mind. If the humanity of Christ was, because of its union to His Divine person, incapable of sinning, then in view of its being Divinely sustained how could it hunger and thirst, suffer and die? and seeing it did, then why was it incapable of yielding to temptation? It is sufficient answer to this impious question to point out that, while the Mediator was commissioned to die (John 10:18), He was not commissioned to sin. The human nature of Christ was permitted to function freely and normally: hence it wearied and wept; but to sin is not a normal act of human nature.

To be the Redeemer of His people, Christ must be 'mighty to save, travelling in the greatness of His strength' (Isa. 63:1). He must have power to overcome all temptation when it assails His person, in order that He may be able to 'succour them that are tempted' (Heb. 2:18). Here then is one of the solid planks in that platform on which the faith of the Christian rests: because the Lord Jesus is Almighty, having absolute power over sin, the feeble and sorely-tried saint may turn to Him in implicit confidence, seeking His efficacious aid. Only He who triumphed over sin, both in life and in death, can save me from my sins.

[10] Leviticus 11:44 For I *am* the LORD your God: ye shall therefore sanctify yourselves, and ye shall be holy; for I *am* holy: neither shall ye defile yourselves with any manner of creeping thing that creepeth upon the earth. 45 For I *am* the LORD that bringeth you up out of the land of Egypt, to be your God: ye shall therefore be holy, for I *am* holy. ... 19:2 Speak unto all the congregation of the children of Israel, and say unto them, Ye shall be holy: for I the LORD your God am holy.

1 Peter 1:16 Because it is written, Be ye holy; for I am holy.

Psalm 99:5 Exalt ye the LORD our God, and worship at his footstool; for he is holy. ... 9 Exalt the LORD our God, and worship at his holy hill; for the LORD our God is holy.

[11] Matthew 27:59-60 And when Joseph had taken the body, he wrapped it in a clean linen cloth, 60 And laid it in his own new tomb, which he had hewn out in the rock: and he rolled a great stone to the door of the sepulchre, and departed.

1 Corinthians 15:4 And that he was buried, and that he rose again the third day according to the scriptures:

[12] Psalm 16:10 For thou wilt not leave my soul in hell; neither wilt thou suffer thine Holy One to see corruption.

Luke 23:43 And Jesus said unto him, Verily I say unto thee, To day shalt thou be with me in paradise.

1 Peter 3:19 By which also he went and preached unto the spirits in prison;

[13] Luke 23:46 And when Jesus had cried with a loud voice, he said, Father, into thy hands I commend my spirit: and having said thus, he gave up the ghost.

[14] Luther, Martin. Graebner, Theodore (Translator). A Commentary on St. Paul's Epistle to the Galatians; Christian Classics Ethereal Library, Grand Rapids, MI. pages 76–80.

[15] Both hymns are in public domain.

CHAPTER 20
CALVARY REQUIRED THE INCARNATION

There are specific phrases that are used in relationship to the sacrifice of the LORD Jesus. Some of those phrases are also used in other passages so that we can compare Scripture with Scripture and understand the application of the phrase. I do not suggest that this is a complete listing, but I do believe that these are among the key passages to understanding the implications of the Incarnation.

Calvary required the Incarnation. By that I mean that the atonement could not have been provided without the Incarnation.

MADE LIKE UNTO

Hebrews 2:17 Wherefore in all things it behoved him to be **made like unto** *his* brethren, that he might be a merciful and faithful high priest in things *pertaining* to God, to make reconciliation for the sins of the people.

Exodus 25:33 Three bowls made like unto almonds, *with* a knop and a flower in one branch; and three bowls made like almonds in the other branch, *with* a knop and a flower: so in the six branches that come out of the candlestick.

Exodus 25:34 And in the candlestick *shall be* four bowls made like unto almonds, *with* their knops and their flowers.

Romans 9:29 And as Esaias said before, Except the Lord of Sabaoth had left us a seed, we had been as Sodoma, and been made like unto Gomorrha.

Hebrews 7:3 Without father, without mother, without descent, having neither beginning of days, nor end of life; but made like unto the Son of GOD; abideth a priest continually.

In each of the other Biblical uses of the phrase, it is clear that the phrase "made like unto" never is intended to convey that one entity is transformed into another entity.

IN THE LIKENESS OF SINFUL FLESH

Romans 8:3 For what the law could not do, in that it was weak through the flesh, God sending his own Son in the likeness of sinful flesh, and for sin, condemned sin in the flesh:

The phrase "in the likeness of" is found five times in Scripture. In no instance is a transformation from one entity to another declared or implied. The phrase has the meaning of "resemblance" or "to become similar." Adam was made in the likeness of GOD, but Adam did not become GOD. The LORD Jesus was indeed made flesh, but it was not sinful flesh. He is GOD manifest in the flesh.[1]

Genesis 5:1 This is the book of the generations of Adam. In the day that God created man, in the likeness of God made he him;

Acts 14:11 And when the people saw what Paul had done, they lifted up their voices, saying in the speech of Lycaonia, The gods are come down to us in the likeness of men.

348

Romans 6:5 For if we have been planted together in the likeness of his death, we shall be also in the likeness of his resurrection:

Philippians 2:7 But made himself of no reputation, and took upon him the form of a servant, and was made in the likeness of men:

TOOK UPON HIM

Philippians 2:7 But made himself of no reputation, and took upon him the form of a servant, and was made in the likeness of men:

Esther 9:27 The Jews ordained, and took upon them, and upon their seed, and upon all such as joined themselves unto them, so as it should not fail, that they would keep these two days according to their writing, and according to their appointed time every year;

Acts 19:13 Then certain of the vagabond Jews, exorcists, took upon them to call over them which had evil spirits the name of the Lord Jesus, saying, We adjure you by Jesus whom Paul preacheth.

For the Son of GOD to take upon Himself "the form of a servant" required the Word being made flesh.

MADE HIMSELF

Philippians 2:7 But made himself of no reputation, and took upon him the form of a servant, and was made in the likeness of men:

Genesis 42:7 And Joseph saw his brethren, and he knew them, but made himself strange unto them, and spake roughly unto them; and he said unto them, Whence come ye? And they said, From the land of Canaan to buy food.

Genesis 45:1 Then Joseph could not refrain himself before all them that stood by him; and he cried, Cause every man to go out from me. And there stood no man with him, while Joseph made himself known unto his brethren.

349

2 Samuel 3:6 And it came to pass, while there was war between the house of Saul and the house of David, that Abner made himself strong for the house of Saul.

2 Samuel 13:6 So Amnon lay down, and made himself sick: and when the king was come to see him, Amnon said unto the king, I pray thee, let Tamar my sister come, and make me a couple of cakes in my sight, that I may eat at her hand.

2 Chronicles 32:27 And Hezekiah had exceeding much riches and honour: and he made himself treasuries for silver, and for gold, and for precious stones, and for spices, and for shields, and for all manner of pleasant jewels;

Song of Solomon 3:9 King Solomon made himself a chariot of the wood of Lebanon.

John 19:7 The Jews answered him, We have a law, and by our law he ought to die, because he made himself the Son of GOD.

BECOME POOR

2 Corinthians 8:9 For ye know the grace of our Lord Jesus Christ, that, though he was rich, yet for your sakes he became poor, that ye through his poverty might be rich.

TOOK PART

Hebrews 2:14 Forasmuch then as the children are partakers of flesh and blood, he also himself likewise took part of the same; that through death he might destroy him that had the power of death, that is, the devil;

Hebrews 2:16 For verily he took not on *him the nature of* angels; but he took on *him* the seed of Abraham.

GOD WAS IN CHRIST

The mystery of the TRINITY is beyond the human mind to grasp completely. Even more incomprehensible is the atonement. The Incarnation is perhaps the greatest mystery of all. The child of GOD is only able to *understand* by faith how that it was possible for GOD to be *in Christ*.

> Not only was GOD in Christ during His *life* on earth, John 14:10, GOD was in Christ in His reconciling *death*, 2 Corinthians 5:19. This ground is holy, yet is it to be approached, albeit with "reverence and awe," for all that GOD has been pleased to reveal is proper subject for the worshipful consideration of His children. Two cautions are needful here, however. We may not go beyond what is written, and we may not expect to eliminate mystery from the Divine sacrifice or to reconcile all that is revealed concerning it; the human point of view is far too low, the human outlook far too limited, to admit of that.[2]

The wonderful statement "God was manifest in the flesh"[3] does not mean that Jesus of Nazareth reflected or revealed GOD; it means that Jesus of Nazareth was GOD in the flesh: the Word became flesh and dwelt among us.[4]

The TRINITY is revealed to us in Scripture as GOD the Father, GOD the Son, and GOD the Holy Spirit. The TRINITY can be described, defined, and, demonstrated, but the TRINITY cannot be explained. The New Hampshire Confession of Faith provides a simple and satisfactory statement explaining the TRINITY.

> We believe that there is one, and only one, living and true GOD, an infinite, intelligent Spirit, whose name is JEHOVAH, the Maker and Supreme Ruler of Heaven and earth; inexpressibly glorious in holiness, and worthy of all possible honor, confidence, and love; that in the unity of the GODHEAD there are three persons, the Father, the Son, and the Holy Ghost; equal in every divine perfection, and executing distinct and harmonious offices in the great work of redemption.

John 14:9 Jesus saith unto him, Have I been so long time with you, and yet hast thou not known me, Philip? he that hath seen me hath seen the Father; and how sayest thou then, Shew us the Father? 10 Believest thou not that **I am in the Father, and the Father in me**? the words that I speak unto you I speak not of myself: but **the Father that dwelleth in me**, he doeth the works. 11 Believe me that **I am in the Father, and the Father in me**: or else believe me for the very works' sake.

2 Corinthians 5:18 And all things *are* of God, **who hath reconciled us to himself by Jesus Christ**, and hath given to us the ministry of reconciliation; 19 To wit, **that God was in Christ**, reconciling the world **unto himself**, not imputing their trespasses unto them; and hath committed unto us the word of reconciliation.

---

[1] *In the likeness of sinful flesh.* That is, he so far resembled sinful flesh that he partook of flesh, or the nature of man, but without any of its sinful propensities or desires. It was not human nature; not, as the Docetae taught, human nature in appearance only; but it was human nature without any of its corruptions. *SwordSearcher, Albert Barnes' Notes on the Bible,* Romans 8:3

[2] Vine, W. E., *Collected writings of W. E. Vine;* Thomas Nelson, Nashville. Galatians 2:20.

[3] 1 Timothy 3:16 And without controversy great is the mystery of godliness: God was manifest in the flesh, justified in the Spirit, seen of angels, preached unto the Gentiles, believed on in the world, received up into glory.

[4] John 1:14 And the Word was made flesh, and dwelt among us, (and we beheld his glory, the glory as of the only begotten of the Father,) full of grace and truth.

CHAPTER 21
TWO BIBLE VERSES THAT ARE NOT

Verse 1: GOD cannot look upon sin.

Verse 2: GOD turned His back upon Jesus when He was on the cross.

Neither verse as written above or as written in words with the same sentiment is found in the word of GOD. The second of the *alleged verses* is an *inference* based upon the first *supposed verse* **when** that first *assumed verse* is connected to 2 Corinthians 5:21 **and when** 2 Corinthians 5:21 is *misconstrued* and *wrested* to make it to be read so as to fulfill the first verse that does not exist. "What a tangled web"[1] is woven when human reasoning is imposed upon Scripture.

The first concept does not exist except as a wresting of Habakkuk 1:13; therefore, the second has no basis in Scripture at all. Thus, both are false assertions and must and should be rejected outright.

I suggest that you read carefully the verse that is wrested from its context and twisted into saying something that is actually the exact opposite of how the verse does in fact read.

> Habakkuk 1:13 **Thou art of purer eyes than to behold evil, and canst not look on iniquity:** wherefore lookest thou upon them that deal treacherously, *and* holdest thy tongue when the wicked devoureth *the man that is* more righteous than he?

Before we explore the proper exposition of the verse, it is appropriate to read the so-called supporting verses for this verse stating that GOD cannot look upon sin.

> Job 15:15 Behold, he putteth no trust in his saints; yea, the heavens are not clean in his sight.

> Psalm 5:4 For thou *art* not a God that hath pleasure in wickedness: neither shall evil dwell with thee. 5 The foolish shall not stand in thy sight: thou hatest all workers of iniquity.

> Psalm 11:4 The LORD *is* in his holy temple, the LORD'S throne *is* in heaven: his eyes behold, his eyelids try, the children of men. 5 The LORD trieth the righteous: but the wicked and him that loveth violence his soul hateth. 6 Upon the wicked he shall rain snares, fire and brimstone, and an horrible tempest: *this shall be* the portion of their cup. 7 For the righteous LORD loveth righteousness; his countenance doth behold the upright.

It is strange indeed to use these verses, which clearly call attention to what the LORD does "behold," have in His "sight," and that "His eyelids try" to advocate that the LORD cannot look upon that which He clearly sees. The Hebrew word given to us in Psalm 11 as *try* and *trieth* has a primary meaning of *to investigate*.[2] The English transitive verb *to try* has the meaning of "to examine or investigate judicially ... to conduct the trial of … to put to test or trial." Obviously, the *trying* requires *looking upon* that which is being tried.

These three passages all declare without equivocation that the LORD not only sees, but that He sees not as in a casual glance with quickly averted eyes, but that He *beholds*—a concentrated viewing, that His sight determines that wickedness is not clean, and that He sees and evaluates judicially what He sees. These verses strongly state that GOD does look upon sin; but that He does not look upon sin with either favor or indifference. This is the precise message that Habakkuk delivers.

> Habakkuk 1:13 *Thou art* of purer eyes than to behold evil, and canst not look on iniquity: wherefore lookest thou upon them that deal treacherously, *and* holdest thy tongue when the wicked devoureth *the man that is* more righteous than he?

The observation and the rejection of *evil, iniquity, treacherous action,* and *wickedness* by the LORD is the specific and exact issue before Habakkuk—notice the word **wherefore** is found immediately after the statement "*Thou art* of purer eyes than to behold evil, and canst not look on iniquity." Habakkuk is explaining that he does not comprehend why GOD "lookest upon" those that "deal treacherously" and those that are "wicked" who are devouring the righteous and does not bring immediate judgment.

He is phrasing the same perplexity that plagued Asaph and that is presented in Psalms 34 and 73. Asaph knows that the GOD of Heaven sees and knows about the wickedness of men, but he is perplexed as to why those wicked men prosper, while he himself is chastened by the LORD on a daily basis.

> Psalm 34:15 The **eyes** of the LORD *are* upon the righteous, and his **ears** *are open* unto

their cry. 16 The **face** of the LORD *is* against them that do evil, to cut off the remembrance of them from the earth.

I include the whole of Psalm 73 because Asaph explains in the Psalm how he came to understand the purpose of GOD in his life and in the life of the ungodly.

Psalm 73:1 Truly God *is* good to Israel, *even* to such as are of a clean heart. 2 But as for me, my feet were almost gone; my steps had well nigh slipped. 3 For I was envious at the foolish, *when* I saw **the prosperity of the wicked**. 4 For *there are* no bands in their death: but their strength *is* firm. 5 They *are* not in trouble *as other* men; neither are they plagued like *other* men. 6 Therefore pride compasseth them about as a chain; violence covereth them *as* a garment. 7 Their eyes stand out with fatness: they have more than heart could wish. 8 They are corrupt, and speak wickedly *concerning* oppression: they speak loftily. 9 **They set their mouth against the heavens**, and their tongue walketh through the earth. 10 Therefore his people return hither: and waters of a full *cup* are wrung out to them. 11 And they say, How doth God know? and is there knowledge in the most High? 12 Behold, these *are* **the ungodly, who prosper in the world**; they increase *in* riches. 13 Verily I have cleansed my heart *in* vain, and washed my hands in innocency. 14 For all the day long have I been plagued, and chastened every morning. 15 If I say, I will speak thus; behold, I should offend *against* the generation of thy children. 16 When I thought to know this, it *was* too painful for me; 17 **Until** I went into the sanctuary of God; *then* understood I their end. 18 Surely thou didst set them in slippery places: thou castedst them down into destruction. 19 How are they *brought* into desolation, as in a moment! they are utterly consumed with terrors.

20 As a dream when *one* awaketh; *so*, O Lord, when thou awakest, thou shalt despise their image. 21 Thus my heart was grieved, and I was pricked in my reins. 22 So foolish *was* I, and ignorant: I was *as* a beast before thee. 23 Nevertheless I *am* continually with thee: thou hast holden *me* by my right hand. 24 Thou shalt guide me with thy counsel, and afterward receive me *to* glory. 25 Whom have I in heaven *but thee*? and *there is* none upon earth *that* I desire beside thee. 26 My flesh and my heart faileth: *but* God *is* the strength of my heart, and my portion for ever. 27 For, lo, they that are far from thee shall perish: thou hast destroyed all them that go a whoring from thee. 28 But *it is* good for me to draw near to God: I have put my trust in the Lord GOD, that I may declare all thy works.

Asaph was perplexed as to why the GOD of Heaven "plagued and chastened him every morning," even though he worked to keep his heart clean and his hands washed, while the ungodly who openly challenge the authority of GOD prosper in this world. He began to feel envious in their not being corrected by GOD and their prospering in their rebellion.

In the Law, Moses had recorded that Israel was to obey and serve the LORD because GOD *chasteneth* as does a Father.

Deuteronomy 8:1 All the commandments which I command thee this day shall ye observe to do, that ye may live, and multiply, and go in and possess the land which the LORD sware unto your fathers. 2 And thou shalt remember all the way which the LORD thy God led thee these forty years in the wilderness, to humble thee, *and* to prove thee, to know what *was* in thine heart, whether thou wouldest keep his commandments, or no. 3 And he humbled thee, and suffered thee to hunger, and fed thee with manna, which thou knewest not, neither did thy fathers know; that he might make thee know that man doth not live by bread only, but by every *word* that proceedeth out of the mouth of the LORD doth man live. 4 Thy raiment waxed not old upon thee, neither did thy foot swell, these forty years. 5 Thou shalt also consider in thine heart, that, as a man chasteneth his son, *so* the LORD thy God chasteneth thee. 6 Therefore thou shalt keep the commandments of the LORD thy God, to walk in his ways, and to fear him. Those that are not His children do not receive chastisement.

The record of the corrective hand of GOD on the children of Israel during the wilderness years and during the days of the judges would have been familiar to Asaph. He, as do we, was seeing his circumstances and not viewing them through the lens of Scripture.

Since the Book of Job was written before the Law, Asaph likely had access to that wisdom also. In Job 5:17, Eliphaz, who misconstrued some things, speaks from his experiences and gives a profound truth that he seems to have meant as encouragement for Job in the midst of his troubles.

Behold, happy *is* the man whom God correcteth: therefore despise not thou the chastening of the Almighty: 18 For he maketh sore, and bindeth up: he woundeth, and his hands make whole.

Asaph had a nature, a mind, and a memory that functioned exactly as does ours. We read and we forget or we do not apply what we know to our own circumstances. While Asaph did not have the Book of Proverbs, Solomon seems to merge the words of Moses and of Eliphaz in Proverbs 3:11-12.

My son, despise not the chastening of the LORD; neither be weary of his correction: For

360

whom the LORD loveth he correcteth; even as a father the son *in whom* he delighteth.

Both James and Paul quote Eliphaz, Moses, and Solomon and are moved by the Holy Spirit to amplify those words so that we might have a fuller comprehension of what is involved.

James 1:12 Blessed is the man that endureth temptation: for when he is tried, he shall receive the crown of life, which the Lord hath promised to them that love him. ... 5:11 Behold, we count them happy which endure. Ye have heard of the patience of Job, and have seen the end of the Lord; that the Lord is very pitiful, and of tender mercy.

Hebrews 12:5 And ye have forgotten the exhortation which speaketh unto you as unto children, My son, despise not thou the chastening of the Lord, nor faint when thou art rebuked of him: 6 For whom the Lord loveth he chasteneth, and scourgeth every son whom he receiveth. 7 If ye endure chastening, God dealeth with you as with sons; for what son is he whom the father chasteneth not? 8 But if ye be without chastisement, whereof all are partakers, then are ye bastards, and not sons. 9 Furthermore we have had fathers of our flesh which corrected *us*, and we gave *them* reverence: shall we not much rather be in subjection unto the Father of spirits, and live? 10 For they verily for a few days chastened *us* after their own pleasure; but he for *our* profit, that *we* might be partakers of his holiness. 11 Now no chastening for the present seemeth to be joyous, but grievous: nevertheless afterward it yieldeth the peaceable fruit of righteousness unto them which are exercised thereby.

Chastisement on the children of Israel perplexed Asaph and chastisement on we believers while the ungodly prosper bewilders, mystifies, and frustrates us. Asaph was made to understand that the feet of the ungodly were *in slippery places.* I find it impossible not to think that Asaph had been directed to Deuteronomy and that he has reference to 32:35.

> To me *belongeth* vengeance, and recompence; their foot shall slide in *due* time: for the day of their calamity *is* at hand, and the things that shall come upon them make haste.

The LORD will handle the matter of the ungodly *in due time.* That is not to be our concern. It is, in fact, none of our business, even if the ungodly are persecuting us.

> Romans 12:19 Dearly beloved, avenge not yourselves, but *rather* give place unto wrath: for it is written, Vengeance *is* mine; I will repay, saith the Lord.

We are to *give place,* to step aside and to get out of the way so that the wrath of GOD might, in due time, repay.

As to the godly being chastised while the ungodly prosper, Peter gives the caution and the admonition that we need in the matter.

> 1 Peter 4:17 For the time *is come* that judgment must begin at the house of God: and if *it* first *begin* at us, what shall the end *be* of them that obey not the gospel of God? 18 And if the righteous scarcely be saved, where shall the ungodly and the sinner appear? 19 Wherefore let them that suffer according to the will of God commit the keeping of their souls *to him* in well doing, as unto a faithful Creator.

---

[1] Oh what a tangled web we weave, When first we practise *[sic]* to deceive! Sir Walter Scott, Marmion, Canto vi. Stanza 17.

[2] *SwordSearcher: Strong's Hebrew Dictionary* 974. בָּחַן bachan "a primitive root; to test (especially metals); generally and figuratively, to investigate:—examine, prove, tempt, try (trial)."

CHAPTER 22

THE SUFFERING SERVANT

THE CONCLUSION OF THE WHOLE MATTER

I cannot accept the premises—that of fearfulness if not cowardice from Jesus of Nazareth in the Garden and that of desertion by the Father and despair by Son at Calvary—as being proper interpretations of Gethsemane and Golgotha. Neither conforms to the prophecies of Scripture. Neither corresponds to the record of the Gospels. Both conflict with the nature and character of GOD the Father and GOD the Son. Both contradict the testimony of the apostles in their later epistles. The Son of GOD did not become fearful or cowardly; He did not seek to avoid dying on the cross. GOD the Father did not abandon His Son.

It is an unavoidable conclusion that one is required to ignore the inspired history of four thousand years[1] of recorded prophecies in order to believe that Jesus of Nazareth knelt three times in the Garden to plead with GOD the Father to provide some alternative to the very circumstances for which He entered into the flesh.[2] It is in-

365

conceivable that as GOD, He did not know before the Garden of Gethsemane the terribleness of the crucifixion. It is impossible that as a Man most familiar with the prophecies of the Old Testament that He would not have understood, for instance, the description of His death from Psalm 22 and Isaiah 53.

It is inescapable to an observant believer that that same record of Scripture and all that we know of the being of GOD must be set aside in order to believe that when Jesus of Nazareth was hanging on that cross during the three hours of darkness that such a transformation occurred in the Son of GOD that the unity of the Father and the Son was broken and that for some unknown length of time Jesus was no longer GOD manifest in the flesh, but that He became sin personified and that when this occurred GOD the Father could no longer look upon Jesus and forsook him. The small case in the previous word is intentional, because if Jesus is not GOD during that time, the capital H, which is reserved or recognition of deity, would be inappropriate.

I consider those two concepts to be a misunderstanding of how they are an affront to the Person of the Son of GOD, whether prompted by a believer who has isolated the words spoken in the Garden or from the cross from the context of all Scripture or promoted as a deliberate maneuver by an unbeliever to discredit the Person of the Son of GOD through portraying Him as having weakness and of being *more human than divine.*

Surely believers who advocate this untenable concept of a faltering Saviour do not comprehend the implications of the teaching. **The LORD Jesus answers the suggestion of His attempting to avoid the cross before it was made.** After the Resurrection, the Son of GOD said that those who did not think that the Messiah would have to accept and to endure those conditions were *fools and slow of heart.*

Luke 24:13 And, behold, two of them went that same day to a village called Emmaus, which was from Jerusalem about threescore furlongs. 14 And they talked together of all these things which had happened. 15 And it came to pass, that, while they communed together and reasoned, Jesus himself drew near, and went with them. 16 But their eyes were holden that they should not know him. 17 And he said unto them, What manner of communications are these that ye have one to another, as ye walk, and are sad? 18 And the one of them, whose name was Cleopas, answering said unto him, Art thou only a stranger in Jerusalem, and hast not known the things which are come to pass there in these days? 19 And he said unto them, What things? **And they said unto him, Concerning Jesus of Nazareth, which was a prophet mighty in deed and word before God and all the people: 20 And how the chief priests and our rulers delivered him to be condemned to death, and have crucified him. 21 But we trusted that it had been he which should have redeemed Israel: and beside all this, to day is the third day since these things were done.** 22 Yea, and certain women also of our company made us astonished, which were early at the sepulchre; 23 And when they found not his body, they came, saying, that they had also seen a vision of angels, which said that he was alive. 24 And certain of them which were with us went to the sepulchre, and found it even so as the women had said: but him they saw not. **25 Then he said unto them, O fools, and slow of heart to believe all that the prophets have spoken: 26 Ought not Christ to have suffered these things, and to enter into his glory?**

367

27 And beginning at Moses and all the prophets, he expounded unto them in all the scriptures the things concerning himself. 28 And they drew nigh unto the village, whither they went: and he made as though he would have gone further. 29 But they constrained him, saying, Abide with us: for it is toward evening, and the day is far spent. And he went in to tarry with them. 30 And it came to pass, as he sat at meat with them, he took bread, and blessed it, and brake, and gave to them. 31 And their eyes were opened, and they knew him; and he vanished out of their sight. 32 And they said one to another, Did not our heart burn within us, while he talked with us by the way, and while he opened to us the scriptures?

Am I to believe that Jesus of Nazareth did not realize what He was to face in Jerusalem before He entered the Garden? Is it possible that any believer would consider that Jesus of Nazareth had been *a fool and slow to believe*? I hope that the harshness of the wickedness of such a terrible accusation will strike a note of *abhorrence* of ever harboring such an ungodly thought or of *repentance* for having done so.

The resurrected Christ reminded His disciples that they ought not to have been taken by surprise by Gethsemane, any of the things that took place between the Garden and Golgotha, or that which took place on the hill of Golgotha.

Luke 24:33 And they rose up the same hour, and returned to Jerusalem, and found the eleven gathered together, and them that were with them, 34 Saying, The Lord is risen indeed, and hath appeared to Simon. 35 And they told what things were done in the way, and how he was known of them in breaking of bread. 36 And as they thus spake, Jesus himself stood in the midst of them, and saith unto them, Peace be unto you. 37 But they were

368

terrified and affrighted, and supposed that they had seen a spirit. 38 And he said unto them, Why are ye troubled? and why do thoughts arise in your hearts? 39 Behold my hands and my feet, that it is I myself: handle me, and see; for a spirit hath not flesh and bones, as ye see me have. 40 And when he had thus spoken, he shewed them his hands and his feet. 41 And while they yet believed not for joy, and wondered, he said unto them, Have ye here any meat? 42 And they gave him a piece of a broiled fish, and of an honeycomb. 43 And he took it, and did eat before them. **44 And he said unto them, These are the words which I spake unto you, while I was yet with you, that all things must be fulfilled, which were written in the law of Moses, and in the prophets, and in the psalms, concerning me. 45 Then opened he their understanding, that they might understand the scriptures, 46 And said unto them, Thus it is written, and thus it behoved Christ to suffer, and to rise from the dead the third day:** 47 And that repentance and remission of sins should be preached in his name among all nations, beginning at Jerusalem.

Is it not obvious that the cross did not come upon Him unawares and it ought not to have taken the disciples by surprise. The LORD Jesus did not hide what was to come from His disciples and He did not obscure the details. He knew and they ought to have known.

> **Matthew** 16:21 From that time forth began Jesus to shew unto his disciples, how that he must go unto Jerusalem, and suffer many things of the elders and chief priests and scribes, and be killed, and be raised again the third day. ... 17:12 But I say unto you, That Elias is come already, and they knew him not, but have done unto him whatsoever they listed. Likewise shall also the Son of man suffer of them. ... 17:22 And while they abode in

Galilee, Jesus said unto them, The Son of man shall be betrayed into the hands of men: 23 And they shall kill him, and the third day he shall be raised again. And they were exceeding sorry. ... 20:17 And Jesus going up to Jerusalem took the twelve disciples apart in the way, and said unto them, 18 Behold, we go up to Jerusalem; and the Son of man shall be betrayed unto the chief priests and unto the scribes, and they shall condemn him to death, 19 And shall deliver him to the Gentiles to mock, and to scourge, and to crucify *him*: and the third day he shall rise again. ... 20:28 Even as the Son of man came not to be ministered unto, but to minister, and to give his life a ransom for many. ... 26:1 And it came to pass, when Jesus had finished all these sayings, he said unto his disciples, 2 Ye know that after two days is *the feast of* the passover, and the Son of man is betrayed to be crucified. ... 26:19 And the disciples did as Jesus had appointed them; and they made ready the passover. 20 Now when the even was come, he sat down with the twelve. 21 And as they did eat, he said, Verily I say unto you, that one of you shall betray me. 22 And they were exceeding sorrowful, and began every one of them to say unto him, Lord, is it I? 23 And he answered and said, He that dippeth *his* hand with me in the dish, the same shall betray me. 24 The Son of man goeth as it is written of him: but woe unto that man by whom the Son of man is betrayed! it had been good for that man if he had not been born. 25 Then Judas, which betrayed him, answered and said, Master, is it I? He said unto him, Thou hast said. 26 And as they were eating, Jesus took bread, and blessed *it*, and brake *it*, and gave *it* to the disciples, and said, Take, eat; this is my body. 27 And he took the cup, and gave thanks, and gave *it* to them, saying, Drink ye all of it; 28 For this is my blood of the new testament, which is shed for many for the remission of sins. 29 But I say unto you, I will not drink henceforth of this fruit of the vine, until that day when I drink it new with you in my Father's kingdom. 30 And when they had sung an hymn, they went out into the mount of Olives. 31 Then saith Jesus unto them, All ye shall be offended because of me this night: for it is written, I will smite the shepherd, and the sheep of the flock shall be scattered abroad. 32 But after I am risen again, I will go before you into Galilee. ... 26:52 Then said Jesus unto him, Put up again thy sword into his place: for all they that take the sword shall perish with the sword. 53 Thinkest thou that I cannot now pray to my Father, and he shall presently give me more than twelve legions of angels? 54 But how then shall the scriptures be fulfilled, that thus it must be?

Mark 8:31 And he began to teach them, that the Son of man must suffer many things, and be rejected of the elders, and *of* the chief priests, and scribes, and be killed, and after three days rise again. ... 9:31 For he taught his disciples, and said unto them, The Son of man is delivered into the hands of men, and they shall kill him; and after that he is killed, he shall rise the third day. 32 But they understood not that saying, and were afraid to ask him. ... 10:32 And they were in the way going up to Jerusalem; and Jesus went before them: and they were amazed; and as they followed, they were afraid. And he took again the twelve, and began to tell them what things should happen unto him, 33 *Saying*, Behold, we go up to Jerusalem; and the Son of man shall be delivered unto the chief priests, and unto the scribes; and they shall condemn him to death, and shall deliver him to the Gentiles: 34 And they shall mock him, and shall scourge him, and shall spit upon him, and shall kill him: and the third day he shall rise again.

Luke 9:21 And he straitly charged them, and commanded *them* to tell no man that thing; 22 Saying, The Son of man must suffer many things, and be rejected of the elders and chief priests and scribes, and be slain, and be raised the third day. ... 9:28 And it came to pass about an eight days after these sayings, he took Peter and John and James, and went up into a mountain to pray. 29 And as he prayed, the fashion of his countenance was altered, and his raiment *was* white *and* glistering. 30 And, behold, there talked with him two men, which were Moses and Elias: 31 Who appeared in glory, and spake of his decease which he should accomplish at Jerusalem. ... 9:21 And he straitly charged them, and commanded *them* to tell no man that thing; 22 Saying, The Son of man must suffer many things, and be rejected of the elders and chief priests and scribes, and be slain, and be raised the third day. 23 And he said to *them* all, If any *man* will come after me, let him deny himself, and take up his cross daily, and follow me. 24 For whosoever will save his life shall lose it: but whosoever will lose his life for my sake, the same shall save it. 25 For what is a man advantaged, if he gain the whole world, and lose himself, or be cast away? ... 9:43 And they were all amazed at the mighty power of God. But while they wondered every one at all things which Jesus did, he said unto his disciples, 44 Let these sayings sink down into your ears: for the Son of man shall be delivered into the hands of men. 45 But they understood not this saying, and it was hid from them, that they perceived it not: and they feared to ask him of that saying. ... 12:50 But I have a baptism to be baptized with; and how am I straitened till it be accomplished! ... 18:31 Then he took *unto him* the twelve, and said unto them, Behold, we go up to Jerusalem, and all things that are written by the prophets concerning the Son of man shall be accomplished. 32 For he shall be delivered unto the Gentiles, and shall be mocked, and spitefully entreated, and spitted on: 33 And they shall scourge *him*, and put him to death: and the third day he shall rise again. 34 And they understood none of these things: and this saying was hid from them, neither knew they the things which were spoken.

John 2:18 Then answered the Jews and said unto him, What sign shewest thou unto us, seeing that thou doest these things? 19 Jesus answered and said unto them, Destroy this temple, and in three days I will raise it up. 20 Then said the Jews, Forty and six years was this temple in building, and wilt thou rear it up in three days? 21 But he spake of the temple of his body. 22 When therefore he was risen from the dead, his disciples remembered that he had said this unto them; and they believed the scripture, and the word which Jesus had said. ... 3:14 And as Moses lifted up the serpent in the wilderness, even so must the Son of man be lifted up: ... 4:34 Jesus saith unto them, My meat is to do the will of him that sent me, and to finish his work. ... 7:6 Then Jesus said unto them, My time is not yet come: but your time is alway ready. 7 The world cannot hate you; but me it hateth, because I testify of it, that the works thereof are evil. 8 Go ye up unto this feast: I go not up yet unto this feast; for my time is not yet full come. ... 7:10 But when his brethren were gone up, then went he also up unto the feast, not openly, but as it were in secret. ... 10:15 As the Father knoweth me, even so know I the Father: and I lay down my life for the sheep. ... 10:17 Therefore doth my Father love me, because I lay down my life, that I might take it again. 18 No man taketh it from me, but I lay it down of myself. I have power to lay it down, and I have power to take it again. This commandment have I received of my Father. ... 12:23 And Jesus answered them, saying, The hour is come, that the Son of man should be glorified. 24 Verily, verily, I say unto you, Except a corn of wheat fall into the ground and die, it abideth alone: but if it die, it bringeth forth much fruit. 25 He that loveth his life shall lose it; and he that hateth his life in this world shall keep it unto life eternal. 26 If any man serve me, let him follow me; and where I am, there shall also my servant be: if any man serve me, him will *my* Father honour. 27 Now is my soul troubled; and what shall I say? Father, save me from this hour: but for this cause came I unto this hour. 28 Father, glorify thy name. Then came there a voice from heaven, *saying*, I have both glorified *it*, and will glorify *it* again. ... 12:31 Now is the judgment of this world: now shall the prince of this world be cast out. 32 And I, if I be lifted up from the earth, will draw all *men* unto me. ... 13:31 Therefore, when he was gone out, Jesus said, Now is the Son of man glorified, and God is glorified in him. 32 If God be glorified in him, God shall also glorify him in himself, and shall straightway glorify him. ... 16:28 I came forth from the Father, and am come into the world:

again, I leave the world, and go to the Father. ...
17:1 These words spake Jesus, and lifted up his
eyes to heaven, and said, Father, the hour is come;
glorify thy Son, that thy Son also may glorify thee:
... 17:11 And now I am no more in the world, but
these are in the world, and I come to thee. Holy
Father, keep through thine own name those whom
thou hast given me, that they may be one, as we
are. ... 17:18 As thou hast sent me into the world,
even so have I also sent them into the world. ...
18:11 Then said Jesus unto Peter, Put up thy
sword into the sheath: the cup which my Father
hath given me, shall I not drink it?

Nothing whatsoever occurred in the Garden or
between the Garden and the tomb that was unexpected, unanticipated, unforeseen, unknown or
unprophesied **by the Son of GOD.** It is not possible that He was ever confounded or confused. The
very words are difficult to contemplate in relationship to the knowledge and the comprehension of
the eternal Son of GOD. However, that is the
substance of the charge that is leveled against
Him when He is accused of becoming fearful of
the cross and seeking to avoid it. His character
and His conduct are challenged.

Certainly, those approaching events would
have been horrible to contemplate facing. However, for the Son of GOD, the cross was not an
academic exercise of potentiality; it was the anticipation of the known reality. Jesus, the Son of
GOD, knew before the creation of the world the
fullness of what the cross would mean to Him.

Revelation 13:8 And all that dwell upon the
earth shall worship him, whose names are not
written in the book of life of the Lamb slain
from the foundation of the world.

1 Peter 1:19 But with the precious blood of
Christ, as of a lamb without blemish and
without spot: 20 Who verily was foreordained
before the foundation of the world, but was
manifest in these last times for you,

It is strange to suggest that the Incarnate GOD did not become fully aware of what He would suffer until He found Himself in the Garden. That idea is not Biblical. It is irreconcilable with the character of GOD.

> Titus 1:2 In hope of eternal life, which God, that cannot lie, promised before the world began;

I do not wish to minimize the horribleness of what was done to *holy, harmless,* Son of man, Who *went about doing good,*[3] and Whose gentleness was remarkable.[4]

He healed the broken-hearted
And set the captive free,
He made the lame to walk again
And caused the blind to see.[5]

What men did to their Creator[6] is terrible to read and very difficult to mediate upon.

THE APPROACHING ABUSE AND MANHANDLING BY THE CHIEF PRIESTS, SOME OF THE ELDERS AND SCRIBES, AND THEIR SERVANTS

Matthew 26:47 And while he yet spake, lo, Judas, one of the twelve, came, and with him a great multitude with swords and staves, from the chief priests and elders of the people. 48 Now he that betrayed him gave them a sign, saying, Whomsoever I shall kiss, that same is he: hold him fast. 49 And forthwith he came to Jesus, and said, Hail, master; and kissed him. 50 And Jesus said unto him, Friend, wherefore art thou come? Then came they, and laid hands on Jesus, and took him. ... 55 In that same hour said Jesus to the multitudes, Are ye come out as against a thief with swords and staves for to take me? I sat daily with you teaching in the temple, and ye laid no hold on me. 56 But all this was done, that the scriptures of the prophets might be fulfilled. Then all the disciples forsook him, and fled. 57 And they that had laid hold on Jesus led *him* away to Caiaphas the high priest, where the scribes and the elders were assembled. ... 59 Now the chief priests, and elders, and all the council, sought false witness against Jesus, to put him to death; 60 But found none: yea, though many false witnesses came, *yet* found they none. At the last came two false witnesses, 61 And said, This *fellow* said, I am able to destroy the temple of God, and to build it in three days. 62 And the high priest arose, and said unto him, Answerest thou nothing? what *is it which* these witness against thee? 63 But Jesus held his peace. And the high priest answered and said unto him, I adjure thee by the living God, that thou tell us whether thou be the Christ, the Son of God. 64 Jesus saith unto him, Thou hast said: nevertheless I say unto you, Hereafter shall ye see the Son of man sitting on the right hand of power, and coming in the clouds of heaven. 65 Then the high priest rent his clothes, saying, He hath spoken blasphemy; what further need have we of witnesses? behold, now ye have heard his blasphemy. 66 What think ye? They answered and said, He is guilty of death. 67 Then did they spit in his face, and buffeted him; and others smote *him* with the palms of their hands, 68 Saying, Prophesy unto us, thou Christ, Who is he that smote thee? **27:1** When the morning was come, all the chief priests and elders of the people took counsel against Jesus to put him to death: 2 And when they had bound him, they led *him* away, and delivered him to Pontius Pilate the governor. ... 11 And Jesus stood before the governor: and the governor asked him, saying, Art thou the King of the Jews? And Jesus said unto him, Thou sayest. 12 And when he was accused of the chief priests and elders, he answered nothing. 13 Then said Pilate unto him, Hearest thou not how many things they witness against thee? 14 And he answered him to never a word; insomuch that the governor marvelled greatly. 15 Now at *that* feast the governor was wont to release unto the people a prisoner, whom they would. 16 And they had then a notable prisoner, called Barabbas. 17 Therefore when they were gathered together, Pilate said unto them, Whom will ye that I release unto you? Barabbas, or Jesus which is called Christ? 18 For he knew that for envy they had delivered him. 19 When he was set down on the judgment seat, his wife sent unto him, saying, Have thou nothing to do with that just man: for I have suffered many things this day in a dream because of him. 20 But the chief priests and elders persuaded the multitude that they should ask Barabbas, and destroy Jesus. 21 The governor answered and said unto them, Whether of the twain will ye that I release unto you? They said, Barabbas. 22 Pilate saith unto them, What shall I do then with Jesus which is called Christ? *They* all say unto him, Let him be crucified. 23 And the governor said, Why, what evil hath he done? But they cried out the more, saying, Let him be crucified. 24 When Pilate saw that he could prevail nothing, but *that* rather a tumult was made, he took water, and washed *his* hands before the multitude, saying, I am innocent of the blood of this just person: see ye *to it.* 25 Then answered all the people, and said, His blood *be* on us, and on our children.

Mark 14:53 And they led Jesus away to the high priest: and with him were assembled all the chief priests and the elders and the scribes. ... 55 And the chief priests and all the council sought for witness against Jesus to put him to death; and found none. 56 For many bare false witness against him, but their witness agreed not together. 57 And there arose certain, and bare false witness against him, saying, 58 We heard him say, I will destroy this temple that is made with hands, and within three days I will build another made without hands. 59 But neither so did their witness agree together. 60 And the high priest stood up in the midst, and asked Jesus, saying, Answerest thou nothing? what *is it which* these witness against thee? 61 But he held his peace, and answered nothing. Again the high priest asked him, and said unto him, Art thou the Christ, the Son of the Blessed? 62 And Jesus said, I am: and ye shall see the Son of man sitting on the right hand of power, and coming in the clouds of heaven. 63 Then the high priest rent his clothes, and saith, What need we any further witnesses? 64 Ye have heard the blasphemy: what think ye? And they all condemned him to be guilty of death. 65 And some began to spit on him, and to cover his face, and to buffet him, and to say unto him, Prophesy: and the servants did strike him with the palms of their hands.

Mark 15:1 And straightway in the morning the chief priests held a consultation with the elders and scribes and the whole council, and bound Jesus, and carried *him* away, and delivered *him* to Pilate. 2 And Pilate asked him, Art thou the King of the Jews? And he answering said unto him, Thou sayest *it*. 3 And the chief priests accused him of many things: but he answered nothing. 4 And Pilate asked him again, saying, Answerest thou nothing? behold how many things they witness against thee. 5 But Jesus yet answered nothing; so that Pilate marvelled. 6 Now at *that* feast he released unto them one prisoner, whomsoever they desired. 7 And there was *one* named Barabbas, *which lay* bound with them that had made insurrection with him, who had committed murder in the insurrection. 8 And the multitude crying aloud began to desire *him to do* as he had ever done unto them. 9 But Pilate answered them, saying, Will ye that I release unto you the King of the Jews? 10 For he knew that the chief priests had delivered him for envy. 11 But the chief priests moved the people, that he should rather release Barabbas unto them. 12 And Pilate answered and said again unto them, What will ye then that I shall do *unto him* whom ye call the King of the Jews? 13 And they cried out again, Crucify him. 14 Then Pilate said unto them, Why, what evil hath he done? And they cried out the more exceedingly, Crucify him.

Luke 22:52 Then Jesus said unto the chief priests, and captains of the temple, and the elders, which were come to him, Be ye come out, as against a thief, with swords and staves? 53 When I was daily with you in the temple, ye stretched forth no hands against me: but this is your hour, and the power of darkness. 54 Then took they him, and led *him*, and brought him into the high priest's house. ... 63 And the men that held Jesus mocked him, and smote *him*. 64 And when they had blindfolded him, they struck him on the face, and asked him, saying, Prophesy, who is it that smote thee? 65 And many other things blasphemously spake they against him. 66 And as soon as it was day, the elders of the people and the chief priests and the scribes came together, and led him into their council, saying, 67 Art thou the Christ? tell us. And he said unto them, If I tell you, ye will not believe: 68 And if I also ask *you*, ye will not answer me, nor let *me* go. 69 Hereafter shall the Son of man sit on the right hand of the power of God. 70 Then said they all, Art thou then the Son of God? And he said unto them, Ye say that I am. 71 And they said, What need we any further witness? for we ourselves have heard of his own mouth.

Luke 23:1 And the whole multitude of them arose, and led him unto Pilate. 2 And they began to accuse him, saying, We found this *fellow* perverting the nation, and forbidding to give tribute to Caesar, saying that he himself is Christ a King. 3 And Pilate asked him, saying, Art thou the King of the Jews? And he answered him and said, Thou sayest *it*. 4 Then said Pilate to the chief priests and *to* the people, I find no fault in this man. 5 And they were the more fierce, saying, He stirreth up the people, teaching throughout all Jewry, beginning from Galilee to this place. 6 When Pilate heard of Galilee, he asked whether the man were a Galilaean. 7 And as soon as he knew that he belonged unto Herod's jurisdiction, he sent him to Herod, who himself also was at Jerusalem at that time. 8 And when Herod saw Jesus, he was exceeding glad: for he was desirous to see him of a long *season*, because he had heard many things of him; and he hoped to have seen some miracle done by him. 9 Then he questioned with him in many words; but he answered him nothing. 10 And the chief priests and scribes stood and vehemently accused him. 11 And Herod with his men of war set him at nought, and mocked *him*, and arrayed him in a gorgeous robe, and sent him again to Pilate. 12 And the same day Pilate and Herod were made friends together: for before they were at enmity between themselves. 13 And Pilate, when he had called together the chief priests and the rulers and the people, 14 Said unto them, Ye have brought this man unto me, as one that perverteth the people: and, behold, I, having examined *him* before you, have found no fault in this man touching those things whereof ye accuse him: 15 No, nor yet Herod: for I sent you to him; and, lo, nothing worthy of death is done unto him. 16 I will therefore chastise him, and release *him.* 17 (For of necessity he must release one unto them at the feast.) 18 And they cried out all at once, saying, Away with this *man,* and release unto us Barabbas: 19 (Who for a certain sedition made in the city, and for murder, was cast into prison.) 20 Pilate therefore, willing to release Jesus, spake again to them. 21 But they cried, saying, Crucify *him,* crucify him. 22 And he said unto them the third time, Why, what evil hath he done? I have found no cause of death in him: I will therefore chastise him, and let *him* go. 23 And they were instant with loud voices, requiring that he might be crucified. And the voices of them and of the chief priests prevailed. 24 And Pilate gave sentence that it should be as they required. 25 And he released unto them him that for sedition and murder was cast into prison, whom they had desired; but he delivered Jesus to their will.

John 18:12 Then the band and the captain and officers of the Jews took Jesus, and bound him, 13 And led him away to Annas first; for he was father in law to Caiaphas, which was the high priest that same year. ... 19 The high priest then asked Jesus of his disciples, and of his doctrine. 20 Jesus answered him, I spake openly to the world; I ever taught in the synagogue, and in the temple, whither the Jews always resort; and in secret have I said nothing. 21 Why askest thou me? ask them which heard me, what I have said unto them: behold, they know what I said. 22 And when he had thus spoken, one of the officers which stood by struck Jesus with the palm of his hand, saying, Answerest thou the high priest so? 23 Jesus answered him, If I have spoken evil, bear witness of the evil: but if well, why smitest thou me? 24 Now Annas had sent him bound unto Caiaphas the high priest. ... 28 Then led they Jesus from Caiaphas unto the hall of judgment: and it was early; and they themselves went not into the judgment hall, lest they should be defiled; but that they might eat the passover. 29 Pilate then went out unto them, and said, What accusation bring ye against this man? 30 They answered and said unto him, If he were not a malefactor, we would not have delivered him up unto thee. 31 Then said Pilate unto them, Take ye him, and judge him according to your law. The Jews therefore said unto him, It is not lawful for us to put any man to death: 32 That the saying of Jesus might be fulfilled, which he spake, signifying what death he should die. 33 Then Pilate entered into the judgment hall again, and called Jesus, and said unto him, Art thou the King of the Jews? 34 Jesus answered him, Sayest thou this thing of thyself, or did others tell it thee of me? 35 Pilate answered, Am I a Jew? Thine own nation and the chief priests have delivered thee unto me: what hast thou done? 36 Jesus answered, My kingdom is not of this world: if my kingdom were of this world, then would my servants fight, that I should not be delivered to the Jews: but now is my kingdom not from hence. 37 Pilate therefore said unto him, Art thou a king then? Jesus answered, Thou sayest that I am a king. To this end was I born, and for this cause came I into the world, that I should bear witness unto the truth. Every one that is of the truth heareth my voice. 38 Pilate saith unto him, What is truth? And when he had said this, he went out again unto the Jews, and saith unto them, I find in him no fault *at all*. 39 But ye have a custom, that I should release unto you one at the passover: will ye therefore that I release unto you the King of the Jews? 40 Then cried they all again, saying, Not this man, but Barabbas. Now Barabbas was a robber.

John 19:1 Then Pilate therefore took Jesus, and scourged *him*.

THE STRIPPING, THE MOCKERY, THE BUFFETING, AND THE SCOURGING BY THE SOLDIERS OF HEROD AND THOSE OF PILATE.

Matthew 27:26 Then released he Barabbas unto them: and when he had scourged Jesus, he delivered *him* to be crucified. 27 Then the soldiers of the governor took Jesus into the common hall, and gathered unto him the whole band *of soldiers.* 28 And they stripped him, and put on him a scarlet robe. 29 And when they had platted a crown of thorns, they put *it* upon his head, and a reed in his right hand: and they bowed the knee before him, and mocked him, saying, Hail, King of the Jews! 30 And they spit upon him, and took the reed, and smote him on the head. 31 And after that they had mocked him, they took the robe off from him, and put his own raiment on him, and led him away to crucify *him.*

Mark 15:15 And *so* Pilate, willing to content the people, released Barabbas unto them, and delivered Jesus, when he had scourged *him,* to be crucified. 16 And the soldiers led him away into the hall, called Praetorium; and they call together the whole band. 17 And they clothed him with purple, and platted a crown of thorns, and put it about his *head,* 18 And began to salute him, Hail, King of the Jews! 19 And they smote him on the head with a reed, and did spit upon him, and bowing *their* knees worshipped him. 20 And when they had mocked him, they took off the purple from him, and put his own clothes on him, and led him out to crucify him.

Luke 22:54 Then took they him, and led *him,* and brought him into the high priest's house. ... 63 And the men that held Jesus mocked him, and smote *him.* 64 And when they had blindfolded him, they struck him on the face, and asked him, saying, Prophesy, who is it that smote thee? 65 And many other things blasphemously spake they against him.

23:6 When Pilate heard of Galilee, he asked whether the man were a Galilaean. 7 And as soon as he knew that he belonged unto Herod's jurisdiction, he sent him to Herod, who himself also was at Jerusalem at that time. 8 And when Herod saw Jesus, he was exceeding glad: for he was desirous to see him of a long *season,* because he had heard many things of him; and he hoped to have seen some miracle done by him. 9 Then he questioned with him in many words; but he answered him nothing. ... 11 And Herod with his men of war set him at nought, and mocked *him,* and arrayed him in a gorgeous robe, and sent him again to Pilate.

John 18:12 Then the band and the captain and officers of the Jews took Jesus, and bound him, 13 And led him away to Annas first; for he was father in law to Caiaphas, which was the high priest that same year. ... 19 The high priest then asked Jesus of his disciples, and of his doctrine. 20 Jesus answered him, I spake openly to the world; I ever taught in the synagogue, and in the temple, whither the Jews always resort; and in secret have I said nothing. 21 Why askest thou me? ask them which heard me, what I have said unto them: behold, they know what I said. 22 And when he had thus spoken, one of the officers which stood by struck Jesus with the palm of his hand, saying, Answerest thou the high priest so? 23 Jesus answered him, If I have spoken evil, bear witness of the evil: but if well, why smitest thou me? 24 Now Annas had sent him bound unto Caiaphas the high priest. ... 28 Then led they Jesus from Caiaphas unto the hall of judgment:

John 19:1 Then Pilate therefore took Jesus, and scourged *him.* 2 And the soldiers platted a crown of thorns, and put *it* on his head, and they put on him a purple robe, 3 And said, Hail, King of the Jews! and they smote him with their hands. 4 Pilate therefore went forth again, and saith unto them, Behold, I bring him forth to you, that ye may know that I find no fault in him. 5 Then came Jesus forth, wearing the crown of thorns, and the purple robe. And *Pilate* saith unto them, Behold the man!

THE CRUCIFIXION

Matthew 27:33 And when they were come unto a place called Golgotha, that is to say, a place of a skull, 34 They gave him vinegar to drink mingled with gall: and when he had tasted *thereof,* he would not drink. 35 And they crucified him, and parted his garments, casting lots: that it might be fulfilled which was spoken by the prophet, They parted my garments among them, and upon my vesture did they cast lots. 36 And sitting down they watched him there; 37 And set up over his head his accusation written, THIS IS JESUS THE KING OF THE JEWS. 38 Then were there two thieves crucified with him, one on the right hand, and another on the left.

Mark 15:15 And *so* Pilate, willing to content the people, released Barabbas unto them, and delivered Jesus, when he had scourged *him*, to be crucified. 16 And the soldiers led him away into the hall, called Praetorium; and they call together the whole band. 17 And they clothed him with purple, and platted a crown of thorns, and put it about his *head*, 18 And began to salute him, Hail, King of the Jews! 19 And they smote him on the head with a reed, and did spit upon him, and bowing *their* knees worshipped him. 20 And when they had mocked him, they took off the purple from him, and put his own clothes on him, and led him out to crucify him. ... 22 And they bring him unto the place Golgotha, which is, being interpreted, The place of a skull. 23 And they gave him to drink wine mingled with myrrh: but he received *it* not. 24 And when they had crucified him, they parted his garments, casting lots upon them, what every man should take.

Luke 23:24 And Pilate gave sentence that it should be as they required. 25 And he released unto them him that for sedition and murder was cast into prison, whom they had desired; but he delivered Jesus to their will. 26 And as they led him away, they laid hold upon one Simon, a Cyrenian, coming out of the country, and on him they laid the cross, that he might bear *it* after Jesus. 27 And there followed him a great company of people, and of women, which also bewailed and lamented him. 28 But Jesus turning unto them said, Daughters of Jerusalem, weep not for me, but weep for yourselves, and for your children. 29 For, behold, the days are coming, in the which they shall say, Blessed *are* the barren, and the wombs that never bare, and the paps which never gave suck. 30 Then shall they begin to say to the mountains, Fall on us; and to the hills, Cover us. 31 For if they do these things in a green tree, what shall be done in the dry? 32 And there were also two other, malefactors, led with him to be put to death. 33 And when they were come to the place, which is called Calvary, there they crucified him, and the malefactors, one on the right hand, and the other on the left.

> **John 19:16** Then delivered he him therefore unto them to be crucified. And they took Jesus, and led *him* away. 17 And he bearing his cross went forth into a place called *the place* of a skull, which is called in the Hebrew Golgotha: 18 Where they crucified him, and two other with him, on either side one, and Jesus in the midst. 19 And Pilate wrote a title, and put *it* on the cross. And the writing was, JESUS OF NAZARETH THE KING OF THE JEWS.

Beginning in the Garden of Eden and continuing through the days of His earthly ministry, the LORD Jesus foretold what was going to transpire in the Garden and between the Garden and the tomb. The very first prophecy of the Messiah is given in the Garden of Eden. Called by Biblical scholars the Protoevangelium, the first Gospel, these words were spoken by the Son of GOD, JEHOVAH Elohim.

> Genesis 3:14 And the LORD God said unto the serpent, Because thou hast done this, thou art cursed above all cattle, and above every beast of the field; upon thy belly shalt thou go, and dust shalt thou eat all the days of thy life: 15 And I will put enmity between thee and the woman, and between thy seed and her seed; it shall bruise thy head, and thou shalt bruise his heel.

Over the next four thousand years, the prophets were moved to give multiple additional prophecies becoming more specific in the details regarding the sufferings of Christ. Is it not worthy of special attention that Peter, moved by the Holy Ghost, speaks of the **sufferings** and not of His miracles or His teachings?

> 1 Peter 1:10 Of which salvation the prophets have inquired and searched diligently, who prophesied of the grace that should come unto you: 11 Searching what, or what manner of time the Spirit of Christ which was in them did signify, when it testified beforehand the

sufferings of Christ, and the glory that should follow.

PROPHECIES OF THE SUFFERINGS OF THE MESSIAH
Isaiah 52:14 As many were astonied at thee; his visage was so marred more than any man, and his form more than the sons of men: 15 So shall he sprinkle many nations; the kings shall shut their mouths at him: for that which had not been told them shall they see; and that which they had not heard shall they consider. 53:1 Who hath believed our report? and to whom is the arm of the LORD revealed? 2 For he shall grow up before him as a tender plant, and as a root out of a dry ground: he hath no form nor comeliness; and when we shall see him, there is no beauty that we should desire him. 3 He is despised and rejected of men; a man of sorrows, and acquainted with grief: and we hid as it were our faces from him; he was despised, and we esteemed him not. 4 Surely he hath borne our griefs, and carried our sorrows: yet we did esteem him **stricken**, **smitten of Go**d, and **afflicted**. 5 But he *was* **wounded** for our transgressions, *he was* **bruised** for our iniquities: the **chastisement** of our peace *was* upon him; and with his **stripes** we are healed. 10 Yet it pleased the LORD to **bruise** him; he hath put *him* to **grief**: when thou shalt make his soul an offering for sin, he shall see *his* seed, he shall prolong *his* days, and the pleasure of the LORD shall prosper in his hand. 11 He shall see of the **travail** of his soul, *and* shall be satisfied: by his knowledge shall my righteous servant justify many; for he shall **bear their iniquities**. 12 Therefore will I divide him *a portion* with the great, and he shall divide the spoil with the strong; because he hath **poured out his soul unto death**: and he was **numbered with the transgressors**; and he **bare the sin of many**, and **made intercession** for the transgressors.

Old Testament	The Gospels
Psalm 41:9 Yea, mine own familiar friend, in whom I trusted, which	Matthew 26:48 Now he that betrayed him gave them a sign, saying,

did eat of my bread, hath lifted up *his* heel against me.	Whomsoever I shall kiss, that same is he: hold him fast. 49 And forthwith he came to Jesus, and said, Hail, master; and kissed him. 50 And Jesus said unto him, Friend, wherefore art thou come? Then came they, and laid hands on Jesus, and took him. Luke 22:47 And while he yet spake, behold a multitude, and he that was called Judas, one of the twelve, went before them, and drew near unto Jesus to kiss him. 48 But Jesus said unto him, Judas, betrayest thou the Son of man with a kiss?
Isaiah 53:7 Yet He opened not his mouth. As a sheep before her shearers is dumb, so He openeth not his mouth.	Matthew 26:63 But Jesus held his peace. And the high priest answered and said unto him, I adjure thee by the living God, that thou tell us whether thou be the Christ, the Son of God. ... 27:12 And when he was accused of the chief priests and elders, he answered nothing.
Micah 5:1 Now gather thyself in troops, O daughter of troops: he hath laid siege against us: they shall smite the judge of Israel with a rod upon the cheek.	Matthew 27:30 And they spit upon him, and took the reed, and smote him on the head. Mark 14:65 And some began to spit on him, and to cover his face, and to buffet him, and to say unto him, Proph-
Isaiah 50:6 I gave my back to the smiters, and	

my cheeks to them that plucked off the hair: I hid not my face from shame and spitting.	esy: and the servants did strike him with the palms of their hands. John 19:1 Then Pilate therefore took Jesus, and scourged him.
Isaiah 53:12 Therefore will I divide him a portion with the great, and he shall divide the spoil with the strong; because he hath poured out his soul unto death: and he was numbered with the transgressors; and he bare the sin of many, and made intercession for the transgressors.	John 19:18 Where they crucified him, and two other with him, on either side one, and Jesus in the midst. Mark 15:28 And the scripture was fulfilled, which saith, And he was numbered with the transgressors.
Psalm 22:7 All they that see me laugh me to scorn: they shoot out the lip, they shake the head, *saying*, 8 He trusted on the LORD *that* he would deliver him: let him deliver him, seeing he delighted in him. ... 16 For dogs have compassed me: the assembly of the wicked have inclosed me: they pierced my hands and my feet. Zechariah 13:6 And *one* shall say unto him, What *are* these wounds in thine hands? Then he shall answer, *Those* with which I was wounded *in* the house of my friends. 7 Awake, O sword, against my shepherd, and against the man *that is* my	Matthew 27:39 And they that passed by reviled him, wagging their heads, 40 And saying, Thou that destroyest the temple, and buildest *it* in three days, save thyself. If thou be the Son of God, come down from the cross. 41 Likewise also the chief priests mocking *him*, with the scribes and elders, said, 42 He saved others; himself he cannot save. If he be the King of Israel, let him now come down from the cross, and we will believe him. 43 He trusted in God; let him deliver him now, if he will have him: for he said, I am the Son of God. 44 The thieves also, which were

fellow, saith the LORD of hosts: smite the shepherd, and the sheep shall be scattered: and I will turn mine hand upon the little ones.	crucified with him, cast the same in his teeth.
Psalm 69:21 They gave me also gall for my meat; and in my thirst they gave me vinegar to drink. Psalm 22:14 I am poured out like water, and all my bones are out of joint: my heart is like wax; it is melted in the midst of my bowels. 15 My strength is dried up like a potsherd; and my tongue cleaveth to my jaws; and thou hast brought me into the dust of death.	Matthew 27:34 They gave him vinegar to drink mingled with gall: and when he had tasted *thereof*, he would not drink.
Psalm 22:18 They part my garments among them, and cast lots upon my vesture.	Matthew 27:35 And they crucified him, and parted his garments, casting lots: that it might be fulfilled which was spoken by the prophet, They parted my garments among them, and upon my vesture did they cast lots.
Isaiah 53:12 Therefore will I divide him *a portion* with the great, and he shall divide the spoil with the strong; because he hath poured out his soul unto death: and he was numbered with the transgressors; and he bare the sin of	Mark 15:27 And with him they crucify two thieves; the one on his right hand, and the other on his left. 28 And the scripture was fulfilled, which saith, And he was numbered with the transgressors.

many, and made intercession for the transgressors.	
Exodus 12:46 Neither shall ye break a bone thereof. Psalm 34:20. He keepeth all His bones; not one of them is broken.	John 19:32 Then came the soldiers, and brake the legs of the first, and of the other which was crucified with him. 33 But when they came to Jesus, and saw that he was dead already, they brake not his legs: 34 But one of the soldiers with a spear pierced his side, and forthwith came there out blood and water. 35 And he that saw *it* bare record, and his record is true: and he knoweth that he saith true, that ye might believe. 36 For these things were done, that the scripture should be fulfilled, A bone of him shall not be broken. 37 And again another scripture saith, They shall look on him whom they pierced.
Isaiah 53:12 He hath poured out his soul unto death. Daniel 9:26 And after threescore and two weeks shall Messiah be cut off, but not for himself: and the people of the prince that shall come shall destroy the city and the sanctuary; and the end thereof *shall be* with a flood, and unto the end of the	Matthew 27:50 Jesus, when he had cried again with a loud voice, yielded up the ghost. Mark 15:37 And Jesus cried with a loud voice, and gave up the ghost. Luke 23:46 And when Jesus had cried with a loud voice, he said, Father, into thy hands I commend my spirit: and having said thus, he gave up the ghost.

war desolations are determined.	John 19:30 When Jesus therefore had received the vinegar, he said, It is finished: and he bowed his head, and gave up the ghost.

The prophecies of the sufferings of the Messiah culminate in the Book of Isaiah. The topic is not a minor inference in the Old Testament; it is a major emphasis. However, this is terribly neglected, almost to the point of being ignored.

In the Old Testament, the glories of the Messiah follow the sufferings of the Messiah. It would seem that the majority of the Jewish people, including the Pharisees, the Sadducees, and the scribes in the days of the earthly ministry of the Messiah, never understood this truth. Peter calls attention to the order of prophecies.

> 1 Peter 1:10 Of which salvation the prophets have inquired and searched diligently, who prophesied of the grace *that should come* unto you: 11 Searching what, or what manner of time the Spirit of Christ which was in them did signify, when it testified beforehand the sufferings of Christ, and the glory that should follow. 12 Unto whom it was revealed, that not unto themselves, but unto us they did minister the things, which are now reported unto you by them that have preached the gospel unto you with the Holy Ghost sent down from heaven; which things the angels desire to look into.

This chronology of suffering before the glories is clearly seen in the order presented in the Suffering Servant section of the Book of Isaiah.

> **42**:1 Behold my **servant**, whom I uphold; mine elect, *in whom* my soul delighteth; I have put my spirit upon him: he shall bring forth judgment to the Gentiles. 2 He shall not cry, nor lift up, nor cause his voice to be heard in the street. 3 A bruised reed shall he not

break, and the smoking flax shall he not quench: he shall bring forth judgment unto truth. 4 He shall not fail nor be discouraged, till he have set judgment in the earth: and the isles shall wait for his law.

49:5 And now, saith the LORD that formed me from the womb to be his servant, to bring Jacob again to him, Though Israel be not gathered, yet shall I be glorious in the eyes of the LORD, and my God shall be my strength. 6 And he said, It is a light thing that thou shouldest be my **servant** to raise up the tribes of Jacob, and to restore the preserved of Israel: I will also give thee for a light to the Gentiles, that thou mayest be my salvation unto the end of the earth. ... 8 Thus saith the LORD, In an acceptable time have I heard thee, and in a day of salvation have I helped thee: and I will preserve thee, and give thee for a covenant of the people, to establish the earth, to cause to inherit the desolate heritages;

50:5 The Lord GOD hath opened mine ear, and I was not rebellious, neither turned away back. 6 I gave my back to the smiters, and my cheeks to them that plucked off the hair: I hid not my face from shame and spitting. 7 For the Lord GOD will help me; therefore shall I not be confounded: therefore have I set my face like a flint, and I know that I shall not be ashamed. 8 *He is* near that justifieth me; who will contend with me? let us stand together: who *is* mine adversary? let him come near to me. 9 Behold, the Lord GOD will help me; who *is* he *that* shall condemn me? lo, they all shall wax old as a garment; the moth shall eat them up.

52:13 Behold, my **servant** shall deal prudently, he shall be exalted and extolled, and be very high. 14 As many were astonied at thee; his visage was so marred more than any man, and his form more than the sons of men: 15

So shall he sprinkle many nations; the kings shall shut their mouths at him: for *that* which had not been told them shall they see; and *that* which they had not heard shall they consider.

53:1 Who hath believed our report? and to whom is the arm of the LORD revealed? 2 For he shall grow up before him as a tender plant, and as a root out of a dry ground: he hath no form nor comeliness; and when we shall see him, *there is* no beauty that we should desire him. 3 He is despised and rejected of men; a man of sorrows, and acquainted with grief: and we hid as it were *our* faces from him; he was despised, and we esteemed him not. 4 Surely he hath borne our griefs, and carried our sorrows: yet we did esteem him stricken, smitten of God, and afflicted. 5 But he *was* wounded for our transgressions, *he was* bruised for our iniquities: the chastisement of our peace *was* upon him; and with his stripes we are healed. 6 All we like sheep have gone astray; we have turned every one to his own way; and the LORD hath laid on him the iniquity of us all. 7 He was oppressed, and he was afflicted, yet he opened not his mouth: he is brought as a lamb to the slaughter, and as a sheep before her shearers is dumb, so he openeth not his mouth. 8 He was taken from prison and from judgment: and who shall declare his generation? for he was cut off out of the land of the living: for the transgression of my people was he stricken. 9 And he made his grave with the wicked, and with the rich in his death; because he had done no violence, neither *was any* deceit in his mouth. 10 Yet it pleased the LORD to bruise him; he hath put *him* to grief: when thou shalt make his soul an offering for sin, he shall see *his* seed, he shall prolong *his* days, and the pleasure of the LORD shall prosper in his hand. 11 He shall see of the travail of his soul, *and* shall be satisfied: by his knowledge shall my righteous

servant justify many; for he shall bear their iniquities. 12 Therefore will I divide him *a portion* with the great, and he shall divide the spoil with the strong; because he hath poured out his soul unto death: and he was numbered with the transgressors; and he bare the sin of many, and made intercession for the transgressors.

It is only the failure to recognize the record of the prophecies of the Suffering Servant that would prompt the proposal of a faltering Messiah or that would see the need for a forsaken Sacrifice. That failure leads to an infringement on the nature GOD.

To allow for a scenario in which the Incarnate GOD becomes *in any fashion* contaminated by sin and in which His Heavenly Father severs the unity of the GODHEAD, a constitutional alteration would be required in the nature of the Son of GOD to make that possible. For the period of existence when Jesus of Nazareth was not "one with the Father" Jesus of Nazareth could not be Incarnate GOD. If He is not Incarnate GOD, then what exactly does He become for that period of time? If for any period of existence, Jesus of Nazareth was changed in His essence, then He would not be GOD. There is no alternative to that dilemma.

Jesus of Nazareth is not half-god and half-man. Jesus of Nazareth was not a split or divided personality able to function at times as a human and at other times as GOD. To make Jesus of Nazareth a divided entity with a GOD-nature that functions in the divine realm and a man-nature that operates in the human sphere is to create a being that is a product of Greek mythology (e.g. Hercules, the purported son of Jupiter and a mortal woman) rather than from a Biblical origin.

The humanity of Jesus is not to be diminished; the deity of Jesus is not to be minimized. It is far beyond my ability to explain that which the Scriptures describe as the great mystery.[7] "Through faith we understand that the worlds were framed by the word of God, so that things which are seen were not made of things which do appear";[8] and by faith we understand that the Word was GOD and the Word was made flesh and dwelt" on this earth that we might behold "His glory, the glory as of the only begotten of the Father." [9]

That babe wrapped in swaddling clothes, lying in that manger at Bethlehem[10] was a *holy baby.*

> Luke 1:34 Then said Mary unto the angel, How shall this be, seeing I know not a man? 35 And the angel answered and said unto her, The Holy Ghost shall come upon thee, and the power of the Highest shall overshadow thee: therefore also that holy thing which shall be born of thee shall be called the Son of God.

The eternal Son took on Him flesh and blood and in the fullness of time was born of a woman.[11] He grew into manhood[12] as a holy man.[13] The uniform testimony of Scripture is that He was holy in life and in His sufferings.[14] The Scriptures do not end with the declaration of His holy life; the testimony continues with the affirmation that He was a holy sacrifice.

> 1 Peter 1:19 But with the precious blood of Christ, as of a lamb without blemish and without spot:
>
> 1 John 3:5 And ye know that he was manifested to take away our sins; and in him is no sin.

There is an even stronger affirmation of the deity of Jesus of Nazareth at the very time of the crucifixion. While I realize that some among preachers and theologians reject the text as it stands in Acts 20:28, I am not one of them. The words are unmistakable; the conclusion is unavoidable. The blood that was shed at Calvary was the blood of GOD. That is the only logical reading of the text.

Take heed therefore unto yourselves, and to all the flock, over the which the Holy Ghost hath made you overseers, to feed the church of God, which he hath purchased with his own blood.

Matthew Poole gave this succinct commentary on the text.

> *With his own blood;* the blood of Christ, called truly the blood of God, there being in Christ two natures in one person, and a communion of the properties of each nature. If Christ had not been man, he could have had no blood to shed: had he not been God, the blood which he shed could not have been a sufficient price of redemption. Oh the depth of the riches of the wisdom and knowledge of God, who found out such a ransom; and the breadth, and length, and depth, and height of the love of Christ, who paid this ransom for us! (Ro 11:33; Eph 3:18-19). *SwordSearcher, Matthew Poole's Commentary on the Holy Bible* Acts 20:28

John Gill wrote somewhat more expansively.

> ... which he hath purchased with his own blood; which being the blood not only of a pure and innocent man, but of one that is truly and properly God as well as man, was a sufficient ransom price to redeem the church and people of God from sin, the law, its curse and condemnation: so that this is no inconsiderable proof of the true and proper deity of Christ; and contains a fresh argument, or reason, why the flock of God and "church of Christ", as the Syriac version reads; or "the church of the Lord and God", as in five of Beza's exemplars: or "of the Lord God", as the Arabic version, should be taken heed unto

and fed; because it must needs be dear to God and Christ, and precious to them, since so great a price has been paid for it. The purchaser is God, Christ who is God over all, blessed for ever, not a creature; that could never have made such a purchase, it could not have purchased a single sheep or lamb in this flock, no man can redeem his brother, or give to God a ransom for him, much less the whole flock; but Christ being God, was able to make such a purchase, and he has actually made it, and given a sufficient price for it; not to Satan, with whom these sheep were a prey, and from whom they are taken in virtue of the ransom given; but to God, from whom they strayed, against whom they sinned, and whose law they broke; and this price was not silver and gold, nor men, nor people: but Christ himself, his life and blood; and which were his "own", the human nature, the blood of which was shed, and its life given being in union with his divine person, and was in such sense his own, the property of the Son of God, as the life and blood of no mere man are theirs: and this purchase now being made in this way, and by such means, is a very proper one; it is not made without price, but with an invaluable one; and it is a legal purchase, a valuable consideration being given for it, perfectly equivalent to it; and therefore is a complete one, there is nothing wanting to make it more firm, it is a finished purchase; and it is a very peculiar one, it is a peculiar people that are purchased, called the purchased possession, Eph 1:14 and a peculiar price which is paid for it; there is no other of the same kind, nor any thing like it, and it is made by a peculiar person, one that is God and man in one person. *SwordSearcher, John Gill's Exposition of the Entire Bible* Acts 20:28

The blood of my redemption and yours is the blood of GOD Incarnate.[15]

Jesus was GOD before the womb. He was GOD in the manger. He was GOD in Nazareth. He was GOD in the ship on the sea of Galilee. He was GOD on the road to Jericho. He was GOD in the Garden of Galilee. He was GOD in Pilate's Hall. He was GOD on the Tree of Calvary. He was never less than GOD in the flesh.

The incarnate Word did not grow weary of His journey and seek to find another path instead of being lifted up to provide redemption.

The GOD of Heaven that sent His Son, giving that Son, to be lifted up did not reject His Son while He was being lifted up. [16]

[1] From the time of the first promise of the Messiah in Genesis 3:15 to the time of the crucifixion is approximately four thousand years using Ussher's chronology.

[2] John 12:27 Now is my soul troubled; and what shall I say? Father, save me from this hour: but for this cause came I unto this hour.

John 18:37 Pilate therefore said unto him, Art thou a king then? Jesus answered, Thou sayest that I am a king. To this end was I born, and for this cause came I into the world, that I should bear witness unto the truth. Every one that is of the truth heareth my voice.

Hebrews 9:11 But Christ being come an high priest of good things to come, by a greater and more perfect tabernacle, not made with hands, that is to say, not of this building; 12 Neither by the blood of goats and calves, but by his own blood he entered in once into the holy place, having obtained eternal redemption *for us.* 13 For if the blood of bulls and of goats, and the ashes of an heifer sprinkling the unclean, sanctifieth to the purifying of the flesh: 14 How much more shall the blood of Christ, who through the eternal Spirit offered himself without spot to God, purge your conscience from dead works to serve the living God? 15 And for this cause he is the mediator of the new testament, that by means of death, for the redemption of the transgressions *that were* under the first testament, they which are called might receive the promise of eternal inheritance. 16 For where a testament *is,* there must also of necessity be the death of the testator.

[3] Acts 10:38 How God anointed Jesus of Nazareth with the Holy Ghost and with power: who went about doing good, and healing all that were oppressed of the devil; for God was with him.

[4] 2 Corinthians 10:1 Now I Paul myself beseech you by the meekness and gentleness of Christ, who in presence *am* base among you, but being absent am bold toward you:

Matthew 12:15 But when Jesus knew *it,* he withdrew himself from thence: and great multitudes followed him, and he healed them all; 16 And charged them that they should not make him known: 17 That it might be fulfilled which was spoken by Esaias the prophet, saying, 18 Behold my servant, whom I have chosen; my beloved, in whom my soul is well pleased: I will put my spirit upon him, and he shall shew judgment to the Gentiles. 19 He shall not strive, nor cry; neither shall any man hear his voice in the streets. 20 A bruised reed shall he not break, and smoking flax shall he not quench, till he send forth judgment unto victory. 21 And in his name shall the Gentiles trust.

Matthew 11:29 Take my yoke upon you, and learn of me; for I am meek and lowly in heart: and ye shall find rest unto your souls.

⁵ I believe this chorus was written by Paul Paino.

⁶ John 1:3 All things were made by him; and without him was not any thing made that was made. ... 10 He was in the world, and the world was made by him, and the world knew him not.

Colossians 1:16 For by him were all things created, that are in heaven, and that are in earth, visible and invisible, whether *they be* thrones, or dominions, or principalities, or powers: all things were created by him, and for him: 17 And he is before all things, and by him all things consist.

Hebrews 1:2 Hath in these last days spoken unto us by *his* Son, whom he hath appointed heir of all things, by whom also he made the worlds; 3 Who being the brightness of *his* glory, and the express image of his person, and upholding all things by the word of his power, when he had by himself purged our sins, sat down on the right hand of the Majesty on high;

Revelation 4:11 Thou art worthy, O Lord, to receive glory and honour and power: for thou hast created all things, and for thy pleasure they are and were created.

⁷ 1 Timothy 3:16 And without controversy great is the mystery of godliness: God was manifest in the flesh, justified in the Spirit, seen of angels, preached unto the Gentiles, believed on in the world, received up into glory.

⁸ Hebrews 11:3 Through faith we understand that the worlds were framed by the word of God, so that things which are seen were not made of things which do appear.

⁹ John 1:1 In the beginning was the Word, and the Word was with God, and the Word was God. ... 14 And the Word was made flesh, and dwelt among us, (and we beheld his glory, the glory as of the only begotten of the Father,) [sic] full of grace and truth.

¹⁰ Luke 2:7 And she brought forth her firstborn son, and wrapped him in swaddling clothes, and laid him in a manger; because there was no room for them in the inn. ... 2:12 And this shall be a sign unto you; Ye shall find the babe wrapped in swaddling clothes, lying in a manger.

¹¹ Hebrews 2:14 Forasmuch then as the children are partakers of flesh and blood, he also himself likewise took part of the same; that through death he might destroy him that had the power of death, that is, the devil; 15 And deliver them who through fear of death were all their lifetime subject to bondage. 16 For verily he took not on him the nature of angels; but he took on him the seed of Abraham.

Galatians 4:4 But when the fulness of the time was come, God sent forth his Son, made of a woman, made under the law ...

12 Luke 2:52 And Jesus increased in wisdom and stature, and in favour with God and man.

13 Acts 4:27 For of a truth against thy holy child Jesus, whom thou hast anointed, both Herod, and Pontius Pilate, with the Gentiles, and the people of Israel, were gathered together, ... 30 By stretching forth thine hand to heal; and that signs and wonders may be done by the name of thy holy child Jesus.

Acts 3:14 But ye denied the Holy One and the Just, and desired a murderer to be granted unto you;

14 1 Peter 2:21 For even hereunto were ye called: because Christ also suffered for us, leaving us an example, that ye should follow his steps: 22 Who did no sin, neither was guile found in his mouth: 23 Who, when he was reviled, reviled not again; when he suffered, he threatened not; but committed himself to him that judgeth righteously:

15 The Textus Receptus, Acts 20:28

προσεχετε ουν εαυτοις και παντι τω ποιμνιω εν ω υμας το πνευμα το αγιον εθετο επισκοπους ποιμαινειν την εκκλησιαν **του θεου** ην περιεποιησατο δια του ιδιου αιματος

With his own blood. Through the agency of (*dia*) his own blood. Whose blood? If **tou theou** is correct, as it is, then Jesus is here called "God" who shed his own blood for the flock. It will not do to say that Paul did not call Jesus God, for we have Ro 9:5; Col 2:9; Tit 2:13 where he does that very thing, besides Col 1:15-20; Php 2:5-11.

SwordSearcher A. T. Robertson's Word Pictures Acts 20:28

16 John 3:14 And as Moses lifted up the serpent in the wilderness, even so must the Son of man be lifted up:

John 8:28 Then said Jesus unto them, When ye have lifted up the Son of man, then shall ye know that I am *he*, and *that* I do nothing of myself; but as my Father hath taught me, I speak these things.

John 12:32 And I, if I be lifted up from the earth, will draw all *men* unto me. 33 This he said, signifying what death he should die. 34 The people answered him, We have heard out of the law that Christ abideth for ever: and how sayest thou, The Son of man must be lifted up? who is this Son of man?

ABOUT THE AUTHOR

Dr. Jerald Manley is married to Julie Hudson; 2014 will be their 50th Anniversary. They have three children and four grandchildren. He has been preaching since 1958 and pastoring since 1962. He has been in his present pastorate since 1975. He has a B.A. from Bob Jones University, a M.DIV. from Louisiana Baptist Theological Seminary, and the Doctor of Divinity from Pensacola Christian College.

He is the founder and editor of *The Baptist Heritage*. He has written *When Sorrows Come, The Imaginative Christianity of C. S. Lewis, Resource of Weights and Measures for the Authorized Version, The Song of songs, which is Solomon's, What the Dead Man Wrote, Between the Valleys, Keep the Ordinances, Avoid My Mistakes, The Wilted TULIP,* etc.

Made in the USA
Columbia, SC
03 May 2021